The Emergence of Capitalism in Early America

UNIVERSITY PRESS OF FLORIDA

Florida A&M University, Tallahassee
Florida Atlantic University, Boca Raton
Florida Gulf Coast University, Ft. Myers
Florida International University, Miami
Florida State University, Tallahassee
New College of Florida, Sarasota
University of Central Florida, Orlando
University of Florida, Gainesville
University of North Florida, Jacksonville
University of South Florida, Tampa
University of West Florida, Pensacola

THE EMERGENCE OF CAPITALISM IN EARLY AMERICA

CHRISTOPHER W. CALVO

UNIVERSITY PRESS OF FLORIDA
Gainesville / Tallahassee / Tampa / Boca Raton
Pensacola / Orlando / Miami / Jacksonville / Ft. Myers / Sarasota

Copyright 2020 by Christopher W. Calvo
All rights reserved
Published in the United States of America

First cloth printing, 2020
First paperback printing, 2023

28 27 26 25 24 23   6 5 4 3 2 1

The Library of Congress has cataloged the printed edition as follows:
Names: Calvo, Christopher W., author.
Title: The emergence of capitalism in early America / by Christopher W. Calvo.
Description: Gainesville : University Press of Florida, 2020. | Includes bibliographical references and index. |
Identifiers: LCCN 2019032955 (print) | LCCN 2019032956 (ebook) | ISBN 9780813066332 (hardback) | ISBN 9780813057446 (pdf) | ISBN 9780813080369 (pbk.)
Subjects: LCSH: Capitalism—United States—History. | United States—Economic conditions—History. | United States—Social conditions—History.
Classification: LCC HC105 .C225 2020 (print) | LCC HC105 (ebook) | DDC 330.973/05—dc23
LC record available at https://lccn.loc.gov/2019032955
LC ebook record available at https://lccn.loc.gov/2019032956

The University Press of Florida is the scholarly publishing agency for the State University System of Florida, comprising Florida A&M University, Florida Atlantic University, Florida Gulf Coast University, Florida International University, Florida State University, New College of Florida, University of Central Florida, University of Florida, University of North Florida, University of South Florida, and University of West Florida.

University Press of Florida
2046 NE Waldo Road
Suite 2100
Gainesville, FL 32609
http://upress.ufl.edu

IN MEMORY OF JORGE ENRIQUE CALVO

CONTENTS

ACKNOWLEDGMENTS IX

1. Introduction: Capitalism and Antebellum Thought 1

2. Laissez-Faire in the American Tradition 27

3. Progress and Poverty: Malthus and Ricardo in America 75

4. The Crisis of Free Society: The Southern and Northern Reactionaries 103

5. An American Political Economy 137

6. Henry Carey, Nature, and the Destiny of Man 180

7. Liberalism, Republicanism, and Finance 192

8. Conclusion: The Old and the New in American Economics 234

NOTES 243

INDEX 291

ACKNOWLEDGMENTS

Historians of Adam Smith are apt to point out that the complexities of the *Wealth of Nations* render the text impervious to concise summation, though its timeless significance compels the serious attention of anyone interested in economics. More than two centuries after its initial publication, Smith's work is still cited as the birthplace of modern economic thought. Its ability to weave seamless and captivating narratives about the phenomena, motivations, systems, interests, and institutions of market societies has helped people understand the economic world around them. This book traces the evolution of American economic thought from the *Wealth of Nations* to the Civil War era, placing special emphasis on the domestic reception and treatment of Smith. It details the early American attempts at completing what Smith's *Wealth of Nations* did, that is, account for capitalism. Early Americans spun a tangled web of interpretative ideologies drawn from Smith precisely as they immersed themselves in the material realities that morphed marketplaces into market society. The cerebral and real-world manifestations of the *Wealth of Nations* in early America assumed hybrid forms. This book is an intellectual history of that story.

Just as the *Wealth of Nations* is commonly taken as a starting point in capitalism, so too did Smith provide me with the launchpad for this project. It began when I was barely an adult in what now seems like the early stages of a previous life. I am grateful that many of the friends and family who assisted at the start are still in my life at the book's completion. The earliest version of this project was presented to a graduate seminar taught by Darden Pyron, who in a very casual way told me, "You may be onto something here." From there the research was guided by Howard Rock, Nicol Rae, and Peter Onuf. Each afforded important counsel, and I am even more thankful today, a decade later, for the time and effort spent at advancing this work. I am also grateful to Sian Hunter and her colleagues at the University Press of Florida. Sian has been a source of advice and encouragement and was instrumental in matching my manuscript with anonymous reviewers whose criticisms and suggestions helped me better conceptualize the project's framing and objectives. And copy editor Ann Marlowe was exceedingly precise and a pleasure to work with.

This book, and my career as a historian, has benefited most especially from the mentorship of Kenneth Lipartito, which has now extended well beyond the conventional period professors are expected to assist in their students' endeavors. When I yielded to Kenneth's urgings and submitted this book to publishers, he helped me write the prospectus, then found time to read sections of the text and offer line-by-line revisions, as well as invaluable advice on getting a book published. For his willingness to help, coupled with his constant professionalism, I will never be able to express my gratitude in full.

Kathleen Stewart, Kevin Bloom, and Donald Gillett offered advice and encouragement on the manuscript. My parents, Carol and Enrique Calvo, listened attentively to descriptions of the publishing process and assisted with proofreading. My brother, Patrick Calvo, helped me realize that I needed to stop talking about the book and just write it. My children, James and Leila, with bright enthusiasm gave me extra incentive for finishing this "neverending story." And my wife, Darcy, endured with persistent elegance and patience a research and writing process stretching across essentially our entire relationship, offering timely, subtle reminders that there are more important things than nineteenth-century economic thought. Having Darcy, James, and Leila in my life will always be my greatest honor.

1

INTRODUCTION

CAPITALISM AND ANTEBELLUM THOUGHT

Antebellum political economists had the distinct historical privilege of penning their works during arguably the two most important developments in modern economics. First, during the early decades of the nineteenth century the Atlantic world matured into a full-fledged capitalist economy. Commercial, financial, and industrial changes traced to early modern Europe initiated world capitalist systems that forever altered the material basis of the human experience. Antebellum America was at the fore of this transformation. Between 1790 and 1860, practically every available economic indicator points to the unprecedented expansion of the domestic economy, and with it the institutions, relationships, ideologies, and cultures that historians find embedded in societies shaped by market values.

To be sure, the economy grew in fits and starts. But between Washington's inauguration and the start of the Civil War, the economy expanded at an average annual rate of between 1 and 4 percent. Cumulative GDP increases of just 1 percent per year over the course of a generation can lead to significant socioeconomic change. In 1776, for instance, the 2.5 million inhabitants of the American colonies were prospering by contemporary standards, but the colonial economy, which was mostly restricted to east of the Appalachians and largely dependent on farming and staple exports, was roughly one-third the size of the British economy. By the Civil War, the population had increased to 31 million, stretched across a free trade zone almost 3 million square miles wide to the Pacific, advanced revolutions in agricultural, commercial, industrial, and financial sectors, and shrunk the gap between the British and

American economies to about one-half.[1] America's revolution against Britain, in short, was followed by an economic revolution.

The trends in antebellum economic growth were partly a continuation of the colonial period, but the scale and scope of capitalist development between 1790 and 1860 were both quantitatively and qualitatively different. The colonial economy lacked, for instance, steam engines, vertically integrated manufacturing enterprises, 50,000 miles of telegraph wire, machine tools, assembly lines, power looms, interchangeable parts, vulcanized rubber, and 30,000 miles of railroad track. The antebellum economy was replete with the industrial features that scholarly and popular histories link to capitalist transformation. During the formative period of American expansion, industrialization emerged as a central feature of the nation's economy. On the eve of the Civil War, approximately 1.2 million workers were employed in industry. They accounted for 21 percent of the nation's GDP and contributed to increases in antebellum labor productivity rates that exceeded those of the late nineteenth century, producing nearly $2 billion in manufactured goods by 1860, a nearly tenfold increase from 1810, and roughly equal to the total value of domestic agricultural products.[2]

Industrialization was, of course, the leading cause of the industrial revolution. But antebellum America was a nation of farmers. At the start of the nineteenth century, approximately 80 percent of American jobs were in farming. Between 1790 and 1860, the number of farms and plantations increased fourfold to more than 2 million, valued at approximately 40 percent of national wealth.[3] The expansion of domestic agricultural markets was aided by improvements in transportation. Historians estimate the canal-digging frenzy of the 1820s and 1830s reduced shipping costs from about 20¢ per ton/mile to 2–3¢ per ton/mile. By 1860, private and public investment in canals reached almost $200 million. The 4,254 miles of canals constructed by 1860 were, however, dwarfed by the almost 12,000 miles of navigable rivers and lakes that took on new significance with the advent of steamboats. From the launching of Robert Fulton's *New Orleans* on the Mississippi River in 1811 to the Civil War, steamboats contributed to a 75 percent average decline in rates on freight sent upstream. And railroads, famously referred to as the "takeoff" industry in the rise of American capitalism, afforded a net social savings bonanza, roughly 4 percent of total GNP at the start of the Civil War. By then, $1 billion had been invested in the iron horse, and half of the world's track was laid in the United States. Farmers capitalized on sprawling transportation networks to conquer space and time and to penetrate new markets, both domestic and foreign. Raw materials and foodstuffs accounted for 85 percent of antebellum export trade, which helped pay for the European, mostly British, imported manufactures for which the nation had a seemingly insatiable demand. At the start of the nineteenth century, the American economy constituted 3 percent of total global trade. In 1860 that number had swelled to almost 10 percent.[4]

Industry and trade are highlighted as seminal features in histories of the antebellum economy, but historians have increasingly elevated finance to the avant-garde of capitalist insurgency. Savings and commercial banks; trusts; insurance; mortgages; personal and business credit and debt; sovereign debt; state, federal, and corporate bonds; "suspension," bankruptcy, and insolvency; joint-stock corporations; "soft" and "hard" money; commercial paper; and stock markets help fill the lexicon of financial revolution. Giovanni Arrighi described finance as the "recurrent phenomenon which has marked the capitalist era." Niall Ferguson discovered that "behind each great historical phenomenon there lies a financial secret." And in 2013 Thomas Piketty pushed the concept of "capital" into mainstream economic discourse.[5] Finance has become the third estate of the capitalist revolution. Antebellum Americans were prodigious consumers of financial services. Conservative estimates place the number of banks by the late 1850s at around 920, but more generous accountings have the number closer to 1,600. Aggregate note issues of commercial banks in 1860 are calculated at $207 million, up from $45 million in 1815. In 1817 the New York Stock and Exchange Board was formally established. Twenty-five years later there were more than a hundred securities listed, with an average daily trading volume of over four thousand shares. America's culture of "credit fetishism" was encouraged by federal and state legislators, and of course financiers.[6] Ordinary Americans seemingly ignored intermittent boom-and-bust cycles of financial crises with uninterrupted calls for more and cheaper credit, so that by the early decades of the nineteenth century, American economic culture was fully financialized.

Industry, trade, and finance are, in essence, the holy trinity of America's capitalist revolution. Over the last century, historians have adopted diverse methods to chronicle the triumph of American capitalism. The material manifestations of capitalism, and more specifically the quantitative expressions of these material manifestations, were given precedence by economic historians throughout the 1960s and 1970s. The New Economic Historians, or cliometricians, combined statistics, history, and neoclassical theory to fill some of the explanatory gaps left by earlier works in economic history. Economists like Robert Fogel, Albert Fishlow, and Douglass North offered empirical expositions that superseded earlier historical narrative formats, fundamentally changing the way historians understood American capitalism. Their works paid less attention to the social, cultural, and political externalities of emergent capitalism—what William Sewell referred to as "forms of economic life"—in favor of a more technical and data-driven pursuit of mathematical abstractions like GDP per capita, supply and demand curves, factor scarcity, and cost analysis.[7]

But the material histories of capitalism capture only part of the story. By the mid-1970s, social historians expanded the reach of the "market revolution," searching for capitalism beyond regression analyses and plotlines to explore the totality of economic life by looking "beyond the official story." These histories helped uncover the hidden relationships between economic imperatives and social, political, and cultural superstructures. Although the social historians drew on the quantitative discoveries of earlier cliometricians, they wrote a "bottom up" approach to history, retelling the personal stories of individuals that did not occupy space in conventional narratives. Charles Sellers's *The Market Revolution* and Sean Wilentz's *Chants Democratic* were seminal works in this exciting new field. Sellers's sweeping account of Jacksonian America featured a *Kulturkampf* aggravated by the commercialization of agriculture and by labor specialization that left farmers, mechanics, slaves, antinomians, and the entire political apparatus of American democracy trampled underfoot by capitalist revolution. Wilentz described the emergence of class consciousness and class conflict among New York City artisans whose worlds were turned upside down by industrialization. Social historians like Sellers and Wilentz relied on traditional Marxist bifurcation of class and ideology, but they extended the scope of capitalist disruption and contributed insightful combinations of social and cultural analyses that were grounded in the economic.[8]

The shift in emphasis initiated by the social historians was given further impetus in the 1980s and 1990s by the "new cultural history." Theoretical structures like neoclassicism and Marxism that piloted earlier research were cast off as subjective attempts to impose a master narrative that advanced either the pecuniary interests of the dominant class or outdated and impractical paradigms. Positivist epistemology and histories of market institutions were replaced with, among other things, analyses of hermeneutics, symbols, gender, relations between power, knowledge, and agency, and studies of the subaltern. Foucault and Derrida supplanted Ricardo and Marx, and the purely economic was relegated to the margins. By combining anthropology, sociology, psychology, gender studies, literary theory, and poststructuralism, the interdisciplinary approach of cultural history refreshed our understandings of the noneconomic consequences of capitalism.

Since the early years of this century, a materialist interest in the history of capitalism has resurfaced. The New Historians of Capitalism have contributed to "the return of the economic."[9] Encouraged by a broader methodological and theoretical mandate, the new literature recovers historical attention on political economy, minimizes conventional demarcations of time and space in supra-narratives of global capitalism, writes labor history without the Marxist focus on proletariats and the wage-labor regime, challenges neoclassical approaches by diminishing the significance of formal market institutions, highlights the commodification and financialization of practically everything, and aims to "de-naturalize capitalism."[10] Informed by the critical insights and perspectives of social and cultural history, the new scholarship pursues a research agenda that cliometricians had once consigned outside the realm of academic economics. Recent volumes summarizing their works indicate the wide range of interests covered, among them politics, society, psychology, and of course economics. Admittedly, these historians have "minimal investment in a fixed or theoretical definition of capitalism," thus arriving at a clear definitional consensus of the "elusive sovereign" is typically not their focus.[11] Instead, the New Historians of Capitalism implore scholars to embrace a more inclusive understanding of what exactly constitutes capitalism.

While economic materialism is fundamental to the history of capitalism, this book is about ideas. Which brings us to the second most important development of modern economics. Antebellum political economists had the distinct historical privilege of penning their works precisely during the age of capitalist revolution *as well as* the period marked by the establishment of economic science. Capitalism is unique among history's economic systems in that at its historical genesis there emerged simultaneously serious scholarly attempts to understand it. Between America's Revolution and Civil War, the iconic works of Adam Smith, Thomas Malthus, and David Ricardo were published, bracketed on one end by eighteenth-century mercantilism and Physiocracy and on the other by Marx.

This book does not intend to contribute directly to the burgeoning field of material histories of capitalism, nor will it offer a precise definition of capitalism. Existing scholarship already offers a vast repertoire of descriptions of antebellum economic realities. Rather, the purpose here is to sharpen our understanding of the history of American intellectual capitalism. The recent spike in scholarly attention given to capitalism opens opportunities for intellectual historians to reassert themselves in the discourse. Historians of economic thought have been studying the central ideas and texts of capitalist political economy since the eighteenth century.[12] In contrast to the ambivalence surrounding recent attempts at defining material capitalism, historians of economic thought enjoy broad agreement regarding the point of origin for capitalist ideology. Smith's 1776 *An Inquiry into the Nature and Causes of the Wealth of Nations* has long been accepted as the foundational text of intellectual capitalism. Although Smith never employed the term, the *Wealth of Nations* established the core values that are conventionally understood as the quintessential representation of capitalist ideology.[13] These include the pursuit of self-interest, the virtues of competition, the tendency for self-regulating markets to facilitate production and distribution efficiencies, the labor theory of value, the sanctity of private property, profit maximization, and, most important, free trade. Smith described these principles working harmoniously according to a natural liberal economic order designed by the Great Superintendent and existing within a wider laissez-faire paradigm complementary to his earlier disquisitions on moral philosophy, history, epistemology, and jurisprudence.

Tracing the origins of intellectual capitalism in the antebellum discourse requires us to understand what Smith accomplished in his text and how it was interpreted in America. First, historians must recognize that intellectual capitalism and material capitalism are oftentimes exclusive phenomena. Whether expressed in texts, symbols, spirits, mentalities, or cultural gestalt, intellectual capitalism does not necessarily precede, follow, or coexist with material capitalism. Historians of economic thought employ Smithian principles as the standard for gauging intellectual capitalism; and short of tabulating rubrics, economic historians are apt to compare material capitalism against the practical suggestions gleaned from the *Wealth of Nations*.[14] Historians of economic thought appreciate the distinctions between Smithian-inspired intellectual capitalism and expressions of subtle alternatives or wholly noncapitalist paradigms. In the same way, because historians have recently discovered or assigned new, expansive meanings to material capitalism, it is incumbent upon them to appoint nuanced substitute classifications, much as historians of economic thought, for example, differentiate between the classical and neoclassical schools.[15] This is especially true for historians of capitalism who extend their analysis beyond the economic sphere and into the intellectual. By expanding the scale and scope of market penetration into practically all aspects of the American experience, material and cerebral, recent trends in the historiography, namely the New Historians of Capitalism, imply that "capitalism in action" existed in everyone and everything, everywhere, at every time.[16] Slavery is capitalist; so too, even, is state intervention in the market. As such, the New Historians of Capitalism submit narratives that resemble the 1950s consensus school interpretation that posited Lockean liberalism, and by extension Smithian political economy, as the dominant feature of American political, social, economic, and intellectual history. Louis Hartz's "'petit bourgeois' giant of America" and more recent descriptions of "capitalism's rise to economic and cultural supremacy" share a historiographical affinity in that both categorically equate America with capitalist material phenomena and capitalist ideology.[17]

Given America's central position in the material history of capitalism, antebellum economists had a unique vantage point to comment on contemporary economic changes, and they were fortunate to share the language with the British thinkers generally thought to have initiated the field of economic science. Antebellum political economists gave capitalism meaning, identity, and significance. They helped determine how capitalism was understood, how capitalism was empowered or discouraged, and through the dissemination of theory and policy they helped shape the course of the capitalist revolution. The proceeding chapters measure and contextualize antebellum economic ideology within the period's intellectual milieu, highlighting comparisons between American thinkers and their transatlantic counterparts, especially Smith. When appropriate, points of distinction between Smithian-inspired economic philosophy and contemporary expressions of capitalist, hybrid capitalist, and anticapitalist ideologies will mitigate liberal consensus tendencies to universalize intellectual capitalism in the antebellum discourse.

"I have begun to write a book in order to pass away the time," Smith casually wrote to David Hume in 1764. Twelve years later he published the *Wealth of Nations* in London. The initial reception of the book gave no indication of an immediate classic. The first edition sold five hundred copies. At around a thousand pages, it is an exhausting read, and it was never intended for mass circulation. Four years after the book's release, Smith summarized the public response: "I have however, upon the whole been much less abused than I had reason to expect."[18] Hume thought the text "requires so much attention . . . that I shall still doubt for some time of its being at first very popular." Hume was right. The eleven editions of the *Wealth of Nations* published between 1776 and 1805 amounted to a total of 5,250 copies. Outside of the British learned class, few took notice. Indeed, at the time of Smith's death in 1790, he was more famous for his earlier work on moral philosophy.

Personal and historical circumstances interfered with the book's initial success. Smith was not disposed to self-promotion, nor did he recruit disciples. And shortly after publication of the *Wealth of Nations*, the American colonies declared independence from Britain.[19] The war in America, the loss of the colonies, and later the extremism of the French Revolution and subsequent wars with France incited reactionary suspicions in Britain aimed at anything hinting of Jacobinism. These events almost certainly hampered the book's early reception. The *Wealth of Nations* was, after all, a revolutionary text. The book struck at established institutions by urging human emancipation from feudal and mercantilist regimes, was inspired by Enlightenment liberalism, and for some conservatives was downright radical. Edmund Burke, for instance, associated Smith with the French *philosophes*.[20] In the face of this opposition, Dugald Stewart's 1793 *Account of the Life and Writings of Adam Smith* initiated efforts to domesticate the *Wealth of Nations* and find it a more regular and positive acceptance in the public sphere. Stewart, a professor of moral philosophy at the University of Edinburgh and a leading Smith advocate, worked to temper the suspected democratic and egalitarian impulses of the *Wealth of Nations*. Smith's book, Stewart wrote, hoping to convince conservatives of its politically and socially benign attributes, has "no tendency to unhinge established institutions, or to inflame the passions of the multitude. The improvements . . . are to be effected by means . . . gradual and slow in their operation."[21]

The ascendancy of the *Wealth of Nations* did not happen overnight. Rather, in the words of one Smithian scholar, "its influence rose like a gradually swelling tide."[22] In his *Account*, Stewart made legend the notion that "the advantages of a free commerce" were in fact first purported by Smith.[23] By the 1830s, Malthus, Ricardo, and J. R. McCulloch helped establish the *Wealth of Nations* as the "museum piece" of both the nascent science and liberal political economy.[24] Malthus's 1798 *An Essay on the Principle of Population* cites "Dr. Adam Smith" as an essential point of reference. Ricardo starts his 1817 *On the Principles of Political Economy and Taxation* with a discussion of Smith's theory of value. And McCulloch's 1828 edition of the *Wealth of Nations* declared Smith the first to systematically challenge the mercantilist tradition. These efforts, as well as the writings of virtually every economist since the early nineteenth century, canonized Smith as the father of political economy (economics) as well as the founder of liberal economics.[25] Indeed, in some circles the entire discipline of economics is synonymous with the Smithian liberal tradition. Smith, without ever intending it or even fully realizing it, completed the intellectual parlay—by writing the bible of capitalism, he had apotheosized himself as the Jesus Christ of economics.

For practical discursive purposes, and in full recognition of the risks of oversimplification, "liberal economics" is defined here as the intellectual system originating with Smith that aims to expand individual economic freedom while simultaneously restricting state intervention within a market-based (capitalist) economy. "Free trade" is the economic ideology that advances freedom of choice for consumers and producers in domestic and international commerce. Early American economists largely adhered to these theoretical and semantic conventions. The points of contemporary ambiguity, nuance, discrepancy, and historical context that provoke alternative definitions of these terms will be explained in the appropriate places below.

Despite the anachronistic and reductionist dangers inherent in concise definition of concepts, especially ideologically sensitive ones with long histories, Smithian liberalism and free trade will be used interchangeably with "laissez-faire." Laissez-faire is commonly ascribed to the eighteenth-century Physiocrats and the movement against French mercantilism (Colbertism). Historians of economic thought appreciate the principled distinctions between the Physiocrats and Smith, but for the purposes of facilitating scholarly dialogue, the literature commonly conjoins laissez-faire, free trade, and economic liberalism.[26] Most antebellum economists enveloped Smithian-inspired economic liberalism, free trade, and laissez-faire into a single ideological category—what will be called here "intellectual capitalism."[27] In its purest form, intellectual capitalism captures the totality of Smithian economic philosophy, which necessitates additional attention to Smith's earlier works in moral philosophy, epistemology, history, and jurisprudence as integral components that help complete our understanding of the economic ideology embedded in the *Wealth of Nations*. Finally, "classical economics" will be used synonymously with "British classicism." Despite the methodological and theoretical differences between Smith and his liberal successors, especially Ricardo, Smith is commonly identified as the progenitor of classical economics, or the British tradition that evolved into Ricardian economics. As John Maynard Keynes noted, "'The classical economists' was a name invented by Marx to cover Ricardo and James Mill and their *predecessors*, that is to say for the founders of the theory which culminated in the Ricardian economics."[28] Antebellum economic thinkers did not refer to a "classical school," but they regularly catalogued the British thinkers, namely Smith, Malthus, and Ricardo, into a single British tradition.

Given their historical, intellectual, and cultural ties with the British, early Americans expressed an affinity for liberal economists, especially Smith. Historians of economic thought emphasize this point to account for the supposedly paltry theoretical contributions made by antebellum Americans to the burgeoning science. Antebellum political economy is described either as stillborn, nonexistent, lacking originality, or, in the words of the economic historian Charles Dunbar, suffering from "general sterility." In Joseph Schumpeter's *History of Economic Analysis*, published posthumously in 1954, the Austrian émigré found in the pool of early American economists "no first-rate man among them, and they made next to nothing of the great opportunity before them." And in 1958 John Kenneth Galbraith, in his international bestseller *The Affluent Society*, echoed what by then was the conventional wisdom: "Only within very narrow limits can one speak of a separate American tradition in economics. . . . The precepts of the central tradition [British classicism] were accepted equally by Englishmen and Americans." Galbraith added a qualifier, but only to confirm that Americans were mostly passive receptors of British authority. "This is not to say there were no distinctively American figures," Galbraith concedes, "but, as compared with the majestic authority of the central tradition, their influence was comparatively small."[29]

The dismissive tones of Dunbar, Schumpeter, and Galbraith, all professional economists who taught at Harvard, gave subsequent generations of historians little incentive to examine antebellum economic thought. It is commonly assumed that the United States perfected the Smithian liberal creed in the economic sphere by way of an instinctual, a priori disposition toward free markets, and that in the intellectual sphere the Americans swallowed Smithian-inspired liberalism whole. The relationship between Americans, Smithian laissez-faire ideology, and capitalism was akin to historical destiny. It was no coincidence that the *Wealth of Nations* was published in the same year as America's birth. According to this narrative, the material expressions of Smithian-inspired liberalism—capitalism—are proof positive of America's natural attachment to the Scotsman, and therefore explain antebellum Americans' lack of interest in theoretical economics.

Joseph Dorfman's encyclopedic postwar work *The Economic Mind in American Civilization* confirmed what the historical imagination had long believed—the American attachment to the laissez-faire matrix was organic, preponderant, and manifested in economic and cerebral realities.[30] Smith, after all, described the liberal bourgeois ideology innate in all Americans. To truck and barter, free from the fetters of state, was the essential feature of American life, both material and mental. "The most potent determinant of economic action and thought was world commerce," Dorfman concluded, "the commerce that gave us treasure, the commerce that brought foreign goods and took our exports, that profited shipper, middleman, and speculator; the commerce, in short, that created the rich urban community and enlarged the money economy." Smith's work simply consecrated what Americans already believed. Dorfman admitted the presence of alternative ideas, but by the end of the antebellum period these had "shifted gradually toward liberalism, democracy, and agrarianism." The latter should not be misunderstood as disrupting the commerce-oriented laissez-faire consensus, Dorfman noted. "Again and again the farmers as well as the relatively unimportant laboring class," he wrote, "appeared in the arena as the auxiliaries of rival business factions for which they provided the bucolic pen names signed to 'capitalistic' pamphlets."[31]

Dorfman's liberal-consensus narrative describes an almost universal acceptance of the laissez-faire model, as an intellectual system and force for commercial and productive organization. His account conformed to wider trends in postwar American culture that still inform the popular understanding of the historical relationship between Smith, capitalism, and America. Richard Hofstadter characterized the liberal-consensus interpretation as emphasizing "the common, bourgeois, entrepreneurial assumptions of most of the effective forces in American political life, and the tendency of these forces to group ideologically around a Whiggish center rather than to be polarized in sharp ideological struggles."[32] After Dorfman, a generation passed before any scholar gave a full rendering of antebellum political economy.[33] In 1980 Paul Conkin's *Prophets of Prosperity* corroborated Dorfman's sweeping consensus view. Conkin conceded that antebellum economists demonstrated an "embarrassing diversity of viewpoints," yet he concluded, "I have been unable to identify in the pre–Civil War period anything close to a distinctive American tradition in political economy."[34] Like Dorfman, Conkin stressed the correspondence between antebellum thinkers and British laissez-faire. The implication of Dorfman's and Conkin's logic is that America lacked a strong intellectual tradition in political economy precisely because domestic thinkers marched in lockstep with British authorities.

This book challenges the popular notion that early American political economists abdicated their intellectual autonomy and agency. Smithian-inspired laissez-faire did not exercise ideological hegemony. In fact, the antebellum discourse demonstrates fundamental theoretical divisions between American thinkers and the larger Smithian tradition. To be sure, by the early decades of the nineteenth century, most American economists recognized Smith as the authority on all things related to political economy. Richard Edwards's study of early nineteenth-century congressional debates over trade, for instance, finds that the *Wealth of Nations* was "required reading" for American statesmen.[35] Smith was the principal source of economic knowledge, and the *Wealth of Nations* provided the intellectual framework for most Americans' thoughts and writings about the economy. Even Smith's strongest detractors could not ignore the *Wealth of Nations*. But by painting a broad liberal intellectual consensus, historians like Dorfman and Conkin have minimized important features, complexities, and discrepancies in antebellum economic thought.

For starters, antebellum thinkers made significant contributions to the development of modern political economy; they were not simply accomplices in the transatlantic dissemination of Smithian-inspired liberalism. In fact, contesting the Smithian laissez-faire model was the decisive element that united much of the antebellum literature. Smith's *Wealth of Nations*, Conkin accurately notes, "quickly established itself in America as a work of tremendous authority," but to suggest that Smith was the only influence does not reflect the historical reality.[36] Antebellum thinkers were sensible of contemporary breakthroughs in economics, especially contributions made by the British authorities. Even so, they articulated serious reservations, both theoretical and ideological, about the laissez-faire paradigm. As much as America's domestic economy grew in accordance with the principles of Smith, antebellum economic thought, as far as it was expressed by the period's most seasoned academics and most polished public intellectuals, did not subscribe to an absolutist laissez-faire ideology. Antebellum thinkers were not, as Conkin judged, powerless "to create their own universe of discourse."[37] Rather they made substantial departures from laissez-faire standards. And they did so with complete knowledge of the authority British laissez-faire exercised in the nineteenth-century economic literature.

This book intends to liberate antebellum political economy from the shadows cast by modern historians and reclaim for posterity the relevance American thinkers enjoyed during their own time. Antebellum economists constructed a dynamic body of thought that shaped American perceptions of the national historical economic experience, engaged with political economists at home and abroad, offered theoretical frameworks that contributed to contemporary understandings of the transformative effects of emergent capitalism, participated in the formation of economic policy, and split from British classical models by formulating alternative, hybrid visions of material and intellectual capitalism. This intellectual ferment informed American capitalism and deflected it from the straightforward market-freedom narrative of consensus historiography, as well as the commodification and assertive appropriation written in the more recent literature on the New History of Capitalism.

Economic intellectual culture offers the most compelling illustration of the countless interactions between the material and nonmaterial of the capitalist economy. Antebellum political economy, the period's most advanced form of economic intellectual culture, reveals the processes of developing capitalist institutions of thought, or the "cultural logic" of capitalism, that contemporaries constructed to give their economic experiences both tangible existence and abstract meaning. "Even when economic events seem beyond the control of any individual," Jessica Lepler notes in her work on the 1837 financial crisis, "the shaping of their meaning remains within our grasp."[38] Material forces were the impetus behind capitalist revolution, but the American intellect determined capitalism's historical significance by organizing systems of thought to better explain economic phenomena. Put differently, the economic transformations of the early nineteenth century created a hybrid capitalist philosophy, but the interpretations of capitalist reality were developed through cerebral processes that were decided by human agency. As we shall see, Americans exercised this agency to carve distinctive intellectual approaches to the emerging transatlantic capitalist world.

Antebellum political economy was, at its very core, a description of an economy transitioning into capitalism. In this manner, antebellum economists wrote the nation's first histories of capitalism. But at the start of the nineteenth century, economics was, in the words of Jacob Viner, a "stepchild of other disciplines," made to correspond with research methods and trends from inside and outside the embryonic science, and with historical and contemporary intellectual "fashions," as well as prevailing policy imperatives.[39] Economic inquiry drew disproportionately from more traditional fields of study like moral philosophy, history, and theology. Antebellum political economy reflected the underdeveloped state of the science, and the American thinkers, like the British, fostered an interdisciplinary approach. Protectionists, for instance, studied national and labor histories as well as economic statistics. Southern pro-slavery reactionaries inserted sociology into economics. Southern liberals integrated political science. Northeastern liberals incorporated moral philosophy and theology. And the financial literature is well stocked with cultural analyses.

The fusion of disciplinary and methodological approaches in antebellum economic thought reflected attempts to give meaning to the material and nonmaterial manifestations of economic phenomena. The American economy was just then taking shape, exhibiting transient forms that sustained both capitalist and noncapitalist designs. The mixed economy occurred at the local and national levels. Southern slaveholders, for instance, shipped cotton across international markets but relied on noncapitalist labor arrangements. American manufacturers, to take another example, competed for labor, resources, and customers in domestic markets, but through protective tariffs they helped organize a noncapitalist "mother of all trusts." Americans engaged in seemingly precapitalist modes of production, like subsistence farming, alongside highly commercialized agriculture. In other cases, they established economic institutions with the explicit purpose of detaching from market society. These distinctly anticapitalist concerns existed within short distances of highly capitalist enterprise. The Fourier-inspired Brook Farm cooperative in Massachusetts, for instance, was about forty miles from the textile mills of Lowell.

History is replete with examples of the functional cohabitation of economic institutions founded on value systems that were subtly different, moderately antagonistic, or even categorically hostile to each other. Seth Rockman's study of antebellum Baltimore labor markets reveals the incongruous yet parallel forms of economic structures in the early republic. Baltimore's highly mixed labor market employed workers of all types, not just according to craft and skill but also with respect to "relations of ruling."[40] "Jilted slaves," convicts, indentured servants, "black jacks," poor whites, women, children, migrant laborers, and the nominally free but legally and socially disadvantaged lived on the margins of economic society and competed and worked for wages in distorted markets, not always as equals but often side by side. Even economic societies conventionally described as capitalistic were, and still are, amalgamations of various forms. The compounded character of early American economic institutions does not comport with conventional historical preference for reductive categorization, but neither does the antebellum economy call for universalistic descriptors.

The cross-fertilization of capitalist with noncapitalist material institutions was reproduced in the period's political economy. Hybrid capitalism invited hybrid capitalist ideologies. The *Wealth of Nations* established the parameters of the discourse, but antebellum economists did not always think and write within those boundaries. Even liberal economists challenged Smithian orthodoxy by creating alternative laissez-faire paradigms. Others mixed and matched complementary and oppositional ideological claims across a dynamic and evolving cerebral plane with seemingly little regard for theoretical consistency. Intellectual capitalism appeared in amalgamated forms and varying degrees—contemporaries created different or hybrid capitalisms. Southern liberals championed laissez-faire to vindicate slavery, northern liberals defended markets with moral philosophy, protectionists aimed at maximizing individual and national liberation through tariffs, and the opponents of finance capitalism embraced competitive markets. These categories were assorted, relying on multifaceted theoretical dialectics, within a discipline searching for methodological consensus, and imitative of capitalism's varied material existence.

The composite grades of intellectual capitalism should not, however, preclude historians from drawing lines of clarity and structure. It is well known to Smithian scholars that the *Wealth of Nations* endorsed state intervention to protect private property, administer justice, and manage defense, public works, and education.[41] This does not mean Smith was a socialist. Certain expressions of economic thought clearly belong to particular ideological classifications. Antebellum economists who denounced Smith and his laissez-faire prescriptions, knowing full well that the *Wealth of Nations* was the representative text of free-market, liberal economic thought, should be identified as the opponents of intellectual and material capitalism. Intellectual historians are periodically confronted with authors, leaders, or movements that were conventionally associated with one ism or another but adopted practices or policies in stark contrast to the very ideology being championed. Southern slave owners, for instance, advocated laissez-faire while in the same breath calling for legislative mandates to preserve slavery. Some protectionists, to take another example, argued that tariffs were temporary measures to advance the ideal of global free trade. Historians of economic thought identify points of qualification and contradiction, gauge authorial intention and authenticity, and assess the impact of external factors, both societal and personal. Theoretical nuance, however, should not encourage intellectual nihilism or ideological relativism. Neither should the appearance of complexity give license to universalistic categorization. The diversity of capitalist, hybrid capitalist, and noncapitalist economic experiences prompted heterogeneity and conflict in contemporary thought. Antebellum debates over industry, trade, and finance drove intellectual wedges between Americans. These differences in ideology ultimately fractured the nation precisely because contemporaries were hostile to rival belief systems.

The antebellum treatment of laissez-faire illustrates the tendency of Americans to construct hybrid capitalist ideologies. American liberal economists borrowed from Smith, Malthus, and Ricardo, but their arguments reveal the unique conditions of American material and intellectual culture more than they show deference to the British authorities. For some, this meant accepting parts of the free trade model, but with distinctive American twists. Chapter 2 shows that even within the antebellum free trade movement, there was no definitive consensus. Americans developed different types of laissez-faire political economy, each suited to the regional interests and economic experiences of the authors. This was especially the case in the South. Southern liberals manipulated the laissez-faire template to match southern traditions. By the 1830s, southern liberals realized laissez-faire complemented the ideal of the negative state. They employed free trade political economy to strike at the North by attacking protective tariffs and combating assertions that the state could claim or destroy private property—notably slaves. Smith had denounced slavery, but the patent incompatibility between a southern political economy of slavery and the revolutionary, enlightened, liberal moral philosophy of Smith did not stop southerners from becoming antebellum America's chief disseminators of laissez-faire. Nor did southerners, generally hostile to industrialization, consider their brand of hybrid intellectual capitalism inconsistent with British classicism and its midcentury pivot to industry. Free traders in the South shaped laissez-faire into an intellectual strategy to promote the political doctrine of states' rights, defend a slave regime, and stall the emergence of a national industrial economy. It was, in short, not the economic liberalism of the British tradition.

Southern pro-slavery liberalism demonstrates the complexities found in the historical interface between material and ideological capitalism. According to the most recent literature on southern slavery, the peculiar institution "became central to and perhaps even constitutive of a particular moment in the history of capitalism.... slavery helped constitute capitalist modernity."[42] Antebellum economic history is flush with evidence indicating the centrality of slavery to the national and Atlantic economies. However, material slavery and ideological slavery existed in parallel universes. Accounting for the distinctions between the material and ideological weighs against universalistic categorizations that diminish the significance of historical, cultural, and theoretical divisions within pro-slavery liberal political economy. Hybrid intellectual capitalism allows for ideological nuance, but outside of the rather narrow commitment to laissez-faire trade policy, pro-slavery ideology was not capitalist. It is possible for the material realities of an economic system to exist in contrast to the ideological tenets purported by the defenders of that economic system. Southern liberals defended an economic institution—slavery—that was condemned as inherently antithetical to established laissez-faire principles. Southerners cited British liberals, even though the British authorities had themselves based their theoretical, economic, and moral opposition to slavery on laissez-faire models. Smith, for instance, explicitly denounced slavery and raised free labor values to the fore of intellectual capitalism. In short, antebellum slavery may have advanced a commercial-oriented market agenda, but antebellum pro-slavery economic thought did not advance capitalist ideology.

Laissez-faire ideology in the Northeast was not disturbed by discrepancies between the material and intellectual, but rather between the temporal and eternal. In northeastern colleges and universities, professors taught a moralist brand of laissez-faire doctrine quite different from southern free trade. The influence of regional institutional and cultural conventions brought northeastern free traders closest to the Smithian tradition, but further from the British successors of Smith. The northeastern free traders emphasized the ethical and religious benefits of markets. There may be some truth in popular notions that the American intelligentsia harbors an anticapitalist bias, but this was not the case with the northeastern clerical economists. They were not leftist, anticapitalist academics. Nor was capitalist ideology at odds with religion. The northeastern economists championed material and intellectual capitalism as a force for social and moral good. In their view, the ethical rewards of capitalism were more important than the material gains. They considered free trade political economy as confirmation of a benevolent Christian deity. Northeastern professors of political economy were typically clergy who might have otherwise distanced themselves from a discipline still partially linked to the materialism of Hume and the skepticism of the *philosophes*. But because free trade in the Smithian tradition was originally a branch of moral philosophy, teaching political economy was made amenable to the clerical style and substance of the region's curricula.[43]

As a consequence, laissez-faire in the American discourse was split along sectional lines and never coalesced into a single intellectual movement. The sluggish pace with which northeastern clerical economists removed elements of moral philosophy and Christian theology distinguished their interpretations of laissez-faire from the more secular and politicized southern versions of free trade. Perhaps more important, divisions in America precluded the formation of an Anglo-American free trade consensus. Southern free traders grew suspicious of British liberals, especially after Parliament turned sharply abolitionist in the 1830s. By midcentury the popularity of British Evangelical laissez-faire had too waned. With the ascendancy of the more technical Ricardian style of political economy, the break between British and American liberals was complete. And by 1850, southern and northeastern liberals were further isolated by the increasingly popular association between British classicism and industrialization. Finally, the northeastern clergy free traders largely rejected, on theological grounds, the perceived pessimism of the classical school. Both the southerners and the northeastern cleric economists drew from British authorities but there were principled distinctions between them, and generally the Americans followed an economic logic that evolved into something categorically different from laissez-faire as it existed in the nineteenth-century British discourse.

The split between antebellum free traders and British laissez-faire was made explicit in the American treatment of Malthus and Ricardo. Chapter 3 demonstrates how liberal antebellum thinkers largely abandoned Malthus and Ricardo or manipulated their logic to suit distinctly American conditions. Antebellum economic and social conditions convinced liberal writers from both the North and South that the theories of Malthus and Ricardo were simply inapplicable in America. The few Americans who accepted Malthus and Ricardo typically distorted the supposed universalistic approach of the British authorities to advance their own special political and social agendas. It is not uncommon to find a liberal American writer stressing certain conclusions of the British economists while flatly denying the legitimacy of others. In this way, antebellum political economists created their own economic discourse—hybrid capitalist ideology—out of the raw material of British classicism. By the 1850s, the tendency of American thinkers to bend British classicism reached its apex. This was especially the case in the South, where the gloomy forecasts of the British pessimists were manipulated to defend slavery.

Liberal America's break from British classicism was largely a response to contemporary assumptions about American exceptionalism. Declarations of American exceptionalism hark back to the colonial period, but during the antebellum era the concept became a cardinal tenet of American culture.[44] To be sure, southern and northern political economists were selective in their application of American exceptionalism values. Southerners, for instance, appropriated American exceptionalism to describe their region's past, present, and future, but often times excluded the North from the narrative. Still, the belief in American exceptionalism contributed to an almost constant invitation for antebellum writers to construct a native political economy. An American economic renaissance was heralded, one that solicited an economic thought penned by indigenous hands and was appreciative of the historically unique circumstances of the American experience.

The task of creating a system of economic thought designed specifically to reflect American conditions fell to protectionists. Chapter 5 traces the intellectual evolution of antebellum protectionism. Protectionism was the most important development in antebellum economic thought, and it has rightly been appointed the American school of political economy. By fusing various strains of domestic intellectual, social, economic, and cultural history, and placing higher value on American exceptionalism, protectionists captured the essence of the antebellum economic mind. Protectionist works abound with buoyant optimism, commitment to national economic development, and a powerful spirit of independence from the Old World. By exchanging the pessimism of the classical tradition for a distinctly American understanding of economic phenomena, the protectionists authored an economics of affluence.

The popularity of protectionist thought and the promulgation of protectionist policy throughout the nineteenth century illustrate the deep disconnect between American political economy and British intellectual capitalism. For protectionists the exceptional conditions of America made permanent economic progress possible according to a hybrid capitalist model. By commanding through the will of human agency and the instruments of the state what for the British thinkers was an uncompromising and arbitrary natural order, protectionists aimed at catapulting the American economy to unprecedented heights. In these ways and others, protectionists challenged the foundational principles of laissez-faire, though protectionists did not consider their economic system inherently at odds with liberal values. Rather they believed that regulating markets through tariffs would in fact increase the personal autonomy of American citizens and augment national sovereignty. The protectionist ontology of freedom consisted of political and economic independence from Britain, but also humanity's emancipation from what Smith referred to as the "natural system of liberty."

As much as protectionists held in disdain free trade ideology and railed against international commerce, protectionist hybrid capitalism managed a defense of an otherwise liberal, competitive, hybrid capitalist industrial regime where capital and labor coexisted harmoniously—an industrial ideal that avoided the dismal outcomes predicted by Malthus and Ricardo. Protectionists appropriated the pro-industrial thrust of midcentury British classicism while simultaneously attacking the theoretical means advanced by Smith, Malthus, and Ricardo toward that industrial end. In antebellum political economy it was the protectionists, not the free traders, who promoted industrial revolution. If industrial capitalism was indeed an economic revolution, then protectionists were the movement's torchbearing revolutionaries. The period's most important protectionist thinker, Henry Carey, is the focus of chapter 6. Carey took protectionist political economy to its furthest logical conclusion. And in doing so, he offered an all-encompassing economic theory that sought to explain human economic evolution. His effort to integrate protectionism into a coherent economic ideology remains the most significant contribution to the antebellum economic discourse.

Protectionists offered a hybrid capitalist model that stood as the most popular and influential antebellum challenge to Smithian-inspired laissez-faire ideology. A far more violent and darker rejection came from a small legion of southern reactionaries and northern laborites. Chapter 4 traces the political economy of southern reactionaries and northern laborites responsible for the period's sharpest critiques of bourgeois ideals. Although southern agitators like George Fitzhugh and George Frederick Holmes and northern labor activists like Langton Byllesby and Thomas Skidmore operated on the periphery of the discourse, they helped shape the contours of antebellum political economy, and they further showcase the lack of a liberal consensus in American thought. Taken together, the writings of Fitzhugh, Holmes, Byllesby, and Skidmore solicit revisions to conventional ideological alignments. Combining these authors into a single chapter reveals these seemingly adverse thinkers as actually having shared affinities. Both groups offered systematic denunciations of the entire laissez-faire paradigm. Their similarity in ideological disposition challenges traditional class-bifurcation analysis typical of Marxist, Progressive, and neo-Progressive histories. United in their opposition to the moral, cultural, and social externalities of intellectual and material capitalism, especially the commodification of labor and what they perceived as the exploitative relationships attendant on the industrial wage regime, the southern reactionaries and northern laborites illustrate how the antebellum economic discourse occupied a cerebral plane that lacked definitive ideological structure, and failed to respect the differences between accepted formulas of liberal and conservative, radical and moderate, and Marxist and bourgeois belief systems.

Southern pro-slavery reactionaries based their opposition to commercial-industrial capitalism on a Tory-like morality, imbued with conservative paternalistic values and an unwavering attachment to plantation slavery. To be sure, southern reactionaries minimized, and in some cases completely ignored, the physical drudgery and human commodification that accompanied slavery.[45] At the same time, they overlooked the highly commercialized character of plantation slavery. Ignorance is no excuse; but the material realities of the antebellum plantation regime should not discount their efforts to capture contemporary anticapitalist thought and construct a representational economic ideology. Readers can assess the authenticity of their motivations and claims, expose manipulation or theoretical hypocrisy, and gauge their disconnect from the more pervasive southern attachment to laissez-faire. Still, the ideas of conservatives like Fitzhugh and Holmes were symptomatic of powerful social, cultural, and intellectual currents in the antebellum South. The northern laborites echoed the criticisms of the southern reactionaries, but their analyses rested on an emerging socialist political economy then gaining favor in America's industrial quarters. They called for the redistribution of property, an end to the perceived abusive tendencies of the manufacturing system, the abolition of economic classes, and a comprehensive reconfiguration of commercial exchange. In short, the northern laborites stipulated an alternative to the material and intellectual capitalist orders.

The association between northern laborites and southern reactionaries is indicative of the rather awkward manifestations of antebellum ideological alliances. Too often social and cultural historians represent capitalist institutions as entrenched conservative forces. Labor protests, agrarian reforms, or censures against finance have been interpreted as leftist-inspired attacks on the capitalist status quo. This narrative imposes modern historical assumptions on antebellum realities. For antebellum Americans, capitalism was the revolutionary impulse, "the relentless revolution" acting upon human societies with radically transformative powers that overwhelmed and impressed contemporaries.[46] "The bourgeoisie, historically," Marx wrote, "has played a most revolutionary part."[47] The capitalist revolution, like all revolutions, strained

American conservatives. The reactions of northern laborites and southern reactionaries, of opponents of finance, even of protectionists, are, in this light, not intellectual expressions of a radical or revolutionary impulse, but rather conservative instincts aimed at preserving traditional institutions. Economic, social, and cultural conservatism joined American political economists of all stripes against the revolutionary imperatives of insurgent capitalism.

While industry and trade were the most heatedly debated economic topics of the era, finance inspired a special kind of panic. Chapter 7 deals with early American reactions to financial capitalism. This chapter argues that most Americans coalesced around a strong opposition to the proliferation of financial capitalism. Perhaps the most abstract and disruptive institutional feature of the modern economy, finance enrolled Americans, in the words of Jeffrey Sklansky, in a "crash course in capitalism."[48] By the Jacksonian era, financial institutions were deeply rooted in the economy, and during this period both the forces sympathetic to and those determined to resist financial expansion matured into full-fledged political, social, and intellectual movements. To comprehend its complexities, antebellum economists compiled an expansive body of literature geared specifically to uncover both the mysterious evils and the blessings of financial institutions.

Historians have paid considerable attention to Americans' suspicions of finance. However, they tend either to reduce antebellum attitudes into neatly organized antagonistic class-oriented camps or simply to paint with a broad stroke an image of consensus.[49] This book concentrates on a middle variant often ignored in the historiography—political economists who were otherwise committed to Smithian laissez-faire but clear in their opposition to financial institutions, fearful of the moral, social, political, and economic residuals attributed to banks, credit, debt, and stock-corporations. The conventional wisdom on the positive ideological relationship between free markets and finance—that is, capitalism and finance are inseparable bedfellows and therefore the advocates of intellectual capitalism universally champion the expansion of financial institutions—was rare in the antebellum discourse. Put differently, the opponents of finance valued free market competition, railed against state-sponsored creation of what they perceived as legislated monopolies, and adhered to the broader theoretical underpinnings of Smithian liberalism. The advocates of finance, mostly the Whig inheritors of the Hamiltonian tradition, promoted state economic initiatives, embraced a paternalistic view of the government's role in the financial sector, and generally rejected Smithian laissez-faire.

A separate but related vein in the opposition literature on finance fused classical republicanism with Smithian liberalism. Bernard Bailyn's *The Ideological Origins of the American Revolution* (1967) and J. G. A. Pocock's *The Machiavellian Moment* (1975) encouraged a generation of historians to uncover a republican style of thought, not only in the literature surrounding the American Revolution and early national period but also across a broader transatlantic spectrum traced to Renaissance Florence. In Augustan England, opposition to financial institutions emerged as a central component of republican ideology and peaked around the time of the South Sea Bubble in 1720. The collapse of the now infamous South Sea Company epitomized the wicked influence of finance over Parliament and, for critics, the potential for financial institutions to undermine England's fragile commonwealth. Like capitalism, "republicanism" has taken on an assortment of historical connotations. But unlike historians of economic thought who can point to Smith's *Wealth of Nations* for a working definition of intellectual capitalism, historians of republicanism are left without a single foundational text, and search for meaning in a much wider historical literature that dates as far back as Virgil's *Eclogues*. Adding to the trouble, republicanism was first and foremost a political ideology, which developed economic undertones only much later in its etymological history, around the time of England's financial revolution. For the purpose of advancing scholarly dialogue, yet in full recognition of the dangers of crude oversimplification, republicanism in the antebellum context will rely on Pocock's understanding of English Whig thinkers like James Harrington, Thomas Gordon, John Trenchard, and Henry St. John, Viscount Bolingbroke. Accordingly, republicanism brought together a nostalgic civic humanism, moderate political liberalism, and social conservatism into an ideological vehicle, in the words of Pocock, "of a basically hostile perception of early modern capitalism."[50] In the antebellum literature on finance, the linguistic and paradigmatic formulas of England's classical republicans were borrowed to help Americans better understand the nuances of financial revolution, as well as to launch criticisms against financial capitalism according to a republican ideological platform that was familiar to most Americans.

Intellectual histories of the American Revolution and early national period have paid significant attention to the discursive continuity between

English and American republicanism, but they have generally balked at extending the republican paradigm beyond the early 1830s.[51] In doing so, historians of republicanism have largely overlooked the subtle differences between individual republican critics of finance, clustering them together under a single Jeffersonian agrarian ideal that was suspicious of most things modern and commercial.[52] These same historians typically pair republicanism and anticapitalism. Republican criticisms of financial institutions have a decidedly anticapitalist tone, yet conventional histories minimize the existence of bona fide antebellum republicans who expressed a strong preference for free markets, void of financial institutions, as well as republicans who envisioned free markets as an instrument to decelerate the expansion of finance. This chapter does not intend to resuscitate debates over the ubiquity of republican ideology in the broader discourse but rather illustrate the compatibility of liberal and republican economic ideologies, specifically in the opposition literature. Laissez-faire and republicanism were joined together to stall the proliferation of finance. Indeed, most antebellum republican critics of finance valued Smithian liberalism, yet they were deeply anxious over what they considered were the shadowy powers of financial institutions. Nor have historians done justice to the opponents of finance—republican, liberal, or conservative—by representing them as radical outliers, misguided traditionalists, or incorrigible anticapitalists. Antebellum critics of finance were essential components of the era's economic thought, who engaged with the virtues of the free market but with a cautionary element that recognized the dangers of unfettered finance.

Americans' response to the expansion of financial institutions embodies the dialectic tensions attendant to the nation's broader economic discourse. This book aims to contextualize the conflicts in which Americans constructed their economic thought. Evidence is drawn from a diverse field of antebellum economic literature, with special consideration given to the more academic, or abstract, writings. The research is largely dependent on literary sources, often elitist, and concentrates on values instead of behaviors. Recognizing the period's lack of professionalization in the field of economics, popular tracts are incorporated into the discussion. No single group monopolized the production or distribution of economic knowledge. It was disseminated by academics, farmers, merchants, craftsmen, industrialists, pamphleteers, journalists, and politicians, many of whom, despite having nothing near what the present age would consider sufficient training, were confident enough in their expertise to claim the title "political economist." This term is used liberally and interchangeably with "economist," conferred upon those who contributed to what stands as a prodigious assemblage of economic knowledge, found in speeches, memorials, journals, newspapers, and academic treatises. Some political economists treated here are central to any history of antebellum economic thought. Alexander Hamilton, John Calhoun, Henry Carey, Jacob Cardozo, and Francis Wayland were principals in the discourse. Still others included here, George Frederick Holmes, Thomas Cooper, Condy Raguet, Henry Gouge, and Langton Byllesby, are not household names in popular American histories. Perhaps the most difficult task of intellectual history is patching together the ideas and passages of disparate groups into a single analytical work. This is particularly the case with American economic thought, where sharp differences encumber the formulation of broad generalizations. It is left for the reader to determine whether the sources are representative of the whole. Still, the selected literature indicates that economic intellectual culture in antebellum America was encouraging and pursuant of an economic discourse, and, when examined closely, improves our appreciation of the psychology of the American *homo economicus* and widens our understanding of the theoretical basis for America's empire of wealth.

2

⁂

LAISSEZ-FAIRE IN THE AMERICAN TRADITION

A few months before Thomas Jefferson wrote the Declaration of Independence, Adam Smith published his *Wealth of Nations*. Contemporaries eager to find connections between the *Wealth of Nations* and America's birth celebrated the concurrence. "The nativity of the science is to be dated from that event, and the coincidence is to be remarked that it was contemporaneous with our Declaration of Independence in 1776."[1] By all accounts Smith's book was positively received in early America. The *Wealth of Nations* helped justify America's revolution, and the Scotsman also had influence over the Constitution framers at Philadelphia. Nearly 30 percent of the personal libraries of the founding fathers catalogued the *Wealth of Nations*. Washington, Jefferson, and Madison each owned a copy, and Hamilton reportedly prepared an extended commentary on it.[2] An American edition of the *Wealth of Nations* was published in 1789. And by the end of the century, it was incorporated into the curricula at colleges in the new nation.

The bonds between America and Smithian laissez-faire, first signaled by the auspicious timing of Smith's magnus opus and America's founding, have become conventional wisdom. Because Smith explained, and in many ways legitimized, free markets, it is believed Americans felt an innate affinity for his work. According to this narrative, the *Wealth of Nations* provided powerful encouragement for the American commitment to private property, competition, free markets, specialization, and most other prescriptions of the capitalist matrix. More than any other author, Smith contributed to the ideological ascendancy of liberal bourgeois principles in the domestic economic and intellectual landscapes. Through policy examples and historical anecdotes, historians of the antebellum economy have perpetuated the understanding that Smith and America enjoyed a special relationship. "Fresh off a rebellion against British controls that favored the interests of the Empire over those of the American periphery," John Lauritz Larson writes, "colonists understandably seized upon Smith's arguments against all policy restraints." Americans encapsulated the Smithian ideal, in both their thinking and action. "The ideas of Adam Smith," writes Roy C. Smith (not a descendant of Adam), "helped form the model for the development of the American economy.... His theories, as it happened, appeared just in time to be of use to the founding fathers." And John Steele Gordon, in his broad study of American economic history, noted "the United States has consistently come closer to the Smithian ideal over a longer period of time than any other major nation."[3] Smith's work furnished the intellectual grid upon which antebellum Americans understood the economy. The *Wealth of Nations* was America's foundational economics text. And for many Americans, Smith's word was scripture.

That said, historians have exaggerated the bond between Smith and America. In search of an intellectual paragon, historians have raised Smith into the pantheon of American political economy, retelling reductionist narratives or ignoring the nuances and complexities in the relationship between the *Wealth of Nations* and American economic thought.[4] The American treatment of Smith varied considerably—there was no single interpretation that dominated the discourse. At nearly half a million words, the *Wealth of Nations* offers something for everyone. It was constructed and deconstructed, pulled and picked, praised and critiqued, in ways similar to how professional and amateur economists dissect the Scotsman today. Even antebellum liberals failed to arrive at an interpretative consensus. Private property, the principle of competition, and the negative state were taken as basic postulates, but antebellum liberals developed particular, oftentimes dissimilar points of emphasis that were simultaneously pulling the American discourse both closer to and further from the Smithian tradition. With equal effect, liberal antebellum economists exploited an inner logic peculiar to the budding discipline, a "building block approach" that reflected the epistemological origins of political economy and the direction in which authorities wished to see the science carried.[5]

To be sure, the *Wealth of Nations* was for most antebellum liberals, and most antebellum economists generally, the starting point. Thomas Jefferson, for instance, wrote that "in political economy I think Smith's *Wealth of Na-*

tions the best book extant."[6] Smith was part of a corps of Enlightenment philosophers whose ideas helped sanction the young nation's liberal course. But the process by which Smithian principles were integrated into the antebellum liberal discourse was marked by paradigmatic challenges typical of the evolutionary maturation of all modern sciences. Even Smith's position in his own native British liberal orthodoxy followed complex, varied designs. If the development of liberal political economy in antebellum America was a disjointed process, hindered by historically and culturally specific institutions that made consensus difficult and reconciliation with British standards problematic, it was in part consequence of, and imitative of, the uncertainties and discrepancies that encumbered economic inquiry in the Atlantic world. The maturation of liberal political economy in America chronicles the challenges contemporary thinkers faced in positioning their brands of liberalism in what was a shifting paradigm. American liberals, to be fair, failed to engender consensus in an economic discourse that was itself struggling to find theoretical coherency. And in consequence, American liberals developed a unique brand of capitalist political economy—hybrid capitalism.

In this intellectual atmosphere antebellum free traders teaching at prestigious colleges in the Northeast instructed generations of students on the advantages of free markets, but they did so by largely ignoring the economic logic of Smithian laissez-faire. Rather the northeastern brand of liberal economics focused on the moral benefits of free markets. Free trade in the Northeast was primarily geared to engineering an economic society based on moral values, not supply and demand. The study intentionally limited student exposure to the materialist countenances of Smith. Instead, political economy was connected to premodern conservative social values more readily accepted in America's clerical schools. Almost all of the region's institutions of higher learning maintained close ties with the Church. The Congregationalists had their Harvard and Yale, the Episcopalians Penn and Columbia, the Presbyterians Princeton, and the Baptists Brown. Faculty were almost always clerical, Federalist, and aristocratic, and the letter of their instruction mostly conservative. Enlightenment thought was held in suspicion. Curricula emphasized theology, moral philosophy, biblical studies, and occasional tutelage in mathematics and the physical sciences.[7]

The intimacy between Church and antebellum colleges worked against the introduction of new curriculum. Far from being in the vanguard of social movements, early American colleges shunned egalitarian and democratic concepts that could upset the status quo. Classroom instruction matched the traditionalist institutional and cultural factors distinct to the region's academia, propagating a conservative economic intellectual culture.[8] Typically when academic instruction in political economy was offered in the Northeast, it was delivered to seniors in what was considered the climax of an early nineteenth-century higher education—a course in moral philosophy. The subject, according to Dorothy Ross, "studied human affairs as the realm within which individuals sought moral improvement."[9] Smithian moral philosophy, and the economic principles that lie within, blended well with the devout and dutiful nature of northeastern curricula. Smith was, after all, a moral philosopher before he became a political economist. His *Theory of Moral Sentiments* was, by the late eighteenth century, an important addition to the field. In it, and more explicitly in the *Wealth of Nations*, Smith wove ethics and economics together, and his insistence on the universality of moral and commercial principles complemented the northeastern clergy professor's predilection for ideological omnipotence. Moreover, the religious character of northeastern academia welcomed Smith's emphasis on the benign qualities of the liberal economic order, established by the "Author of Nature," along with the cosmopolitan character of free trade that encouraged mutually advantageous exchange. Finally, the version of Smithian economic liberalism taught in the Northeast intimated the conservative interpretations of the *Wealth of Nations* made popular by Dugald Stewart. The merchant patricians who made up college boards of trustees reflected regional commercial interests that were suspicious of Jeffersonian republicanism. Smithian liberalism was accepted in the classroom only if its lessons comported with a socially conservative agenda. Laissez-faire among northeastern clergy-academics was, in the words of one historian, "a sedative, not a stimulant," employed to advance "defensive social campaigns."[10] Clerical professors manipulated Smithian political economy to promote the status quo, especially after the rise of Jackson, and even more so during the early decades of industrialization and the emergence of organized labor.

Throughout the antebellum period, northeastern clergy-professors, Protestant churchmen, and Protestant laity in general coveted moral and material balance between God and Mammon. Holy scripture, centuries' worth of liturgical damnation of materialist ambition, suspicions against Enlightenment philosophy, and the conservative bent of intellectual culture in the Ivy League were overcome, however, not by cerebral machinations but rather by subtle adaptations and adoption of middle-class bourgeois values which included liberal economics. The clerical professors taught how Smith made markets moral. In the early twentieth century, Max Weber made famous the intellectual and practical connections between Protestantism and capitalism. Weber explained how Protestantism "helped deliver the spirit of modern capitalism, its specific ethos: the ethos of the modern bourgeois middle classes."[11] The northeastern clerical economists showed how market values fostered Christian piety. Protestant economic thought, the historian Daniel Walker Howe has shown, "attempted to infuse the marketplace with moral meaning" and sustained Christian doctrine as the primary frame of reference to understand emergent capitalism.[12] In antebellum America, where monetary donations to Protestant churches in 1860 were approximately $35–40 million, equal to roughly 70 percent of that year's federal income, and the number of churches was more than double the number of post offices, it seems sensible for intellectual capitalism to have been forced into compliance with Protestant values.[13]

In this way, northeastern liberals pulled Smith backward, to the fundamentals of moral philosophy from which his inquiry into economics was originally launched. By midcentury this brand of laissez-faire had lost popularity, supplanted by the materialist, technical, and utilitarian abstractions of Ricardo and John Stuart Mill. Still, northeastern intellectual capitalism clung to a distinctly religious, moral, and traditional strain in transatlantic free-trade thought. Freeing political economy from theology and moral philosophy took almost a century longer in America than it did in Britain.[14] "Modernization of American society," according to Howe, "was not accompanied by a corresponding secularization."[15] But by incorporating sacred and ethical principles into free trade analysis, the northeastern clerical economists helped assimilate liberal economics within America's religiously oriented colleges otherwise reticent to accept the nuances of the Enlightenment. If laissez-faire political economy was censored by some critics for its materialism, then presenting free-trade doctrine as evidence of a higher power abetted the discipline's acceptance into northeastern curricula before it was ultimately permitted to stand as an independent field of study.

This is not to say American clerical free traders were in complete isolation from the secular turn in the transatlantic liberal discourse. British liberal political economy was also challenged with a crisis of faith. An evangelical strain of free trade associated with Malthus and Thomas Chalmers persisted through the early decades of the nineteenth century. Malthus, for instance, advocated liberal policies to promote ethical behavior and encourage social stability—"to watch and ward." Like the American clerical free traders, Malthus and Chalmers were concerned more with social and economic stability than growth. The coexistence of an American and a British free trade movement that accentuated the spiritual over the material illustrates the intellectual ties between the two nations. It also indicates that the northeastern clergy-academics were actively engaged in shaping the new science, as well as active participants in the ideological trajectory of laissez-faire doctrine, if only by steering political economy to its original course in moral philosophy and religious orientation.[16]

Columbia College professor John McVickar exemplified the connection between Christian piety, moral philosophy, and free trade political economy in antebellum America. Born in 1787 into an elite New York City Federalist merchant family, he entered Columbia as a student at thirteen and graduated four years later at the top of his class. Ordained by the Episcopal Church in 1812, McVickar preceded his years at Columbia by serving as rector of the Church of St. James in Hyde Park, New York. In 1817 he returned to his alma mater as professor of moral philosophy.[17]

McVickar helped popularize free trade doctrine in America. His 1825 *Outlines of Political Economy* republished with extensive editor's notes J. R. McCulloch's essay "Political Economy."[18] In 1828 McCulloch was appointed the first professor of political economy at the University of London, where he became a leading advocate for Ricardian economics. His "Political Economy" was in essence a more accessible adaptation of Ricardo's *Principles of Political Economy* (1817). McVickar's textual platform for disseminating laissez-faire seems unusual, given McCulloch's unequivocal declaration that political economy was not a "moral science . . . the production of material wealth is the only question."[19] Still, McVickar's version of free trade was cast in the language of moral philosophy. He employed McCulloch's work to advance the cosmopolitan vision of Smithian laissez-faire. Liberal cosmopolitanism complemented the minister's religious disposition and was by the 1830s easily connected to Ricardo's theory of comparative advantage. Free trade, McVickar argued, spread universal fraternity and worked in particular toward the reunification of American and British minds. "It may serve to moderate the hasty zeal ... by showing how nearly reflecting men on both sides of the Atlantic arrive at the same conclusions, and thus tend to draw together two kindred nations, whom an unwise and illiberal policy has too often disunited." Free trade advanced humanity in its epic quest to eliminate the evil tendencies that separated men. "It inclines them to drop the sword from their hands, by demonstrating to them, that they are about to plunge it into their own bowels."[20] Free trade, in short, promoted peace between nations.

During the early modern period, mercantilism provided European powers with a global economic regime of regulated commerce. But mercantilist policy also evolved into a weapon of war during the seemingly endless conflicts between the British, French, Dutch, and Spanish. The British Navigation Acts, for instance, outfitted mercantilism to justify violations of the trading rights of neutral powers engaged in "illicit" trade. During the Napoleonic Wars, American shipping was routinely harassed and attacked on the high seas. Washington, Adams, and Jefferson demanded that Europe's warring powers respect American commercial neutrality, but the United States was ultimately drawn into the conflict, first during the quasi–naval war with France, and then during the War of 1812 against Britain. Americans like McVickar advocated commercial liberalism in part because mercantilist policy engendered what must have appeared to contemporaries as perpetual war. Laissez-faire may have undermined commercial order and stability within an imperial trade regime, but for liberals it engendered an economics of peace.[21]

McVickar's pontifications on the macro moral benefits of global commerce were extended to the micro level. Clergy and political economists, according to McVickar, did essentially the same thing—rescue individuals from a life of moral depravity.[22] What scripture revealed to be man's duty, market phenomena rewarded with riches. Economic success was predicated on individual virtue. Like Smith, McVickar argued that free market exchange strengthened morals. Smith's *Theory of Moral Sentiments* tied market institutions to a more righteous commonwealth through, among other things, the prospect for harmonious socialization and the countless opportunities for inducing shared perceptions, mutual approbation, sympathy, and the correspondence of internalized fellow-feeling sentiments.[23] For Smith, "the road to virtue and that to fortune ... in most cases [were] very nearly the same."[24] In a similar vein,

McVickar admitted that although "it be but the science of wealth, yet does it show that wealth to be the result of the moral and intellectual, as well as the physical powers of man. It demonstrates that to man, ignorant and vicious, there is no road to wealth." Political economy was illustrative of divine scripture. "Gold and virtue," McVickar wrote, are not "balanced against each other in opposite scales." Indeed, he continued, "the greatest pursuit of wealth is still the greatest safeguard of virtue."[25]

McVickar's free-market moralism was fundamentally different from liberal texts that stressed the material benefits of market competition. It was also distinct from the more pessimistic strains of early nineteenth-century British Evangelical economics. The northeastern interpretation of the free-market order was not the dismal science of Malthus with its vengeful, punishing, catastrophic template of Old Testament divine retribution.[26] Rather McVickar highlighted the economics of benevolent progress. Like Smith, McVickar was ultimately an optimist. The natural economic order spread benefits, not misery; the natural system of liberty was a force of moral, social, and economic good. His version of laissez-faire found kinship with the contemporary transatlantic liberal movement that was, according to one historian, "loosely linked with a whole set of values—freedom of religion, of knowledge, of land, of education, freedom from oppression, war, drink, slavery—which served to identify free trade with a wider range of public goods instead of simply that of free markets."[27]

To be sure, the northeastern clerical liberals of the early antebellum period sympathized with abolitionists, especially after the Second Great Awakening, but they were not firebrand antislavery men. McVickar's free-trade moralism was not tied to the transatlantic free-trade antislavery crusade.[28] From his post at Columbia, McVickar was cognizant of New York's commercial dealings in southern cotton. The sons of the plantation elite enrolled in his classes. His writings contain almost nothing on the subject of abolitionism. And student records of his lectures indicate the subject was rarely entertained in course discussions. Abolitionism strained America's Protestant churches. The Presbyterians (1838), Methodists (1844), and Baptists (1845) all split over the slavery controversy. Francis Wayland, whose free-trade moral economic philosophy occupies the following pages, was also ambivalent on abolition. In 1835 Wayland prohibited student discussion of abolition on the campus of Brown University, where he was president. Despite being considered the nation's premier moral philosopher, Wayland favored maintaining ties between Southern and Northern Baptists over moral denunciations against slaveholders. "And where is Dr. Wayland?" William Lloyd Garrison reproved the professor over his silence in the slavery debate. It was not until 1854 that Wayland addressed abolition in public, and he did so in an innocuous fashion.[29]

Since Eric Williams's *Capitalism and Slavery* (1944), historians have debated the connection between free-trade political economy, industrialization, and abolitionism. Williams posited, among other things, that the shift in British intellectual and political culture from mercantilism to laissez-faire was orchestrated to disguise the pecuniary ambitions of industrialists. In the early nineteenth century, British industrial interests advocated abolition and divestment of West Indian plantation assets, including slaves, as well as the reallocation of capital toward domestic manufacturing in order to transform the British economy into an industrial hegemon. According to Williams, abolitionism was advertised as a humanitarian appeal to moral sentiments, when in fact it was an ideological and cultural deception, employed to enrich free-trade industrialists who realized slavery was more costly than wage labor, and ultimately unprofitable. Although Williams focused on the British West Indies, historians of colonial and early national America have extended the implications of his arguments to the United States. The New Historians of Capitalism, for instance, have encouraged the application of Williams's thesis to highlight the centrality of slavery in the history of American economic development.[30]

The implication of Williams's argument for this study is that free-trade ideology, notwithstanding its original motivations, should exhibit ties with antebellum abolition. However, antebellum academic expression of laissez-faire, emanating precisely from the rapidly industrializing Northeast, was not motivated by abolitionist concerns. While Williams's description of the links between British abolition and laissez-faire is significant for that nation's political history, there is little evidence in the American discourse to support the wider narrative. Antebellum free traders like McVickar and Wayland were not abolitionists, and the southern advocates of laissez-faire were slaveholders who worked against industrial culture. Moreover, McVickar's and Wayland's texts were far more sympathetic to merchants than to manufacturers. And although their brand of laissez-faire was based on humanitarian appeals and encouraged individual economic autonomy, these values were not extended to southern slaves.

Finally, northeastern liberals balked at an alliance with Richard Cobden's free trade abolitionists, regardless of their shared affinity for moral economic liberalism. Despite what some historians have suggested, free trade cosmopolitanism in the Northeast avoided the slave controversy, even as British liberalism confronted it. And the region's ideological commitment to laissez-faire political economy was not born at the founding of the American chapter of the Cobden Club in 1866. Cobden did not "enlist" American liberals to a British-led free trade movement.[31] Rather, McVickar, Wayland, and others illustrate that American liberal moralism developed organically, for reasons separate from the Anti–Corn Law League. The reluctance to engage abolitionism, even into the 1850s, however, should not be interpreted as evidence of free trade unity between southern and northeastern liberals. Quiet over slavery does not indicate support. Still, it demonstrates the gap between the northeastern and southern brands of laissez-faire. Northeastern and southern liberals largely ignored each other, or at least failed to communicate on the most critical issue of the day. Northeastern liberals were alienated from both abolitionists and planters. In this regard, northeastern laissez-faire existed in its own cerebral universe.

Neither is McVickar's version of Smithian laissez-faire Jeffersonian. Contrary to conventional historical thinking, not all antebellum strains of free trade were tied to Jefferson's agrarian ideal. McVickar was not a mouthpiece for merchant capital, but his brand of liberalism does reflect the ideological and policy inclinations of someone who matured intellectually in the commercial-mercantile Northeast of the early national period.[32] Commercial networks that were developed during the colonial period and maintained after America's independence found merchants, bankers, sailors, and commodities passing between Europe and America with regularity. But when trade wars erupted across the North Atlantic, inflamed by Napoleon's Berlin decree, Britain's Orders in Council, and Jefferson's Embargo of 1807, northeastern shipping and mercantile interests were ruined. Peace in the Atlantic world was a fleeting aspiration, and conflict galvanized the merchant's call for liberal exchange. McVickar's brand of intellectual capitalism offered a solution, based not on the agrarian homilies of Jeffersonianism but on mercantile values couched in Christian cosmopolitanism. Free trade "teaches among nations and federative states," McVickar wrote, "the all-important lessons of peace and mutual benefits.... It unites nations, not by treatise or federations... but by the laws of mutual interest."[33] Laissez-faire inspired fraternal intercourse, not economic conflict. Furthermore, the connection made by some historians between free trade policy and late nineteenth-century imperialism does not exist in McVickar's version of laissez-faire. McVickar's merchant capitalist, held suspect by traditional agrarians and Marxist historians of modern imperialism, stood at the fore of Atlantic amity, offering commercial exchange as a harbinger of peace.

At Brown University, Wayland strengthened antebellum attachments between Christianity, cosmopolitan fraternity, and liberal economics. Wayland was born in 1796 in New York City. Like McVickar, Wayland served the church before entering the academy. The five years prior to Wayland's accepting the posts of president and professor of moral philosophy at Brown were spent at the First Baptist Church of Boston. When he started teaching at Brown in 1827, Wayland supplemented his lectures on moral philosophy with economics. The following year political economy was added to the university's course listings. In 1837 Wayland authored what became antebellum America's most popular economics textbook, *The Elements of Political Economy*. The text went through eighteen editions before the Civil War, selling nearly 60,000 copies.[34] And like McVickar, Wayland fastened Smithian laissez-faire to Christian values and moral philosophy. "The principles of political economy are so closely analogous to those of Moral Philosophy, that almost every question in the one, may be argued on grounds belonging to the other." The natural economic order established a direct correlation between virtuous behavior and the accumulation of wealth. "The circulation of the scriptures, the inculcation of moral and religious truth upon the mind of man, by means of the Sabbath schools, and the preaching of the gospel, are of the very greatest importance to the productive energies of a country."[35] Wayland's integration of Christianity into political economy was more explicit than McVickar's. In some passages Wayland's economic lessons invoke Sunday sermon. "In the sweat of thy brow shalt thou eat bread" was characteristic of Wayland's doctrinal disposition.[36] "If a man complain because God made him to labor; it is a difficulty which the complainant must settle with his Maker." In his discussion of paupers and poor relief, Wayland concluded that "the fault lies, not in their wages, but in themselves." And, he continued logically, "of course, the correction must come, not from a change in wages, but from a change in habits."[37] Connecting laissez-faire to a Protestant ethic, Wayland believed free-trade political economy compelled the masses to righteous and industrious behavior.

For Wayland, free trade was demonstrative of a providential order. The object of clerical sermon was, after all, to illustrate manifestations of Divine Providence. Separated by wide distances, humanity relied on each other for sustenance. "The aptitudes of different nations for the creating of different products, has, in many cases, been fixed by unchangeable, geographic, and physiological laws." Thus, the Almighty arranged a cosmopolitan trade regime that compelled humanity to cultivate Christian fraternity. Natural economic laws governing free exchange were intended so "that men should live together in friendship and harmony." The theory of comparative advantage was for Wayland akin to divine revelation. "I suppose it unnecessary to state," Wayland wrote, "that nations, that is, people, if left to themselves, are like individuals, disposed to avail themselves of the peculiar advantages bestowed upon them by their Creator."[38]

Trade between nations extended benefits beyond wealth. Like McVickar's, Wayland's version of laissez-faire did not accentuate the material benefits of free exchange. Trade spreads culture, promotes amicable relations through mutually advantageous intercourse, and weakens those wicked prejudices that dispose men to national rivalry and acts of war. Capitalism, according to this view, is magnanimous. Wayland held an enlightened, non-Hobbesian worldview where nations worked peaceably toward a universal commonwealth based on reciprocal benefit. "From this universal dependence, we learn that God intends nations, as well as individuals, to live in peace, and to conduct themselves towards each other upon the principles of benevolence."[39]

Wayland's strand of economic liberal moralism, like McVickar's, looked externally, beyond America's borders, to benign global markets coordinated to foster a humanitarian ethic. Laissez-faire ideology was not monetized; rather priority was given to the positive moral, social, and political externalities engendered by free trade. In this way Wayland and McVickar found Smithian liberal moralism a complementary fit to American economic intellectual culture. Only toward the middle decades of the nineteenth century did British liberalism begin emphasizing the dynamism of market economies and the potential economic benefits of free trade. But in the earlier part of the century, most British liberals conformed to the traditional view that the economy was static, and understood free-market policy as an instrument to decelerate economic growth, or restrict excessive and "unnatural" economic expansion, and stabilize what to some contemporaries appeared as uncontrollable commercial and industrial development. Malthus's rejection of the Poor Laws, for instance, was in part an effort to restrict growth, foster social balance, and encourage ethical behavior—"goading men to be good." Wayland and McVickar broke with these stationary economic views. Wayland's economic optimism was more in line with Smith. Although Wayland concentrated on the spiritual, moral, and social benefits of liberal markets, his faith in a benevolent creator promised material benefit. Humanity, Wayland argued, was not destined for the lowly and somber conditions described by Malthus, Chalmers, and other British Evangelical economists. Rather, the providential order intended for each successive generation to enjoy greater prosperity. "It is thus that a society, age after age, grows rich, and each successive race of men leaves the world more richly provided with means and facilities of production, than it found it."[40] Improvement is the permanent condition. Through the more efficient application of labor, the discovery of new technologies, and augmented investments of capital, those who in earlier times might expect to suffer privations enjoyed comfort. Economic progress was predicated on free markets. Wayland pontificated conventional liberal precepts against state intervention, consecrated free trade, and damned tariffs. "Every man is more interested in his own success, than any other man can be interested in it," Wayland wrote. Unfettered pursuits of self-interest were the surest means of augmenting the wealth of individuals and nations. Legislation never increased capital; neither could state interposition channel labor to profitable avenues. Duties raised prices, diminished productivity, redistributed property, depressed trade, and increased unemployment. Governments, Wayland concluded, "can do much, by confining themselves to their appropriate duties, and leaving every thing else alone. Interference of society with the concerns of the individual, even when arising from the most innocent motives, will always tend to crush the spirit of enterprise, and cripple the productive energies of a country."[41]

Free markets were essential to Wayland's brand of laissez-faire, but like most American liberals he was not an absolutist, and in some cases his economic philosophy was inconsistent. When Wayland perceived tension between Christian values and economic freedoms, his faith prevailed. This devotion is evident in his seminal work *The Elements of Moral Science* (1837).

Considered the first American textbook in moral philosophy, it sold 100,000 copies by the end of the century.[42] Therein Wayland confessed the authority Christian moralism had over his political economy when he reverted to a premodern form of economic thought in a critique of self-interest. Self-love was sometimes least productive of social and individual happiness. The economic order "was not constructed to secure the happiness of any single individual," Wayland sermonized, "and he who devises his plans with sole reference to himself must find them continually thwarted by that Omnipotent and Invisible Agency, which is overruling all things."[43]

Colonial economic thought, fastened deliberately to Christian ethics, exercised influence over Wayland, as well as McVickar. The latter's discussion of acceptable criteria for restricting trade demonstrates the lasting impact of a colonial Christian moralism that inhibited economic behavior. "If . . . individual gains may be pursued to the detriment of national wealth," McVickar wrote, "then must the guardians of the national welfare be ever upon the watch against individual encroachment." McVickar struck a tone reminiscent of seventeenth-century economic thought when he censured "home speculation," as well as those occasions when "individual profits are . . . extracted from the miseries of other, from the vices and passions of society."[44] Theological imperatives played a powerful role in colonial political economy. Puritan settlers calculated a "just price," applied the Golden Rule to economic exchange, and filled broadsides with anti-merchant rhetoric critical of the corruptive and misanthropic tendencies of commercialization. Influential thinkers like John Winthrop of Massachusetts employed scripture to defend public economy over private, advocated state surveillance and control over the distribution of wealth, cursed interest, and railed against the notion of buying cheap to sell dear. Pennsylvania Quakers looked to sacred texts for economic guidance as well, crafting sumptuary laws and legislative control of prices.[45]

The transition from medieval scholasticism to secular rationalism was a cumbersome trail for political economy. Wayland and McVickar gave sharp expression to the dialectic between Christianity and economic thought, and in doing so the northeastern free traders signaled their opposition to the analytical transformations of midcentury British classicism.[46] McVickar and Wayland failed to march in lockstep with the methodological developments ushered in by the more secular Ricardo and the utilitarianism of Jeremy Bentham and John Stuart Mill. Instead, the region's reticent intellectual culture, sustained by the prolonged relationship between academic and religious institutions and pursuant to the methodological tendencies of moral philosophy, compelled northeastern liberals to resurrect the imperatives of divine explanation and reinforce standards of ethical propriety in intellectual capitalism. They should not be faulted, however, for failing to predict that the trajectory of political economy was splitting from its Smithian roots toward more technical and materialist modes of analysis that ultimately excommunicated economics from Christianity.

For Wayland and McVickar, Christianity and laissez-faire were similar in another significant way: both laid claim to universality. Economic laws presided over practically every liberal account of the free market. Margaret Schabas has noted that political economy of the early modern period "regarded the phenomena of their discourse as part of the same natural world studied by natural philosophers. Not only were economic phenomena understood mostly by drawing analogies to natural phenomena, but they were also contiguous with physical nature."[47] McVickar and Wayland wrote in this tradition. From labor and land to money and trade, economic laws arranged an uncompromising order, similar in scale and scope to the formulas that governed earthly matter and the celestial bodies. Moreover, since natural laws were designed by the higher power, man had a moral obligation to follow them. Natural law theorists, led by John Locke, gave additional credence to the natural order by attaching moral qualities to scientific theorems. The rules that governed the material world were reasonable, observable, inflexible, and beneficial to their adherents. Failure to correspond with the natural order, legislative or otherwise, precipitated damaging consequences and ran counter to God's will. By the middle decades of the eighteenth century, economic philosophers described market tendencies as ordained regularities, prompting consistent patterns of human conduct attributed to man's constitution and his station in the cosmological order. Few things were considered more natural than individuals acting on their private interests. Stimulated by automatic impulses, Economic Man manifested an innate acquisitive spirit capable of constructing rational and orderly economic relations that not only augmented personal and national wealth but encouraged social stability by making commercial behavior predictable. Natural-law theory afforded the underpinnings of transatlantic laissez-faire, including antebellum American expressions.[48]

Perhaps it is only fitting that the cosmopolitan jurist Francis Lieber became one of the principal advocates of antebellum liberal universalism. Born at the turn of the century in Prussia, he fought against Napoleon at Waterloo, studied in Berlin, and eventually settled in America after fleeing prosecution for inciting German nationalism. An eclectic thinker, Lieber took a universalistic approach to scholarship. His first major text, a thirteen-volume translation of a popular German encyclopedia, brought him professional accolades and contacts with prominent Americans. These connections, particularly with Nicholas Biddle, helped Lieber secure the professorship of political economy and history at South Carolina College in 1835.[49]

In his course on political economy, Lieber instructed students from J. B. Say's free-trade *Treatise on Political Economy* (1803). The progress of civilized society revealed the inevitability of the natural liberal order, according to Lieber. Individual freedom was on the march, claiming victory first against despots, then in a political defense of private property. It was man's destiny not merely to exist but to "become civilized," and civilization according to Lieber rested on the natural law foundations of property rights.[50] Private property, separate and predating the social compact, was for Lieber a universal inalienable right. According to his understanding of legal history, one's property was the fundamental expression of individual autonomy. After private property, Lieber's liberal narrative turned to free trade policy. "Free trade has arrived at that period . . . when it is universally acknowledged within each country. The next period will be when it is acknowledged within our entire race, and people will speak of protection as we now speak of the beauty patches of the last century."[51] Because of the inherent correlation between political and economic institutions, laissez-faire, grounded on the tenets of property rights, best complemented the political formula of liberalism, since both ideologies instructed freedom from government interference. "Free trade is nothing more than protection against obstruction," Lieber argued. And for Lieber, it was that simple. Unfettered exchange was, he wrote, "no system, no theory, no wicker-work of slender concepts; it is simply unencumbered exchange."[52]

But for Lieber liberalism was more than a temporal force; free trade carried spiritual connotations. Providence established laws governing commercial society, and free trade was one of them. "Free trade is the principle of the gospel of peace and goodwill, carried out in the world of exchange." Nature required that individuals exchange the products of their labor to perpetuate the existence of the human race. Trade was not only natural but also necessary. The "Law of Inter-Dependence," as Lieber called it, "is a truth of great importance for natural theology."[53] Restrictions, whether mercantilist or protectionist, were akin to blocking divine will; "in reality they interfere with God's own laws and commands."[54] The omnipotent wisdom of providential reciprocal dependence ensured that those who populate the earth would engage in mutually beneficial social interactions.

In 1855 Lieber, passed over by the trustees to fill the vacant presidency at South Carolina College, resigned his professorship, sold his slaves, and left the South for good. This was probably best. Lieber suffered from what he called "utter mental isolation" in the South. In 1856, despite repeated complaints that his teaching responsibilities left him with an empty feeling, he accepted the chair of political economy and history at Columbia College. There he established himself as one of the premier American jurists of the nineteenth century. A devoted Unionist during the Civil War, he was commissioned by Lincoln's War Department to draft directives on wartime treatment of freed and escaped slaves, prisoners of war, spies, and the management of civilians in Union-occupied territories. Today the Lieber Code, or Lieber Instructions, is considered the first systematic attempt to codify the rules of war.[55]

Despite his attachment to nationalist concerns, Lieber never abandoned liberal principles for Republican protectionism. He described protectionism as "petty statishness," "veiled communism," and interference with the "Divine Law of Inter-Dependence." From his lectern at Columbia, Lieber argued that the changes in political and economic conditions wrought by the Civil War did not alter the universality of liberal political economy. "The laws of production, exchange, and consumption do not alter any more than the laws of electricity," Lieber continued; "we are human beings placed on the same globe with other people, subject to the same physical and moral laws, liable to the same penalties for running counter to the dictates of wisdom, and bound by the same duties toward others and ourselves." Though Lieber was not an extraordinarily religious man, his political economy was guided by a sense of propriety. From a moral standpoint, commercial restrictions were comparable to ethics violations, since they inhibited man's ability to acquire sustenance. "To interfere with consumption is really as preposterous as an attempt would be to interfere, by sapient laws, with free respiration." Natural economic laws, Lieber contended, were designed for the "essential welfare of mankind" through material comfort and the fostering of amicable relations, as well as to direct the human race in its quest for higher civilization.[56]

At Columbia Lieber taught alongside McVickar. The new post brought Lieber additional teaching responsibilities, increased from eight hours a week at South Carolina to fifteen hours at Columbia. Perhaps he found consolation in the political sympathies of his new colleagues. Like McVickar, Lieber was a political conservative, in the Hamiltonian mold. "Democratic absolutism" was Lieber's great fear. Before the Civil War he lambasted Jacksonians, challenged states' rights advocates, privately condemned slavery as a moral evil, but thought abolitionism foolish.

In many ways Lieber straddles the sectional divide in antebellum free-trade ideology and in doing so embodies the intellectual conundrums of the American free-trade movement. Liberals in the North and South were estranged from one another. Despite advocating the same policy, neither side seemed interested in what the other was saying. Like the northeastern version, the southern strain of laissez-faire was consistent with its intellectual heritage, social customs, and institutional traditions and gave force to preserving the region's political and economic strength in national affairs. Southern colleges were decidedly more secular. Southern liberalism was not disseminated from the pulpit or the lectern of the moral philosopher. Free trade texts in the South were, therefore, less inclined to emphasize the merits of moralist erudition, lest those discussions raise the ethical responsibilities of southern institutions.

Most critically, slavery was at the center of southern laissez-faire. Free-trade economists in the South extracted from the cosmopolitan fraternalism of the enlightened Smith a theoretical vehicle to advance states' rights and defend slavery. This precipitated a practical, politically charged, and policy-oriented defense of free trade. Economics served the political, and the political served the planters. Thomas Cooper and John Calhoun cemented this association during the nullification crisis, and as the nation moved toward civil war, the bond between pro-slavery, states' rights, and free trade grew inseparable. In consequence, the domestic free-trade movement lacked national cohesiveness, mitigated promulgation of free trade legislation, and ultimately contributed to a cerebral and political void filled by protectionism.

Attempts at an alliance were made, but these endeavors were short-lived. They illustrate the ideological discrepancies and confusion within antebellum free trade rather than the potential for consensus. The single most important effort to unite national laissez-faire was the Free Trade Convention at Philadelphia in September 1831. The meeting organized by Condy Raguet came mostly in response to the so-called Tariff of Abominations of 1828. Born in Philadelphia in 1784, Raguet was a merchant and journalist by trade. He sat in the Pennsylvania state senate as a Federalist and had a brief stint as American consul to Brazil. When Raguet returned to Philadelphia from diplomatic service, he found himself in the lion's den of protectionism. To counter protectionist momentum he established the *Free Trade Advocate* in 1829. Lacking subscriptions, Raguet renamed the journal *Banner of the Constitution* and, in an effort to better organize free trade voices at the national level, moved its place of publication to Washington, DC, then New York, and finally back to Philadelphia.[57]

Raguet's writings on trade, published mostly in his failing newspapers, are a compilation of biting short essays designed to refute protectionist claims. Though Raguet was sometimes cited as an authority, he was not a systematic thinker. His criticisms of legislative interdictions on commerce were little more than recitations of popular liberal arguments typical of the period. Restrictions promoted smuggling that undermined the authority of the state, discriminated against the poor by taxing common necessities, limited exports, diminished domestic capital and employment, and promoted distrust among the populace by bloating the size and expense of government with trained "inquisitors" in the art of regulatory "espionage."[58] Raguet's narrative of American history points to 1816 as a pivotal date. Prior to this year, "the American Government was in the hands of political economists," honest statesmen who appreciated "that individuals are better judges of the most advantageous mode of employing their labor and capital." From this point forward, however, Congress was infiltrated by "political arithmeticians," or protectionist politicians keen at manipulating statistics and their constituents to sneak through high tariff legislation. He accused protectionists of aggregating quantitative data to not only confound unsuspecting legislators but also artificially enhance the scientific basis of protectionism. Raguet defended theory over facts, one of the ancillary debates in the antebellum economic discourse. "Any one may thus see that an acquaintance with figures is not enough to qualify a man to reason correctly upon matters which require a depth of thought." The protectionist, Raguet discovered, "very often so completely buries himself up in figures, that he hardly knows himself to what conclusions his premises lead." It was unfortunate, Raguet lamented, "that the statistical collectors would not confine themselves to their proper vocation, and avoid meddling with political economy, which they do not understand."[59]

At the Philadelphia convention arranged by Raguet, attended by more than two hundred delegates from fifteen states, sectional interests, disputes over the constitutionality of tariffs, the specter of nullification, and arguments over what constituted appropriate modifications to existing tariff levels hampered progress.[60] Still, the convention produced a memorial, attributed to former treasury secretary Albert Gallatin, that was read to both houses of Congress in 1832. The memorial transmitted a policy-oriented review of contemporary free trade positions, noting the sectional favoritism embedded in high tariffs and the trouble with diverting capital "from profitable to unprofitable pursuits," and it described protectionism "as the last relic of that system of general restrictions and monopolies, which had its origins in barbarous times."[61]

What progress was made toward the unification of domestic laissez-faire was quickly overshadowed by the nullification crisis later in 1832. It is important for historians to avoid overstating the influence of the Free Trade Convention. It was certainly not the seminal event in antebellum free trade history. Many of the leading spokesmen of American free trade did not attend. And the publications associated with the convention, mainly the *Memorial*, did not become, as one historian has suggested, "the textbook for free traders of the day."[62] Only 5,000 copies of Gallatin's memorial were printed. In comparison, Wayland's liberal textbook sold 60,000 copies. The convention contributed to a temporary spike in interest in free-trade doctrine. But to suggest that the origins of the American liberal discourse should be traced to the 1831 convention places too much trust in accounts by the event's promoters. By then, liberal economics was taught in political economy courses offered in at least fourteen American colleges. Smith's *Wealth of Nations* had gone through two American printings, and Malthus's essay on population was published in the United States in 1809. The 1821 English translation of Say's *Treatise on Political Economy*, in the words of one historian, "dominated the United States textbook market until after 1837," and several important domestic free-trade texts had already been published.[63] In short, the Philadelphia convention did not "provide the nation with a comprehensive manifesto setting forth the American strand of free trade." To be sure, the Free Trade Convention energized the movement. However, to conclude the meeting "was at once the culmination and the foundation of the unique principle of American free trade thought" implies the absence of earlier contributions. As this chapter illustrates, American liberals presented a dynamic and sophisticated economic dialogue with origins stretching to the earliest decades of the nineteenth century. More important, exaggerating the consensus of the Free Trade Convention discounts the deep divisions within what was a heterogeneous and intellectually conflicted body of American laissez-faire ideology. There is no "distinctly American" version of free trade, and some of these divisions were evident at the convention itself. Any consensus of thought was confined to Gallatin's *Memorial*, which was limited in scale and scope as well as circulation.[64]

Finally, the Philadelphia convention demonstrates more the frustrations of free-trade policy than its triumph. Historians recognize nineteenth-century America as one of the most protectionist economies in modern history. Debates over what exactly constitutes a "protective tariff" have their own place in the historiography, but beginning in 1808 and stretching through the remainder of the century, American tariffs were high, in some cases exceedingly high. And the Compromise Tariff of 1833 was motivated primarily by the constitutional crisis surrounding nullification, not a "liberal awakening" prompted by Gallatin's *Memorial*. The Compromise Tariff cut duties to the revenue level of 20 percent over the following decade. This legislation, along with the moderate revenue tariffs of 1846 and 1857, represent the extent of free-trade policy in nineteenth-century America.

Gallatin's policy-oriented *Memorial* indicates the influence of the southern attendees at the convention, who numbered nearly twice the northerners present.[65] Southern laissez-faire was far more inclined to integrate discussions of contemporary politics and society, mainly slavery, than metaphysical abstractions. Southern liberals offered analysis that was more secular, and tended to tout the material benefits of free trade. George Tucker is perhaps the exception to the southern inclination for policy-minded free-trade ideology. Born into a prominent merchant family in Bermuda in 1775, Tucker left the island as a young man on the advice of relatives. After studying at the College of William and Mary, he settled in Williamsburg for legal training under the tutelage of his uncle, St. George Tucker. Poor investments, a gambling addiction, and a lottery scheme he orchestrated that ended in his imprisonment burdened Tucker's life with financial hardships. These troubles did not prevent him from serving six years in Congress, nor did they seem to hinder his intellectual output, much of which he produced as professor of moral philosophy at the University of Virginia.

When Jefferson established the university in 1819, he stressed the importance of teaching political economy. Despite Tucker's Federalist politics, Madison recommended him to the faculty in 1825 after reading some of Tucker's essays. He served the university in various capacities and exhibited administrative and pedagogical foresight. But as a professor, according to one student, his lectures were "dull and uninteresting," and his courses "confusion worse confounded." In 1845 at age seventy, Tucker retired from teaching, but he continued writing. He published *Political Economy for the People* while in his eighties. In 1861, on board a ship waiting to depart Mobile Bay, he was struck by a bale of cotton, leaving him temporarily unconscious. He died three months later, two days before the attack on Fort Sumter.[66]

Of the entire assemblage of antebellum American political economists, Tucker deserves special attention for drawing the closest philosophical affinity with Smith. What Smithian scholars today consider an imperative for appreciating the totality of Smith's thought—that is, tying together the Scotsman's earlier essays on epistemology, ethics, and language and giving fair treatment to his earlier *Theory of Moral Sentiments* before coming to grips with the *Wealth of Nations*—was largely overlooked by antebellum economists. This is true, to some degree, even of McVickar and Wayland. Antebellum liberals in the South especially either ignored, did not have access to, or entertained only a blinkered reading of Smith's earlier publications and, therefore, neglected the connection between Smith's political economy and his moral philosophy. Tucker's works, however, showed that in his metaphysical disposition he closely resembled the Enlightenment economic thinkers. And by merging economics within lengthy expositions on moral philosophy, sociology, and psychology, Tucker presented a style of thought that corresponded, more so perhaps than any other antebellum economist, with the ideological nuances of Smithian intellectual capitalism.

In *Theory of Moral Sentiments*, Smith wrote extensively about epistemology, or the history of the accumulation of knowledge.[67] Like many Enlightenment philosophers, Smith expressed skepticism about man's mental faculties. The *Theory of Moral Sentiments* is a culmination of his earlier works that described humanity's fickle relationship with knowledge, forever plagued, according to Smith, by its inability to accurately comprehend natural phenomena. Governed by base human passions, even our most immediate self-interests are but clouded assessments, riddled with deceptions and stymied by the complexities of nature's grand design. Reason, awareness, and familiarity with the natural world bring temporary mental tranquility, cultivating human understanding, or the "connecting chain" of ideas that flow "gradually and easily into the heart, without violence, pain or difficulty."[68] Novelties, however, evoke surprise, wonder, and admiration and disrupt cerebral balance. From birth, humanity stumbles through an epic quest to decipher its natural surroundings. Sympathy, or the correspondence between individuals in their observations made of the natural world, are favored over disagreement and, for Smith, engender a fellow feeling that serves as the basis for moral sentiments. Even when confronted with incontestable facts, or positive, accurate knowledge, individuals favor the temporary soothing of their imagination and thus cling to long-standing beliefs. Certain cosmological work of Descartes and other early modern pioneers in science, Smith noted, "regarded by a very ingenious nation, for near a century together, as a most satisfactory account . . . has been demonstrated, to the conviction of all mankind, that these pretended causes of those wonderful effects, not only do not actually exist, but are utterly impossible, and if they did exist, could produce no such effects as are ascribed to them."[69]

From this subtle yet striking conclusion stems Smith's entire defense of laissez-faire. The natural order is too perplexing to measure and too powerful for mortals to master. Even when vested with the most sophisticated, reasoned systems of human intellect, "the natural causes of things can not be entirely controlled by the impotent endeavors of man," a race, Smith argued, that is "allotted a humbler department . . . one much more suitable to the weakness of his powers, and to the narrowness of his comprehension." Suspicions of man's capacity for intelligence were amplified when Smith considered statesmen, whose policies often encouraged consequences beyond all reasonable expectations. If individuals experienced difficulty understanding their own immediate reality, and with it their economic self-interest, then certainly politicians, even those trained in the "science of the legislator," had very little chance. Smith's skepticism about humanity's mental faculties is the philosophical root of his contempt for mercantilism. "Amidst the turbulence and disorder of faction, a certain spirit of system is apt to mix itself with that public spirit ... intoxicated with the imaginary beauty of this ideal system, of which they have no experience, but which has been represented to them in all the most dazzling colours in which the eloquence of their leaders could paint it. Those leaders themselves ... become many of them in time the dupes of their own sophistry."[70] Smith concluded his description of legislative fetters inhibiting the system of natural economic liberty in the *Wealth of Nations*: "The sovereign is completely discharged from a duty, in the attempting to perform which he must always be exposed to innumerable delusions, and for the proper performance of which no human wisdom or knowledge could ever be sufficient."[71] Most important, from the standpoint of a moral philosopher, the greatest benefit of free exchange is the unlimited opportunity for sensual consensus, or fellow feeling. Put differently, free trade offers consumers, workers, butchers, bakers, and brewers a chance for mental tranquility occasioned by correspondence in their mutual assessment of values.

Although most antebellum economists did not incorporate the full extent of Smith's logic into their own thought, exploring the theoretical subtleties of their epistemological roots is an important metric to decipher ideological predispositions. Like Smith, antebellum liberals expressed a complacent optimism about the economic behavior of private individuals, found security in a benevolent natural order, and deprecated political institutions for their incompetence in managing the national economy. The ascendancy in American culture of economic and political individualism, as well as the expansion of the suffrage, rested partly on the widespread social belief in the existence of an enlightened self-interest. Doubly safeguarded by Madison's concept of contending factions and the stabilizing force of the Constitution, an invisible hand of government supervises socially benign competition, preserves harmony between opposing interests, and begets spontaneous order, or in the language of Smith, "without intending it, without knowing it, advance[s] the interest of society."[72] Economic thinkers from Hume to Milton Friedman have commented on the correlation between free markets and free political institutions. By conceptualizing the economic sphere as occupied by individuals who exercise reason in private judgment, and organizing society according to Bernard Mandeville's supposition that private vices occasion public benefits, faith in the liberal regime is encouraged. That Americans experienced economic success only confirmed the growing consensus for liberal institutions domestically, as the accumulation of wealth was believed the reward for rational behavior.[73]

Tucker's economic intellectual culture is intimately connected to Enlightenment dialogues on human psychology, moral philosophy, sociology, and epistemology. His chief philosophical concern was "mental philosophy," or investigating the cerebral instruments of man. He seemed especially influenced by Smith's best friend, Hume. Tucker's early writings are set in a speculative cast, intrigued by the whimsical and often erroneous nature of the human intellect. Guided by "fancy," humanity passed through a misinterpreted reality detached from the actual state of things. "They prattle of visits they never made; repeat conversations they never heard; and describe objects they never saw—all this too, without the smallest consciousness of falsehood." Even well-tested convictions were more expressions of fabricated confusions than reasoned truth. "Sometimes we see the imagination so lively, so completely the master of the mind, that it prevails over the plain and direct communications of the senses." He recommended that all accepted forms of knowledge be approached with a cautionary temperament—trust but verify. "If imagination is capable not only of substituting its own copies of the perception of senses for those of memory, but even of cheating us out of these perceptions themselves, how much and how often must it pervert judgment. . . . How liable is every chain of reasoning to be turned this or that way from the right line of truth, when every link is so likely to be distorted."[74] Accurate assessments were nearly impossible, particularly in areas dealing with the interconnected web of causes and consequences that characterized market economies.

Like Smith, Tucker set his understanding of epistemology at the core of his laissez-faire position. Statesmen were no more gifted in discerning the intricacies of economic phenomena than laymen. But traces of Tucker's skepticism extend into other aspects of his political economy. He offered something comparable to a psychological measurement in his theory of value. If economic evaluations are subjected continually to inaccurate estimations, then what is valuable to one may be worthless to another. Tucker's definition of value was not determined exclusively by supply and demand, or the labor input, but according to the individual's unique desire for an object. "Value, being a feeling of the mind, is as various as the diversified and ever-changing wants and tastes of men. It is different in different objects, in the same object at different times and places, with different individuals, and with the same individual, on different occasions."[75] Economic value reflected emotional measurements based on personal appraisals of satisfaction and utility expected in a product, approximations that were real or imaginary.

As Tucker's political economy matured, it integrated the old with the new. What separated political economy from other disciplines, and what drew Tucker to the study, was its supposed propensity for scientific truth. Toward the end of his life, Tucker developed a penchant for statistics, a tendency that brought him closer to the quantitative nature of later economic inquiry. He synthesized the empirical and metaphysical, writing in his *Progress of the United States in Population* that the "unerring logic of numbers" was an invaluable addition to the nascent science.[76] Tucker's political economy is symptomatic of wider, transatlantic shifts in methodology within the discipline. His nuanced methodology was an important distinction from southern and northeastern free traders who favored theory over data, as well as from the Smithian emphasis on moral-economic philosophy that had originally coincided with Tucker's own epistemological style.

But like most antebellum economists, Tucker was not an absolutist. His commitment to free trade grew conditional with age. Though he used Say's work in his course, by the 1850s he turned increasingly protectionist, acknowledging the potential for tariffs to cut American dependence on European imports, pay down the national debt, encourage diversity in industry, and foster infant manufacturing. The latter, according to Tucker, could help the South by absorbing the region's surplus labor. Unlike other southern liberals who emphasized the role of international commerce, particularly the trade in cotton, Tucker expected America to grow rich not with Atlantic trade but from the expansion of the domestic market.[77] Tucker was unique in the antebellum liberal discourse. But his writings are also characteristic of the complexities that mark much of antebellum hybrid capitalist political economy. The flexibility of his ideological and methodological constitution makes definitive categorization almost impossible. Tucker's varying positions on slavery illustrate this point. As a young adult, he opposed slavery as a moral evil. His 1837 *Laws of Wages, Profits and Rents Investigated* argued that free labor was more productive than slave, blamed the South's peculiar institution for the region's stunted industrial growth, and declared it an anachronism.[78] The agitations of abolitionists, however, alarmed Tucker enough that by the 1840s he became a slave apologist, just before emancipating his five domestic slaves and moving to Philadelphia.

Tucker's writings belong more to the age of Jefferson and Smith. During the colonial and early national periods, southern intellectual culture flourished under the leadership of an aristocratic class of Enlightenment thinkers. "Gentlemen" like Tucker and Jefferson drew from the Atlantic store of eighteenth-century philosophy. For a time equal to, if not exceeding, their northern counterparts, the South's contributions to the early national philosophical milieu were hardly negligible. And the South was more engaged in contemporary economic discourse, argues Michael O'Brien, than any place besides Scotland. Then, beginning in the 1820s, southern liberals initiated the process of linking laissez-faire, states' rights, and pro-slavery into a single cohesive ideology, mainly in response to the threat of northern interference in southern institutions. The region's commitment to slavery pulled southern liberals away from northeastern liberals, and it compromised their ideological relationship with Smith and other Enlightenment figures. This is arguably the most important development in antebellum laissez-faire. By the 1850s, southern politicians and economists effectively monopolized free trade in the national political discourse. The partisan atmosphere surrounding the nullification crisis, exacerbated by the agitations of New England abolitionism, the Missouri question, the menace of slave insurrection, British abolitionism, and the increasing profitability of King Cotton, pushed southern liberals into a kind of intellectual isolation, whereby the defense of slavery became the principal object of southern thought. Their devotion to economic liberalism hardened. Jeffersonian egalitarianism was abandoned, Enlightenment ideas were censured, and subtle expressions of abolition prompted intolerant, paranoid, and violent reactions.[79]

The irony of pro-slavery intellectuals vindicating a conservative, archaic slave regime by referencing Smith and the overtly liberal, revolutionary precepts of laissez-faire ideology was missed by southerners. Smith explicitly noted the economic inefficiencies of slavery. "From the experience of all ages and nations, I believe, that the work done by free men comes cheaper in the end than the work performed by slaves. Whatever work he does, beyond what is sufficient to purchase his own maintenance, can be squeezed out of him by violence only, and not by any interest of his own."[80] For Smith, slavery was unprofitable, stunted the division of labor and innovation, and most important, countered the natural system of liberty. This did not stop pro-slavery southerners from championing Smith's doctrine. "In our opinion the minds of the people of the South are coming to be much more united upon this subject of free trade," a leading southern journalist declared in 1857; "let the South unite upon this movement."[81]

The material realities of the southern economy indicate that Smith grossly miscalculated the inefficiencies of slavery. The literature on American slavery is marked by competing interpretations that are not necessarily mutually exclusive. The debate is sometimes framed in the context of the South's response or rate of integration into the national market economy. Capitalist-oriented plantations, highly commercialized port cities like New Orleans and Charleston, reform-minded planters and cotton merchant factors piqued by profits, and international market imperatives coexisted with subsistence and semi-subsistence petit planters of the Old South, indifferent to profits, isolated from markets, and repulsed by the commercialization of Yankee capitalism. Slaveholders were a mixed lot, to be sure. Most slave owners lived on properties with five or fewer slaves, but most slaves lived on estates with more than twenty slaves. James Oakes's history of American slavery finds that "timeless stability never really characterized the slaveholding experience in America."[82] Slaves were exploited for a variety of purposes. And the slave economy was not a stationary, homogeneous enterprise. There were intermittent market fluctuations, predicated on national and international commercial, financial, and political developments, occasioning violent swings in cotton and commodity prices and provoking flush times and gluts across a southern economy with important regional distinctions.[83]

One thing is sure: slavery served as a significant source of national economic growth, and cotton was one of the most important export commodities of antebellum America.[84] Kenneth Stampp's *The Peculiar Institution* helped demonstrate that antebellum planters were fully engaged in a capitalist economy. Slavery, according to Stampp, was as much a commercially oriented "systematic method of controlling and exploiting labor" as the northern industrial regime. "In the 'race for wealth' in which . . . all were enlisted, few proprietors managed their estates according to the code of the patricians." Planters, conventionally understood as slaveholders with more than twenty slaves, were "entrepreneurs," "calculating," and imbued with "the businessman's interest in maximum production without injury to their capital."[85] Stampp's interpretations of antebellum slavery have since the early 2000s been given a powerful and updated exposition by the New Historians of Capitalism. Edward Baptist's *The Half Has Never Been Told*, Sven Beckert's *Empire of Cotton*, and Walter Johnson's *River of Dark Dreams* not only reposition slavery as the "true narrative" in American history but place slavery at the very center of American capitalism.[86] The slavery-is-capitalism thesis highlights, among other things, the centrality of southern slavery in the history of the "capitalist world-system," especially Atlantic industrialization, the "shock of the whip" and "calibrated torture" that accelerated southern cotton output, the ubiquity of "scientific management" on southern plantations, the role of slavery in the expansion of finance, and the national and even transatlantic unity between slaveholders, financiers, and statesmen working to advance planter interests across the globe.[87] If separated from the North and West, the South was the fourth most prosperous economy in the world in 1860. Cotton plantations resembled early models of large managerial enterprises that conditioned the scale and scope of cotton production according to international commodities markets. Encouraged by Britain's insatiable demand and Whitney's cotton gin, "white gold" drove slavery's expansion west to Louisiana's border with Texas, and with it the ecological and imperial transformation of the Mississippi Valley that followed the War of 1812, ceding Jefferson's Empire of Liberty to, in the words of Johnson, "the emergent overlords of the Cotton Kingdom."[88]

Global demand for cotton swelled in 1818, peaked again in the 1830s, and climaxed in the 1850s. By the 1820s, southern cotton monopolized global markets, providing 80 percent of the world's total. In 1860, 5 million 400-pound bales of cotton were picked by southern slaves.[89] That year, cotton exports reached $191 million, nearly 60 percent of the nation's total. Southern slaves were worth $1.3 billion, roughly 14 percent of national wealth in 1850.[90] And on the eve of the Civil War, the almost 4 million slaves represented about 14 percent of the nation's population. "All told," Thomas Piketty notes, "southern slave owners in the New World controlled more wealth than the landlords of old Europe."[91] Anticipating the New Historians of Capitalism by almost half a century, Douglass North developed the Cotton Staple Growth Theory to explain cotton's role in antebellum economic growth. "It was cotton that initiated the concomitant expansion in income, in the size of domestic markets, and creation of the social overhead investment . . . in the Northeast which were to facilitate the subsequent growth of manufactures. Cotton also accounted for the accelerated pace of westward migration as well as for the movement of people out of self-sufficiency into the market economy." North concludes, "in this period cotton was indeed king."[92] Although North's theory has been challenged, few deny what antebellum pro-slavery tracts touted—slave-picked cotton was instrumental to the American and Atlantic economies. Southern cotton fed textile manufacturers in Britain, accounting for 70 percent of John Bull's cotton imports. Industry in Britain must have cotton, and only the South could meet the demand. "His Majesty, King Cotton, therefore, is forced to continue the employment of his slaves," David Christy wrote in a widely read article published in 1860. "Slave labor products have now become necessities of human life, to the extent of more than half of the commercialized articles supplied to the Christian world."[93]

For antebellum southern liberal economists, the economic preponderance of King Cotton required that the United States maintain open and reciprocal trade with the world, but especially Britain. Trade restrictions threatened the region's economic relevance, with far-reaching political and social consequences. Hence the importance of free trade in the southern mind, and the necessity to fit free trade into a wider defense of southern institutions. Thomas Cooper was the principal intellectual force behind the ideological matrix of laissez-faire, slavery, and states' rights. Born in 1759 in London, Cooper emigrated to the United States in 1794. Critical of almost everything, he was an enemy of clerics, aristocracy, democracy, Federalists, tariffs, and banks. He first won notoriety in America through a series of stinging attacks in 1799 on President John Adams. Cooper scoffed at the administration's Sedition Act, the statute under which he was later charged with libel. In 1800 he was sentenced to six months in prison for an article published in the *Northumberland (Pennsylvania) Gazette*.[94] Cooper taught at Carlisle College (now Dickinson) and later the University of Pennsylvania, eventually settling at South Carolina College as professor of chemistry. He became the college's president in 1821, serving until 1834. Cooper died five years later in Columbia. Jefferson praised him as "the greatest man in America in the power of the mind."[95] His seminal economic text, *Lectures on the Elements of Political Economy*, was published in 1831 during the nullification crisis. For Cooper, the 1828 Tariff of Abominations extended the debate over trade policy into a more serious examination of the nature of representative government. The *Lectures* propelled Cooper to the fore of the national economic discourse, and in the process he became, along with John Calhoun, the symbolic head of South Carolina's nullification movement.

More than any other southerner, Cooper merged laissez-faire and states' rights into a single cohesive doctrine. His work crystallized the intimacy between politics and economics in the southern mind. Like Tucker, Cooper tied economics to a metaphysical logic with affinities to the philosophical skepticism of Smith. Cooper questioned man's capacity for rational thought. "Temptations, from caprice, from prejudice, from flattery, from temporary excitements . . . from imperfect apprehensions of the questions before them . . . [and] from sudden impulse," he wrote, drives humanity to irrational behavior and obscures comprehension of an enlightened self-interest. "When I was young," Cooper reminisced, "I took for granted, that every man, and every body of men, would act uniformly on the obvious motive of self-interest. I was mistaken. The fact is otherwise; not in a few, but in a majority of cases."[96]

Cooper reiterated Smith's cynicism toward the legislator's capacity to judge the interests of individuals. This skepticism, as we saw with Tucker, served as a foundational principle for intellectual capitalism. But Cooper broadened the scope of Smithian laissez-faire to be inclusive of all public policy—political, social, and economic. Cooper's philosophical skepticism intensified in his discussion of elected officials. Legislators, Cooper wrote, "promiscuously chosen, who have neither the same means of minute information, the same imperious motives to use them, or the same experience," should exercise deference in economic matters, for "every man who has dedicated his whole time and attention to the business by which he supports himself and his family, must have more perfect and accurate knowledge." Laissez-faire and states' rights were natural allies. If individuals were best suited to determine and act on their economic self-interest, then those same individuals knew best their local political interests. Cooper sought the wholesale transfer of legislative power from federal to state institutions in the same way that Smith undermined mercantilist ministers by placing economic agency in the hands of ordinary individuals. Having attacked the practical value of legislators' judgments, Cooper moved to deny the moral and historical value of nations. The tendency of contemporary philosophers to exaggerate the significance of states by finding in them "some existing intelligent being" drew Cooper's ire. "Every nation is composed of its individual citizens; the terms nation, state, community, are words merely—they do not denote any thing separate from the individual members whose aggregation and association has received these names."[97] Far from being the "terrestrial divinity," the state was simply a practical, necessary evil to "protect nothing but the laws affording a common protection."[98] Southern free traders deconstructed the state.

In pro-slavery antebellum thought, states' rights philosophy is the political manifestation of laissez-faire, advancing extreme localism approaching direct democracy, binding instructionalism, political devolution, and the disintegration of representative government. Regional, state, or municipal affairs were only understood by officials with immediate knowledge and a vested stake in the community. Sovereignty was found in the halls of local government, and legislators perched atop Capitol Hill in distant Washington, DC, knew nothing of life in the South. Threats to individual autonomy emanated from within the national political system, mainly majority rule and broad interpretations of the Constitution. From this point Cooper constructed a case for the negative state. He doubled down on the popular liberal assertion that politics has no place in economics. Say had divorced politics from economics in his *Treatise on Political Economy*. "Since the time of Adam Smith," the Frenchman wrote, "it appears to me, these two very distinct inquiries have been uniformly separated; the term political economy now being confined to the science which treats wealth, and that of politics, to designate the relations existing between a government and its people, and the relations of different states to each other."[99] Since political imperatives, crafted by ill-advised legislators, were powerless in the face of universal economic laws, the state was impotent in effecting economic phenomena. But Cooper expanded Say's logic by combining laissez-faire and the negative-state doctrine, arguing that, in fact, political institutions need not interfere in the day-to-day operations of society more generally. Removing politics from economics, for Cooper, was an established convention. Extending this logic to spheres beyond the economic illustrates the breadth of Cooper's commitment to liberal ideology.

In their defense of slavery southerners exhibited a capacity for philosophical flexibility, which occasioned seemingly contradictory attitudes toward state and federal powers. Historians have exposed the hypocrisy of southerners "rushing to the storm cellar of states' rights" at the slightest suggestion of federal interference with their peculiar institution, while simultaneously calling for draconian measures to defend slave property. The three-fifths compromise, the censoring of southern mails, the House gag rule on abolitionist petitions, the Fugitive Slave Act, and the Kansas-Nebraska Act illustrate the South's encouragement of statist legislation to prop up slavery. Matthew Karp has demonstrated how southern planters were largely responsible for enlarging the antebellum federal military apparatus and directing that power to advance hemispheric and global slavery. The annexation of Texas was, according to Karp, the "quintessential achievement of the foreign policy of slavery" and emblematic of how planters "almost universally looked to the federal government as the natural savior of slavery, both at home and abroad."[100] John Majewski's history of southern political economy extends the implications of the statist narrative to the Civil War era, discovering that secessionists were in fact full-blown statists. "Far from endorsing laissez-faire," Majewski writes, "most secessionists believed that some form of collective action would strengthen the long-term prospects for slavery and the southern economy." The "modernizing impulse" in secessionist thought, according to Majewski, included broad support for protectionist trade policies that drew southerners into an ideological alliance with protectionists like Alexander Hamilton and Friedrich List. Majewski's work focuses on secessionists in Virginia and South Carolina during the late 1850s, but his analysis stretches to the 1840s. The implication of his argument is that secessionist economic thought captured a wide swath of southern economic ideology. "In many respects," Majewski notes, "the secessionist economic imagination fit well with the general mentality of southern slaveholders."[101]

In the years preceding the Civil War and certainly during the conflict, elements of southern thought turned decidedly statist. And while secessionist planters constituted a relatively small faction of the South's population, they exercised considerable influence over the region's discourse, especially as the nation moved closer to war. Still, southern expressions of statism, and specifically criticisms of free-trade political economy, are more illustrative of a discursive and ideological instrument employed by a small set of reactionary Fire Eaters. In his study on Civil War–era political economy, Richard Bensel conceded that the hyper-statist measures of the Confederacy were "so extensive that they call into question standard interpretations of southern opposition to the expansion of federal power in both the antebellum and post-Reconstruction periods." Bensel, however, correctly distinguished antebellum opposition to statist elements and the centralizing tendencies of the Confederacy as separate but corresponding efforts at "defensive strategies directed against the hegemonic influence of the northern industrial economy."[102] Confederate statism, in short, was a practical wartime policy. It was not the manifestation of an embedded, dormant philosophical disposition with deep roots stretching across antebellum southern thought. Moreover, Majewski's argument that secessionists favored a tariff on southern imports at 15–20 percent indicates more a commitment to Smithian laissez-faire than Listian protectionism. During the antebellum period, restrictions set at those levels were understood as reasonable efforts to raise federal revenue and were, therefore, not protectionist. Participants at the Free Trade Convention of 1831, for instance, suggested uniform tariff rates at 20–25 percent, while South Carolina's nullifiers negotiated a revenue tariff of 20–26 percent, and the so-called free trade Walker tariff of 1846 set rates at 26 percent.[103] Even the most committed free traders in the North and South recognized the necessity of a tariff for revenue. Finally, "King Cotton diplomacy," or the Confederate cotton-exports embargo intended to compel Britain and other European powers to extend diplomatic recognition to the South, reflected delusions of economic grandeur rather than a secessionist commitment to protectionism. Indeed, the employing of embargoes or boycotts has a long history in American commercial protests. During the colonial and Revolutionary eras there were similar exaggerated estimations of American economic significance, first within the British Empire, and again in the wider Atlantic economy during Jefferson's and Madison's administrations. And similarly, many of these early attempts at economic blackmail were called for by advocates of laissez-faire.[104]

If the secessionists who directed Confederate war efforts were modern liberals, as Majewski has suggested, then they could not also be protectionists. And if they were Listian protectionists, then these same southerners could not also be liberal Smithians.[105] Chapter 7 below shows how protectionists like Henry Carey considered tariffs a means of national and individual economic liberation. But Carey arrived at this point through a fairly sophisticated, decades-long metaphysical exercise that extended Smith's ontology of freedom beyond adherence to a natural economic order and the pursuit of personal self-interest. Carey still considered himself a protectionist, and rightly so. By the Civil War, the imperatives of military conflict drove states' rights and laissez-faire southerners into uncomfortable and paradoxical ideological confines. Still, statism and protectionism were anomalies impressed on the southern economic mind by the exigencies of war rather than reflections of the totality of southern ideology.

In the antebellum economic discourse, Cooper offered the strongest case for the negative state. He combined philosophical skepticism and the discounting of state authority with two key economic tenets. First, Cooper presented a narrow definition of what constituted national wealth. Antebellum economists argued exhaustively over what exactly were the components that contributed to the wealth of nations. Protectionists believed each nation possessed a preponderant, overarching national economic interest, which they measured according to a variety of institutions, including industrial capacity, internal improvements, defense, employment, and a favorable balance of trade. Cooper argued national wealth was simply the collective of that which was possessed by individuals. "The wealth, the capital of every nation, is nothing else than the aggregate of the wealth and capital of the individuals who compose it." Liberals like Cooper deconstructed the significance of the state by denying the existence of a common, national economic good. Second, his political economy was based on the buy-where-you-can-buy-cheapest principle. "If I can buy of my neighbor any commodity, cheaper than I can make it at home, I save the difference of expense of buying it; and I am more profitably employed in making some exchangeable commodity for my neighbor, cheaper than he can make it, than by making the article that I want from him."[106] The state had no place in commercial exchange. By 1830 states' rights, and even nullification, were the natural political adjuncts of Cooper's version of laissez-faire. He helped shape economic and political narratives over the legal exercise of central-state authority by devaluing the role of all political institutions and undermining national prerogatives in the economic sphere. In short, the individual trumped the state.

But Cooper's attachment to southern institutions also drove him to articulate a version of laissez-faire that was, contrary to mainstream liberal expressions in Europe, completely without reference to industrialization. In fact, he celebrated a traditional Jeffersonian agrarianism. Although Cooper had been an industrial chemist as a young man in his native England, he also studied mineralogy and was a member of the Academy of the Natural Sciences. "If any profession is to be fostered," Cooper asserted, "let it be the tiller of the earth, the fountain head of all wealth, and all power, and all prosperity."[107] Manufacturers gave birth to monopolies and moneyed aristocrats, exacerbated inequities in the division of wealth, and encouraged luxury and idleness. "The whole system," Cooper wrote of manufactures, "tends to increase the wealth of a few capitalists, at the expense of the health, life, morals, and happiness of the wretches who labor for them ... we want in this country, no increase of proud and wealthy capitalists."[108] Simply put, the establishment of manufactures threatened the republican character of American society.

Southern tirades against industry reflected what pro-slavery liberals perceived as sharp divisions in the national conscience over the trajectory of the American economy.[109] Southern liberals believed two incompatible national economic programs had emerged. Northern protectionists encouraged rapid state-sponsored industrial growth, while southern free traders imagined a zero-sum game playing out in the national economy, whereby northern industrialization in combination with a leveraged northern democracy empowered Yankee legislators to undermine the plantation economy and hasten slavery's demise. The southern attachment to states' rights and free trade and the intellectual and policy creation of nullification as a viable option were in part reactions to the increasing influence that protectionists, and northerners in general, wielded over national political economy.[110] To defend southern institutions, liberals like Cooper drew on long-standing free trade values that accentuated the political consequences of economic policy. The southern version of laissez-faire became arguably the most important political challenge to federal authority. And by doing so, southern free traders transformed laissez-faire into a formidable political defense of slavery.

More than any figure, John Calhoun popularized the connection between laissez-faire and slavery in the political discourse.[111] Calhoun loaded Cooper's economic analysis with political and sectional overtones. In speeches, papers, and letters written before, during, and after the nullification crisis, he integrated selective principles of laissez-faire into a tightly woven political doctrine. Calhoun developed an affinity for laissez-faire, but he was more concerned with the political ramifications of policy than its theoretical or economic rationale. He employed the standard assumptions of laissez-faire as a defensive strategy aimed at preserving the South's economic and political significance in national affairs. And like Cooper, Calhoun extended his criticisms of tariffs into an antistatist and anti-industrial political economy.

Born in 1782, Calhoun matriculated at Yale and the prestigious Litchfield Law School in Connecticut. He had a long and distinguished career in national politics stretching from 1811 to his death in 1850. He served terms in the House and Senate, was vice president under two administrations, and was secretary of war and secretary of state. He was one of the most important political figures of the middle period and, arguably, the most sophisticated theoretician to serve in Congress. Under Jackson, he led South Carolina in the nullification crisis of 1832. By then the South was experiencing seismic shifts in its economy. The Central Plains, Sand Hills, and Piedmont regions of the Old South were covered with soils of lower fertility, which contributed to higher production costs and shrinking yields. This led to the net export of slaves and capital to the more alluvial fields of northwestern Alabama, Mississippi, Louisiana, and Arkansas. During the five decades preceding the Civil War, the American Middle Passage transported approximately one million slaves from the Old South to the Mississippi Valley. Although South Carolina was once the nation's leading cotton exporter, after 1826 its cotton production actually declined for some years.[112] The region experienced a precipitous decrease in wealth. By 1840 the South Atlantic economy was the poorest in the nation.[113] Calhoun communicated this despair in a letter written to a friend in the summer of 1828. "My property has ceased to give profits, which I believe is true of 9/10 of our planters."[114] He nailed the protective tariff as the cause of the malaise. "The whole of our profits are intercepted at the Customs House, through high duties on what we consume," Calhoun figured.[115] "We are the serfs of the system," he charged, "out of whose labor is raised, not only the money paid to the Treasury, but the funds, out of which are drawn the rich reward of the manufacturer and his associates in interest. Their encouragement is our discouragement."[116]

The 1828 Tariff of Abominations was the catalyst in the evolution of Calhoun's economic thought, but it was not its genesis. Calhoun entered Congress just as hostilities between the United States and Britain were moving the nations toward war. A staunch Anglophobe, Calhoun railed against British impositions on American trade neutrality, as well as the Crown's impressment of American vessels and sailors. At the convening of the 12th Congress in 1811, Calhoun was one of several southern congressmen backing protectionist policies as a means of liberating the young republic from the neocolonial yoke of Britain. Lacking a domestic industrial sector, credit, and an internal transportation infrastructure, American agriculture had grown dependent on British export markets, akin to commercial relations of the colonial era. Calhoun called for the immediate suspension of trade with Britain. For Calhoun, trade restrictions were a means to an end, not an ideological commitment. An embargo would compel Britain to recognize the importance of trade between the two nations and to respect American demands for the free intercourse of neutral powers.[117]

The antistatist, provincial elements that were later central to Calhoun's free trade ideology had not yet taken shape. Calhoun and other southern National Republicans, whose Anglophobia reached fever pitch by 1812, launched a hawkish defense of American independence, calling for the creation of a "federated" market, securing for northern merchants an effective monopoly of the coastal trade, and protection of domestic (mostly northern) mercantile and shipping interests. Calhoun implored the South to temporarily sacrifice its immediate economic interests, forgoing profitable cross-Atlantic trade in cotton and agriculture, in order to secure American sovereignty and inter-sectional harmony and to confirm what some perceived as the nation's commitment to the revolutionary principles of liberal economics.[118] When northern Federalists and Republican merchants turned against the embargo, Calhoun's nationalist idealism faded. Southerners felt betrayed. And in the postwar period, when northern manufacturers demanded protection for the region's infant industries, Calhoun and other southerners realized their wartime offerings were made in vain. From this point, Calhoun interpreted American trade history through the lens of southern martyrdom. He adopted a sectional understanding of the tariff. The South was falling under a northern neocolonial economic regime comparable to America's earlier dependence on imperial Britain.[119]

By the mid-1820s, Calhoun had adopted an uncompromising stance against tariffs. Protectionism, he figured, enriched the North at the expense of southern producers and consumers, subsidized northern industry and labor, and fleeced planters by spending federal tariff revenue on internal improvements based primarily in the northern states. "The very acts [sic], which imposes the burden on the consumers gives to the labour of one section the power of recharging and more than recharging the duty, while to the other it is a pure unmitigated burden, which cannot be shifted to the shoulders of others." For every cent paid in tariffs, northern labor was awarded higher prices for their products and, thus, higher wages. "Almost every man to the North, let his employment be what it may . . . hopes to receive more from the tariff by the increased price of his labor, or his property than what he pays in duties, as a consumer."[120] Since trade was merely a transfer of commodities and labor, paying an additional tax diminished the exchange value of southern staples and slaves, weakening the South's competitive advantage in global markets and encouraging the region's reliance on the North.

Calhoun's ally in Congress, George McDuffie, contributed to growing southern claims that planters were the colonial wards of northern economic imperialists. McDuffie was active in South Carolina politics since the 1810s, serving successively as a congressman, governor, and senator. He chaired the House Ways and Means Committee during the nullification crisis. Conflict between the McDuffie-led Ways and Means Committee and the more recently Clay-established and overtly protectionist House Committee on Manufactures became a political flash point in congressional debates over tariff legislation and illustrated tensions between northern industry and southern plantations.[121] By the late 1820s planters focused much of their irritation against tariffs targeting imports of slave clothing. They argued that restrictions on coarse woolens worn by slaves were blatant examples of legislative favoritism. Rhode Island's burgeoning woolen manufacturers marketed their cloths to southern planters as an alternative to British textiles. The failure of the Woolens Bill in 1827 energized protectionist forces, culminating in the organization of a cross-sectional New England, mid-Atlantic, and western congressional alliance that won passage of the Tariff of Abominations the following year. Western farmers were enticed by duties on raw wool and by promises to use tariff revenue to expand internal improvements.[122]

"Any burden imposed upon these manufactures [imports]," McDuffie declared in Congress in 1831, "must consequently operate upon the planter, and upon the value of cotton too, precisely as if it had been imposed upon the cotton itself at the time of its exportation, or at any previous or subsequent period."[123] Duties on imports were equivalent to taxes on southern exports. McDuffie's Forty Bales Doctrine gave formal expression to what Calhoun had suspected. That is, tariff schedules determined exactly the amount of cotton expropriated through federal taxation. Additionally, tariffs burdened the South with added costs on articles necessary in the production of staples, undermining the region's leverage against foreign competitors.[124] By diminishing American imports, the tariff also restricted access to foreign cotton buyers. And since foreign commerce almost always involved reciprocal exchange, British manufacturers, McDuffie surmised, would trade in southern cotton an amount equal to what Americans purchased in British wares. Southern fears of economic vulnerability and victimization were heighted by contemporary perceptions of the region's growing dependence on northern capital and commercial services. The tariff made planters reliant upon either heavily taxed British imports or overpriced northern wares. The necessity of resorting to the latter incensed Calhoun. "You compel an exchange with you by taxing our exchanges with the rest of the world."[125] Legislation imposing habits of consumption to boost pecuniary advantages for a specific class of producers reeked of privilege and sectional favoritism.[126]

With the theory of nullification, McDuffie and Calhoun raised free-trade economics into a full-fledged political doctrine. In essence, they synthesized states' rights and laissez-faire. Calhoun interpreted tariff legislation as having grown from practical measures to stabilize federal receipts and remit government debt into schemes that doled out privilege to northerners and enhanced the authority of national institutions. The tariff, Calhoun lectured Congress, "extracts from the South a large portion of the proceeds of its industry, which it bestows upon the other sections, in the shape of bounties to manufactures."[127] Calhoun added to his argument principles of classical republicanism. Excessive duties provided the central state with revenue to spread patronage and ultimately corrupt the republican character of the American polity. It made no difference that tariff laws were promulgated by democratic legislatures. According to Calhoun, majority rule was the most dangerous form of all governments. "No government, based on the naked principle, that the majority ought to govern, however true the maxim in its proper sense, under proper restrictions, ever preserved its liberty even for a single generation." Calhoun's constitutional reasoning brought him to the theory of state interposition. The reserved rights of the states implied "a veto or control within its limits on the action of the General Government, on contested points of authority," or put simply, the right to nullification.[128]

Laissez-faire complemented other important facets of Calhoun's political philosophy. Like Cooper, he challenged the positive state. "That all governments are actuated by a spirit of ambition and avarice, and that there is a universal tendency in consequences to the abuse of power, be the form of government what it may, monarchical, aristocratical, or republican, and which, if unchecked, must lead to tyranny and oppression, is a truth so well established by uniform experience, that it may be considered an axiom in political science."[129] Calhoun's distrust of government extended beyond conventional republican fears of legislative abuse of power and corruption; like Smith he doubted the legislator's ability to manage the economy.[130] In an 1842 article published in the *Southern Quarterly Review*, Calhoun cautioned, "In view of the errors to which legislators are subject . . . it appears to us that the benefits that may flow from it are more than counterbalanced by the ill consequences that may arise from unadvised attempts to foster an unnatural growth, which no care or protection can naturalize." However genuinely interested the impartial, seasoned legislator might be, the intricate webs of commerce permeating throughout and beyond the economy made any attempt at supervision impossible. Drawing on Smithian skepticism that highlighted the unintended consequences of economic legislation, Calhoun asserted that "the ramifications of trade are so extensive, the circumstances that combine to make any manufacture in this or that position, likely to succeed, or the contrary, are so numerous, that it is altogether beyond the grasp of human intellect to adjust to nice calculation."[131]

Calhoun's thought also underscores the nineteenth-century interface between laissez-faire and agrarianism. Southern free traders like Calhoun were part of an earlier free-trade tradition with ties to, among others, the Physiocrats, Smith, and Jefferson.[132] Smithian historians have highlighted the complexities in the personal and intellectual relationships between Smith and the Physiocrats. Had François Quesnay, the founder of Physiocracy, lived to see the publication of the *Wealth of Nations*, Smith would have dedicated it to the Frenchman. The Scotsman's expositions on the economic and social benefits of agriculture are well known to Smithian scholars. For Smith, manufacturing, and even foreign trade, was never as productive as agriculture. "The capital of the landlord," Smith explained in the *Wealth of Nations*, "which is fixed in the improvement of his land, seems to be as well secured as the nature of human affairs can admit of." Moreover, Smith wrote in a tone later echoed by Jefferson, "the beauty of the country besides, the pleasures of a country life, the tranquility of mind which it promises . . . to cultivate the ground was the original destination of man, so in every stage of his existence he seems to retain a predilection for this primitive employment."[133]

Accommodating intellectual capitalism to manufacturing and machine-based systems of social production was hardly Smith's intention. It was not until Ricardo's defense of manufacturers, or more accurately his argument that Parliament should abolish the Corn Laws, decultivate marginal lands, increase European grain imports, move British labor from country to town, and rely more heavily on British industrial exports, that the association between free trade and industrialization emerged. Binding laissez-faire ideology and industrialization was owed to the political adjustments and market convulsions that shook the post-Napoleonic Atlantic world. In Britain, the task of synthesizing laissez-faire with the industrial order fell not to academics but to a mixed bag of manufacturers and political entrepreneurs who rose to prominence in the 1830s by targeting the Corn Laws. When members of Parliament realized Britain could not feed itself, authorities initiated plans to move British labor into manufacturing and design reciprocal trade agreements to promote industrial exports in exchange for foodstuffs. Simultaneously, industrialists reckoned free trade in agriculture might cheapen the cost of labor, making British manufactures less expensive for foreign trade. Together, these forces launched a campaign that tied intellectual capitalism to the industrial ethos.[134] Transforming laissez-faire into the ideological adjunct of industrialization took several decades and, as Boyd Hilton has indicated, was "not a dogmatic application of economic theory, but a flexible adaptation of means to consistent pragmatic ends—food supply, monetary, and economic stability."[135]

By the 1820s the Corn Laws debate was at the fore of British politics. Activists organized the Manchester-based Anti–Corn Law League in 1839, with the free-trade abolitionist Richard Cobden at its head. The League, and its mantra the "cheap loaf," matured into a political machine the likes of which had never before been seen in Britain, and shortly after its establishment it spun off a subsidiary organization popularly known as the Manchester School of Economics. These groups propagated laissez-faire in British intellectual and political culture. British free traders railed against conservative, protectionist Tories, the landed gentry, and farmers. The crusade against the Corn Laws was encouraged by parliamentarians who wished to advance the industrial reach of Britain, or in the words of Joseph Hume, MP, "render all the world tributary to us."[136] The repeal of the Corn Laws in 1846 signaled the culmination of decades' worth of political, social, and cultural shifts in British public opinion over trade policy. By then, free trade was posited as the most effective policy to develop Britain's industrial economy, and for its critics, it became the economic ideology of British imperialism.

While free trade mutated into an ideological and policy instrument of industrialism in Britain, in the American South it remained attached to an agrarian regime, at least through the Civil War era. Conversely, nineteenth-century British protectionists echoed their American counterparts, the distinction being that American protectionists championed industrialization. British protectionists favored tariffs for agriculture and decried free trade as special-interest legislation benefiting manufacturers. Anna Gambles has shown how protectionism in the British discourse, much like the American version, promised a more balanced home economy with higher domestic wages, was imbued with nationalistic sentiment, and attacked the universalism of classical doctrine while urging a more historicist understanding of political economy.[137] The differences between British and American protectionists and British and American liberals showcase the malleability of nineteenth-century political economy to serve divergent interests. By and large, the advocates of laissez-faire in the British discourse were typically social and political liberals, and abolitionists. In the American South, economic liberalism was fastened to agrarian institutions, namely slavery, that to the outside world seemed anachronistic, or at least conservative. Southern free traders borrowed from British free traders, but, as this chapter has shown, only those ideas that suited their interests. Like Cooper, Calhoun pushed the southern free-trade movement against industry and away from the style and purpose of laissez-faire in the Mancunian tradition. The agrarian temperament of southern free trade, however, was not restricted to the South. North of the Mason-Dixon line, liberals in the mid-Atlantic states favored agrarian pursuits as well, and were generally skeptical of industrialization. Raguet, for instance, dedicated space in his *Banner of the Constitution* to issue dire warnings about the expansion of northern industry, imploring Americans: "Look at the robust, hardy, yeoman of the West, seated on his farm of eighty acres, with his table groaning under the weight of the meat, bread, vegetables, and fruit. . . . See him, healthful and sprightly, go through his daily work, master of his own actions, accountable for the steady employment of his time to no earthly superior, and enjoying himself."[138]

For Calhoun the potential for industrialization to undermine agrarian cultural values paled in comparison to the dangers of industry's social and political externalities. Industrialization, according to Calhoun, weakened the nation's republican foundations by radicalizing the working class and upsetting the traditional social relations. In his "Exposition and Protest," Calhoun stressed the social hazards of the industrial regime, forecasting a decline in wages to below subsistence levels until civil strife descended on the North "between the capitalists and the operatives; for into these classes it must, ultimately, divide society. The issue of the struggle here must be the same as it has been in Europe."[139] Northern workers were beginning to realize their condition was comparable to, if not worse than, the slaves'. Leveling elements would inevitably seize the private property of all Americans. Calhoun was not sincerely interested in the plight of northern industrial workers; rather he feared the spread of labor radicalism. These fears prompted Calhoun to propose a partnership between conservative "gentlemen" of the North and southern planters. The Lords of the Lash would help silence labor if the Lords of the Loom helped hush abolitionists. There was, however, more to Calhoun's suggested union between northern capital and southern slaveholders. Calhoun's version of laissez-faire was compatible with classical republicanism. Tariffs abetted the assembly of a manufacturing aristocracy antithetical to America's republican mission. What he feared most was an alliance between capitalists—manufacturers and bankers for Calhoun—and the federal government. As Lacy Ford has pointed out, "Calhoun fought in defense of economic liberalism against a potentially reactionary alliance of government and capital."[140] He dreaded equally the revolutionary inclinations of industrial workers and the ability of capital to wield the powerful arm of the state and subvert the republican nature of American government.[141]

Calhoun's free-trade ideology featured a counterrevolutionary and Torylike disparagement of industrialization, couched in Jeffersonian agrarian republican idealism.[142] It compels historians to revisit conventional associations between laissez-faire and industrial capitalism in the nineteenth-century discourse. The southern version of laissez-faire was not, in twenty-first-century parlance, an expression of anticapitalist thought, but its version of free trade was a social, political, and ideological enemy of capitalist industrialization. To be sure, reform-minded free-trade planters of the later antebellum period were locked into market institutions, sponsored widespread commercial development, and harangued the South for failing to foster diversity in the region's economy. These coexisted with a more traditional southern commitment to slavery that effected ideological tensions upon antebellum laissez-faire. Commercial expansion along decidedly capitalist lines and slavery were not incompatible, as recent studies have illustrated. Still, when taken to its furthest logical conclusion, the South's brand of free-trade ideology perpetuated economic institutions as they existed, conserving a mostly staple-export agrarian economy, resistant to full-fledged programs of economic modernization, and designed to thwart northern ambitions to catapult America into the industrial age. In the antebellum economic discourse the strongest advocates of free trade—the southerners—were some of the strongest advocates against industrialization. It is perhaps the essential feature of American liberal hybrid capitalism—a slave-based free-market regime without industry.

The relationship between southern laissez-faire and agrarianism is one of several marks of the erratic relationship between the American free-trade movement and Atlantic free-trade ideology, especially British laissez-faire. By the 1830s, Parliamentary abolitionists broadened the schism between southern and British free traders. Britain had invested mightily in Atlantic abolition. Between 1820 and 1870, the Royal Navy expended approximately £12.5 million to capture almost 1,600 slave vessels and to free more than 150,000 slaves.[143] Karp's work on pro-slavery influence over American foreign policy argues that southerners interpreted Parliament's turn toward free trade, signaled by the repeal of the Corn Laws, as a transatlantic admission of the economic potency of King Cotton. This implies widespread consensus on both sides of the Atlantic over the inevitability that the modern economy would feature slavery and global free trade. "The liberalization of commerce all across the Atlantic world, southerners argued, was more than just a technical adjustment on the part of world markets. It reflected a larger ideological transformation: the American political economy of slavery and free trade defeated the rival British model of abolition and mercantilism." Southerners were prone to wild exaggerations of the importance of slave-picked cotton in the world economy. But as indicated above, free-trade policy in Britain was the product of wide-ranging historical forces. In other words, southern slavery did not defeat British mercantilism. Hyperbolic manifestos common to the southern discourse represented important strains in the region's political economy, but perhaps Karp invested too much authority in planter promotionalism when he concluded, "King Cotton, not King Coal, still commanded the world market; the decline of global tariffs testified equally to his might."[144] Histories of Britain's mid-nineteenth-century trade debates show scant evidence of southern cotton playing an instrumental role in Parliament's decision to liberalize trade. Cotton planters were not Parliament's sovereign. British textile manufacturers were hardly dependent on southern slave cotton during the formative years of industrialization before the nineteenth century; neither were they during

Jefferson's embargo or the "cotton famine" years of the Civil War, and certainly not in the postbellum period.[145]

When Parliament emancipated slaves in the British colonies in 1833, southern free traders like Calhoun reverted to their traditional Anglophobia. After passage of a free-trade revenue tariff in July 1846, in a show of unity an English merchant in Charleston sent a bust of Calhoun to the Anti–Corn Law League.[146] Parliament had repealed the Corn Laws earlier that spring. This temporary confluence in the Anglo-American free-trade movement does not, however, constitute a transatlantic "liberal awakening." In fact, anti-British sentiment on southern plantations reached fever pitch following Parliament's proposal to recognize Texan independence on the condition that the young republic join the abolitionist cause. Two days before the Corn Laws were repealed, Congress declared war with Mexico on May 13. By the end of 1846, rumors circulated of a London-based plot to incite abolitionism in Texas, elevating southern suspicions of their British trade partners. Feelings of distrust persisted through the 1850s, mostly on account of southern paranoia over the specter of Atlantic abolitionism, especially after France emancipated slaves in its West Indies colonies in 1848. On the eve of the Civil War, British free traders showed little sign of supporting slavery still. Parliament did not reflexively craft trade policy according to southern demands. During the Civil War, Britain balked at officially recognizing the free-trade Confederate States of America, much to the surprise of southerners, who were convinced King Cotton would act as a powerful diplomatic force. During the "cotton famine" years of the Civil War, Britain supplanted southern cotton by tapping a global bumper crop just before the conflict, then supplemented these stocks with imports from India, which more than doubled between 1860 and 1863.[147] By then, any chance for an Anglo-American free-trade alliance had long expired.

American free traders followed a unique course in the intellectual and historical development of laissez-faire political economy. And as this chapter has illustrated, the domestic free-trade movement was divided. There coexisted two fundamentally incompatible articulations of laissez-faire ideology. If the United States did indeed symbolize in practical terms the ideal of a free-market domestic economy, the nation did not actually harbor a singular, synthesized expression of free-trade ideology. Southerners attached a secular, economic justification of free trade to their defense of states' rights and slavery. Still, they failed to incorporate the values of the midcentury

Cobdenite Mancunian tradition. They were also isolated from the free trade moralism of the clergy academics of the Northeast. Moreover, southern free trade was part of a wider, highly politicized regionalist movement associated with manifest destiny and, later, southern imperialist expansionism, both of which were in sharp contrast to the cosmopolitan visions of British and northeastern laissez-faire. The sectional and partisan nature of southern thought compelled men like Cooper and Calhoun to engage the laissez-faire discourse pursuant to interests and ideas fundamentally different from all other nineteenth-century liberal economists. Tucker is the exception in American laissez-faire, but even his ambivalence over tariffs and slavery, as well as his expressed favoritism for empirical over theoretical analysis, brings him closer to and further apart from the Smithian tradition, and thus positions him on an isolated intellectual plane.

The meteoric rise of southern laissez-faire is matched only by the rapidity of its decline in the postbellum period. The agrarian, pro-slavery, states' rights brand of southern laissez-faire was eclipsed by the industrial-commercial ideological regime that dominated postwar American intellectual capitalism. The South did, after all, lose the Civil War. Relegated to the fringes of the American economic mind, the totality of the demise of southern laissez-faire is perhaps comparable only to the lack of influence suffered by northeastern liberal moralism during the same postwar period. If intellectual capitalism is driven by selfish values void of moral imperatives, as Marxist critics are apt to point out, then the northeastern clerical emphasis on an ethical laissez-faire was an anomaly. The industrial-capitalist ethos tied to Herbert Spencer and William Graham Sumner was profoundly different from the cosmopolitan, moralist liberalism of McVickar and Wayland. In short, as American free traders moved into the Gilded Age, they largely abandoned their intellectual heritage.

American free traders were, in this way, awkwardly arranged. Both sects of American liberals were social conservatives. Calhoun's and McDuffie's commitment to slavery does not strike historians as liberal. And McVickar's and Wayland's insistence on preserving Christian values in economic society seems dated in a modern world turning increasingly secular. Although the northeastern and southern free-trade brands were both Smithian in their genesis, it is hard to find a single American liberal who exhibited an absolute commitment to the Scotsman, and there was even less interest in conforming to the British authorities who succeeded Smith. These figures are the focus of the next chapter. Antebellum Americans were insolent in their treatment of Malthus and Ricardo, or, as with the northeastern and southern packaging of Smith, the American liberals who reviewed Malthus and Ricardo were not theoretical purists; they either manipulated or rejected in full the British giants. The belief in American exceptionalism inhibited antebellum economists from agreeing with the perceived apocalyptic forecasts of Malthus and Ricardo. In consequence, a distinctly liberal American political economy emerged, a hybrid capitalism of sorts, independent of contemporary currents and without intellectual precedent. American liberals discovered their own discourse, suited to the American experience and fit for the American mind.

3

PROGRESS AND POVERTY

MALTHUS AND RICARDO IN AMERICA

The flexibility of Adam Smith's principles accommodated laissez-faire to the intellectual cultural traditions of the northeastern and southern free traders. During the first several decades of the nineteenth century, Thomas Malthus and David Ricardo incorporated important nuances into the laissez-faire discourse, some of which precipitated substantial departures from the Smithian model and thus incited mixed interpretations. Taken together, their works merged theories of production and distribution into an interlocking system that forms the basis of classical political economy. American liberals tied to versions of the Smithian paradigm were reluctant to accept the Malthusian and Ricardian shifts. This is not to say that liberals ignored the substance of Malthusian and Ricardian political economy. Both authors' texts circulated well across the North Atlantic discourse, and American liberals maintained critical engagement with the British thinkers. But the pessimistic implications abstracted from Malthus's and Ricardo's works did not correspond to the American economic mood. Antebellum liberals twisted, turned, and transformed Malthusian and Ricardian logic to comport with contemporary perceptions of American material conditions, as well as to advance their own sectional interests. They did so while thinking and writing within the wider laissez-faire paradigm, crafting hybrid capitalist ideologies that broadened the theoretical boundaries of nineteenth-century intellectual capitalism. Some northern liberals wrote wholesale denials of Malthusian population theory. And they pointed to existing circumstances to refute Ricardian forecasts of diminishing returns and inevitable class conflict. In the partisan atmosphere of the later antebellum period, northern rebuttals of Malthus and Ricardo were meant to showcase the region's economic primacy. Southerners interpreted these same rebuttals as thinly veiled polemics aimed at slavery. Southern liberals fired back, advancing Malthusian thought as an ideological vehicle against northern criticisms of slavery, isolating carefully selected Malthusian principles to explain southern economic growth, highlight the social and material benefits of slavery, and make gloomy predictions about the future of northern society. Both sides matched regionally specific brands of hybrid capitalism to regionally specific versions of American exceptionalism, and in the process they altered and undermined the supposed universal economic order and natural laws of the classical tradition.

Smith's *Wealth of Nations* helped launch political economy into the mainstream of the transatlantic public sphere. On population he relied on what by the late eighteenth century had become the conventional materialist explanation of growth.[1] "The produce of the soil maintains at all times nearly that number of inhabitants which it is capable of maintaining," Smith wrote in *The Theory of Moral Sentiments*, anticipating Malthus, adding that landlords "are led by an invisible hand to make nearly the same distribution of the necessaries of life . . . had the earth been divided into equal portions among all its inhabitants . . . and afford means to the multiplication of the species."[2] At the time of Smith's writings, England suffered acute social afflictions attendant on the nation's industrial revolution. Peter Linebaugh, a historian of early modern England, has described the age as "a time when economists have been hard put to explain how the labouring people could actually live given the wage rates that prevailed."[3] Beggars, prostitutes, paupers, workhouses, poor laws, enclosure acts, crime, food scarcity, and food riots blighted the Georgian landscape. Poverty was pervasive. And grain shortages hastened by the wars with France, first in 1795–1796 and again in 1799–1800, brought England to the brink of social and political calamity.

By the publication date of Malthus's *Essay on the Principle of Population* (1798), political economy featured population studies. At the turn of century, Europe was experiencing explosive population growth, Britain especially. Between Britain's inaugural census in 1801 and Malthus's death in 1834, England's population had doubled to 13 million, growing faster than at any other time in its recorded history, and faster than any other nation in Western Europe. The American population was growing even faster, and by the 1830s it was roughly equal to the population of England and Wales combined. Most understood the population was rising, but they did not have an accurate count on the extent of growth. Malthus, for instance, estimated the population at approximately 35 percent less than what it actually was.[4]

In 1805 Malthus was awarded the first academic post in the world bearing the name political economy, at East India College in Hertfordshire. Born in 1766, at eighteen Malthus enrolled at Jesus College, Cambridge, to study for a clerical career, and shortly after graduation he was ordained in the Church of England. He became something of a celebrity following the first edition of *Essay on the Principle of Population*.[5] The work went through six editions during Malthus's lifetime, incorporating important revisions that reflected contemporary criticisms of the book as well as changes in his thinking. He published several other works in political economy, but Malthus is largely remembered for his text on population.

What set Malthus's account apart from earlier discussions was the extent to which the *Essay on the Principle of Population* carried materialist population theory to its furthest and darkest conclusion. Malthus condemned much of humanity to a life of depravity and melancholy. The benign deity that Smith relied on was absent. Providence arranged natural laws, Malthus argued, with no regard for human happiness. The most insensitive and pressing of nature's dictates was the rapidity with which humanity populates the earth and the inability of the food supply to keep pace. "These two laws," Malthus wrote, "ever since we have had any knowledge of mankind, appear to have been fixed laws of nature; and, as we have not hitherto seen any alteration in them, we have no right to conclude that they will ever cease to be what they are now."[6] Mankind increases its numbers geometrically, but the means of subsistence increase by arithmetical progression, or simple addition. Confronted with this ominous calculation, Malthus penned what became one of his most famous passages:

> A man who is born into a world already possessed, if he cannot get subsistence from his parents on whom he has a just demand, and if society do not want his labour, has no claim of right to the smallest portion of food, and, in fact, has no business to be where he is. At nature's mighty feast there is no vacant cover for him. She tells him to be gone, and will quickly execute her own orders, if he do not work upon the compassion of some of her guests. If these guests get up and make room for him, other intruders immediately appear demanding the same favour. The

report of a provision for all that come fills the hall with numerous claimants. The order and harmony of the feast is disturbed, the plenty that before reigned is changed into scarcity; and the happiness of the guests is destroyed by the spectacle of misery and dependence in every part of the hall, and by the clamorous importunity of those who are justly enraged at not finding the provision which they had been taught to expect. The guests learn too late their error, in counteracting those strict orders to all intruders, issued by the great mistress of the feast, who, wishing that all her guests should have plenty, and knowing that she could not provide for unlimited numbers, humanely refused to admit fresh comers when her table was already full.[7]

Malthus predicted little better for the United States. In America, where labor was well compensated, the masses avoided immediate suffering, but, he cautioned, "It may be expected that in the progress of the population of America, the labourers will in time be much less liberally rewarded. The numbers will in this case permanently increase, without a proportional increase in the means of subsistence."[8]

The third edition of *Essay on the Principle of Population* was published in the United States in 1809 and was widely referenced in the domestic discourse. Although, with few exceptions, American economists rejected his population theory, Malthusianism was not, in the words of one historian, "a side attraction."[9] Antebellum liberals recognized Malthus as a central figure in British intellectual capitalism, and they treated the Englishman's thought in a serious manner. But American liberals rejected parts of Malthus on the basis of an independent logic and the belief that domestic realities existed without historical precedent.[10] Antebellum liberals integrated distinctly American understandings of population growth into a wider defense of laissez-faire, but one that was not rigidly confined to the strictures of the British classical paradigm.[11]

Benjamin Franklin's 1755 "Observations Concerning the Increase of Mankind and the Peopling of Countries" was the first systematic attempt made by an American to deal with population theory.[12] Franklin anticipated Malthus's materialist understanding of population, but without the ominous forebodings. Material conditions determined population growth, Franklin argued, and thankfully colonial circumstances precluded redundant numbers. Even if the population doubled every twenty years, a rate calculated by Franklin and one that proved true until the Civil War, there was no need to fear overpopulation. "Notwithstanding this increase," Franklin wrote, "so vast is the territory of North America, that it will require many ages to settle it fully."[13] The seemingly infinite supply of fertile land, combined with the scarcity of labor, meant colonialists would not compete for dwindling resources. Rather, wages would be kept high enough to afford a decent standard of living and support future population increases. "A laboring man," Franklin found, "can in a short time save money enough to purchase a piece of new land . . . whereon he may subsist a family."[14] Rules appropriate for Europe, he concluded, were inapplicable to America.[15] Thus, population studies "formed on observations, made on full-settled old countries, as Europe," Franklin wrote, would not "suit new countries, as America."[16]

Franklin helped set the tone for antebellum population theory. The breach between the Americans and Malthus was based largely on perceptions of American exceptionalism that can be traced back to seventeenth-century colonial promotionalist literature. By emphasizing American exceptionalism, antebellum liberals signaled their willingness to pursue an alternative economic narrative, acknowledging the potential for iron laws, in this case population, to bend according to prevailing domestic circumstances. On some occasions, the belief in American exceptionalism undermined the internal consistency of their logic. If British classicism delineated axioms applicable to all, then historical conditions were immaterial. The natural order could be compromised, and the otherwise holistic, interlocking system of intellectual capitalism deconstructed and made to account for the American experience.[17]

The belief in American exceptionalism had a powerful influence on northern interpretations of Malthus. Northeastern liberal clergy like Wayland rejected Malthusianism out of belief in American exceptionalism combined with faith in a benevolent God.[18] Providence intended man to be fruitful and multiply. Capital determined population, Wayland contended, but American prosperity guaranteed that "the increase of capital more than keeps pace with the natural and imported increase of the human race."[19] Wayland's denial of Malthusianism was based on his understandings of the potential for American productive capacities. Moreover, population crises in Europe, Wayland found, were the result of corrupted political institutions that burdened the laboring poor and misdirected otherwise productive capital toward government superfluities.

Protectionists like Daniel Raymond and Henry Carey, discussed here in later chapters, countered Malthus with an explicitly optimistic vision of America.[20] Their rebuff of Malthus was founded on several points of criticism. First, protectionists quelled contemporary anxieties by arguing that even if the Malthusian trap was possible, overpopulation was not "for centuries to come."[21] Many flatly denied the supposed universal law of perpetual population increase. In fact, few antebellum Americans could see any benefit to restricting domestic population growth.[22] Besides, western lands provided a "safety valve" for redundant numbers. Second, Malthus viewed each increase in humanity as an addition to the pool of consumers, but he failed to calculate the potential each human addition had for increasing productivity. Population pressures spurred Americans toward greater production through specialization, the mechanization of labor, and ultimately a more effective cultivation of the soil. Combined, these developments promised higher yields and higher wages. Population density was not something to fear; rather, it reflected American progress. The future held higher standards of living as production gains would outpace population pressures. Put differently, capital accumulations would exceed population growth. Finally, protectionists, like their liberal northeastern counterparts, argued that Malthusian overpopulation was evident only in countries with corrupt political and social institutions. The European masses faced population crisis because their governments were instruments of the aristocracy. Reared in Old World England, Malthus was incapable of imagining the ancillary benefits afforded to ordinary citizens under a democratic republic.[23]

Loammi Baldwin, Harvard graduate and renowned engineer, composed one of the earliest antebellum writings on population in an essay anticipating the release of the census of 1810. The framers established the census to help balance apportionment of political power among the thirteen states.[24] For Baldwin, the census enumerated essential data pertaining to population, geography, agriculture, and industry that enhanced the science of political economy. By facilitating discovery of more efficient methods in the production of national wealth, legislators too would profit from the information. Baldwin expected the census to confirm the unprecedented material circumstances of America. Indeed, national material progress advanced with great haste, surpassing outdated patterns in the stages of economic growth typical of European societies. Variation in American demography, culture, and geography meant so-called universal principles conjured up by Old World philosophers were irrelevant in the United States.[25] Novel techniques in political economy were thus necessary, Baldwin wrote: "nothing can be applied here by copying from others; every thing relative to political economy must be original. Without recurrence to the past we have to consult futurity."[26] Baldwin predicted American population growth would exceed any ratio seen in Europe. Without primogeniture, aristocracy, or poor laws, and blessed with an extraordinary spread of unclaimed and bountiful land and with political and economic systems that encouraged the individual pursuit of self-interest, the "positive" or "preventative" checks portended by Malthus were absent in America. Baldwin's treatise was more a promotional piece than a systematic presentation of population theory. But the centrality of optimism and American exceptionalism was typical of what almost every antebellum economist already believed—that Malthusianism was simply inapplicable in the United States.

Samuel Newman, Harvard graduate, clergyman, and professor both of Latin and Greek and of rhetoric and oratory at Bowdoin College from 1819 to 1839, offered in a series of lectures in political economy what became conventional wisdom in antebellum population theory. Newman relayed stock liberal views on most economic issues. Individual and communal interests were identical, private property was sacred, and on free trade he wrote, "there can be no doubt, that were this system fully adopted by the nations of the earth, the peace and happiness of the human race would be promoted." He accepted the standard Ricardian logic on wages, but on population Newman was more sanguine. Nature's bounty, he figured, depended on the "guidance of man to develop it and make it efficient." In civilized societies, humanity's aptitude for manipulating nature was well matured, thus augmented returns on labor afforded each successive generation a more easily gotten subsistence, and labor a more direct employment of productive capital and still larger yields. Only restrictions on personal freedom, regulations "unnecessary and injurious, being detrimental to the public good, and often oppressive to individuals," could stall America's advance.[27]

Newman found Malthus's fears grossly exaggerated. And like Wayland and McVickar, Newman combined scripture and economics. Although pertinent to nations where land was limited and labor redundant, Malthus failed to credit the abundance of vacant lands both in America and throughout the world as indicative of Providence's benevolent design. "The period when the surface of the earth should be covered with inhabitants, that population will equal the means of subsistence," Newman estimated, "is so distant, and all calculations and reasoning relating to this state of things so indefinite and shadowy, that the whole subject is one of no practical importance." Besides, Malthus's reasoning was more revealing of Britain's institutions than illustrative of the universal order. There, the difficulty labor experienced in acquiring necessities was not attributable to a deficit in land, "but may be traced to some existing abuses of civil institutions, or to some unwise neglect of nations to avail themselves of the productive resources within their power."[28]

J. D. B. De Bow carried optimism over American population growth into the southern discourse. By the later decades of the antebellum period De Bow had emerged as a seminal voice in southern political economy. Born in Charleston in 1820, he moved as a young man to New Orleans, where in 1846 he established the popular journal that carried his name. Two years later he was appointed professor of commerce and statistics at the University of Louisiana (now Tulane). In 1853 De Bow was made head of the United States census. His three-volume work *The Industrial Resources, Statistics, &c, of the United States and More Particularly of the Southern and Western States*, published in 1854, was a monumental achievement in statistical economics.[29]

A southern nationalist and staunch supporter of slavery, De Bow molded his treatment of Malthus to celebrate what he believed were the exceptional features of the region's socioeconomic condition. De Bow was a vocal proponent of southern commercial values. His *De Bow's Southern and Western Review* became the principal organ for promoting the progressive wing of planter ideology. As the historian James Oakes has shown in his work on antebellum planters, most slaveholders were imbued with a materialist impulse. The relentless pressure to succeed that filled much of southern economic culture fostered a disciplined work ethic, social mobility, and the incessant desire to expand westward.[30] Although historians have traditionally associated entrepreneurialism and the Horatio Alger complex with northern free labor ideology, by the later decades of the antebellum period southern promotionalist and reformist literature was replete with instructions for improving plantation management, advice on implementing the latest discoveries in scientific agriculture, and prescriptions for the expansion of commercial cotton production.

This was especially the case in De Bow's New Orleans. By the 1850s the Crescent City had grown to the third largest in the nation, the fourth largest port in the world, and the epicenter of commercial slavery.[31] Planter expositions defending slavery's central role in the national economy were motivated in part by an increasing barrage of abolitionist attacks on the supposed inefficiencies of the southern economy. But the capitalist instincts described by reform promotionalists like De Bow were not knee-jerk reactions to contemporary partisan politics; rather the region's commercial milieu can be traced back to the colonial period.[32] Progressive planter intellectual hybrid capitalism was predicated on slavery. Individual, regional, national, and, for some pro-slavery thinkers, global economic prosperity hinged on the southerner's right to own property in slaves. Wealth and bondage were inexorably linked. Commercially oriented planters measured slaves as economic units of production, a view premised on widespread assumptions of black inferiority and on ideological conventions that legitimized the dehumanization and exploitation of slave labor.

Southerners like De Bow couched their understanding of population growth on the foundational belief that the master class exercised unqualified authority over its labor source, which included opportunities to manage slave numbers, and thus preclude theoretical concerns of population redundancy. Antebellum plantation slavery attached novel paradigmatic formulas to nineteenth-century intellectual capitalism. Southern economists conceptualized slaves as both capital and labor. They combined factors of production into a single theoretical value illustrative of the historically abnormal material and cerebral circumstances attendant on a highly commercialized plantation ideology that coexisted on the far edges of a transatlantic intellectual capitalist discourse that otherwise presumed the existence of an ostensibly free labor market. In this way, southern labor values precipitated a fundamental ideological breach from the Smithian-inspired labor-theory-of-value matrix. Smith, Malthus, Ricardo, and the economists who wrote in the classical tradition presumed labor enjoyed at least some level of understanding and autonomy over their economic self-interests. In contrast, southern political economy denied slaves' individual freedom in part on the assumption that blacks were incapable of a wide range of cognitive functions, including recognition of an enlightened reason. Southern economic thought combined these intellectual components with the legal ownership of human property and its productive powers that denied slaves control over their labor resource, thus engendering a niche theoretical understanding of labor markets that classical economists did not fully account for in their population studies.

The day-to-day authority southern masters exercised over slaves helped elicit an alternative theoretical labor component in antebellum economic thought, one that was not considered in classical population doctrine. As the historian Amy Stanley has shown, plantation management and exploitation of slave labor intruded on even the most intimate concerns of human relationships. "Thus slaves gave new meaning to biblical injunctions about being fruitful and multiplying.... The wealth of the plantation plainly lay in a measure of solicitude for the breeding body, if not the heart or soul."[33] The extent of antebellum slave breeding is difficult to quantify. Southern slaves experienced natural increases as early as the 1710s and actually surpassed population growth rates of white Americans by 1840.[34] Questions surrounding the control and supervision of slave propagation occupied space in contemporary literature and congressional debates. Frederick Douglass and William Lloyd Garrison both contributed to abolitionist writings that considered "slave-growing" the epitome of human commodification. These reflected cultural assumptions, stated explicitly and implicitly in antebellum abolitionist and pro-slavery tracts, that the master class considered superintendence of slave numbers an economic prerogative.

The control that masters wielded over slave labor inspired in southern political economists like De Bow optimistic assessments of the region's population trajectory, and in the process they effectively established an alternative paradigm distinguished by a genuinely southern appreciation of economic phenomena. According to De Bow, the republican nature of the southern polity, dependent on the existence of slavery, cultivated "habits" of a robust industrious spirit. Southerners were compensated for their virtuous commercial and industrial characters with augmented provisions of capital and increased wages. Thus, labor and capital were given constant improvement in their condition.[35] The natural order, De Bow argued, issued laws "just as fixed and unalterable as those that presided over the motions of planetary masses, or that regulate chemical affinities."[36] But for the South, nature's system did not portend the population trap described by Malthus. In the southern economic mind, there were regional exceptions to the universality of laissez-faire principles. De Bow discovered a substitute natural order in the South, and the laws governing that region's universe offered charitable bounties, providing opportunity rather than peril.

This appreciation was grounded in southern optimism and faith in the political economy of slavery. Southern agricultural reformers like De Bow believed they were near to perfecting the exploitation of nature. "Speed the plow," De Bow ordered, "raise the capacity of the earth, say we, to satisfy the requisitions of a rapidly augmenting population." Southerners commanded nature's treasures. "The innate faculty of our people to subdue the physical world, their energy and self-reliance, their habitual disregard of discomfort, difficulties and dangers, have made other nations say of us, that we alone could instill heroism in the common pursuits of life." De Bow touted the industrious spirit of southerners and celebrated the region's agricultural resources. "Let two blades of grass shoot up where but one grew before. Let one man conduct the previous operations of two men."[37] In southern political economy, slavery was the juggernaut, disrupting otherwise universal laws, contributing to unprecedented growth, negating important principles of British classicism, and affording southerners the logic behind an otherwise unusual understanding of the philosophy of capitalism.

De Bow, however, interpreted northern conditions in a more ominous Malthusian tone. Employing Malthusianism as an intellectual strategy to defend southern institutions, De Bow predicted the population of the industrial North moving inevitably toward redundancy. "The mining and manufacturing operatives of the North . . . labor there from early dawn until after candlelight, from one year to another, for a miserable pittance, scarcely above the starvation point and without hope for amelioration."[38] But in the South, slavery provided a social and economic safeguard. Slavery boosted wages and the social status of the South's white workers and precluded its free labor force from finding "employment in crowded cities and . . . competition in close and sickly workshops and factories, with remorseless and untiring machinery."[39]

The peculiar uses of Malthusianism in the South found another clever though inconsistent expression in George Tucker. Like De Bow, Tucker denied the nineteenth-century convention that bound Malthus with laissez-faire universalism. Early in his career, Tucker offered an early critique of Malthus, but in his later writings, in the words of Joseph J. Spengler, he "out-Malthuses

Malthus."[40] Tucker's version of laissez-faire was malleable, and toward the end of his life was driven by a will to defend slavery. As chapter 2 showed, Tucker was symptomatic of the southern tendency to eschew theoretical discipline. "The laws of population, as laid down by Malthus must be considerably modified," he wrote in 1855, for "it is clear, then, that moral causes—probably by producing a slight retardation of marriage—constitute the operative check in the United States, and that the extraordinary facility of subsistence which exists here, seems to exert no influence."[41] Americans deferred nuptials and procreation until sustenance was secured. In fact, Tucker's analysis of the 1840 census concluded that fertility rates were declining. Moral restraint curtailed the geometrical growth anticipated by Malthus. But Tucker's criticisms of Malthus also rested on a secular belief in a benevolent system of natural liberty. "Liberty seems to have been productive of so much good in whatever it has been fairly tried . . . that we are encouraged to hope it would not occasion a mischievous excess of population."[42] The natural laws that governed Tucker's economic order were markedly different from those described by Malthus. Large populations stimulated human progress through increased specialization, a more effective exploitation of markets, and by encouraging literature and the fine arts. The Whiggish tone of Tucker's thought reflected his belief in American exceptionalism. The young nation fashioned a New World economy. "There is seldom a day that the most indigent person among us does not eat animal; and it is next to impossible for many to suffer seriously here from the want of employment."[43] He attributed these material circumstances to the prudent character of the nation's republican citizenry. In sharp contrast to the violent and foreboding curbs nature imposed in the Malthusian cycle, population checks in America operated as subtle, almost voluntary social forces.

Like many southern liberals, Tucker's political economy reflected the ebbs and flows of the nation's political pressures. His understanding of population grew increasingly Malthusian during the partisan sectional debates over slavery. The earlier optimism that imbued his accounts of American exceptionalism waned. In the words of one biographer, Tucker "recognized the principle of economic relativity."[44] During the controversy surrounding the Missouri question, Tucker borrowed Malthusian logic to defend slavery against abolitionists. There was no need for immediate emancipation, Tucker posited, since the vanishing of the western safety valve combined with the proliferation of industrial technologies would in the not-too-distant future cut the wages of free labor, and therewith the value of slaves. Put differently, free labor would emerge as the more efficient and lower-cost factor of production. Tucker's intermittent optimism over population was replaced by Malthusian fatalism in an extensive correspondence with the well-known Boston protectionist Alexander Everett, a northern anti-Malthusian, published in the late 1840s and widely circulated in Everett's *Democratic Review*. Tucker had earlier admitted to Everett that upon first reading Malthus, he "revolted at it, and felt assured that it was founded on fallacies." Only after later readings did he change his views and, having "thought much, on the subject . . . persuaded myself that . . . Malthus's premises are in the main true."[45] Tucker now better understood that the natural limitations on fertile land coupled with humanity's propensity to multiply would depress wages to subsistence levels. With civilization came decay as redundant numbers exerted a slow, agonizing effect on the food supply, passing from animal to vegetable to grain and eventually potatoes. "Food cannot go on increasing," Tucker concluded in his latest theoretical reversal; civilization had productive limitations.[46] Labor would suffer disproportionately as provisions, unevenly distributed among the masses, shrank to quantities unable to support life.[47]

Other southerners, mainly Thomas Cooper and Thomas Roderick Dew, offered a more consistent application of Malthusianism to fit the southern worldview. Southern economists, according to the sociologist Dennis Hodgson, "were attracted to Malthusianism . . . because it allowed them to project a bleak future for the 'free-labor' system."[48] As the nation moved closer to civil war, southerners manipulated Malthusian logic and laissez-faire principles to portend the failure of free labor society and bolster the legitimacy of southern slavery.[49] As was shown in chapter 2, Cooper invoked free-trade ideology to defend states' rights during the nullification crisis. On population, Cooper warned that man's "tendency to increase is a law of nature: it may be checked, controlled, counteracted: by natural causes, by artificial means; but it can not be stopped. . . . if there be more human beings than food to support them, some of them must starve."[50] The pro-slavery movement shifted lines of logic and argument to match contemporary political and social currents. In Cooper's political economy, Malthusianism complemented his analysis of the social and economic malfunction of northern society as well as the moral superiority of slavery. This mode of attack grew popular as the North struggled to deal with the social ramifications of industrialization, including the emergence of a more stratified and permanent class structure. Contemporary reports from England detailing pauper conditions and abject poverty suffered under wage slavery laid bare proof that free labor society was collapsing. Cooper envisioned the South moving confidently into the modern world, since slavery acted as a positive check on overpopulation. Northern free society permitted labor to multiply with wanton rapidity, but in the South masters deftly managed slave numbers and, if necessary, restricted their generation. Furthermore, because capital (master) in the South owned its labor, the slaveholder was more likely to afford a decent sustenance to slaves, since by doing so he enriched his own assets.[51]

Dew developed southern Malthusianism into a formidable defense against state-sponsored interference in his native Virginian peculiar institution. Born in 1802 into a prominent slave-owning family, Dew was, in the words of one biographer, a "Southern touchstone" of pro-slavery philosophy.[52] In 1827 Dew returned to his alma mater William and Mary as professor of history, metaphysics, and political economy.[53] "The South," according to Michael O'Brien, "sat in his classroom and was told what to think."[54] He was elected president of the college the following year and served in this capacity until his death in 1846. Historians often credit him for helping reorient the pro-slavery argument from the "necessary evil" principle to the "Slavery is a positive good" maxim. A free trade fundamentalist, Dew instructed his students from the *Wealth of Nations* until he published his own lectures. Dew's laissez-faire axioms were given full exposition in his course curricula. He was a Ricardian on wages and profits, celebrated international commerce and the principles of comparative advantage, railed against state meddling in the individual pursuit of an enlightened economic self-interest, denied the possibility of general gluts, and argued that protectionism "infringes the natural rights of man" by "throwing obstacles in the way of a free circulation of labor and capital." The principles of laissez-faire, Dew discovered, "may truly be compared to the great law of gravity in the material world; powerful in its agency, frequently counteracted by other forces, but in consequence of the constancy and steadiness of its operation, overcoming every other power in the end." Perhaps most important, Dew concluded, laissez-faire had won "the sanction of enlightened philosophy . . . the highest sanction which any measure can obtain, whether moral, political, or economical."[55] Dew's free trade credentials earned him an invitation to the Philadelphia Free Trade Convention as a representative from

Virginia. There he exerted powerful influence over the proceedings and likely helped Gallatin pen the convention's *Memorial*.[56]

Dew's population theory was interwoven with conventional antistatist laissez-faire principles. He weaponized Malthusian rationale to strike at federal and state legislative attempts to regulate slavery. For Dew, Malthusianism evidenced the impenetrable authority of the liberal market order, which included the inalienable right to own slaves. The free-trade regime was not only nature's prescribed economic system; it was beyond the scope of statutes, and fortuitously consistent with the pecuniary interests of slaveholders.[57] "The energies of government," Dew declared in legislative debates, "are for the most part feeble or impotent" in their attempts to counter the inexorable natural economic order.[58] The complexities of the economy precluded statesmen from attempts at central planning. In fact, given the myriad of factors that shaped commercial exchanges, there was hardly any point of rational management or theorizing about economic systems.

The Philadelphia Free Trade Convention coincided with Dew's involvement in Virginia debates over proposals for the gradual emancipation of the state's nearly 500,000 slaves. The controversy encouraged Dew to formulate a more systematic expression of population growth, which was communicated in his *Review of the Debate in the Virginia Legislature of 1831 and 1832*. He argued against legislative initiatives to raise revenue intended for purchase of Virginia's slaves. Upon manumission, the freed blacks would be deported. Since, according to Dew, "Malthus has clearly shown population depends on the means of subsistence," the sluggish pace at which the state's white population increased would grind to halt, as taxes reduced the availability of basic necessities, encouraging white flight.[59] State purchases of slaves would in fact unintentionally augment demand, and thus supply, luring enterprising masters to breed slaves at prodigious rates, counteracting the purpose of the legislation.

Legislative schemes intended to curtail Virginia's slave population, and therefore expand the state's free labor market by promoting economic diversification and white immigration could, in an ideal scenario, level the state's racial imbalance and lessen the threat of slave rebellion. But Dew reminded Virginia's reformist planters that the threat of race war would inevitably be supplanted with Malthusian population traps and Ricardian class conflict. "The mandate of scripture would here be liberally complied with. Man would increase, and multiply, and fill the land ... capital and population would thus increase to such an extent, that they could no longer be employed on the first soil." Wages and profits would diminish accordingly, Malthusian logic explained, until Virginia's white free workers organized "mobs and violent commotions." Here Dew resorted to a Jeffersonian agrarian idealism that matched wider trends in antebellum laissez-faire. "In agriculture, the labor is much more varied, and calculated to give greater play to the imagination," Dew rhapsodized; "he is never employed so long at any one thing, as to lose wholly his relish for it; and all the external scenery too of nature, is well calculated to enlarge and liberalize the mind."[60] In the southern mind, lessons on the benefits of agriculture were translated into criticisms of northern industrialization. Malthusian population theory laid bare the potential dangers of moving Virginia away from slavery. Industrialization hastened population redundancy, setting conditions primed for Ricardian social catastrophe and separating "society into two distinct classes, capitalists and laborers, who are separated at too great a distance from each other." Factory operatives suffered mental degeneration and "serious moral disadvantage." Working-class insurrections then common in England and brewing in the North foreshadowed Virginia's fate and hastened the necessity for a "rigid and energetic police force" to monitor free white labor, creating a social regime "hostile to genuine liberty."[61] Slavery bent the otherwise unyielding laws of classical political economy. Prolonging the plantation regime quelled fears of overpopulation, encouraged social stability, and guaranteed white freedom.

As the Civil War drew closer, Dew and other laissez-faire southerners increasingly tied Malthusian population theory to the pro-slavery cause. This was not Malthus's intention. Malthus was an abolitionist. When he learned his earlier appraisals of slavery's effect on Africa's populations were employed by anti-abolitionists in parliamentary debates, he rushed into print an appendix to the third edition of the *Essay on the Principle of Population* to defend British abolitionism and, in his own words, "rescue my character from the imputations of being a friend of the slave trade."[62]

Crafting a defense of slavery out of Malthusian logic occasioned theoretical irregularities among southern thinkers. In the same way, northeastern liberals countered Malthusian laws with their interpretation of American exceptionalism, but they wrote with confidence about universal principles tied to the larger edifice of intellectual capitalism. If liberal political economy professed scientific precision and advertised the universality of its axioms, then its principles would ostensibly be applicable to all systems of human organization. Southern and northern liberals, for their part, confirmed the existence of an economic order determined by natural laws in their discussions of free trade; however, political and sectional exigencies forced them to deny the existence of that same unyielding natural order in their discussions on population. The antebellum treatment of Malthus is suggestive of the unprincipled character of antebellum liberal political economy vis-à-vis mid-nineteenth-century British classicism. American liberals were not obedient conformists to the internal logic of the classical paradigm. It was not unusual for contemporaries to endorse particular aspects of Malthusianism while at the same time refuting others. This would not have struck contemporaries as especially contradictory, either, since it is not entirely clear that every antebellum economist understood fully the totality of the classical system, nor had British authorities themselves finished working out the kinks in their own intellectual arrangement.

The lack of consensus between British and American liberals is given a more profound exposition in the antebellum treatment of Ricardo.[63] By the mid-nineteenth century reputable economists could not write on economic matters without discussing Ricardo. "Ricardo's influence on economic thought in the United States of the nineteenth century," Joseph Dorfman wrote, "was enormous."[64] Dorfman's assessment, however, perpetuates the notion of liberal unanimity by glossing over the complexities of intellectual capitalism in the antebellum discourse. American liberals treated Ricardo similarly to how they handled Malthus. Southerners balked at accepting the sum of Ricardo's doctrine, while most northerners denied practical application of Ricardian principles in the American environment. Ricardo, in short, did not dominate the domestic discourse. The prevailing optimism in American intellectual hybrid capitalism invoked a noncompliant attitude that engendered a powerful sense of theoretical autonomy and ultimately the construction of a distinctly native, if incredibly varied and disjointed, version of laissez-faire.

Ricardo was born in London in 1772. The third of seventeen children, at fourteen he joined his father on the London Stock Exchange. Shortly thereafter, Ricardo renounced his Jewish faith to marry a Quaker, which left him estranged from his family. Ricardo began his own brokerage business, made a fortune, and retired at age forty-two as a country gentleman in Gloucestershire. At age twenty-seven, by chance Ricardo came across Smith's *Wealth of Nations*. This was his first exposure to the subject, and, in his own words, he "liked it so much as to acquire a taste for the study."[65] In 1819 he became a member of the House of Commons representing Portarlington, Ireland, a seat he held until his death in 1823. He wielded considerable influence in parliamentary debates that dealt with monetary issues, and his arguments were frequently cited in the controversies surrounding the Poor Laws. But it was during the outrage attending the Corn Law dispute that Ricardo's authority came to be regarded as absolute. By the mid-nineteenth century, conventional wisdom on political economy tied Malthusian population theory to the Ricardian system in what became known as classical economics. By the end of the century, classicism was elevated to sacrosanct status. Subtle but important differences between Ricardo and Malthus occasioned disagreements between the two, which were sometimes published in contemporary newspapers and journals. Ricardo got the better of these debates, Malthus later admitted: "I have so very high an opinion of Mr. Ricardo's talents as a political economist, and so entire a conviction of his perfect sincerity and love of truth, that I frankly own I have sometimes felt almost staggered by his authority, while I have remained unconvinced by his reasonings."[66] The exchanges were always cordial; in fact the two developed such an affinity for one another that when Ricardo died he bequeathed Malthus a small fortune.

Ricardo introduced a new level of theoretical abstraction to nineteenth-century economics. The long-winded historical narratives that characterized the works of Smith and earlier economists were replaced with condensed, technical, and rigid logic that made Ricardo's writings a cumbersome read. Moral philosophy was extracted, as the study grew increasingly ahistorical and the methodological approach more secular. Critics charged that Ricardo's stubborn attachment to abstraction severed economics from practical experience. He wrote on a wide range of economic topics, but his theories on distribution—mainly rent, wages, and profits—distinguished his writings.

In his *Principles of Political Economy and Taxation* (1817) Ricardo defined rent as "that portion of the produce of the earth which is paid to the landlord for the use of the original and indestructible powers of the soil." Rent is paramount to Ricardo's analysis since it determines income distribution. When population expands, greater sums of labor are required to cultivate less fertile lands. As it becomes more difficult to extract food from marginal lands, the costs of food, labor, and rent increase. Over time, labor competes for a smaller real wage and plows less fertile soils. "The fate of the laborer will be less happy," Ricardo surmised; "he will receive more money wages, it is true, but his corn wages will be reduced; and not only his command of corn, but his general condition will be deteriorated, by his finding it more difficult to maintain the market rate of wages above their natural rate"—that is, the Iron Law of Wages.[67]

Labor is not the only sector disturbed by increased rents. Because labor's compensation is determined by a wages-fund, what the manufacturer pays in wages he subtracts from profits. As food costs eat away at profits, manufacturers suffer declining returns. "Each man may, and probably will, have a less absolute quantity; but as more laborers are employed in proportion to the whole produce retained by the farmer, the value of a greater proportion of the whole produce will be absorbed by wages, and consequently the value of a smaller proportion will be devoted to profits." Tensions between rents (landlords) and profits (industrialists/capitalists), combined with Malthusian overpopulation, keep labor at subsistence levels and cut profits for manufacturers. Capital, Ricardo posited, "will diminish with every diminution of profit, and will cease altogether when their profits are so low as not to afford them adequate compensation for their trouble"—that is, the Law of Diminishing Returns. In the Ricardian system, capitalists (industrialists), labor, and the proprietors of land are at odds, precipitating social conflict. "The interest of the landlord is always opposed to that of the consumer and manufacturer."[68] Ricardo's version of the natural economic order bound commercial society by the same rules that determined the behavior of plants and animals.[69] Market forces are comparable to scientific formulas. The Iron Law of Wages, the Law of Diminishing Marginal Returns, and the Law of Comparative Costs, for instance, are ungovernable, indiscriminate in their application, and "rendered permanent by the laws of nature."[70]

In the North, the immediacy of industrial development brought upon its liberal economists a special urgency to review Ricardo's work. More than any northerner, Henry Vethake exhibited the sharpest appreciation of the Ricardian system. Born in 1790 in British Guiana, Vethake moved to the United States at an early age. After graduating from Columbia, he enjoyed a long and illustrious academic career, teaching a variety of subjects and serving in various capacities at a number of northeastern institutions of higher learning including Columbia, Queen's College (Rutgers), College of New Jersey (Princeton), Dickinson, University of the City of New York (New York University), and the University of Pennsylvania. A well-regarded savant in his own time, Vethake was awarded honorary degrees by the College of New Jersey and Columbia, edited a volume of the *Encyclopedia Americana*, and is often considered the first professor in America to teach students political economy. At the 1831 Philadelphia Free Trade Convention, Vethake served as a delegate from New Jersey. He died in 1866 as professor of mathematics at Philadelphia's Polytechnic College.[71]

Vethake's 1838 *Principles of Political Economy* drew heavily from Ricardo, but a sensibility for American exceptionalism precluded him from accepting the totality of Ricardo's system.[72] Vethake, according to John Turner's study on American economic thought, was "not... limited by the orthodox teaching."[73] On free trade, Vethake recited stock liberal tenets, in a parlance aligned with Smith. Free trade was natural law, Vethake wrote, "as immutable as the will of Him who has ordained them."[74] Unrestricted commerce advanced civilization, spread peace and prosperity, and secured individuals the greatest command over the necessities of life. Vethake echoed the underlying optimism that marked the northeastern liberal discourse, but his confidence did not rely solely on a materialistic foundation. Like many of his colleagues teaching in the Northeast, Vethake was a devout man. His *Principles of Political Economy* opened with jeremiads on the evils of drink. Moral decency and republican simplicity, according to the Presbyterian Vethake, were determinant factors in an individual's economic fate. Studies in the wealth of nations, Vethake wrote, exhibit "to us the moral relations of political economy; relations which confer upon it a peculiar dignity, and I do not hesitate to say, elevate it to the highest rank among the branches of human knowledge." Uniting religious and moral values with instruction in political economy not only augmented material riches; it promoted spiritual and social tranquility. The belief in a benevolent creator, combined with a subtle appreciation of American exceptionalism made Vethake an economic optimist. The economic order, Vethake found, was governed by an "Author of nature... co-operating" with humanity to ensure the greatest amount of happiness possible.[75] His unwillingness to admit that God rewarded pious workers and steadfast capitalists with economic hardship and social disorder allowed Vethake to remain convinced of a more positive economic future.

Religion was not the only factor that influenced Vethake's writings, however. His economic thought reflected the social and political context of the Jacksonian era. Vethake's academic posts brought him in close proximity to the epicenters of American industrialization. There he discovered, unlike in Ricardo's England, capital and labor moving in harmony, encouraging prosperity and stability rather than poverty and strife. The entrepreneurial ethos that characterized antebellum culture prevented Vethake from forecasting the class tensions explicit in Ricardo's work. A Jacksonian Democrat, his ideal was a middle-class society where laissez-faire benefited those of an industrious spirit. Vethake was drawn to political economy because the discipline offered practical lessons to improve labor's condition without resorting to solicitations of the politician's "superficial views of expediency."[76] Teaching the nascent science would inspire the rich to accept moderate reforms and help labor understand the futility of radical militancy.[77] All things being equal, wages, profits, and rent tended toward equilibrium. Even calls for workers' trade unions, for instance, were misguided. Labor agitation might temporarily spike wages, but artificially inflated pay shrunk profits, Vethake explained along Ricardian lines, slowed capital accumulation, and triggered widespread unemployment.[78]

A desire for social balance framed the ideological parameters of Vethake's brand of intellectual capitalism. He anticipated an alternative industrial course, with increasing returns to manufacturers helping to dull labor's transition into the industrial regime.[79] His theory of distribution was buttressed by a belief in American exceptionalism and a Jacksonian ideology of equal-opportunity capitalism. Ricardo's influence is unmistakable in Vethake's political economy, but the American professor never fully accepted the Englishman's three-tiered economic class structure, for "the same person may unite in himself the characters of landlord, of capitalist, and of laborer, or of any two of them."[80] Vethake's descriptions do not comport with contemporary realities, however. In the so-called Age of Egalitarianism, the distribution of wealth was becoming increasingly marked by inequality. This was especially true in the Northeast where Vethake taught. Edward Pessen's histories of class and riches in Jacksonian America dispelled the antebellum rags-to-riches legend. Despite what Alexis de Tocqueville and other foreign visitors described as essentially a classless society where fortunes and status were in a constant state of flux, Pessen's study of the available data indicates that income disparity was the "central feature" of the antebellum economy.[81] When Vethake accepted a teaching position at the University of the City of New York in 1832, the richest 1 percent owned roughly 35 percent of the city's wealth. By 1845, one year after Vethake published his *Principles of Political Economy,* this same one-hundredth of the population had increased its share of the wealth to 47 percent.[82] Similar inequities existed in most other antebellum cities, much as in contemporary Europe, and the fortunes of the rich were born primarily through family inheritance rather than individual grit or merit.

The appearance of growing class stratification in America's urban Northeast was given some attention in Vethake's account of the inverse relationship between wages and profits. Here Vethake espoused a tempered version of Ricardian orthodoxy, while still maintaining an underlying optimism about American circumstances.[83] Although he found little proof of the supposed inherent hostility between labor and capital, Vethake did acknowledge the struggle between workers and capitalists over what remained of national income after rent payments. Population growth would direct labor and capital to less fecund soils with diminishing yields and augmented rents. At the same time, industrialists compensated labor with wages that matched increased demands for foodstuffs. The law of diminishing returns detracted from industrialists' profits, stunted the accumulation of savings, and shrunk the wages-fund from which labor was paid.

These sequences were explained in Ricardian parlance, featuring dry, technical abstractions.[84] But Vethake's final act avoided the Ricardian nihilism of class war. Rather Vethake, who genuinely seemed concerned for the sober mechanic and prudent middle-class entrepreneur, avoided narratives inclusive of the types of social conflicts that beguiled radicals. Vethake's political economy offered Americans a shimmer of light. Domestic conditions could save the young republic from debilitating poverty, class stratification, and social tumult. The latter seems to have been of special concern for Vethake. In 1842, while serving as president of Washington College (now Washington and Lee University), Vethake was attacked by a suspended student. A chemistry professor shielded Vethake from the assailant with a pair of tongs. And earlier in his career, when he was a professor of mathematics and natural philosophy at Dickinson in Carlisle, Pennsylvania, student violence forced the entire faculty to resign and temporarily close the college.[85]

Perhaps the threat of social disorder encouraged Vethake to adopt an almost serene, sedate, matter-of-fact prose in his *Principles of Political Economy*. Like most northeastern liberals, Vethake employed political economy to advance a conservative social agenda. He stressed the potential for greater worker productivity and increases in capital accumulation as a means to safeguard higher wages. "The consequences which have been deduced are, however, modified, and in certain cases altogether counteracted, by the effects resulting from the development of the powers of human invention.... the labor of man is thus rendered more efficient to produce... and the effects of the diminishing returns... be either partially or entirely counteracted." Wages were determined by capital's advance, so workers had no reason to protest swelling profits. Technological improvements in agriculture and industry promised labor higher standards of living. These advancements, combined with a nondistributive tax system, the spread of popular education, the enlargement of the suffrage, and the encouragement of prudent behavior, shielded Americans at least temporarily from the social and economic headwinds forecast by Ricardo and Malthus. Vethake, like most antebellum Americans, remained positive in an otherwise glum Ricardian context.[86]

On rent, however, Vethake struck a more deliberate Ricardian tone, suggesting that his understanding of classical doctrine assumed malleable forms. Rent was "that portion by which they [profits] may exceed in amount those yielded to the capital invested most disadvantageously in the same employment." Since rent, profits, and wages naturally settle toward equilibrium, rent is distinct from profits and wages in that it originates as "compensation for the use of the natural powers of the soil." In the Ricardian dialectic, rent yields progressively larger returns to proprietors as population grows redundant, forcing labor to contend for food. Because Ricardo held labor as the source of value, nature's order prejudiced landlords with higher yields and thus a greater share of income without having to expend additional labor. Vethake acknowledged that "no one can consistently deny rent to be likewise the product of labor," but he said nothing of the potential moral impropriety of an economic system that awarded the propertied class increasing returns without attendant sacrifices. Instead, Vethake implicitly questioned the authority of Ricardian rent by highlighting the supposed parity in domestic income levels, the apparent ubiquity of antebellum land ownership, and the purported classless nature of American society.[87]

Vethake merged Ricardian orthodoxy with a fleeting optimism that sprung from his moral idealism, his belief in American exceptionalism, and his unwillingness to accept the portended misery of the working poor. He was one of the few northern liberals to systematically review Ricardian principles, and his work in many ways symbolized the region's inability to swallow whole the dire conclusions reached by the Englishman. Vethake's political economy represents a uniquely hybrid form of intellectual capitalism. While Ricardian economics was in this way adapted to the burgeoning industrialism of the North—and in a context of Yankee piety—the southern treatment of Ricardo was not as clearly tied to the region's institutional and cultural traditions. A few radical fire-eaters interpreted classical doctrine as proof positive of the impending collapse of free labor society, but the more objective, levelheaded southern economists found in Ricardo's theories little of relevance to American conditions.[88] Like most Americans, southern liberals were not categorically committed to the classical paradigm. Rather they borrowed bits and pieces from their British counterparts to construct a distinctly American understanding of intellectual capitalism.

Jacob Cardozo illustrates this point. Like Ricardo, Cardozo was of Sephardic Jewish heritage. He was born in Savannah, Georgia, in 1786 but spent most of his life in Charleston. There he published the free-trade organ *The Southern Patriot*.[89] He ran the paper until his death in 1873. As a journalist, according to one biographer, he exercised tremendous influence on public opinion and "reveals southern intellectual thought at its highest level."[90] An ardent free trader, he threw himself into the debate over the 1828 tariff by helping draft a memorial to Congress on behalf of the Charleston Chamber of Commerce. In the heated political atmosphere of the early 1830s, Cardozo was unique among southerners in offering tempered analysis. He estimated the average American paid a little over two dollars in duties per annum,[91] hardly enough to justify secession. Cardozo cautioned his South Carolina neighbors against disunion, arguing "we are for getting rid of this system [tariffs] by no means that will place the Union of these states at hazard. . . . We should prefer making a larger sacrifice even to the odious spirit of monopoly, sooner than break up and scatter, never to be re-created, the elements of this glorious scheme of Republican Federative Government." He figured South Carolina paid a nominal share of the national revenue collected from duties. Moreover, the Palmetto State owed its economic troubles not to tariffs but to planter absenteeism and westward migration. The collapse of cotton prices in the years preceding the

Tariff of 1828 was, according to Cardozo, "entirely disconnected with the supposed operation of the protecting duties." Rather it was the result of a glut in Liverpool markets derived chiefly from overproduction of cotton in the American South and the East Indies.[92]

This is not to say Cardozo was sympathetic toward tariffs. Cardozo was a free trade disciple. Liberalism maximized efficiency in the allocation of labor and capital, stimulated the economy, encouraged reciprocity between nations, and established cost-effective lines of international credit. But eliminating tariffs would not provide South Carolina with the economic panacea promised by its politicians. Cardozo argued that the abolition of slavery and economic diversification were more likely to rescue the ailing Old South. Tariffs hurt the South, but the real danger to the region's economy would come when Britain no longer demanded southern staples.[93] Cardozo borrowed from Smith the standard liberal critique of slavery, calculating free labor two or three times more productive, and as early as the 1840s he advocated the development of southern industry as an adjunct to King Cotton.

Cardozo's 1826 *Notes on Political Economy* was written largely in reaction to the growing influence Ricardian economics had over the Atlantic discourse. He was the first American to systematically attack Ricardo's paradigm.[94] Hardly a paragraph passes in his *Notes on Political Economy* without referencing the classical authorities, often in critical terms. "We are . . . convinced that if the principles of this theory," Cardozo wrote of Ricardian orthodoxy, "should be adopted as texts for lectures in our Colleges and Universities, it will greatly retard the progress of this important science among us."[95]

Cardozo challenged the two most fundamental precepts of Ricardian economics. First, he rejected the labor theory of value. He argued that wayward intellectual traditions and European conditions gave the labor theory of value its vaunted authority in nineteenth-century political economy. "The notion, therefore, that capital is nothing but accumulated labor, is as erroneous as the idea that labor is the sole element and only regulator of value," Cardozo asserted, "or, that the agency of Nature does not add to value in exchange, which, in fact, is what Mr. Ricardo has positively asserted." What Cardozo called "natural agents and natural substances" figured just as importantly as labor "among the elements of value, and every system of Political Economy that omits either of these constituents must be imperfect." In European societies with populations pressed on soils already becoming less productive, economists were inclined to overstate labor's importance in wealth creation. The determinant of value was, according to Cardozo, never absolute; rather it was decided by an array of factors. Moreover, neither labor nor capital had absolute claim to a nation's wealth. Cardozo offered a subtle counter to standard Ricardian logic that argued rent was requisitioned from wages and profits.[96] Capital and labor are not squeezed from rent, Cardozo found. Neither are wages lost profits for capitalists. Wages, profits, and rent could increase simultaneously in Cardozo's optimistic economic world.

Second, Cardozo attacked Ricardian rent. He was far more sanguine than the Englishman. "What evidence is there, that skill, science and ingenuity are not, in all stages in the progress of society, able to overcome that natural inferiority of soil which refuses to yield, without the co-operation of these powerful human aids, an increase of the means of subsistence?" In fact, man's propensity for expanding productive powers knew no limit. There was the remote possibility that posterity might suffer from decreased social production, but, Cardozo assuaged his readers, this period is "so distant indeed that we may not trouble ourselves." Cardozo also censured Ricardo for integrating into his rent theory a Physiocratic partiality that exaggerated the importance of land and agriculture.[97] "The larger portion of the produce of the soil transferred, in the form of rent, in consequence of the social arrangements that have taken effect throughout Europe, has given rise to the idea of a net surplus that is peculiar to Agriculture." This bias reflected an implicit social value prevalent in the Old World where land was monopolized by an aristocratic regime. "Where more natural arrangements prevail," that is, in America, "there is no surplus for rent, in the sense of this term as it is generally understood."[98] But the understanding of stagnant or circumscribed growth that was typical of European political economy also reflected a prejudiced perspective of nature's capacity as somehow limited. Diminishing returns were absent in Cardozo's version of intellectual capitalism. The vast unclaimed and fecund soils of America, combined with advances in the fields of agricultural and mechanical production, the cooperation between capital and labor, and the myriad of other facets of nature that man has yet to discover, promised material prosperity without the attendant sacrifices traditionally expected from the laboring classes.

Cardozo's criticisms of Ricardian rent were expanded to cover more generally the methodology by which political economists conducted the science.

He emphasized the role of historical circumstances in economic analysis, treated political economy as culturally specific, and rebutted Ricardo's claims of universality. Cardozo was one of the only free traders in the antebellum period to explicitly call for an absolute American divorce from European models. The British authorities had formulated economic principles based on assumptions of economic scarcity, ignoring New World conditions. Ricardian rent was applicable to conditions in the Old World, but it was irrelevant to the United States. Malthus too was apt to state certain principles "positively as a law of nature, which, for what we know to the contrary, may be the result of imperfect social organization." Cardozo advocated for the construction of a distinctly liberal American political economy. The nascent science, Cardozo wrote, could be more properly investigated here than in Europe, since American "institutions and laws have done less to derange the natural order of things than where a vicious social organization has resulted either from military violence or a selfish policy."[99]

The political economy of Vethake and Cardozo exemplified the American reception of Ricardo. Antebellum economists were not passive recipients of classical orthodoxy. They did not, as Conkin asserts, attempt to "amend and revise" Ricardo's system "in ways that only illustrated how much they remained within the same analytical tradition."[100] The Americans operated within an alternative laissez-faire paradigm. Vethake's doctrine was simply more optimistic than Ricardo's, and Cardozo initiated his economic analysis from an entirely different set of liberal precepts. In the process of refuting Malthus and Ricardo, antebellum economists forged a new brand of laissez-faire, essentially an entirely new understanding of intellectual capitalism. The failure to fall in line with the Malthusian-Ricardian regime does not exclude the antebellum economists from the transatlantic free-trade movement. Rather it illustrates the lack of consensus within that movement.[101] The tent under which liberal thinkers found shelter was broader and more complex than traditionally believed, welcoming a plurality of personalities whose understandings of the laissez-faire ideal varied considerably. In the antebellum literature it was perfectly acceptable to be anti-Malthusian, anti-Ricardian, and yet still be labeled a free trader. The treatment of Malthus and Ricardo is also indicative of how many antebellum free traders did not take seriously the perils British economists ascribed to economic growth and industrialization. The Americans had a different understanding of material and intellectual capitalism. Overpopulation, class warfare, and other hazardous features of the modern economy were attributed to the aristocratic qualities of British political and social systems. These dangers were neutralized by the exceptionality of American circumstances.

As the following chapter will show, however, the forecasts of Malthus and Ricardo were taken seriously by minority sects. These groups rejected contemporary notions of American exceptionalism, refuted liberal bourgeois values, and broke decisively from the theoretical nuances of American laissez-faire economics. Although divided along regional lines, they shared an affinity of ideas that provided an alternative expression of American economic intellectual culture. In the South, George Fitzhugh and George Frederick Holmes struck at Smith, Malthus, Ricardo, and all that was sacred to intellectual capitalism. In the North, the Jacksonian-era race toward industrialization cultivated the philosophical origins of domestic socialism. Although the northeastern and southern expressions of liberal intellectual hybrid capitalism occasioned differentiated theoretical trajectories and were, in some instances, seemingly operating in parallel universes, they still wrote within the broadening spectrum of the nineteenth-century laissez-faire template. The southern reactionaries and northern laborites, however, operated outside the liberal tradition, encouraging instead a fundamentally different social, political, and economic system, founded on a diametrically hostile set of principles, and providing antebellum America with its most vicious challenge to the free-market paradigm.

4

THE CRISIS OF FREE SOCIETY

THE SOUTHERN AND NORTHERN REACTIONARIES

During the middle decades of the antebellum period, the expansion of short-staple cotton production across the Mississippi Delta brought a highly commercialized form of the plantation complex to the border with, and ultimately into, Texas. In the Northeast, industrialization precipitated sweeping economic and social transformation. These twin developments coincided with a sprawling network of internal improvements extending into the Ohio River valley that linked that region's commercial farming to swelling urban markets in the New England and mid-Atlantic states and integrated the South's slave regime into a single domestic economy still marked by sectional distinctions. The material successes of slavery and industry, the historical prevalence of slavery in southern history, but also the more recent manifestations of commercial prosperity credited to plantation slavery in the so-called New South, combined with the rapidity with which the industrial order was becoming embedded in northern society, heightened the public's focus on the attendant social externalities of both systems. These factors pushed plantation slavery and industrialization to the fore of the American economic mind.[1] As slavery and industry both grew more prosperous, contemporary discussions about them became more politicized. In the process, both required from their proponents nuanced justifications to fend off criticisms from detractors and to convince audiences of the purported improprieties of the economic regimes of their sectional rivals.

Within this body of literature, a small but vocal group of northern labor advocates experimented with profound theoretical alterations to industrial society. They appealed to Americans outside of academia and government, mostly urban workers frustrated by capitalist transformation and interested in seeing elements of the industrial revolution stalled, reversed, or torn asunder. They broke sharply from the more established versions of liberal intellectual capitalism then being taught in northeastern institutions of higher learning, fomenting instead a decidedly anticapitalist ideology penned by machinists and artisans with bona fide working-class credentials and based on the real-life experiences shared by those coming of age in the nation's industrial headquarters. The northern laborites exemplified antebellum working-class mentality, and they made important contributions to an organic, domestic version of early socialist thought. They were, in essence, America's first anticapitalists. Langton Byllesby and Thomas Skidmore were the foremost representatives of this movement. They found something akin to an intellectual alliance with southern pro-slavery theorists, such as George Fitzhugh and George Frederick Holmes, who were simultaneously presenting southern audiences with sharp denunciations of bourgeois institutions and an economic ideology designed to stop the spread of material and intellectual capitalism. The supposed internal inconsistencies of laissez-faire political economy, particularly British classicism, the degradation and commodification of labor exacerbated by industrialization, the perceived callousness of market competition ruled by the cash nexus, and the emerging class stratification in the North were featured in both laborite and pro-slavery attacks that struck at the core of intellectual capitalism.

Labor advocates like Byllesby and Skidmore and pro-slavery conservatives like Fitzhugh and Holmes occupied different social positions in American society, but they shared space on the anticapitalist cerebral spectrum. Both groups introduced a conservative brand of political economy aimed at preserving traditional social mores and economic institutions that they believed were threatened by emergent capitalism. Contrary to conventional narratives that posit capitalist-oriented interests at the core of an American conservative faction arranged to preserve or advance an industrial and commercial status quo, the northern laborites and southern reactionaries indicate that in the antebellum discourse there existed conservative intellectuals working to undermine capitalist revolution. The similarities between the northern laborites and southern firebrands never developed into an organized cross-sectional political movement. And despite southern conservatives offering explicit appeals to domestic industrial labor, and northern labor advocates often comparing their station to the chattel slave, they seemed, like the northern and southern liberal economists, to be speaking around each other. Still, they represented essential expressions of antebellum conservative political economy, and they further illustrate the lack of a liberal consensus in American thought.

In the decades leading up to the Civil War, pro-slavery militants popularized contemporary perceptions of the incompatibility of industry and slavery. Reactionary pro-slavery economists grew unreceptive to intellectual capitalism and its industrial, Ricardian offshoot. They gave voice to a strain of intellectual pro-slavery that helps historians better situate the ideological divisions between North and South. Their writings illustrate that anticapitalist ideology was not monopolized by the working class. Moreover, pro-slavery conservative thought was distinct from the more established pro-slavery laissez-faire orthodoxy. Earlier criticisms of industrial society by liberals like Calhoun and Cooper were moderate, almost affable censures when compared to the vitriol of Fitzhugh, Holmes, and other southern fire-eaters. Finally, reactionary pro-slavery authors of the 1850s expressed the period's most violent rejection of intellectual capitalism, in all its hybrid forms, as well as British classicism, industrialization, and practically every bourgeois institution historians typically associate with the free-market order.

To Fitzhugh and Holmes fell the task of articulating conservative pro-slavery political economy in its most essential form. Their writings hardly constitute well-honed scientific studies, and most historians of antebellum southern thought place their ideas outside of the mainstream. This should not, however, discount their cultural significance. Pro-slavery conservatives like Fitzhugh and Holmes exercised authority across the region, especially in the Old South. Fitzhugh touted this influence in an exchange with Holmes just before the Civil War. "You, [Henry] Hughes, and I have revolutionized public opinion at the South on the subject of slavery."[2] To be sure, Fitzhugh was prone to exaggeration. "My friends tell me that I lead the Southern mind," he wrote President James Buchanan in 1858.[3] The historian James Oakes pegs the cultural impact of pro-slavery conservatives to the social, political, and economic power this group wielded at the "points of entrance" into southern high society—"perimeter conservatives" whose wealth afforded them prestige and clout, enabled by intergenerational transfers of estates that were largely immune to the fluctuations of international cotton prices and western migration mania. "Within this perimeter," Oakes writes, "a conservative, paternalistic slaveholding ideology survived long after most masters, even those in the perimeter itself, had adopted the prevailing principles of political liberalism and free-market commercialism."[4]

The southern conservatives subscribed to a political economy that seems anachronistic, nervously defending a bygone era swept aside by the South's sharp turn toward commercial slavery and the North's industrial expansion. They were displaced, isolated, alienated, and afraid. Their writings were, according to Oakes, marked by "personal idiosyncrasy," and on the whole, their dying breed of paternalistic slavery was passed over by their more commercially minded southern contemporaries. Yet a study of Fitzhugh, Holmes, and the entire cohort of fire-eaters that contributed to conservative reactionary planter ideology broadens the scope for understanding the internal struggles within the southern mind between progressive and paternalistic slaveholders. Moreover, historical appreciation of conservative pro-slavery thinkers, even if their ideas represent a minority sect, widens appreciation of the divisions within the American economic conscience, precisely as the nation moved toward political dissolution.

Fitzhugh was born in 1806 near Brentsville, Virginia. He received little beyond a common education, rarely traveled, and spent much of his time reading from his personal collection of books and pamphlets. Before the Civil War he held minor government posts in the Attorney General's office, and during the conflict he worked in the Confederate Treasury. In the Reconstruction Era he served alongside an ex-slave, presiding as an associate judge in the Freedmen's Bureau. He later moved to Kentucky and then to Texas, where he died in 1881. In the prewar era Fitzhugh's ideas circulated widely in articles written for *De Bow's Review* and in his two main books published in the 1850s, *Sociology for the South* and *Cannibals All!*

Fitzhugh's critique of intellectual capitalism was the platform from which he launched southern reactionary planter ideology. "He stripped away many of the contradictions and hesitations and brought those assumptions into the open," Eugene Genovese wrote, and "he took a major step toward the formation of a coherent slaveholders' world view."[5] Fitzhugh's attack on material and intellectual capitalism offered sweeping denunciations of the foundational principles of bourgeois society. First, Fitzhugh struck at the liberal assumption of the "right of private judgment," or personal intellectual sovereignty and the right to act on that judgment. For Fitzhugh, the right of private judgment was the glue holding together the liberal ideological template, and he traced it to the radical, antiauthoritarian underpinnings of the Protestant Reformation and the English Civil War. In American liberalism, the right of private judgment found expression in the "enthusiastic speculative philosopher" Thomas Jefferson, who with wanton disregard for traditional institutions invented ethics that were both socially and morally hazardous. All men were not created equal, Fitzhugh declared. But there were natural and universal rights, chief among them the right "to be taken care of and protected, to have guardians, trustees, husbands, or masters; in other words . . . a natural and inalienable right to be slaves."[6] Fitzhugh mocked personal sovereignty and self-reliance as impractical ideals. Indeed, he estimated that nineteen out of twenty individuals were incapable of self-care. The one in twenty was fitted for authority, the others for slavery. His program was indiscriminate; Fitzhugh advocated slavery for blacks and whites. "The weak in mind or body require guidance, support and protection," and society's leaders were obligated to afford them protection.[7] Caring for the weak, whether free or slave, was the most sacred moral tenet in conservative government. "Instead of relaxing more and more the bounds that bind man to man, you must screw them up more closely," Fitzhugh declared in a tone decidedly statist and antiliberal, reminiscent of an earlier age; "instead of no government, you must have more government."[8]

Fitzhugh inverted intellectual capitalism, following the rudimentary axioms of laissez-faire to their supposed dismal ends, illustrating what he believed were its theoretical inconsistencies, and accomplishing what he thought was the overthrow of the entire system of Smithian-inspired political economy. He dubbed Smith "absent, secluded, and unobservant," but the Virginian did share with the Scotsman deep skepticism about the human intellect. While Smith's philosophical skepticism was employed to defend free markets, and tied to an optimistic faith in a benign natural order, Fitzhugh's explicit, exaggerated, and pessimistic expressions of skepticism went beyond heads of state to ordinary individuals, to discredit economic liberties and point out the supposed fallacies of organizing society on the principle of self-interest. Ministers and monarchs were badly mistaken in their understanding of the economy, but so too were the hewers of wood and drawers of water. "Nature has made them slaves," Fitzhugh wrote, "to protect men, not merely from wrong and injustice from others, but from the consequences of their own vices, imprudence and improvidence."⁹ In short, most of humanity was incapable of discerning an enlightened self-interest, and with it the capacity for self-care.

Showcasing the internal inconsistencies of laissez-faire ideology was one of Fitzhugh's main pursuits. His target was almost always Smith. He abused Smith rhetorically and took special pride in supplying a litany of inflammatory moral declamations against Smithian liberalism. The *Wealth of Nations*, which Fitzhugh judged the most influential book since the Bible, substituted for Christian piety a struggle for survival where the cunning exploit the obtuse. "A beautiful system of ethics this," Fitzhugh noted sarcastically, "that places all mankind in antagonistic positions, and puts all society at war."[10] The danger of Smith's teachings, according to Fitzhugh, was its application as both an economic and a moral system. "The morality . . . is one of simple and unadulterated selfishness," Fitzhugh complained. We saw in chapter 2 that northeastern clerical liberals stressed the potential for commerce to engender cosmopolitan fraternity. Fitzhugh found more sinister forces at work. "The public good, the welfare of society, the prosperity of one's neighbors, is, according to them, best promoted by each man's looking solely to the advancement of his own pecuniary interests."[11]

By the 1850s, conservative reactionaries across the South were highlighting the supposed sociological and psychological damage wrought by industrial capitalism. Fitzhugh's *Sociology for the South* (1854) was the first American treatise having in its title the term "sociology." He seemed genuinely convinced that contemporary southern inquiries into the nature of the American experience advanced nineteenth-century studies of society. By emphasizing the deleterious social consequences of free labor industrial regimes, Fitzhugh fashioned sociology as a rhetorical device to attack abolitionist claims of the moral superiority of northern society. The underlying cultural factors inherent in relations between industrial capital and labor elicited Fitzhugh's attention. His description of labor's condition drew strong parallels to antebellum northern labor literature.[12] Labor's social-psychological woes evidenced the moral bankruptcy of free markets. Contemporary reports described industrial labor in a miserable state, locked in satanic mills, toiling without end, living hand to mouth, and forever susceptible to capital's abuse. "We do not know whether free laborers ever sleep. They are fools to do so; for, whilst they sleep, the wily and watchful capitalist is devising means to ensnare and exploit them." Capital stalks labor, Fitzhugh found, into "every recess of domestic life, infects its food, its clothing, its drink, its very atmosphere, and pursues the hireling, from the hovel to the poor-house, the prison and the grave. Do what he will, go where he will, capital pursues and persecutes him."[13] Labor's material exploitation aggravates its mental degradation. Capital's inhumane treatment of workers is driven by greed, is methodical, organized, and efficient, with booty taking the shape of profits won from a "moral Cannibalism" that free society celebrated as the gentleman's reward.

More cognizant of the totality of white supremacist values embedded in pro-slavery ideology, modern readers might deduce from conservative planter opposition to industrialization deep-seated anxieties over the potential for the modern economy to upset white hegemony. Fitzhugh's position, which was atypical, that slavery should be extended to whites should not distract from the more pervasive conservative logic that industrial capitalism destroyed the social and economic primacy of white workers. African slavery was defended with and helped maintain white supremacy. At the same time, reactionary planters combined anticapitalist animus that imitated the concerns of contemporary socialists about the plight of workers—white workers—with warnings directed against abolitionists, who ostensibly aimed at leveling the races. Although reactionary planters never explicitly combined these points, racial attitudes were a determinant factor in their ideological superstructure. Industrial capitalism, conservative planters feared, could accomplish the historical racial-economic trifecta, that is, hasten slavery's natural demise with the spread of a cheaper, more competitive, industrial labor input, elevate the status of blacks through emancipation, and by way of Malthusian and Ricardian processes, reduce white workers to wage slaves and, worse still, force whites to compete with blacks.

Advocating the well-being of workers was cut short when Fitzhugh and most of the southern intelligentsia wrote about the European rebellions of 1848. Conservatives were struck with horror over the disorder and general affronts to traditional values that the uprisings represented. For Fitzhugh the social and political troubles in Europe were the natural consequences of modernity's twin evils—liberalism and industrialization. As free labor grew more cognizant of "their own numbers and strength," Fitzhugh wrote, "all the reasoning in the world will not satisfy them that they who produce every thing should starve, in order that a handful of lords and capitalists should live in wanton waste and idle luxury."[14] Liberal and egalitarian ideals purported to offer unprecedented benefit to the masses, but it was precisely this segment of society that suffered under free-market systems. "The little experiment of universal liberty that has been tried for a little while in a little corner of Europe, has resulted in disastrous and appalling failure."[15] Like many southerners', Fitzhugh's ire against all things British, including classical political economy, intensified as Parliament's crusade against slavery grew more determined. And the specter of labor insurrection buttressed southern claims that slavery was the more effective form of social organization. In Britain, free markets drove wages to subsistence levels. In Ireland, English capitalists starved peasants. In France, the people won *liberté, égalité, fraternité*, but begged for bread. And in the American North, the laborer was without a "home of his own; he is insecure of employment; sickness may overtake him at any time and deprive him of the means of support; old age is certain to overtake him, if he lives, and generally finds him without the means of subsistence; his family is probably increasing in numbers, and is helpless and burdensome to him."[16] Liberty and equality, what Fitzhugh called "new things under the sun," had given international license for the rich to destroy the poor.[17]

Fitzhugh's critique of industrialization drew him into an awkward alliance with Atlantic socialism. "We, too, are a Socialist," Fitzhugh declared.[18] The affinity Fitzhugh and other pro-slavery writers of the 1850s entertained for socialism is one of the peculiar features of antebellum economic thought.[19] Fitzhugh expressed sharp opposition to industrial capitalism at almost exactly the same time European socialists codified their creed. The lines separating European and domestic socialists from southern conservative reactionaries were blurred. To be sure, Fitzhugh's disparagement of laissez-faire was influenced more by Carlyle than by Marx, but it indicates the extent to which pro-slavery theorists were willing to stretch their logic to defend southern institutions, as well as the intellectual elasticity of the antebellum conservative-reactionary mind. Fitzhugh's sympathy toward socialism was, however, mainly for rhetorical purposes. "I never read a socialist author treating his subject philosophically in my life," he wrote in 1855.[20] And workers' revolution, precisely the type advocated by some socialists, was for Fitzhugh and other like-minded pro-slavery conservatives a perilous evil.[21]

Still, the apparent demise of industrial capitalist society abroad, illustrated by European labor unrest and forecast in the writings of Malthus and Ricardo, assured southern reactionaries of the virtues of plantation slavery. Indeed, the ability to cultivate harmonious relations between capital and labor—that is, master and slave—solved the quandary affecting nineteenth-century industrialization. Slavery, Fitzhugh wrote, is a "benign and protective institution," founded on a mutuality of interest between labor and capital that "begets domestic affection on the one side, and loyalty and respect on the other."[22] Under slavery the masses, blacks and whites, were guaranteed security and happiness. Slavery sheltered labor in sickness, infancy, and old age. "We tell those who ask for or require protection and support that 'they must submit to be controlled, for that price of security has ever been, and will be, the loss of liberty.'"[23] The master will defend his slave, Fitzhugh wrote in a patronizing tone, as he would any of his personal possessions. "A man loves not only his horses and his cattle, which are useful to him, but he loves his dog, which is of no use. He loves them because they are his." Such was the omnipotent design of Providence, to make "the selfishness of man's nature the protecting aegis to shield and defend wife and child, slaves and even dumb animals."[24]

Pro-slavery conservatives ignored the physical drudgery imposed on slave labor, while simultaneously shaming the northern industrial regime for degrading free labor. The highly commercialized version of material plantation slavery that existed across the Mississippi region, characterized by the abject exploitation, commodification, and traumatization of slave labor, was not featured in Fitzhugh's defense of the peculiar institution. Elements of the southern reactionary understanding of antebellum slavery comport with post–Civil War apologist narratives, and even modern histories have found the master-slave relation primed with benign values.[25] Where paternalistic ideals did exist—or at least where planters believed paternalism existed, notwithstanding the reality—the slaveholder's guilt was likely dulled. The perception of paternalistic slavery was bolstered by antebellum assumptions of African racial inferiority, as well as widespread depictions of the slave's character and faculties as childlike, and thus the necessity for the enslaved to abide by the master's instructions. Relations on the typical antebellum plantation were also likely influenced by demographic differences between master and slave. In 1850 most slaves were under the age of eighteen, while the typical master was in his mid-forties. The consensus among modern historians is that the self-serving paternalistic ideal Fitzhugh waxed enthusiastic over was uncommon on plantations devoted to maximizing profits. Slaves were thought of primarily in a commercial context. The reality was, most planters knew very little about their slaves and probably rarely developed meaningful bonds of affection.[26]

The fact that pro-slavery conservative thought was disconnected from reality should not, however, discourage historians from taking contemporary understanding of paternal slavery seriously. The editors of the South's most influential journals considered high-minded pro-slavery ideals legitimate enough to regularly publish articles penned by Fitzhugh, Holmes, and other conservative authors. These were printed in the decade leading up to the Civil War, presumably when southerners were most attentive to arguments defending slavery. Fitzhugh encapsulated the intellectual culture of the reactionary planter of the Old South, and in the process widened the gap between northern and southern economic thought. Although it is difficult for historians to measure the practical or policy consequences of reactionary literature, men like Fitzhugh were complicit in setting the tone for secessionists, or at least they helped establish the parameters for debate. Fitzhugh's attacks on industrial capitalism rattled northern bourgeois culture, galvanized the Yankee North, and presumably helped field an army in defense of southern institutions.

But Fitzhugh's thought is also reflective of regional differences within the southern economy, and the subtle differences in how southerners responded to market expansion. Commercial development, and the commercialization of slavery, pursued a highly uneven course across the South. Historians sometimes refer to these regional differences as the "dual economy," or the coexistence of market-oriented plantation economies and isolated subsistence or semi-subsistence farmers and petit slaveholders of the Old South.[27] By the 1840s, reform-minded planters in western Alabama, Louisiana, and Mississippi entrenched commercial plantation slavery deep into a wider transatlantic economy, driven by market imperatives and increasingly tied to the financial, industrial, and commercial services of the North. These were not the planters that Fitzhugh spoke for. In the Old South, especially Fitzhugh's Virginia, slavery had been reduced to less commercial and less prosperous forms. Fitzhugh's own residence, described by a neighbor as a "rickety old mansion, situated on the fag-end of a once noble estate," was indicative not only of Fitzhugh's own family's fall from economic fortune but also the region's general decline from national economic prominence.[28] His hometown of Port Royal, once a bustling commercial center on the Rappahannock River, had suffered economic decay. By 1860 its population was 323. Western migration of slaves and capital left some upland parts of Virginia, the Carolinas, and Georgia underdeveloped and isolated, populated by what Louis Hacker aptly called "'sand-hillers,' 'crackers,' and 'clay eaters' . . . those unfortunates who, because of poverty, had become isolated in nonproductive pine barrens and sandy coastal plains zones; who lived in a misery and squalor that has rarely had its equal in human history; and whose low physical and mental state was due to inadequate diets, malaria, hookworm, and constant inbreeding."[29] Add to those parts the remote frontier hill counties of Alabama and the swampy backcountry of Louisiana and Mississippi, inhabited mostly by subsistence farmers and masters of a few slaves who had grown apathetic toward developers and promoters.

Yeomen, petit planters, squatters, vagrants, day laborers, poor farmers, and other rural types that occupied the South manifested different levels of resistance to market encroachments and material culture. To some of Fitzhugh's southern readers, emergent markets destroyed time-honored values, customs, and institutions. Although most large planters were keen on commercialization and the accumulation of riches, some took pride in austere, almost destitute, living conditions. Abolitionists argued that slavery bred contempt for labor and made some masters lazy, neglectful tenants of dilapidated homes with poor furnishings, dressed in worn clothes, perpetually filthy, surviving on unrefined diets, and imbued with a frontier sense of self-denial.[30] In 1861 one fire-eater, Senator Louis T. Wigfall of Texas, told a British journalist: "We are an agricultural people. . . . We have no cities—we don't want them. We have no literature—we don't need any yet. We have no press—we are glad of it. . . . We want no manufactures: we desire no trading, no mechanical or manufacturing classes."[31] Such words capture what our historical imagination tells us these people must have feared about the commercial excess of Yankee capitalism. They were, according to the historian Harry L. Watson, "an ever more eager audience for sectionalist fire-eaters and a mounting political pressure for secession."[32] It was the fathers and sons of these regions who filled the Confederate front lines, fighting the "poor man's fight," in part to preserve southern institutions from what Fitzhugh described as the vile depravity of Yankee cannibalism.[33]

In the postwar period Fitzhugh published articles in *De Bow's Review*, where he predicted the spread of "Yankee isms" (socialism) in the North. "We have little hope for the future," Fitzhugh lamented; "the American Republic is near its end." The nation's only hope rested in a "conservative reaction . . . effected by the untrammeled aid of the South."[34] Fitzhugh aimed to stop capitalist revolution before what he imagined was its inevitable descent into socialism. Although an uncompromising, cantankerous voice in the eyes of historians, Fitzhugh's position as an outlier should not be exaggerated. Louis Hartz's depiction of Fitzhugh as "a mad genius" is in some ways accurate, but it implies that Fitzhugh's ideas were well beyond the antebellum mainstream. To be sure, Fitzhugh was not the archetypal antebellum political economist. He admitted to never having read a full-length text on some of the topics he covered in his own writings. His scattershot presentation suited his personal anti-philosophical disposition. "Philosophers," he wrote, "are the most abstracted, secluded, and least observant of men. Their premises are always false because they see but few facts; and hence their conclusions must be false."[35] In this way Fitzhugh reflected a broader reactionary anti-intellectual strain in American culture. Still, Fitzhugh's articles and books circulated fairly well. In his history of American conservatism, Clinton Rossiter labeled Fitzhugh the "high-point of reaction" in antebellum society. This characterization better captures Fitzhugh's brand. It would be an exaggeration to claim Fitzhugh was the spokesman for the South. Rather his writings should be sampled within the broader context of anticapitalist American conservatism and compared with similar antiliberal movements that sprung up across the North Atlantic in response to Enlightenment philosophy, intellectual capitalism, the French Revolution, and industrialization.[36]

In this intellectual environment George Frederick Holmes presented his critique of material and intellectual capitalism. Holmes was born in 1820 in British Guiana and educated in England before arriving in America at age eighteen. He taught languages, history, and political economy at Richmond College and William and Mary before, at age twenty-eight, he was elected first president of the University of Mississippi. His time at Mississippi was brief, however. Much of the remainder of Holmes's career was spent at the University of Virginia, where he taught a variety of subjects for forty years until his death in 1897.[37] In countless articles published in the South's most influential journals, Holmes offered conservative expositions on all that was wrong with intellectual and material capitalism. His criticisms were more learned than Fitzhugh's. Holmes stood closer to the genteel planter-cavalier intellectual ideal than any other southern thinker. His writings are methodical and tempered, and his descriptions of northern bourgeois society are scholarly in nature. This infused Holmes's works with an element of objectivity that was missing from the propagandist style of other southern fire-eaters like Fitzhugh.

Holmes's critique of bourgeois ideology assumed several forms. Like Fitzhugh, he was interested in the enduring social consequences attendant on large-scale industry. But Holmes also paid special notice to the development of laissez-faire as an intellectual system. Free-trade political economy, Holmes argued, lacked the basic standards by which scholarly inquiry is customarily handled and could therefore make no claims to scientific objectivity. Even the most central concepts—capital, labor, and value—lacked precise definition. "The obscurity and fluctuation of their terms arise from the previous want of lucidity in their conceptions, and they generate in the progress of speculation further obscurities and fluctuations, and very frequently fallacies which are neither discerned nor suspected." This criticism was often leveled against British classicism, which, to be fair, by the mid-nineteenth century was still experiencing internal disputes over fundamental principles. Holmes contended that political economy could not reach definitive conclusions; "the house is built upon sand," he declared.[38]

Challenging the theoretical basis of intellectual capitalism was a strategy pro-slavery writers employed to undermine northern free-labor society. They also figured the intellectual hollowness of laissez-faire was symbolic of the degenerated nineteenth-century liberal mind. Like most southerners writing just before the Civil War, Holmes was suspicious of liberal intellectual culture. The South grew less and less tolerant of Enlightenment ideas.[39] This anti-intellectual bent resonated across American culture, but it was palpable in the South. "We are, indeed," Holmes declared in an 1850 article for the *Southern Quarterly Review*, "no great believers in 'the march of the intellect' in the nineteenth century." Laissez-faire political economy was the most conspicuous and harmful philosophical fiasco of the era, Holmes insisted. Indeed, Smith, Ricardo, and Malthus were little more than charlatans clothed in learned dress, servants to the prevailing commercial-industrial order. "Political economy," Holmes wrote, "must be regarded as the grand Catholicon of social evils; admirable within its range, it is ruin, to body and soul, beyond it."[40] The British economists penned treatises that gave a false air of theoretical prestige to "the Gospel according to Mammon," legitimizing the impetuous desires of humanity by inventing an ideology marked by "the immediate gratification of the most important number—Number One."[41]

From this point Holmes launched a systematic critique of the psycho-social consequences of free markets. His writings indicate that the differences between the antebellum liberal North and conservative South were as much cultural as they were economic. In free-market societies, "individual life is swallowed up in . . . business avocations:—the lust of gold is the main-spring of . . . actions."[42] The human spirit was transformed, according to Holmes, its social and moral faculties retooled as monetary scales. Moral conventions were determined not by tradition or ethic but by the ability to satisfy base pecuniary wants. Material gain governed the human spirit, Holmes wrote; now society "rapidly degenerates into a curse."[43] The moral necessities of the human race were abandoned, "given place to gain and expediency:—immutable right and unchangeable wrong are measured and tested by the surplus or deficit of their aggregate money returns." Cast in an all-engrossing chase for wealth, the individual has "overlooked everything else."[44]

Like many pro-slavery critics of industrial society, Holmes appealed directly to northern workers, and by highlighting the exploitative tendencies of industrial capitalism, he strengthened the intellectual bonds between socialists and conservative planter reactionaries. Unlike Fitzhugh's, Holmes's treatment of socialist thought was not simply a rhetorical ruse; rather he harbored sincere affection for socialist-inspired reforms. "The first grand aim then of social amelioration," he wrote, "should be to establish a more thorough and equal distribution of the means of sustaining life—of productions—by a natural, healthful, and orderly modification of the laws of property."[45] His interpretation of the historical development of labor was consistent with contemporary socialist and Tory narratives. The transition from slave to feudal to free labor was initiated only after the early-modern commercial-capitalist class realized that free labor optimized profit. "The more it has been released from legal restrictions or deprived of legal protection," Holmes wrote of labor, "the worse has become the condition of the laborer, the more precarious his support, and the more stringent and crushing the pressure of the circumstances—that ever burning circle of fire—by which he is surrounded." The emancipation of serf and slave was prompted not by a pious, enlightened, or compassionate heart but by capital becoming more cognizant of new opportunities to exploit labor with scarcely any attendant responsibilities. "The principle which occasioned the substitution of free for slave labor was the prospect of diminished expenditure and increased gain. . . . Look into their declamations, contemplate their tactics, survey the whole literature of political economy, and it will be manifest that the real argument is simply that free labor is cheaper and more productive or profitable than slave labor."[46]

Comparisons between the costs of slave and free labor were a persistent feature in the antebellum discourse. Holmes's position on the higher costs of slave labor reinforced paternalistic arguments that posited slavery as more ethical than free labor. Here Holmes was criticizing the industrial order, but he was also censuring southern commercial planter reformers for disparaging slaveholders who supposedly failed to make the most effective use of the comparative cost advantages of cheap slave labor. Holmes's argument also comported with and appealed to northern labor advocates who commonly argued that factory operatives were the "wage slaves" of the industrial regime. Modern historians show that slave labor was in fact more expensive than alternative labor systems, at least when compared with agricultural labor costs in other cotton-producing economies like mid-nineteenth-century India. Alan Olmstead and Paul Rhode relay cliometric studies indicating that American slave labor annual costs were approximately ten times Indian agricultural wage labor circa 1850. Moreover, when hired out, antebellum slave wages in the decade before the Civil War were cheaper than northern wages for unskilled and skilled labor, but comparable to wages earned by female workers in cotton textiles.[47]

For Holmes, the early-modern transition toward free labor constituted a dereliction of moral duty whereby society's elite abandoned their traditional and sacred responsibilities to the poor. Southern reactionaries imagined themselves global crusaders charged with rescuing the masses from the perils of free labor industrialization and the race toward societal cannibalism. "It is to be feared that capital is applied most diligently to the procurement of a cheaper substitute for human labor, and to its exclusion. The steam man is the competitor of the human man."[48] Echoing antebellum workers' protests against the mechanization of labor, Holmes argued that the wonders of science and technology inevitably led to the displacement of workers, since machines would in time supplant humans as the more cost-effective alternative. Human exploitation was turned into a technical science, soliciting more proficient methods to profit at the expense of humanity, and in the process undermine conservative values that emphasized social responsibility and Christian morality. Reiterating a form of Malthusian pessimism, he anticipated that the spread of industrial machinery would "reach speedily the limit when the masses, not of one country, but of the whole commercial world will be pauperized, and unable to keep up with the production . . . and enfeebled by disease so as to be unable to supply the physical force required for the creation of the raw material."[49]

Increasing incidents of worker strife foreshadowed the North's inescapable plunge toward social conflict. "The different classes are arrayed against each other," Holmes warned; "the rich dread and scorn the power of the masses. . . . The multitudes envy, hate, and menace the wealth:—they threaten agrarianism or the less sweeping remedies of violence and fraud:—for they feel that inherent discrepancy has grown into bitter hostility and inexplicable wrong."[50] Slavery was the obvious alternative. While the rest of Western society shamed the moral absenteeism of planters, pro-slavery conservatives helped popularize nineteenth-century British parliamentary reports that laid bare the degraded conditions of that nation's working poor. Details of British pauperism, below-subsistence-level wages, dangerous working environments, urban crime and overcrowding, and the growing body of anecdotal evidence depicting the abject poverty that blighted America's very own industrial quarters evidenced how much better off materially the southern slaves were than the factory operatives. Like Fitzhugh, Holmes was partial to descriptions of southern plantations that featured paternal relations between master and slave. He voiced the southern maxim that slavery was a positive good, chiefly because the institution accomplished what no other economic system could. It brought together in harmonious accord the interests of capital and labor.[51]

Engaging intellectual capitalism afforded pro-slavery reactionaries opportunities to launch broader criticisms of political liberalism, which were often packaged into multilayered polemics against northern institutions. Mixing economics and politics was common in early nineteenth-century tracts, so antebellum economic literature was typically accompanied by lengthy discussions on political and social theory. In this way southern conservatism offered an all-encompassing counterrevolutionary ideology. Although they were confident in local white southern majorities to fend off national legislative intrusions by an expanding northern democracy, conservative planters were also surely cognizant of the 10 percent decline in the number of slaveholding families between 1830 and 1860. The democratic base of the plantation regime was shrinking. By the later decades of the antebellum period, conservative planters had already abandoned many of the Enlightenment ideals embedded in the principles of 1776, and they were also becoming increasingly antidemocratic.[52] A Tory disposition engendered a Federalist political temperament, which in some cases fostered an affinity for authoritarianism.

In the mind of the southern reactionary, intellectual capitalism and the doctrine of political individualism were intellectual siblings. "But the cry of the capitalists for the Laissez faire system," Holmes wrote, "in order that their acquisition of gains might be unrestricted, has led to the supposition that the entire absence of political restraints was the Utopia of political organization, and the surest evidence of Democratic principles."[53] What were traditionally constructed as independent bodies of thought—political, social, moral, and economic—were consolidated by nineteenth-century liberalism into a single ideological program that demanded the maximization of freedom in all categories of life. Liberalism, in short, aimed to remodel practically every aspect of the human experience. For conservative thinkers like Holmes, laissez-faire doctrine served as the intellectual springboard that threatened to flip the world upside down. Free-trade economics, Holmes argued, finds some truth "within the narrow range of their legitimate application; but when we see it wrenched from its just employment, as an explanation of the increase of wealth, into a cannon for the government of nations," it endangered all that was sacred to conservatives. Too much freedom promised to destroy the human race. By the 1850s radical pro-slavery authors denounced everything associated with Yankee culture. Like Fitzhugh, Holmes gave voice to what other opponents of liberalism had only hinted at. "There is one great delusion of political economy, not as a science, but as a practical rule, that it conceives the world will steadily pursue what is best, not what seems best."[54] Intellectual capitalism and the doctrine of individual sovereignty left society open to chance. Enlightened self-interest was a philosophical farce.

The breadth of Holmes's conservative reach was given further expression in his antiliberal views on private property. Here Holmes struck at the capstone of Lockean liberalism. Traditional property rights were not sacred. "In all ages, the forms in which it [property] must be confined, have been a legitimate subject of legislative and constitutional enactment."[55] In this regard Holmes articulated the extent to which reactionary southern economic thought was divorced from bourgeois liberalism. The social transformations wrought by political individualism and material and intellectual capitalism required that nineteenth-century conservatives rethink conventional principles. "The wants of modern societies," Holmes wrote, "have outgrown received formulas; . . . the existing elements of social organization have in consequence been thrown into fatal anarchy and discord."[56]

Holmes was not an intellectual alien disseminating ideas into a reactionary vacuum. During his own time, he was regarded enough to teach at the nation's second largest university for four decades. Along with Fitzhugh, fire-eaters like Henry Hughes, James Hammond, and Edmund Ruffin filled the southern discourse with anticapitalist reactionary scorn. Henry Hughes, an eccentric attorney in New Orleans, packed his 1854 *Treatise on Sociology, Theoretical and Practical* with repudiations of individualism, vindications of slavery, or what he called "warranteeism," and justifications for an authoritarian state. "A man has no right to use his mind and body as he will," Hughes wrote in a parlance soaked in hyper-statist values; rather all have an equal obligation to labor under the direction of a powerful central administrator, as "the moral theory of any economic system, is the assistance of all for the subsistence of all."[57] James Hammond of South Carolina famously declared on the Senate floor in 1858 that in all civilized societies "there must be a class to do the menial duties, to perform the drudgery of life . . . it constitutes the very mud-sill of society." Fortunately, Hammond continued, the South had its slaves, "hired for life and well compensated . . . elevated from the condition in which God first created them . . . happy, content, unaspiring, and utterly incapable, from intellectual weakness, ever to give us any trouble by their aspirations." For Hammond the North had its own slaves, but by another name. "Yours are white, of your own race; you are brothers of one blood . . . equals in natural endowment of intellect, and they feel galled by their degradation." Empowered by the ballot box, the wage slaves of the industrial North threatened to turn on their capitalist masters. Hammond warned abolitionists that slavery's role in preserving the conservative order not only was essential to southern society but was effectively the final bulwark preventing nationwide anarchy.[58]

And Edmund Ruffin, acclaimed agronomist, zealous fire-eater, and Virginian aristocrat, offered a polished defense of slavery by attacking free society in his 1853 *The Political Economy of Slavery*. Slavery, according to Ruffin, advanced civilization, improved the condition of the masses, promoted the common good by forcing humanity to perform what it least enjoys, and mitigated the spread of pauperism or what he called the "class-slavery" of industrial societies. The historical ubiquity of the institution proved its aptitude for productivity and self-sustainability. In modern industrial societies, redundant populations subject labor to unremitting competition, depreciate wages to Malthusian subsistence levels, and attain "the most perfect and profitable condition of industrial operations for the class of capitalists and employers." Soon slavery would prove economically untenable, "for sharp want, hunger and cold, are more effective incentives to labor than the slaveowner's whip."[59] The wage-slavery system, after all, was only adopted because it was discovered to be a more effective method to exploit labor. But by compelling workers to toil at subsistence wages, free society drives labor into a position akin to slavery, while releasing master capitalists of their otherwise natural moral responsibility to care for their underlings.

If modern historians have a difficult time taking the hyperbole of planter conservatives at face value, men like Ruffin certainly took themselves and the cause they championed seriously. At age sixty-five, Ruffin enlisted as a private in the Palmetto Guard of the South Carolina militia. He is often credited with having fired the first shots on Fort Sumter, a 64-pound shell from a columbiad iron cannon. During the Civil War, Ruffin and his family were escorted by Union troops from one of their Virginia plantations. When Ruffin returned, he was shocked to learn his slaves had fled, but perhaps less surprised to see his plantation looted and vandalized. Union soldiers had inscribed in charcoal and tobacco juice on an interior wall: "You did fire the first gun on Sumter, you traitor son of a bitch."[60] At the news of Lee's surrender, Ruffin wrapped himself in a Confederate flag and committed suicide.

Fitzhugh suffered during the war as well, forced to take refuge in Richmond when his home at Port Royal was bombarded. After all, according to Abraham Lincoln's law partner and biographer William H. Herndon, Fitzhugh's *Sociology for the South* "aroused the ire of Lincoln more than most pro-slavery books."[61] The Civil War strained Holmes's personal life too. He described the conflict as a "crusade of anarchy, corruption, and agrarianism." British citizenship and blindness in one eye disqualified Holmes from military service. Student enrollment in his courses at the University of Virginia dropped suddenly after Fort Sumter. In 1862 only three students attended his lectures, and thus the professor's income declined. The war forced his family to relocate to the Appalachians of southwest Virginia, leaving Holmes in Charlottesville worried for their safety. Toward the war's end Holmes grew more certain that the North was headed toward military dictatorship, and at Lincoln's death he predicted revolution and the spread of "all the furies of agrarianism and anarchy."[62] Most southern conservatives believed abolitionism was simply cover for widespread property expropriation. Neither of Holmes's ominous predictions came true, of course. He took the oath of amnesty shortly after Appomattox and returned to teaching and writing. His obituary in the *American Historical Review* observed that the professor had "published little, but was of note as a teacher."[63]

Posterity consigned Fitzhugh, Holmes, Hughes, Hammond, Ruffin, and the entire legion of southern reactionaries to an intellectual culture reminiscent of centuries past. At a time when America was at the fore of Atlantic liberal capitalist transformation, southern conservatives gave voice to a counterrevolutionary movement best suited for the waning years of the Old Regime. But they remind historians that in the antebellum discourse, material and intellectual capitalism was perceived as the radically transformative movement. They also remind historians that the forces aligned against capitalism did not necessarily emanate from the left. Now buried deep in the American popular historical consciousness, even their successors in modern conservative intellectual history have relegated the planter reactionaries to the far fringes of its ideology. "The final clue to the southern ideology is the way America managed to forget it," Hartz wrote in his "Feudal Dream of the South" chapter, "and who can deny that the rejection of capitalism has been forgotten as much as any part of it?"[64] The antidemocratic, antiegalitarian, antiliberal, anticapitalist, pro-slavery southerners constituted a minority in the region's otherwise commercially oriented brand of antebellum free-trade slavery. But they were an intellectual force to contend with. And even if conservative planters conformed in their day-to-day lives to the imperatives of material capitalism, their intellect did not.

"The reactionary enlightenment" of radical pro-slavery ideology was, as Hartz wrote, "the great imaginative moment in American political thought." But conservative planter ideology was not rejected or neglected.[65] Nor was its demise as an ideological movement inevitable because it captured an anti-modernity perspective antithetical to what most historians equate with progress.[66] To be sure, the conservative planter paradigm was anticapitalist, and so far as historians regard market relations and intellectual capitalism as the dominant matrix that advanced modern societies and material progress, then the southern reactionaries were traditionalists, or, put differently, antimodern. Neither was conservative planter ideology destined for destruction because the economic system grown from it was less efficient than free labor. Economic historians have shown that slavery, despite its antebellum prosperity, was dependent on westward expansion and therefore was not an especially sustainable economy.[67] Still, systems of economic organization have existed for extended periods despite their inefficiencies. Plantations managed according to paternalistic values, we have to imagine, were less productive than commercially oriented plantations and, in this sense, likely to have died an earlier death. But the midcentury collapse of American slavery, both paternal and commercial, was not necessarily an inevitable outcome wrought by meta-historical, supranational forces, driven by Enlightenment waves of progress, modernity, and the social-spiritual gestalt of industrial capitalism. The real reasons for the defeat of both brands of antebellum slavery were the superior numbers and resources of the Union Army.

The material and intellectual forces of Yankee capitalism ultimately excluded planter conservatism from the lexicon of American political economy. Still, Holmes and Fitzhugh and the others illustrate the breadth of the antebellum discourse. And contrary to liberal consensus historiography and the New Historians of Capitalism, the reactionary pro-slavery writers were not aliens in an otherwise free-market environment. The North had its own cohort of critics that issued stinging rebuttals of intellectual and material capitalism. Although the northern anticapitalists were oftentimes abolitionists and prescribed reforms that were quite different from the southern reactionaries', the two groups shared an ideological base explicit in the desire to reconstruct America in accordance with pre-market values.

The postponement of an American edition of Marx's *Communist Manifesto* until 1871 did not prevent circulation of socialist literature in America. European labor intellectuals who migrated to the United States after the revolutions of 1848 found in the industrial North an indigenous working-class movement. In the 1820s, trade and craft associations organized two separate groups called Working Men's Party, one in Philadelphia and the other in New York. Leadership within the Working Men's Party, as well as the region's broader labor movement, was drawn from a variety of classes and trades. The rank and file were an eclectic bunch, including dock workers, journalists, physicians, teachers, attorneys, printers, master craftsmen, apprentices and journeymen in the building and metal trades, shoemakers, tailors, cabinetmakers, grocers, dry goods merchants, and wage laborers of all kinds. In short, the propertied and propertyless, the working and professional classes. According to one estimate, by the mid-1830s approximately 35,000 workers were active in the labor movement.[68] As Sean Wilentz has shown in his study of antebellum New York City, workers organized according to a fluid, dynamic set of social relations that adjusted to an equally shifting set of production systems. The expansion of manufacturing restructured centuries-old artisan traditions to conform to emerging bourgeois ideals of labor, land, and markets. Combined with religious and ethnic distinctions, these forces helped determine class associations and ideology in antebellum America. In a process involving, Wilentz notes, "the possible coexistence of several tendencies and outlooks, sometimes in a single movement or in the minds of individual participants," class formation and class consciousness never assumed a linear trajectory and in fact saw an amalgamation of different peoples and ideas.[69] There was widespread opposition, however, to the perceived destruction of preindustrial craft labor, or what Wilentz described as the bastardization of the artisan system, namely, the subcontracting of production processes to unskilled wage labor, the replacement of paternal, almost guildlike master-apprentice tutelage with more efficient alternatives, the decline of the "just price" and "just wage" values, and the increasing mechanization and commodification of what were once independent artisans.

The shifts in manufacturing production processes that started at the end of the eighteenth century were pervasive by the 1840s.[70] The early labor movement championed a broad platform, including public education, curtailing the issue of banknotes, the restructuring of lien laws, a ten-hour workday, an end to monopolies and licensing restrictions, abolition of imprisonment for debt, termination of prison labor, reforms to the two-party political system, and, in New York specifically, countering the influence of the entrenched Tammany and Albany Regency political machines.[71] Party alignments were ultimately determined by the exigencies of local politics, co-optation, and intrigue. By the election of 1832, the Working Men's Party, beset by infighting and partisan wrangling, split its votes between the Jacksonian Democrats, the supporters of Clay, and the anti-Mason party.

Northern laborites of the 1830s and 1840s focused a great deal of energy on land reform as well. In the Jeffersonian-republican tradition, a virtuous citizenry could be fostered only through yeoman proprietorship. Luckily America was blessed with a vast continental expanse. Mounting perceptions of the moral and social degradation inherent in urban-industrial environments, combined with the threat of increasing rents and the monopolization of land, led reformers to land distribution schemes that promoted western settlement. Opening western lands would mitigate what northern workers believed was a growing labor surplus, exacerbated by unprecedented immigration and mechanization. Leaders in the movement like George Henry Evans and Robert Dale Owens, both British emigrants, equated land reform with traditional cultural values like self-sufficiency, family coherence in a patriarchal hierarchy, and personal responsibility.

The agrarian reform movement was not unique to antebellum America. The Americans participated in what one historian describes as a "cross-fertilization" of ideas, an agrarian internationalism transcending Atlantic waters through open lines of communication with European, but especially British, land reformers. In Britain, land reform movements also grew out of existing labor movements. Overcrowded labor markets, dismal working and living conditions, and successive failures at political radicalism made land reform seem like a practical alternative. In early America, the agrarian movement similarly worked in unison with various labor organizations, often shared the same leadership, and occasionally invoked the "agrarianism" of earlier working-class spokesmen. But by 1850, land reformers had largely abandoned the radical demands of earlier labor agitators; instead they advanced programs sympathetic to bourgeois free-market ideology. Their chief accomplishment, the Homestead Act of 1862, was imagined by supporters in line with the principles of 1776 and in the mode of a Jeffersonian-Jacksonian bourgeois middle-class ethos.[72]

Labor intellectuals of the early antebellum period were frequent critics of the so-called land monopolists, but they more often injected socialist values into the debate and in some instances disavowed the Jeffersonian petit-bourgeois values of land reformers. Chief among these was Langton Byllesby. Born in Philadelphia in 1789, Byllesby was just an infant when his parents died of cholera.[73] He served as an editor for a local newspaper in western Pennsylvania before moving his family to New York City. There Byllesby worked as a journeyman proofreader for Harper Brothers. In 1826 he published *Observations on the Sources and Effects of Unequal Wealth*. The work is considered the first American attempt to understand the consequences of technology on social inequality and unemployment levels. And according to Conkin, Byllesby's *Observations* was "the first angry American economic treatise," initiating "a tradition of class-conscious economic advocacy by those who identified themselves with an American working class."[74]

Byllesby assumed the charge of articulating the concerns of the disaffected journeyman mechanic. From his perspective, entrepreneurial masters subordinated long-established labor traditions to the interests of capital. His political economy gave voice to an emerging working-class ideology that aimed at reversing labor's condition to a preindustrial age. He did not advocate a moderate strain of Jeffersonian agrarianism.[75] Land redistribution and imposing limitations on accumulation were part of his program, but these were ancillary to a comprehensive reorganization of the urban craft economy. Byllesby's economic thought was set in an alternative paradigm from the laissez-faire model. Indeed, he sought the complete overthrow of the foundational principles of material and intellectual capitalism, or in his words, an "absolute revision of the present system of the arts of life; and distribution of the products of labor." His work is as much a critique of industrial capitalism as it is a conventional inquiry in political economy. He was, however, familiar enough with the nineteenth-century economic discourse to weaponize his criticisms against the central tenets of classical doctrine. Like Fitzhugh and Holmes, Byllesby borrowed Ricardian logic to launch a powerful attack on the entire edifice of intellectual capitalism. His analysis began with reaffirmations of the Ricardian labor theory of value. "Labor alone is the source of all wealth," Byllesby declared, and all have a natural right to the fruits of their labor and the sustenance it provides. But in the prevailing free-market system "the products of labor belong to almost any other than the producer, who generally obtains from the application of his power no more than a bare subsistence."[76] The sequestering of labor's wealth by a parasitic few forced American workers into conditions comparable to chattel slaves and European paupers. Moreover, it cemented the class stratification then emerging in the nation's industrial quarters.

Byllesby was one of the first Americans to argue that permanent class divisions were an inherent feature of free-market society. Class stratification was precipitated by gross disparities in the distribution of wealth, accumulated by capital through the exploitation of labor. Byllesby highlighted four market institutions responsible for exacerbating income inequities and aggravating class relations. In doing so, he assailed the foundational elements of material capitalism. He struck first at the banking industry. Byllesby preempted Jackson's war on banks by declaring financial institutions the chief culprit in accelerating economic inequality. Financiers perpetrated an array of frauds on the working class. Currency was originally intended to facilitate fair exchange and promote the general good. Instead, banks circulated notes to advance avarice, destroying community bonds in the process. The moneyed interests combined with middlemen and merchants, or those engaged in what Byllesby called "trafficking," forcing workers to sell their labor and wares for a fraction of their worth.[77] Compelling workers to accept an amount below the fair value of their productive powers was tantamount to slavery. Intermittent fluctuations in currency values, suspensions of payments, and the seemingly incessant desire of banks to undermine the common good ensured that the owners of capital would live off the sweat and toil of the laboring masses.

After finance and commerce, Byllesby challenged the ethical propriety of profits, based in part on his understanding of the labor theory of value. All profit, he declared, was a morally depraved value expropriated from workers. Finally, Byllesby projected that machinery would hasten unemployment crises, reduce wages, weaken consumer purchasing power, and initiate general gluts.[78] The impact of technology on the distribution of wealth was of special interest to Byllesby. Increases of production attributed to machinery were confiscated from labor, allocated instead to the idle few. Industrial machinery, Byllesby estimated, produced more than the entire human race could ever consume. Still, poverty was a persistent problem.[79] Production levels should not be determined by market imperatives but rather by society's needs, especially the guarantee to provide all with steady employment.

The reforms suggested by Byllesby would have abolished the market system. His Association for Securing Equal (or Mutual) Advantages (or Interests) designed a program of "equalization."[80] This included the organization of industrial communities in the form of joint-stock corporations. These labor associations would harness the productive powers of industry, secure high employment, guarantee a just reward for labor, and eliminate poverty. Labor should, Byllesby figured, when combined with industrial machinery, find four to five hours a day sufficient for the production of a subsistence. Under the new regime, trade would be based rightfully on the principle of reciprocity, ruinous competition curtailed, and all would have equal entitlement to the land. Finally, Byllesby advocated for the abolition of inheritance, the prohibition of interest, and the requirement for all to work.

Joseph Dorfman minimizes the significance of Byllesby by suggesting his reforms were simply a Jacksonian-style protest "against privilege and invidiousness."[81] By casting Byllesby as a laissez-faire type, Dorfman places too much emphasis on contemporary politics, and thus neglects the totality of Byllesby's intentions. Like the southern reactionaries, Byllesby's political economy was wholly antithetical to the laissez-faire model. Its purpose was to return society to a precapitalist era. The burgeoning working class that Byllesby gave voice to reminisced on old-fashioned fraternal bonds that celebrated a producerist ethic—an idealized time when social production was organized around the community's needs, much as they imagined it had been during the premodern age with masters and apprentices sharing the "mysteries" of craft, often living and working under the same roof, and shouldering equally the responsibility for a moral economy. To historians, the sentimentalist accounts of craft labor relations are obviously different from the romanticized planter descriptions of paternal slavery. Journeymen and apprentices, historians reason, must have understood that their relations with master craftsmen were fundamentally different from the supposed familial bonds between slaves and planters. In the same way, comparisons made by planters and northern workers between industrial working conditions and those of antebellum slaves seem misguided. But these comparisons were real for contemporaries. And they brought critics of material and intellectual capitalism together under a shared desire to return America to a precapitalist age.

In his study of American conservatism, Rossiter described elemental forms of "temperamental conservatism" as "man's 'natural' disposition to oppose any substantial change in his manner of life, work, and enjoyment." This is typically accentuated, Rossiter continued, by "the fear of change, which dislocates, discomforts, and worst of all, dispossesses."[82] Byllesby, like the planter reactionaries, was a conservative in a time of capitalist insurgency. The guild-like communal organization of social production that Byllesby advocated was based more on fraternal values than on the paternal ethos of men like Fitzhugh and Holmes; still, it emphasized the social advantages of organizing economies according to communal benefits and moral responsibilities. To be sure, Byllesby's brand of labor radicalism frightened southern conservatives, but in their point of original criticism, the two groups expressed a shared revulsion at what they considered a vile and self-defeating capitalist system based on the exploitation of man.

Unlike the southern reactionaries, however, Byllesby was genuinely committed to a socialist agenda. He admitted an intellectual debt to the British neo-Ricardian/Ricardian Socialists, in particular the Scottish economist John Gray. The neo-Ricardian/Ricardian Socialists extrapolated principles from British political economy, mainly the labor theory of value, to undermine the logic of classical doctrine. According to their calculations, if the value of commodities equaled the quantity of labor embodied in them, yet capitalists acquired the lion's share of income through interest, rent, and profits, then labor's recompense was unjustly appropriated. Gray calculated that workers were typically compensated at roughly 20 percent of their actual labor value. Moreover, the central problem with industrial society was that demand determined production. Since capitalist exploitation, mechanization, and market competition combined to reduce wages, workers consumed less, thus social production reached only a fraction of its potential.[83] After having read Gray, Byllesby discovered a clear "similarity of ideas" and rushed to include protracted quotations from Gray's 1826 *Lecture on Human Happiness* in his own *Observations*.[84] Byllesby's work must be treated beyond the context of the Jacksonian war on banks. Antebellum economists were deeply engaged in the transatlantic discourse and often exchanged ideas with European thinkers. Byllesby voiced workers' hostility to free markets and industrialization, and a determination to craft economic society along ideological lines that reflected the period's burgeoning working-class conscience. As Wilentz noted, "with Byllesby . . . we witness the acceleration of a fundamental shift in language and sentiment . . . toward a recognition that a deeper matrix of exploitation and unequal exchange for labor was responsible for the plight of the mass."[85]

The socialist impulse behind Byllesby's thought was given powerful impetus by Thomas Skidmore. Son of a Connecticut farmer, Skidmore spent his early adult years searching for work in the Northeast. In 1819 he settled in New York City, educated himself with the works of Jefferson, Locke, and Rousseau, and became active in local politics. Journalist, teacher, printer, carpenter, and listed as a "machinist" in the catalogues of New York's Working Men's Party, the otherwise obscure craftsman had by 1830 became the intellectual head of the antebellum labor movement before his premature death in 1832 at the age of 42. Skidmore articulated a mature expression of working-class antagonisms toward intellectual and material capitalism.[86] His criticisms were as incendiary as Fitzhugh's. In his 1829 *The Rights of Man to Property!* Skidmore proposed wholesale transformations to antebellum society. He intended, in his own words, to "entirely remodel the political structure of our state, and make it essentially different from anything else."[87] He scoffed at the notion of private property, attacked the foundational principles of classical doctrine, and aimed to reconstitute America along pre-bourgeois-capitalist lines.

The Jacksonian era was replete with suggestions for economic and social reforms couched in the laissez-faire tradition. This was not the case with Skidmore. His criticisms of market institutions were entirely at odds with intellectual capitalism. He advanced what he described as a political economy founded on rational principles, meant to educate a republican citizenry, and directed at a democratic legislature. Skidmore's first target was the justification for property rights that stemmed from the labor theory of value. Although labor adds value to property, it does not imply ownership. "Why will not labor bestowed upon property in possession give title: Because the property *itself*, is another's, and before any labor can be honestly bestowed upon it, that other, who alone owns it, must give his consent." Land is the original source of all property. Labor transforms the earth's resources into manufactured wares, but in the process, the general ownership over the original natural asset is not conferred on individuals. In fact, no man can determine how God's creation ought to be divided. From this conclusion, Skidmore demanded the abolition of private property. All men have equal claim to nature's provisions. "The soil," Skidmore declared, "belongs . . . equally to all who are found upon it." Only through communal consent can individual property rights exist. Moreover, property rights are neither sacred nor inalienable. Rather they are entirely conventional: "to-day, there is one rule for determining these rights, and to-morrow there is another." And the accumulation of property by one should never inhibit another's claim to sustenance, for this entailed a violation of the most basic human right to the necessities of life. Under bourgeois property rights, however, "a part, and that a very great part, of the human race, are doomed, of right, to the slavery of toil, while others are born only to enjoy."[88]

The logical consequences of Skidmore's program separated his economic ideology from other laborites. He envisioned a classless society. "It is time, now, that he should begin to live for himself; and, not like a slave as he truly is, for the benefit of another." In no uncertain terms, Skidmore called for immediate working-class rebellion. "Is it not time for the people," Skidmore asked, "those who have rights as well as the rich, to interpose in their own behalf?" His measures targeted the rich. "Let us look then upon the rich man . . . rather as a curse, than as a blessing; rather as a something, himself, which it is proper to exterminate . . . Nor let the word *exterminate*, be thought a harsh one. *Both rich and poor ought to be exterminated:* the latter by being made what we may call rich; and the former by being brought to the common level." The urgency of Skidmore's reforms was precisely the type of labor extremism that southern reactionaries feared and led them to infer the failure of free society. "All governments may and ought to be put down, which do not preserve" equal rights to property. To "unclench the hand of avarice, and make it give up its dishonest possessions," Skidmore urged a sweeping reconfiguration of the economic experience, to block what he believed was the inequitable distribution of property attendant on the transformative effects of material and intellectual capitalism.[89]

The first practical step toward a more just distribution was the abolition of inheritance. An individual's lease on property ended with death. Just as succeeding generations do not interfere with those who have come before them, the dead have no claim over the destiny of the generations that follow. God's resources shall be returned to a common pool upon an individual's death. "The system which I thus place before the world," Skidmore declared, "will rigidly maintain the principle, that no man or generation of men, have property, or the disposition of property, either as to who shall own, or shall not own it, or as to the use that shall be made of it, one moment after they cease to exist." Every adult member of society was entitled to the property of the deceased, distributed by the state, placing each on an equal footing at the attainment of adulthood. "There is no truth more indisputable than this; the soil of any and every country, belongs wholly and equally to all who are found upon it."[90] The revolutionary character of Skidmore's agenda is difficult to exaggerate. Skidmore, as Wilentz wrote, "carried the questioning and ambitious temperament of the American artisan radical to new heights... in a relentless assault on institutions and hierarchies even his most radical predecessors did not challenge."[91] To suggest, as Dorfman has, that Skidmore pursued "business ends" is inaccurate.[92] Dorfman's evaluation is based in part on Skidmore's support for tariffs. Skidmore's protectionism, however, was designed to shield domestic labor from foreign competition. Prohibiting importation of foreign manufactures secured what Skidmore argued was a social compact that obligated Americans to purchase the products of their countrymen—it was not intended to advance the interests of an industrial elite.[93] Neither is it accurate to represent Skidmore's political economy as alien to antebellum economic intellectual culture. His platform found a receptive audience. On October 19, 1829, Skidmore presented his ideas to a New York Working Men's Party convention. The party endorsed Skidmore's reforms and nominated him for the New York state assembly. When the final tallies of the 1829 election were posted, Skidmore was short of victory by only twenty-three votes.[94]

In the American economic discourse there were dozens of labor intellectuals who echoed Skidmore's resistance to industrial capitalism. Stephen Simpson, a Philadelphia-based journalist, onetime bank clerk, and politician who as a young man served under Jackson at the Battle of New Orleans, endorsed much of Byllesby's and Skidmore's working-class consciousness and abhorrence of inequality. Simpson was to the Philadelphia branch of the Working Men's Party what Skidmore was to New York's. His 1831 *The Working Man's Manual: A New Theory of Political Economy* described how modern economic science was composed primarily by "the champions of capital.... Among the foremost of these apologists of tyranny, and deceivers of the populace, stands Adam Smith," who convinced the masses that starvation conditions were natural and just. Simpson propounded the labor theory of value, denouncing capital as the passive agent, existing only to exploit workers, as "a tyrant; always standing on the alert to grind down the mere operative." Simpson was not a systematic thinker. In the introduction to his *Working Man's Manual* he conceded that "metaphysical refinement has been studiously avoided." The work was dedicated to Jefferson, but he later wrote of Hamilton, "no writer on economy is superior."[95] Simpson did not, however, advocate an equality of condition, or the abolition of free markets. He railed against monopolist bankers while simultaneously defending the Bank of the United States. Like the southern reactionaries, the northern laborites offered American audiences an assortment of ideological dispositions that likely did not appear contradictory to contemporaries. Still, Simpson contributed to a growing awareness among Philadelphia's workers that capital was the enemy of labor, and in doing so he challenged the fundamentals of intellectual capitalism.

By the 1850s the working-class movements of earlier decades had largely fizzled out. So too did much of the momentum of earlier attempts at land reform. Perhaps the last influential contributor to the agrarian-labor reform discourse was John Pickering. Like the writings of Byllesby and Skidmore, Pickering's 1847 *The Working Man's Political Economy* offered a systematic attempt to account for the distinctions between capital and labor, as well as the potential for class war. "Working men, wake up, wake up," Pickering demanded. "To us belongs the task of commencing the work of moral reform; we have trusted our self-made masters too long." Between sarcastic attacks against land monopolists, jeremiads against finance soaked in biblical allegory, and moralist rants against "merchant princes," Pickering reiterated what by the 1840s were standard working-class charges against free-market society. Chattel slaves were better off materially than workers under the "free slave system," labor was the source of value, and contemporary political economy was "devoted to the interests of the king and the capitalist." Capital he described with rhetorical flair as "a blighting curse in the land; it is a grievous canker, that eats out the poor man's substance; it is a vile and loathsome incubus, that corrupts and corrodes the human heart, by making it callous to the sufferings of our fellow men."[96] Pickering inherited his agenda for land reform from Evans and Owens. He advocated an inalienable right to proprietorship through homestead grants, the abolition of land speculation, and legal protections for settlers against foreclosure. The right to the soil, after all, is the same as the right to breath the air and feel the warmth of the sun. But Pickering, like most antebellum spokesmen for the National Reform Association, couched his demands in a Jeffersonian bourgeois style of thought. Indeed, most of his measures were in line with contemporary Jacksonian equal rights.

In some ways the northern laborites and the southern reactionaries served as the intellectual bookends of antebellum economic literature. Combined, they offered the most penetrating critique of industrial capitalism, both as an intellectual system and a practical socioeconomic system. The northern laborites and southern reactionaries were the counterrevolutionaries. In the antebellum discourse, "liberalism" was appropriated by those who followed the Enlightenment brand of Smithian economics, based on their original opposition to mercantilist restrictions and, in the early nineteenth-century American context, the celebration of free trade and the negative state. The cerebral connection between northern laborites and southern reactionaries may be owed to what Holmes called the "anarchy and confusion" of the nineteenth-century discourse.[97] It is possible, within the context of antebellum thought, that by returning to more traditional economic, social, and political forms, both groups genuinely believed they were advancing humanity's cause. Antebellum Americans considered economic freedom across a broad intellectual spectrum. The paternal slavery advocated by southern conservatives and the socialism of northern laborites were both intended to liberate the masses from the physical drudgery of industrial labor and the mental slavery of the cash nexus. Northern socialists and southern reactionaries were, at least ostensibly, equally interested in optimizing some forms of human freedom. To many contemporaries and historians alike, both camps, but especially the pro-slavery reactionaries, seem either disingenuous in their concerns or pursuing a contorted logic. But to contemporaries, like the secessionists whose vision of freedom was predicated on slavery and who advocated rebellion in 1861 for liberty's sake, or like Skidmore's voters who agreed with his plans to abolish private property in order to emancipate workers from wage slavery, liberalism assumed different meanings. Antebellum labor leaders popularized comparisons between "factory slavery" and chattel slavery much as Fitzhugh employed the term "wage-slave" in his descriptions of northern free labor; liberty was guaranteed only through the abolition of the industrial order, not the abolition of slavery.

"Strange as it may seem," Holmes wrote, "the Socialists, the Communists . . . are precisely those who most loudly proclaim their desire to establish a concentrated and consolidated government, which shall constantly interfere in all the affairs of private life. . . . this is to one set of admirers of the nineteenth century an indication of the progress of freedom."[98] Holmes's description of socialism is certainly not liberal; rather it seems to depict a premodern feudal society. Socialism promised, according to Holmes's interpretation, liberation from market forces, freedom from the industrial regime, an end to labor's suffering, and mitigation of the dismal conditions of the poor that classical doctrine described as natural and inevitable. In the logic of socialists like Byllesby and Skidmore, independence from the natural economic order of Smith, Malthus, and Ricardo represented the ultimate form of human liberty. For the southern reactionaries, freedom was interpreted as safety from capital's exploitation, security from want, and, oddly enough, the preservation of slavery.[99] The differences between the socialist understanding of liberty and that of the southern reactionaries may be obvious to twenty-first-century historians, but in the context of nineteenth-century economic thought, the distinctions were not clear. "The slave receives a permanent and fixed amount of maintenance; the wage-labourer does not," Marx wrote in 1865. "If he resigned himself to accept the will, the dictates of the capitalist as a permanent economical law, he would share in all the miseries of the slave, without the security of the slave." Slavery is socialism under a more efficient system of labor coordination, Ruffin wrote. "Socialism proposes to do away with free competition," Fitzhugh wrote, "to afford protection and support at all times to the laboring class; to bring about, at least, a qualified community of property, and to associate labor. All these purposes, slavery fully and perfectly attains."[100] Like Ruffin, Fitzhugh believed slavery was the most perfect form of socialism.

Smithian-inspired intellectual capitalism was grounded in Enlightenment values like civic equality, skepticism, secularism, and in some instances even representative democracy. This environment shaped the post-1776 world. The southern reactionaries withdrew from this world, and they wrote against the liberal Smith in full knowledge of the ideology that the Scotsman had come to represent. For them, slavery was the tried and tested economic system; its presence in all forms of human civilization, ancient and modern, was proof that the institution was not outdated. After all, for most conservatives, the ancient is worth preserving. In a similar way, the communal economic sensibilities of laborite socialism harkened back to a preindustrial age. The northern laborites accepted the liberal political and social adjuncts to the modern world, but they too retreated from the essential conventions of the capitalist order, mainly finance, industry, private property, and profits.

In the antebellum era both groups were economic counterrevolutionaries. Their shared principles resist traditional Marxist bifurcation of class ideology. American political economy offered opportunities for intellectual synchronicity from writers of fundamentally distinct socioeconomic backgrounds. Moreover, social history that posits leftist-inspired labor movements as acting against entrenched conservative capitalist forces ignores the dynamism of antebellum economic thought as it matured during America's market revolution. Capitalism was then recognized as the insurgent agent, refiguring society along revolutionary lines, undermining traditional institutions, and placing the economy on a trajectory that overturned the existing order to which workers and planters had grown accustomed. The southern reactionaries and northern laborites are the essential representations of this antiliberal movement, or American conservatism, in a time when the nation was undergoing its most revolutionary changes.

It was also in this discursive setting that antebellum protectionism emerged as a full-fledged alternative to intellectual capitalism. Protectionists, like the free traders, the northern laborites, and the southern reactionaries, constructed a political economy that promised to augment American freedoms. But the protectionists did not demand a complete overthrow of material capitalism; rather they worked within the parameters of intellectual hybrid capitalism. They argued that by restricting Smith's "natural system of liberty" in international trade, Americans would find their personal and national economic freedoms enlarged. The protectionist version of hybrid capitalism advocated domestic market economies divorced from international markets. In the antebellum discourse it would not have appeared contradictory for protectionists to argue for an economic system that preserved individual economic and national freedoms while simultaneously sealing off the home market from foreign competitors. Protectionists were, in this sense, championing an economic order that offered both a similar and a different set of freedoms from those proposed by the northern laborites and southern reactionaries. Within the protectionist framework, restrictions were conceived as liberal measures. When taken together, the various strains in American political economy, anticapitalist and hybrid capitalist, illustrate that the domestic discourse functioned in its own unique cerebral sphere, with contributors occasionally writing in what seem to be parallel universes.

5

AN AMERICAN POLITICAL ECONOMY

Among the petitions read to Congress in its inaugural session in March 1789 were recommendations on how best to repair the economic damages occasioned by the break from Britain, years of revolution, and the Confederation period. A number suggested measures to encourage domestic manufacturing. Drawing on contemporary patriotic sentiment, one submitted "that America, freed from the commercial shackles which have so long bound her, will see and pursue her true interest, becoming independent in fact as well as in name; and they confidently hope that the encouragement and protection of American manufactures will claim the earliest attention of the Supreme Legislature."[1] One month later James Madison introduced the nation's first tariff bill, which passed both houses after some debate on July 4, 1789. Its preamble read: "Whereas, it is necessary for the support of the Government the discharge of the debts of the United States, and the encouragement and protection of manufacturers, that duties be laid on goods, wares and merchandise imported."[2] The press of the day hailed it as America's second Declaration of Independence. It was a fairly moderate measure, with ad valorem duties ranging from 5 to 10 percent on about ninety articles. The following year President Washington, symbolically draped in an American-made coat, delivered his first annual address to Congress. Speaking in tones sensitive to national security and economic welfare, Washington declared: "The safety and interest of the people require that they should promote such manufactures as tend to render them independent of others for essential, particularly military supplies."[3]

From this point forward, tariff policy was fundamental to antebellum political economy. In almost every decade between America's founding and its civil war, tariffs were at the center of political debate. Although historians recognize the importance of tariffs in antebellum politics, only in the later decades of the twentieth century did the literature begin to pay serious attention to the ideology that undergirded protectionist thought.[4] Much of what has been written on protectionism comes from economic historians of a liberal disposition, who obstruct serious discussion of protectionism as a legitimate economic philosophy because it falls outside neoclassical orthodoxy. These histories minimize the value protectionist thinkers contributed to the nineteenth-century discourse, dismiss protectionist ideology as incoherent, or pin the mercantilist pejorative to every trade restriction as an example of the inefficiencies of forced allocation of capital and labor resources. Since practically every respectable nineteenth-century economist advocated free trade, the burden of proof, this narrative holds, has always rested on the protectionists.[5] Adjunct to these charges is the notion that tariffs are the product of political corruption—the "pocket-book interest"—devised by scheming industrialists to convert Congress into a paper mill for lobbyist-inspired legislation intended to monopolize domestic markets. This charge was common among Progressive historians of the early twentieth century who tied Republican tariff legislation to robber-baron political sleaze of the post–Civil War era. Matthew Josephson offered what was then the typical description in his 1938 book *The Politicos*: "Led by the first alert organizers of industrial associations or lobbies ... the cleverer and more learned politicians who could read trade reports and account sheets and write tax laws ... found reward ... in the pleasing labor of heaping high the profit margins of manufacturers of wool, cloth, glass, marble, copper, and iron products."[6] Additionally, liberal historians of antebellum America have downgraded the significance of protectionism because it challenges broader assumptions about the nation's historical attachment to laissez-faire.[7] Liberal consensus narratives dismiss antebellum tariffs as "islands in a laissez-faire stream," and thus devalue the intellectual, political, and cultural importance of protectionist ideology.[8] And while producer interests certainly helped write tariff legislation, these interpretations give greater credence to free-trade ideas than Americans at the time did, and they ignore the complex of interests and thinkers who developed and supported the protectionist position.

Marxist historians have contributed to conventional liberal hostilities toward tariffs. In his *Critique of Hegel's Philosophy of the Right* (1844), Marx equated the "system of prohibitions" with thinly veiled attempts at constructing a "sovereignty of monopoly."[9] Marx encouraged generations of left-leaning historians not to find a friend in the enemy of laissez-faire; rather they charged protectionists with abetting the industrial order that led to the exploitation of man by man. And more recently, historians have expanded their criticisms by making individual protectionists complicit in undermining republican egalitarian ideals, prolonging antebellum slavery, fortifying white supremacy, and lacking the forethought to prevent "another great source of human inequality, greed, and exploitation: the world of largely unregulated, untrammeled, and only at times creative destruction that was nineteenth-century American capitalism."[10]

A subset of the literature written primarily by cliometricians has, perhaps unintentionally, further diminished the significance of protectionism by urging scholars to avoid exaggerating the impact of tariffs. The dynamics governing economic society comprise a multitude of interests, actors, and institutions, making it virtually impossible to effect intended policy results. This being so, economic historians have reached the conclusion that antebellum tariffs were in fact of little consequence. Despite the United States enjoying arguably some of the most impressive periods of industrial expansion precisely while it traded under protectionist regimes, most economic historians find that adjustments in commercial policy did not alter profit, wage, or price levels, had little to no impact on domestic manufacturing output, typically followed rather than preceded periods of economic crisis, and likely did nothing to alter the direction of American industrial progress. Frank Taussig, an early twentieth-century economic historian whose chronicles of American tariffs vastly improved our understanding of nineteenth-century commercial legislation, concluded that "the sober-minded investigator will be slow in laying too much stress on a single cause, slow in generalization, and slowest of all in prediction."[11] Implicit in these arguments is that because tariffs had little direct economic influence, they were enacted strictly to serve the political interests of the legislators responsible for them and were based not on measured economic assessments but rather crass political calculations designed to dupe voters and win elections.

Whatever the interpretative consensus among economic historians, antebellum Americans took tariff schedules quite seriously. And protectionism exercised a commanding influence over antebellum economic thought. More than any other economic ideology, protectionism represents the quintessential features of a distinctly American brand of intellectual capitalism—hybrid capitalism—and it best captures contemporary Americans' response to the emerging industrial order. Protectionism was also the period's most systematic and successful challenge to classical orthodoxy. And it was antebellum America's main theoretical contribution to the transatlantic discourse. In short, protectionism was the American political economy. Hamilton fathered the movement, but it was not until the 1850s that Henry Carey consolidated protectionist thought into a coherent ideology. During this period protectionism passed through several stages of theoretical maturation. At each juncture, protectionists incorporated principles at the core of the American economic, political, and social experience. The successful integration of widely shared antebellum values into protectionist ideology helps explain the political and cultural triumph of protectionism. These values included, among others, American exceptionalism, free-labor entrepreneurialism, national industrial expansionism, Anglophobia, and an explicitly optimistic view of the potential for hybrid capitalist economic growth. Each of these occupied a principal position in American intellectual capitalism and facilitated the spread of capitalist and hybrid capitalist institutions and culture. Protectionists were not apologists for an emerging factory regime, either; rather their arguments reflected a sincere appreciation for the overall vitality of the domestic economy. Finally, more than any other economic ideology of the antebellum period, protectionism asserted America's ambitions for economic, political, and cerebral independence from the Old World.

The evolution of protectionist thought corresponded to several seminal political and economic events that stretch back to the Revolutionary era. During the early stages of America's breach with Britain, a symbiotic ideological relationship developed between political and economic liberal values. In the economic minds of many Americans, laissez-faire was the natural economic accessory to a broader set of political and social principles grounded in eighteenth-century liberalism. Generations of historians have shown how the War of Independence was fought to free colonials from the impositions of British mercantilism. But American declarations of commercial independence coexisted in contemporary thought with an already well-established preference for state activism. The works of Edward Peskin and other historians of Revolutionary-era economic culture indicate that many Americans welcomed an interventionist state, especially during times of crisis.[12] After the Seven Years' War, colonials grew more receptive of collectivist initiatives to counter what were increasingly viewed as the suffocating policies of the British system. Politically rebellious mechanics and merchants of the 1760s and 1770s filled broadsides and speeches with developmentalist rhetoric and neo-mercantilist strategies that included nonimportation, homespun, and autarkic values. As America transitioned from colony to nation, attacks on British mercantilism were balanced against colonial economic activism that featured encouragement of domestic manufacturers. Both were cast as patriotic endeavors designed to emancipate the colonies from metropolitan fetters and work practically toward managing the wartime economy.

Colonial and Revolutionary promotionalist literature expressed in germane form many of the themes that were later highlighted in the central texts of nineteenth-century protectionism. As Peter Onuf and Cathy Matson have shown, during the early national period "productivity and patriotism merged" into the Federalist economic program, which was given full exposition in Hamilton's 1791 *Report on Manufactures*.[13] The essay was commonly referenced by antebellum protectionists as the movement's founding document. In it Hamilton mixed contemporary economic thought, materials collected on the state of domestic manufacturing, and a pragmatic nationalist sensibility that addressed the young nation's strategic vulnerabilities. Although the *Report* was initially requested by Washington to determine how best to avoid the scarcity of supplies that beleaguered the army during the Revolutionary War, Hamilton took the opportunity to present a capstone policy paper that laid bare his vision for the future of the American economy. The *Report*, combined with Hamilton's essays on credit and the national bank, afforded the young nation an industrial, commercial, and financial horoscope.

First, Hamilton dispelled what was then the popular Physiocratic convention on the advantages of agriculture and the disadvantages of industry. Conditions in America, he admitted, gave the appearance that the nation was well suited for agrarian pursuits, but, Hamilton argued, the idea that agriculture should be allotted "any thing like an exclusive predilection, in any country, ought to be admitted with great caution." Hamilton's refutation of Physiocracy was an implicit swipe at Jeffersonian agrarianism and helped lend legitimacy to industrial pursuits in the domestic discourse. He figured no modern nation could realize its full economic potential if tied to an agrarian regime. In fact, Hamilton found that human labor could be more effectively applied if independent from nature's unsteady, seasonal, and sometimes uncooperative cycles. "It is very conceivable," Hamilton posited, "that the labor of man laid out upon a work, requiring great skill and art to bring it to perfection, may be more productive, in value, than the labor of nature and man combined, when directed towards more simple operations and objects." More important, agrarian nations were most vulnerable in what Hamilton believed was a perpetually Hobbesian world at war.

Second, in what popularly became known as the home-market argument, Hamilton explained how the expansion of manufacturing complemented agrarian economies by providing an "extensive domestic market for the surplus of the soil."[14] The agricultural sector was assured of a steady domestic demand from northern industry, thus cementing the states into a harmonious economic and political union.

Third, encouraging manufacturing would augment America's productive capacity. Here Hamilton deftly employed Smith's *Wealth of Nations* to illustrate how, when compared to husbandry, industry engaged more machinery and capital, advanced the specialization of labor, promoted immigration and investments, and made economies more diverse and competitive. Industry also brought idle women and children into the workforce, lest this labor source be squandered. Finally, to critics who charged that trade restrictions inflated prices for manufactured wares, Hamilton reasoned that tariffs actually increased the number of domestic manufacturers, facilitating competition, lowering prices, and preventing the establishment of monopolies.[15] In a perfect world, Hamilton admitted, free trade would govern commerce, but in the real world "the system which has been mentioned is far from characterizing the general policy of nations. The prevalent one has been regulated by an opposite spirit."[16]

Nationalist and statist overtones saturate Hamilton's economic writings. Promoting national unity and defending American sovereignty were his principal concerns. Hamilton linked the nation's political strength and national identity to its economic power. The encouragement of manufacturing would further synchronize the complementary values of fostering an independent national economic culture and constructing a state apparatus.[17] In the Hamiltonian matrix, the tariff was one of several economic instruments intended to create a visible hand of government that regulated economic forces to safeguard the newly minted central administration. Hamilton initially favored bounties over tariffs for this purpose, but the prospect of increased federal expenditures and a bloated national debt was politically precarious. Jefferson and Madison were then issuing long harangues against Hamilton's supposed corrupt alliance with northern finance and the prospect of perpetual debt. Customs duties proved more benign and, at the moderate levels that Hamilton suggested, would hardly be noticed by consumers and would avoid protests from northern merchants interested in normalizing trade with Britain. During the antebellum period, tariffs accounted for 90 percent of federal revenue, which Hamilton found essential for funding national liabilities, placating domestic and foreign lenders, securing the young nation's credit standing, and encouraging investments.[18]

Hamilton settled on tariffs as a practical policy to pursue these fiscal ends. Antebellum protectionists regularly cited Hamilton's *Report* as a source of authority, but as an economic instrument, he intended tariffs to offer temporary encouragement, not permanent protection. If tariffs were too high, imports and the revenue collected by customs officials would shrink, jeopardizing Hamilton's financial system. Still, much in the same way that some liberals elevated Smith to sainthood, antebellum protectionists discovered in Hamilton the movement's prophet. By then, however, Jefferson would probably have been better suited. Despite Jefferson's well-known espousal of economic liberalism, the exigencies of Atlantic conflict precipitated by the French wars and the subsequent Federalist turn toward free trade following Jay's Treaty (1796) with Britain shifted domestic political support for manufacturers to the Republican camp. Anti-English sentiment featured in pro-manufacturing colonial diatribes comported with Jeffersonian Republicanism, but it irritated the merchant elite that influenced Federalist politics. Hamilton had always considered maintaining commercial ties with Britain essential. Moreover, his successors within the Federalist Party grew increasingly uncomfortable with the "change economy," which some conservative New England merchants viewed as a plot to undermine established commercial interests, alienate Britain, and forge a dangerous alliance with French radicalism.

After Republicans' victories in the election of 1800, they set about cutting internal excise taxes, making federal revenue essentially dependent on tariffs, which were raised in 1804 to a maximum ad valorem rate of 22 percent on dutiable goods. Jefferson's Embargo (1807) and Madison's Non-Intercourse

Act (1809) were celebrated by domestic manufacturers, but they incensed Federalist merchants. These measures were followed by an almost absolute prohibition on imports through the peace at Ghent in 1815.[19] Manufacturing interests had by then shifted en masse behind the Republicans, encouraged by average wartime tariffs that taxed dutiable imports at as high as 49 percent. The War of 1812 encouraged protectionists to collate the earlier Hamiltonian economic nationalist program with the furiously anti-British sentiment of the Jeffersonian Republicans, which was extended beyond the policy realm of commercial relations to include criticisms of British political economy. The result was a more refined and systematic defense of protectionist policies that expanded on Hamiltonian precepts like the so-called infant industries argument, the claim that industrialization bolstered agricultural production, and the notion that tariffs benefited American labor. The economic arguments were, however, secondary to assertions that protectionism secured the republic's political independence from Britain.

During the War of 1812, imports shrunk by an average of 80 percent. This provided a boon to domestic manufacturers. Peace brought the normalization of trade and successive dumping of cheap British wares that started in the spring of 1815, leading to a spike in imports, a 28 percent drop in prices, and a decline in domestic industrial production. The nation's burgeoning manufacturing sector was threatened. For protectionists, this sequence was proof positive of the need for restrictive legislation. Protectionist petitions flooded Congress, and legislators responded with the tariff of 1816. Historians consider the bill the first decidedly protectionist tariff in American history. Its passage received crucial support from the mid-Atlantic states. In an indication of the decline of merchant influence in the region, New England congressmen backed the measure. And although the South split its vote, war hawks like Calhoun signed on. The tariff included a 25 percent tax on cotton and woolen goods, provisions for pig iron to be admitted under an ad valorem duty of 20 percent, and regulations against imported hammered and rolled iron. In all, the bill restricted importation of dozens of articles—stockings and buckles, pins and needles, tin and lead, glass and cutlery, pickles, carriages, and canes.[20] Jefferson's now famous 1816 letter from Monticello signaled the growing protectionist consensus. He wrote: "The grand inquiry now is, shall we make our own comforts or go without them at the will of a foreign nation? He, therefore, who is now against domestic manufactures must be for reducing us, either to a dependence on that nation, or to be clothed in skins, and live like wild beasts in dens and caverns—I am proud to say I am not one of these. Experience has taught me that manufactures are now as necessary to our independence as to our comfort."[21]

The generation of protectionists that lived through the War of 1812 infused the literature with the Hamiltonian economic nationalist vision that stressed patriotism, but it also relied more heavily on tariffs as the primary defensive mechanism to guarantee American sovereignty. Few could ignore the recurrent military hostilities between America and Britain. Anglophobic sentiment during the early decades of the nineteenth century matched that of the Revolutionary era. Toward the end of Jefferson's second term, many perceived London and Washington engaged in a kind of commercial cold war, with both sides competing for markets and asserting their commercial rights. Anti-British sentiment did not subside in the years following Ghent. Throughout the antebellum period Anglophobia was a national cultural phenomenon. Much of protectionist ideology hinged on anxieties that Britain was the eternal existential threat to American independence.[22] Antebellum protectionists broke sharply with the pro-British sensibilities of Hamilton and instead clamored for aggressive policies that confronted Parliament's attempts at neocolonialism. "We were," one protectionist testified, "as much bound to Britain after the Revolution as before."[23] Protectionists based several of their claims on the perceived threats of British imperialism. "What all have at present most to fear," a protectionist warned, "is the industrial supremacy of England."[24] Britain was master of the economic universe, accelerating its commercial and industrial hegemony through the expansion of the world market, and from the protectionist perspective, should be guarded against with all that America could muster. "The gigantic power of England . . . the wonder of the world," that mighty nation was powerful enough to bring the world to its knees.[25] "All states," a protectionist warned, "have a common interest in defending themselves against the damage that England, enjoying world economic supremacy, can arbitrarily inflict upon their industries."[26] The ostensible threat of British colonialism persisted deep into the antebellum period, even as American manufacturing emerged as a competitor to British industry.

The notion that British commercial policy intended an economic "war of extermination" drummed up fears, and protectionists were keen on exploiting these fears.[27] Parliament, one protectionist wrote, sought to "revive the old system of colonial dependence," capturing the young nation with a "manufacturing and commercial yoke." Free commerce with Britain meant Americans would essentially "cede their political power in order to render British productive and political power omnipotent."[28] High tariffs, protectionists pled, were critical to assuring national sovereignty. But it was the exercise of British "soft power" through the dissemination of Smithian intellectual capitalism that provoked special angst among protectionists. Penetrating American markets undermined American material and political sovereignty; the *Wealth of Nations* subverted American intellectual autonomy. Smith's free-trade brand of universal fraternalism was cover for turning Britain into "the workshop of the world." "Well might Napoleon dispense with arms when he had conquered the world," a protectionist warned, "and well might Mr. Huskisson recommend free-trade when it would make the world tributary to England."[29]

More than any figure, Mathew Carey infused protectionist thought with an Anglophobic tone. He had a long personal history of hating all things English. Dublin born in 1760, as a youth he worked as a pamphleteer campaigning for Irish independence. In 1784 Carey's writings caught the attention of Parliament, and warrants for his arrest were soon issued. After selling everything he owned, and dressing like a woman to evade the authorities, Carey boarded the ship *America* sailing for the new republic. He settled in Philadelphia, where, with help of a loan from the Marquis de Lafayette, he launched what would become one the nation's leading publishers. The success of Carey's publishing business brought him into Philadelphia's literary high society and helped him establish relations with, among others, Hamilton's assistant and coauthor of the 1791 *Report*, Tench Coxe. In 1819 Carey joined a small group to found the pro-tariff Philadelphia Society for the Promotion of National Industry.[30] By then Carey was recognized as one of the leading voices in the protectionist movement, advocating the promotion of small producers, entrepreneurs, and investments in domestic manufacturing. These measures were highlighted in newspapers and magazines, as well as several full-length texts printed mostly through his publishing house, until his death in 1839.

The volume of pro-tariff literature churned out by Carey's press elevated his position within protectionist circles. But it was Carey's belligerent, hyperbolic Anglophobic pitch that became a staple in antebellum writings. His brand of protectionism was geared primarily at inciting anti-British fervor. American political culture was especially receptive to Carey's economic nationalism following the War of 1812. He wrote frequently of Irish suffering under British rule, often with great hyperbole, cautioning Americans about the dangers that came with failing to guard their economic sovereignty. Freedom for Carey was synonymous with economic independence from Britain. By opening its markets to British competition, the United States, according to Carey, had "voluntarily adopted the colonial policy of England." Antebellum Americans were well aware of the past and current commercial warfare between the United States and Britain. "It was vain for any man to shut his eyes against the active rivalship and persevering hostility of British manufacturers," Carey warned.[31]

Carey's anti-British tone was given further expression in the middle decades of the antebellum period by Calvin Colton. Born in 1789 in Longmeadow, Massachusetts, Colton graduated from Yale, served as a minister in the Episcopal Church, and was later a Whig propagandist. He was popular among Whigs for his partisan ten-essay *Junius Tracts* published in 1840. His major literary accomplishment, however, was the six-volume *Life and Times of Henry Clay*, which Colton was commissioned to write in 1844 and released two years later.[32] His seminal economic treatise *Public Economy for the United States* (1848) offered little refined analysis. Instead Colton stroked the nationalist key by exposing what he believed were British commercial strategies aimed at colonizing the United States. It was "simply a question of justice, as the American revolution was a war of justice—and precisely, identically the same interests are at stake now as then. 'Free trade' would give up all which American independence acquired—all that is worth having."[33] For evidence of British plans to sabotage the American economy, Colton referenced speeches in Parliament. Henry Brougham, an influential British statesman, was a favorite culprit. Colton believed Brougham laid forth the British plot. Speaking to the House of Commons in 1816 on the state of American industry, Brougham declared that "it was well worth while to incur a loss upon the first exportation in order by the glut to stifle in the cradle those rising manufactures in the United States which the war had forced into existence contrary to the usual course of things."[34] The British, it seemed, were using instability in global markets following the Napoleonic Wars as economic disguise to ruin American attempts at developing an industrial base.

The threat of British economic imperialism was amplified by a supposed free-trade intellectual offensive on the American mind. Following the War of 1812, paranoia grew over the circulation of British laissez-faire in antebellum literature. Alexander Everett accounted for the popularity of free-trade thought in an 1830 article published in *Niles' Weekly Register* by pointing to the general regard Americans had for British philosophy. "Their [British] means of information upon matters of pure science and literature are superior to ours; and it is consequently very natural that we should look to the results of their inquiries with curiosity and confidence."[35] Colton offered similar explanations for the influence of free-trade ideology in America. Like Everett, he pointed to the "habit of the American mind—too much so, perhaps—to defer to European, especially to British, authority, in matters of science." Acquiescence to British intellectual traditions was the result of a desperate American search for what protectionists considered were the simplified theories of free traders to explain otherwise complicated issues. "They want something that will strike the fancy, something that will prove itself; they want the philosopher's stone that will turn everything to gold; and this they find in Free Trade."[36]

For protectionists neither merit, tradition, nor a shared cultural heritage fully accounted for the reverence British economists were awarded on domestic soil. There seemed to be more sinister forces at play. The growing popularity of free trade, especially in institutions of higher learning, was propagated by academics naïve to British schemes, or worse, orchestrated attempts to subvert the republic's independence. Carey estimated the works of Smith and Say to have sold more than seven thousand copies in America. "The doctrine of free-trade is a fraud," Colton declared, "imposed upon the world by pensioned writers for the benefit of Great Britain chiefly, which originated the fraud."[37] Allegations that Smith and a cabal of British free traders acted on behalf of Parliament were standard among protectionists. That Smith began his economic treatise while commissioned by a member of Parliament was evidence enough. "Was he not paid for it?" Colton asked. Colton worked harder than any other protectionist to delegitimize Smith as a charlatan. The Scotsman, Colton charged, was a "pensioned economist" responsible for perpetrating a "great conspiracy against mankind."[38] Free trade literature, according to Carey, was intended "to paralyze our industry."[39] And American free traders were instruments, accused one protectionist, of "British manufacturers and their agents and representatives."[40] With the passage of the liberal Walker tariff in 1846, protectionists argued British free trade imperialists had successfully infiltrated Congress. "Our anti-tariff politicians," another wrote, "are as much playing into the hands of the English, in all their measures, as if the words were put into their mouths by England, and our laws penned by her too.... No two nations ever existed, that could have played into each other's hands so completely, as this country and England."[41]

Although British writers were by the early nineteenth century at the fore of the laissez-faire movement, for centuries Westminster had promulgated mercantilist policies, and British authors had previously published a steady stream of mercantilist texts. Indeed, before Smith, the British wrote almost exclusively in the mercantilist tradition.

Since time immemorial, Everett reported, Britain had kept her ports "hermetically sealed" as if "every bale and parcel of manufactures from every part of the world had been infected with the plague."[42] Now that Britain was the industrial Goliath, its economists clamored for free trade. This was a historic about-face. Colton published his *Public Economy* two years after Parliament moved toward a more liberal trade policy, accentuated by the abolition of the Corn Laws in 1846. Colton and other protectionists connected ideology and policy to a wider British conspiracy. "And how should it happen that nearly all British writers on this subject, from Adam Smith down to this time, and nearly or quite all the lecturers of the universities, and almost the entire periodical press ... should have become one solid phalanx of Free-Trade advocates.... This, certainly, is a very extraordinary spectacle."[43] Smithian laissez-faire was nothing more than an adversarial ideology, projected to advance an industrial and commercial Pax Britannica, so that Britain might "become the richest nation in the world—in that way, the most powerful—and to maintain that ascendancy." Free trade, another wrote, "had not been intended for home consumption. It had been intended for export."[44] Historians debate the legitimacy of these claims. By most accounts Smith was a disinterested scholar. Historians have, however, noted how Parliament tied, quite expectedly, trade policy to British interests. "The parliamentary free traders," one historian writes, echoing the claims of antebellum protectionists, "strove not so much to achieve a cosmopolitan system ... but to preserve Britain's industrial predominance, and, if possible, to achieve a virtual monopoly for a British Workshop of the World."[45]

Criticisms of British free-trade imperialism were typically combined with charges that laissez-faire political economy lacked scientific rigor. In this regard, Smith again was consistently targeted by protectionists. "Whilst he treats detached matters with great ingenuity and experience," one protectionist wrote, "his system, considered as a whole, is so confused and distracted, as if the principal aim of his books were not to enlighten natives, but to confuse them for the benefit of his own country."[46] Carey found that "in no science, are the general maxims of mere theorists more delusive, and more to be distrusted, than in political economy. This branch of knowledge is yet in its infancy. . . . Its principles are not yet established. Those which have been considered as the most fixed, have been overthrown; those which have been taught as self-evident, are questioned; and the whole are the subject of ardent discussion." Carey quoted Smith's *Wealth of Nations* at length, picking apart passages that he found riddled by "much sophistry and unsound reasoning . . . and there is likewise, as in all the rest of the doctor's work, a large proportion of verbiage, which is admirably calculated to embarrass and confound common understandings, and prevent their forming a correct decision."[47] Protectionists disparaged Smith for indulging in speculative abstractions and said the Scotsman's background as an Enlightenment savant inclined him to specious metaphysical assumptions on human psychology and morality that clouded his assessments of economic systems. "The casual association of its teaching with moral philosophy," one protectionist alleged, "is the circumstance to which is to be attributed that metaphysical bias, manifested by almost all Economical writers, in their method of investigation, and which has conducted them to such vague, hypothetical, and unsatisfactory results."[48]

Deductive reasoning was, protectionists charged, a critical flaw in British intellectual capitalism. Public policy and a stronger regard for the empirical sciences were superior analytical tools in economic inquiry. "This science is in its nature essentially practical, and should be treated in a plain, practical way. Adam Smith, Mr. Say, and others who wrote upon this subject, were too abstract and theoretical for common use."[49] Carey found Smith "to have been duped by his own system," a sophist confused by webs of abstractions and an idealistic cosmopolitanism out of touch with real-world conditions.[50] A "fool's gold," Colton wrote, with assumptions passed off as natural laws, able only to "prove itself by itself."[51] The free trader was a "speculative professor, who concocts abstract theorems of political economy in his closet," fashioning a doctrine "profligate, false, and absurd," based on "dreamy hallucination, made up of fallacies, sophistical assumptions," and contorted logic.[52] "It is against such visionary projects," Carey declared, "that we have raised our hands; it is to warn you from the closet speculations of theorists, to invite you to common sense practice, founded on the nature of things."⁵³

Protectionist attacks against the metaphysical tone of laissez-faire were indicative of the pragmatic bent of antebellum intellectual culture. Beginning in the colonial period, a seemingly endless stretch of unsettled lands encouraged Americans to adopt a more practical mindset. Their energies focused on the constant application of a pragmatic resolve. Time and effort consumed in pensive speculation did little for a people requiring a frontiersman's survival instinct. The American knack for common sense was raised above the abstract "book wisdom" of laissez-faire philosophers. Distrust of the privileged, cloistered philosopher devising intangible theories in an ivory tower was ingrained. Even during the so-called Age of Reason, Americans held in suspicion the metaphysical musings of Enlightenment thinkers. They found more to their liking the Scottish School of Common Sense. Thomas Reid was favored over Hume. Reid's Common Sense philosophy, conceived to temper the "metaphysical lunacy" and "excess of refinement" of Enlightenment skepticism, was taught in American colleges and was popular with the nation's learned classes.⁵⁴

Henry May referred to the American penchant for pragmatic inquiry as the Didactic Enlightenment. Intellectual pursuits were intended mostly for instruction, not abstract inquisition. Moderate in temper, the no-nonsense character of American thought emphasized function over form. The popularity of this brand of thought mirrors the general hostility Americans held for academic institutions. Establishments of higher learning in the Old World were regarded as arms of an oppressive Church. Americans harbored these prejudices against their own institutions of learning. When the cultural dimensions of American anti-intellectualism are taken together, they offer a potential point of origin for the nontheoretical basis of some protectionist writings. Protectionism, according to one historian, was an "economics of the street."⁵⁵ By placing at the fore regard for American conditions and keeping as a central goal for economic inquiry the discovery of practical policy, protectionism conformed to domestic intellectual traditions.⁵⁶

The cultural tendencies that shaped protectionist skepticism of laissez-faire philosophy were reinforced by antebellum political events. During the Jacksonian era anti-intellectualism reached new heights. Jackson himself was a product of the Tennessee frontier, his formal education minimal, his literacy sometimes questioned, and his capacity for reason sometimes overcome by an impassioned Scotch-Irish temperament prone to gambling, confrontation, and physical violence. Jackson's landslide victory in 1828 over the sophisticated Harvard-educated son of the learned John Adams speaks volumes to the American distrust for men of culture.[57] The "era of the common man" that Jackson is said to have ushered in reflected the egalitarian thrust of democracy that engendered a society where the refined elite were held in suspicion. A political milieu with an I'm-as-good-as-you population of equals worked against elevating the status of academics.[58] Amid distrust of the scholar's counsel, knowledge was sought not in books or philosophy but in home-grown intuition and folkish wisdom.

In the protectionist North, intellectualism was trumped by a competitive business culture and a wild scramble for riches.[59] True men of genius were those clever enough to win pecuniary gains in the competitive marketplace. What, a Jacksonian paper queried, "has intellect to do with man, except in helping him to cast compound interest and loss and gain?"[60] Historians have noted that the principal object of mental activity during the Jacksonian era was commerce. In consequence, scholarship was not awarded the same social esteem as in European societies. "They will not afford to let their young men study till two or three and twenty," Fanny Trollope recorded to her travel journal in 1832. Fewer than six hundred students, according to contemporary reports, attended college during the 1820s.[61] "At sixteen, often much earlier," Trollope continued, "education ends, and money-making begins; the idea that more learning is necessary than can be acquired by that time, is generally ridiculed as obsolete monkish bigotry."[62]

To reconcile the antimetaphysical, practical bent of the American mind with their own demands for scientific rigor, protectionists incorporated into their works a bounty of economic data.[63] "Of all sciences," Colton argued, "public economy, to be safe and useful, claims, more, if possible, than any other, to be based on facts; all its deductions should be founded on facts, and facts alone; and any theory, passing under this name, which has not such a basis, is worthy of no respect."[64] Protectionists extolled the value of historical details in political economy, stressing the importance of formulating legislation only after scrutinizing quantitative analysis of prevailing economic conditions. This served the dual purpose of toughening their claims to scientific legitimacy while simultaneously challenging and offering an alternative approach to free-trade ideology. In doing so, protectionists believed they initiated a methodological revolution in economic inquiry. While laissez-faire was based on "the invisible, the mysterious, the fluctuating internal nature" of moral philosophy and deductive reasoning, protectionism "pursued the opposite method; to have started from facts, and not assumptions."[65] Protectionists steered economic inquiry away from Ricardian technical abstractions and criticized analyses that started with a prior deduction for having skewed objective reasoning and widened the gap between political economy and the positive sciences.

Statistics were for protectionists a natural bridge to the more inductive-based attributes of economic history. Blending economic history with theoretical economics is one of the lasting contributions protectionists made to the transatlantic discourse and represents a significant methodological challenge to the growing acceptance of Ricardian intellectual capitalism. Protectionists engaged the epistemological evolution of the budding science by spearheading a reversal of research methods. Smith's *Wealth of Nations* seamlessly linked economic analysis with historical narrative. According to the historian of British political economy T. W. Hutchison, however, Ricardo and later John Stuart Mill "shattered" the historicism of Smith, precipitating nothing less than a "revolution" in method relegating economic history to the works of "rebels and outsiders."[66] The Historical School—that is, the enrichment of economic study by emphasizing history, institutions, sociology, politics, and culture—became a seminal feature in American economic thought throughout the nineteenth century.[67]

Friedrich List is considered "the earliest example on American soil of the Historical School of Economic Thought."[68] Born in 1789 in Württemberg, List came to the United States in 1825 at the suggestion of Lafayette, whom he met in Paris while in exile. German unification was his life's passion. As a young man, he wrote articles demanding reforms, slandered judges and civil servants, and advocated a pan-German customs union. List's activism attracted the ire of Württemberg authorities. In 1822 he was arrested and sentenced to ten months in a fortress prison. Rather than serve the stint he fled, in his own words, "like a thief in the night," settling in Strasbourg, where he was kept under surveillance, then Paris, then back to Württemberg, where he was imprisoned. As a condition of his release, List agreed to leave Württemberg for good.[69] He settled first as a farmer near Harrisburg, Pennsylvania, then worked in Reading as a journalist until his return to Europe in 1832. Later, in Paris, he wrote his seminal text, *Das Nationale System der Politischen Oekonomie* (1841), generally thought to be the original statement of economic nationalism.[70] But after a series of business failures List fell deathly ill, and in 1846 he checked in to a small provincial hotel and committed suicide. The report submitted by local authorities at the time of his death described List as "suffering from such a degree of melancholia as to render him incapable of thinking clearly or of acting rationally."[71] He is remembered today as the architect of the Zollverein, a customs union established in 1834 that brought eighteen German states under a single trade administration. In the words of one List scholar, he was "the driving force behind the Zollverein.... In a very real sense he was the Alexander Hamilton of his people."[72] The organization existed in various forms and eventually incorporated both German and non-German states across central Europe until its dissolution in 1919.

During his American sojourn List became a prominent voice in the protectionist movement. His relationship with Lafayette brought him meetings with practically every prominent man in 1820s America, including John Adams, Jefferson, Madison, Monroe, John Quincy Adams, Daniel Webster, John Marshall, and of course the leading figures of the protectionist movement. His influence in America and abroad helps illustrate a nineteenth-century transatlantic resistance to British intellectual capitalism, as well as the extent to which antebellum protectionists were engaged in a supranational antiliberal discourse.[73]

At the invitation of Charles Ingersoll, List drafted a pamphlet for the protectionist Harrisburg Convention in 1827. The essay was originally intended to challenge the free trader Thomas Cooper, but at the request of the Pennsylvania Society for the Promotion of Domestic Manufacturers, it was expanded into a series of letters syndicated in more than fifty newspapers and later compiled in List's *Outlines of American Political Economy*. Because *Outlines* was published in the hyper-politicized sectional buildup to nullification, the work attracted the attention of protectionists and free traders alike. Cooper's ally in Congress, James Hamilton, sarcastically noted in House debates, "We appear to have imported a professor from Germany, in absolute violation of the doctrines of the American system."[74]

The *Outlines* do not constitute a systematic inquiry, but by emphasizing nationalist economics, historicism, and a more relativist approach to political economy, List's values matched existing trends in antebellum protectionist culture. For List, political economy comprised three distinct but interconnected fields—philosophy, politics, and history. The most critical was history, since it encouraged the formulation of policy based on national experiences.[75] Economic principles were relative, according to "how nations, endowed by nature with all the means of reaching the highest degree of wealth and power, can, without inconsistency, and should, change their system in proportion as they advance." Nation-states were for List history's most important actors. "The highest association of individuals now realized," List declared, "is that of the state, the nation."[76] And by focusing on the past and present practical economic necessities of the state, a more historicist- and nationalist-oriented commercial policy avoided the confusion engendered by British classicism and "the illusions of ideology."[77] History proved how protectionist regimes abetted national power through industrial expansion. "Without interference of national power there is no security," List exhorted his American audience. "Industry, entirely left to itself, would soon fall to ruin, and a nation letting every thing alone would commit suicide."[78] List called Cooper the Coryphaeus of American free trade and said he wrote a "castles in the air" version of political economy as if man was not separated by borders, thus leaving national productive powers to either "hazard, nature, or Providence," and almost certainly vulnerable to British manipulation.[79]

As with Hamilton, List brought questions of national sovereignty to the fore of political economy. "Between the individual and the whole human race there is the nation," List wrote. Citizens were bound to a common will that compelled individuals to contribute toward national economic power. Political sovereignty, after all, rested on a nation's ability to control its economic destiny free from foreign influence—in List's case, mainly British. German economic independence, like America's, was threatened by British industrial hegemony. In the post-Napoleonic era, "the English government favored very efficiently the inundation of the continental markets with manufactured goods, for the purpose of smothering in the cradle the infant manufactures of the continent."[80] List contributed to contemporary anti-British sentiment in America by explaining Parliament's two-prong approach of material and cerebral colonization. "The Scot's theory," referring to Smithian free trade, was the modern "Trojan horse."[81]

Although expressed in economic terms, List's nationalist ideals were more political and cultural than economic. They reflected the cultural nationalism typical of nineteenth-century German thought and an inclination already present in American protectionist circles. List argued the nation-state deserved special notice in political economy. This was a direct challenge to the cosmopolitan ideals advanced in British intellectual capitalism, as well as to contemporary southern free traders who employed states' rights philosophy to deconstruct the national political authority. "*National Economy*," as List labeled his brand of economic thought, "teaches by what means a certain nation, in her particular situation, may direct and regulate the economy of individuals . . . to increase the productive powers within herself . . . in order to grow in power and wealth."[82]

List's economic nationalism, however, should not be confused with imperialism. As Giovanni Arrighi noted in his history of capitalism, contrary to the eighteenth- and nineteenth-century British imperialism that sought economic supremacy through world territorial expansion and global market formation under the banner of a liberal trade regime, American protectionism interpreted economic nationalism as an instrument for domestic territorialism. Economic prosperity was found at home, not abroad. Hamilton's home market argument captures the essence of protectionists turning inward. Protectionist "domestic territorialism" drew affinities with what Gustav von Schmoller, a leader of the German historical school of economics, in his description of early modern mercantilism, called "state-making and national-economy-making."[83] Antebellum protectionists, in this regard, sought the extension of home markets while simultaneously restricting exposure to foreign competition, namely British, which from their perspective jeopardized national economic development and undermined the domestic prerogative of the central state. List's objectives, like almost every antebellum protectionist's, addressed the economic needs of citizens by developing industrial productive powers as a means to reinforce patriotism and cultivate national identity. His influence in antebellum protectionism illustrates the importance nationalist and statist-centered sentiments played during the formative years of the movement. List emphasized the role of the state in industrializing economies. The state, after all, had a natural political obligation to instruct and patronize the economic needs of its citizens. Moreover, the state was best suited to discern the historical and future needs of society. "Every nation," List argued in direct contrast to the universalism of free trade, "has its particular political economy."[84] British laissez-faire, List contended, written largely in reaction to early modern mercantilism, discounted the concept of nationalism and ignored the responsibility of the nation-state in advancing growth-oriented policies.

List's national political economy also helped refresh in antebellum protectionism a Hamiltonian/realist perception of foreign affairs. This was a diametrically opposed worldview from British cosmopolitan intellectual capitalism.[85] Free traders, especially in the Northeast, posited a world moving toward peace, harmonious trade, and a fraternal order where nations were obsolete. "In the actual world," List wrote, humanity was divided into nations competing for economic power. To defend American sovereignty from foreign aggression List advocated well-measured trade policies that favored national over personal interests. Laissez-faire considered only "how the economy of the individuals and of mankind would stand, if the human race were not separated into nations." With its failure to appreciate the essential correlation between individuals and nations, and moreover the centrality of the nation-state in the modern world, List found laissez-faire misguided by "a chimerical cosmopolitism, which does not comprehend nationality, and which has no regard for national interests."[86] In his nationalist brand of political economy, coordination and cooperation at the macro level were essential. "An individual, in promoting his own interest, may injure the public interest; a nation, in promoting the general welfare, may check the interest of a part of its members. But the general welfare must restrict and regulate the exertions of the individuals."[87] Economic policy ought to promote national concerns, nurture a nation's productive powers, and if necessary inhibit personal behavior.

The emphasis protectionists gave to national economics marked another important ideological contrast with laissez-faire. List was not concerned with maximizing private wealth. Put differently, he inverted laissez-faire logic that argued national wealth trickled upward from individual wealth. List believed there was a higher, national calling for the burgeoning science. Rather than teach individuals how to amass personal fortunes, political economy should focus on national economic policy. List stressed the interplay between economic and political institutions. Political economy, List argued, "should be concerned as much with politics as with economics." He challenged the standard free-trade maxim that political and economic inquiries were two distinct fields of study. Rather the study was one of several branches of knowledge statesmen should reference in the composition of national objectives. British advocates of laissez-faire, List wrote, "in spite of the very name they chose to give their science, . . . will make us believe that there is nothing of politics in political economy. If their science is properly called *political economy*, there must be just as much *politics* in it as *economy*, and if there is no *politics* in it, the science has not got the proper name, it is then nothing else but *economy*."[88]

On this point List was not entirely original. His visit to the United States came shortly after the publication in 1820 of the first full-length treatise on political economy written on America soil, Daniel Raymond's *Thoughts on Political Economy*. Raymond issued a second edition with significant revisions under the title *The Elements of Political Economy* in 1823. The text was read by John Jay, John Marshall, and Mathew Carey, and John Adams wrote to Raymond that he had "never read any work upon Political Economy with more satisfaction" and that the book stood as "a proud monument of American literature."[89] Cardozo reviewed the book in Charleston's *Southern Patriot*, and Dew referenced Raymond in his *Lectures on the Restrictive System*. Still, Raymond's work did not reach an especially wide audience. Only 750 copies were issued, and of that number more than 200 were sold at auction. A copy did reach List, and historians have suggested that Raymond had a powerful impact on the German.[90]

Born in Connecticut in 1786, Raymond attended the prestigious Litchfield Law School and eventually settled in Maryland, where he was admitted to the bar in the Baltimore County Court. He did not enjoy success as a lawyer, which left him time to write on various subjects. Raymond drew some notoriety with an 1819 pamphlet, *The Missouri Question*, where he wrote disparagingly on slavery, blaming the institution for the South's economic troubles. He ran on three occasions as an anti-slavery candidate for the House of Delegates of Maryland, losing each time. Southern congressmen accused Raymond of being a paid agent of abolitionists. He advocated widespread manumission, but only to ensure the gradual extinction of the race. According to Raymond's logic, freed blacks were incapable of obtaining the necessities of life. In 1842 he moved to Cincinnati and established a weekly paper, but the endeavor lasted less than six months. He died in 1849 of cholera. An obituary in the local paper noted Raymond "had become reduced in his circumstances, and has resided here for several years, but little known."[91]

A romantic nationalist sentiment guided Raymond's economic thought.

He treated economics from a research paradigm squarely at odds with laissez-faire cosmopolitanism. "Political economy is a science which teaches the nature and causes of public or national wealth . . . the most effectual means of promoting a nation's wealth." Raymond anticipated List by censuring British intellectual capitalism for being fixated on the individual accumulation of riches. "Instead of treating of public economy they in fact treat of private economy; instead of talking about nations they talk about individuals."[92] He defined private wealth as an individual's capacity to obtain the necessities and comforts of life. This style of economic inquiry reflected an individual's temporary, fleeting pecuniary ambitions, or what Raymond described as "the narrow contemptible principles of private interests." In Raymond's vernacular, political economy is the science of the legislator, a higher calling tasked with understanding the public's well-being while taking into account that a nation might last into perpetuity. Political economy understood that national wealth is comprised of several elements—political, economic, social, and cultural—each contributing toward national production in the present and future. The science is not a second-rate branch of knowledge intended for maximizing the accumulation of personal property. Raymond's definition of what constituted political economy captured the basic ideological schism between protectionism and intellectual capitalism. Raymond targeted Smith in his criticisms over semantics. "Adam Smith has not, in the whole of his voluminous work on 'the wealth of nations,' given a definition of national wealth."[93] By confusing private and public economy, free traders obscured important differences between the two, and had thus initiated their analyses from false pretenses. "It is most unfortunate for the science of political economy, that the word wealth has been applied indiscriminately, to nations and to individuals."[94]

Raymond's attention to terminology was meant to illustrate the immaturity of contemporary economic inquiry, as well as to demonstrate what he considered the rather unscientific approach of the classical school. The fundamental error in language regarding individual and national wealth led to other points of logical disorder regarding private and public interests, according to Raymond. Laissez-faire assumed that what was good for the individual was beneficial to the nation. Smith's invisible hand concept equated the liberal pursuit of private interests with the wealth of nations. Raymond found this association erroneous. An individual's interest could be opposed to the national interest, just as the nation's prosperity could undermine an individual's private economy. "The sophistry of Dr. Smith's reasoning consists in a great measure," Raymond wrote, "in his not discriminating between national and individual interests. He considers the interests of some particular class of citizens, as identical with the interests of the nation, when in reality they are, perhaps, directly opposed."[95] The failure of laissez-faire to provide clear direction for legislators on how best to maximize national wealth originated in its reasoning from individuals to nations.

Like Hamilton, Raymond's political economy transmitted the concerns of a newly independent nation still debating the role of the central state. Government had the right and obligation to place the national economy ahead of its citizens. Personal economic freedoms were not sacred, especially if they undercut national prosperity. "It is ever to be remembered," Raymond wrote, "that the public interests are paramount to individual interests ... and that when a political economist has shown that public and private interests are opposed, he has made out a case, in which the interposition of the government is necessary; he cannot be required to prove that private interests ought to give way—this is to be taken for granted." Even property rights were conventional and, according to Raymond, should be limited to quantities needed to obtain the necessities of life. Like most antebellum protectionists, Raymond did not fear the power of the legislator. Rather he held statesmen in high esteem. Legislators were "the vicegerents of God on earth; and, as he regulates and governs the world, by the laws of eternal justice and wisdom, in regard to the future, as well as the present; by the same laws, ought legislators to regulate and govern the earth, over whom they preside."[96]

The thrust of Raymond's work was intended to refute British intellectual capitalism in general and free-trade policy in particular. Smith was his favorite foil. And like most protectionists, Raymond wrote explicitly against the Scotsman in full understanding that Smith's work represented the laissez-faire ideal. Raymond's political economy was not, however, anticapitalist. Neither was he an absolute protectionist. Each nation should craft a practical commercial policy, according to its historical necessity. Raymond enumerated the possible dangers of protectionism, namely its monopolistic tendencies, as well as the potential for subsequent increases in domestic production to exacerbate inequality. Without government interference, gaps in the distribution of wealth were the natural consequence of economic growth. To limit exaggerated accumulations of property, Raymond constructed an understanding of the social compact that required native consumers to purchase wares from native producers. American manufacturers, in essence, should be guaranteed a domestic demand.[97]

Raymond's work was published at a pivotal time in the nation's debate over tariffs. Congress was then setting the stage for the fracas that culminated in the constitutional crisis surrounding Calhoun's nullification movement. In 1820 the recently established House Committee on Manufactures, chaired by Henry Baldwin of Pennsylvania, brought to the floor a decidedly autarkic tariff bill that passed the House but was defeated in the Senate. In the partisan atmosphere initiated by the Missouri crisis, votes on the aborted 1820 Baldwin tariff were cast along sectional lines. By then the patriotic sentiments that had earlier inspired southern leaders to acquiesce around legislative encouragements of domestic manufacturing on the basis of national security had waned. In the House, fifty of the fifty-three southerners voted nay on the Baldwin tariff, and in the Senate only one southerner voted in favor. Sectionalism carried the day.

The defeat of Baldwin's bill forecast the sectional tone on all future antebellum tariff legislation. Perhaps southerners figured the 1820 census would corroborate their fears that the North's population growth outpaced the South's. Missouri's recent admittance into the Union as a slave state was balanced in the Senate with Maine. But congressional reapportionment based on the 1820 returns meant that the newly minted House seats would be filled by representatives from protectionist-leaning states in the North. Southerners increasingly argued that tariffs favored manufacturing interests at the expense of planters. In chapter 3, the protests of Calhoun and Cooper were featured, with the latter arguing parts of what modern economists refer to as the Lerner Symmetry Theorem. Developed in the 1930s by Abraham Lerner, the theorem holds that a tax on imports operates as a tax on exports.[98] Since most early nineteenth-century international commerce depended on a relatively equal exchange of imports for exports, and because merchant ships rarely made the return sail without cargo, the tariffs that restricted imports also, in effect, restricted exports. Douglas Irwin's history of American trade shows how the political ramifications of antebellum tariffs often aligned export-oriented producers against import-competing producers. Antebellum congressional vote tallies evidence this divide well. Southerners voted almost unanimously in opposition to tariff increases, while northerners mainly voted in favor. Western states held the swing votes, but representatives from Kentucky, Ohio, and Tennessee could be enticed to support tariff legislation with restrictions on agricultural products like hemp and flax. Plus, protectionists often packaged tariffs as revenue measures intended to aid in the extension of western internal improvements.

When the 18th Congress convened in 1823 the seats were allocated according to the 1820 census totals. The Senate remained balanced, but in the House the protectionist states won the majority of new appointments. Henry Clay was named Speaker, and the following year the Kentuckian delivered his American System speech, much to the chagrin of southerners. Clay prescribed a fundamental reorganization of American political economy that bound northern and western interests together with protective tariffs, internal improvements, and the recharter of a national bank. Political dynamics in the early 1820s were influenced by fresh memories of the Panic of 1819. This was arguably the nation's first economic emergency that manifested the modern business cycle phenomenon of postwar boom, inflationary expansion, contraction, crisis, and depression. Evidence of British dumping galvanized protectionists, but a glut in international cotton markets that sent prices plunging by 60 percent stirred planters.[99]

In this hypersensitive political and economic environment, the tariff of 1824 was presented in the House by Clay's recent appointee to head the Committee on Manufactures, the Pennsylvania protectionist John Tod. Congressional votes were again cast along sectionalist lines. The tariff of 1824 passed both the House and Senate on razor-thin margins, with representatives from western states casting the pivotal votes. As Jonathan Pincus has shown in his work on antebellum tariff politics, the 1824 tariff signaled an ideological divorce between tariffs and revenue. By that time tax revenues were high enough to limit the appeal and logic of tariff arguments for the purpose of raising federal receipts. It was then clear that protectionists intended tariffs to guard against foreign competition. Moreover, the financial Panic of 1819, according to protectionists, was hastened by dramatic increases in specie outflow, mainly to pay for British imports. Raymond, like Hamilton, connected commercial policy to domestic finance. His *Thoughts on Political Economy* came on the heels of successful efforts to recharter a national bank. Raymond paid considerable attention to financial institutions in his work. He suggested that a favorable balance of trade, guaranteed by high tariffs, was imperative in restricting specie exports and thus maintaining sound currency. Free trade, according to Raymond, encouraged wanton increases in consumer purchases of foreign wares, paid by specie, depleting the nation's reserves and thus upsetting national finance.[100]

The 1824 bill raised rates from 38 percent to 42 percent on an expansive range of dutiable goods. Agricultural products like hemp, butter, lard, pork, wheat, flour, beef, and potatoes were included in the measure, which helped win the support of representatives of northern and western farmers. Tariffs on cotton manufactures were raised to 33 percent, but schedules on woolen textiles were increased proportionally less than rates on raw wool. This incited protests from New England's woolen manufacturers, culminating in the Woolens Bill of 1827, which passed the House but failed in the Senate when Calhoun, then the vice president, cast the deciding nay vote. The proposed rate increase on woolen textiles incensed southerners, who were the chief consumers of kerseys, the coarse woolens that planters purchased for their slaves. As Seth Rockman has shown, the row over woolens brought to the fore the intersection of northern manufacturers and southern plantation owners. Through legislative fiat the central government picked economic winners and losers, with "Congress devoting its power of taxation to the question of who would dress the nation's slaves."[101] By then, tariff policy had grown inseparable from the large debate over the future of slavery.

The aborted Woolens Bill had another, more immediate impact. The Harrisburg Convention of July 1827, organized by the Pennsylvania Society for the Promotion of Manufactures and the Mechanical Arts, brought together almost a hundred of the nation's leading protectionist statesmen, industrialists, and public intellectuals. In all, 13 of the 24 states were represented. Carey attended; so too did List. The five-day conference invigorated protectionist forces and offered an opportunity for woolen manufacturers and wool producers to reach a compromise over tariff schedules. This they did, and in 1828 after a series of political machinations, backroom chicanery, and an eleventh-hour rate increase on woolen manufactures that helped win support from New England, the so-called Tariff of Abominations passed along sectional lines and was signed into law by President Adams that spring.

Tariffs had become a political football. The 1828 tariff, for instance, was wedded as much to the presidential ambitions of Jackson and Van Buren as it was to economics. Neither side was especially pleased with the 1828 bill. Protectionists were confounded by the rate increases on raw materials. Carey referred to the legislation as a "crude mass of imperfection."[102] Southerners were enraged over higher minimum valuations on cotton manufactures, which threatened the export cotton trade with Britain. In his study on American tariffs, Taussig describes the 1828 minimum valuations schedules on textile imports best: "The bill provided that all goods costing less than 40 cents a square yard were to pay duty as if they had cost 40 cents; all costing more than 40 cents and less than $2.50 were to be charged as if they had cost $2.50; all costing between $2.50 and $4.00 to be charged as if they had cost $4.00."[103] Later amendments to the original bill made restrictions more permanent and had by 1830 raised the average tariff on dutiable goods to 62 percent, the highest in antebellum history.

Calhoun had seen enough. The nullification crisis was followed by Jackson's Force Bill and ultimately the so-called Compromise Tariff of 1833. The latter quelled South Carolina's secessionists. Introduced by Clay, the agreement restructured tariff schedules by gradually reducing rates over the next decade to a universal revenue-only level of 20 percent. But on September 1, 1842, the schedules worked out in the Compromise Tariff were dropped after only two months for a more protectionist bill passed by insurgent Whigs. What Democrats called the Black Tariff of 1842 was connected to President John Tyler's divorce from the Whigs, a growing fiscal crisis that protectionists tied to lower tariff receipts, and the Panic of 1837, as well as sectional disagreements that further cemented commercial policy in the controversy over slavery. The measure included planned uniform rate increases to 37 percent by 1844.[104]

Jacksonian-era conflict over tariffs contributed to the already politicized tone of the antebellum economic discourse. Allegiances on both sides hardened. The debate on trade was couched in arguments about who would exercise influence over the future of the American economy. Free-trade ideology grew affixed to southern slavery at almost the same time that protectionism emerged as the policy corollary to northern industrialization. But as protectionists provided legislators with the economic logic behind higher tariffs, they devised a more organic, polished, and multifaceted interlocking economic philosophy that laid bare American industrial hybrid capitalism. The growing presence of free-trade intellectual capitalism in contemporary domestic literature—disseminated, according to protectionists, by British agents—further compelled protectionists to sharpen their reasoning, expand their criticisms of laissez-faire political economy, and connect commercial policy to larger questions about the role of government in the economy. The protectionist version of hybrid capitalism promised Americans industrial growth and economic security without the social hazards foreshadowed by Malthus and Ricardo. With a keen eye for American history, protectionists anticipated the course of American politics and economic development. They argued that British laissez-faire was incompatible with the past, present, and future of the republic, and developed what they regarded as an alternative vision of industrialization grounded in the exceptional character of the American experience.

Both List and Raymond echoed antebellum nationalist currents, particularly in the North, but perhaps ironically, it was the German-born List who entreated Americans to recognize that the United States was perfectly situated to assert its economic independence. Indeed, America was presented with an "unexampled" opportunity to self-determine its economic destiny. "The condition of this nation cannot be compared with the condition of any other nation," List declared.[105] Like many European visitors to antebellum America, List articulated a feeling that the national economic experience offered something positively different. A number of laissez-faire thinkers employed American exceptionalism as a device to negate specific tendencies of Malthus and Ricardo. These laissez-faire economists did not, however, make American exceptionalism a foundational element of their ideology. More than any antebellum school of economic thought, the protectionists made American exceptionalism a central tenet of their political economy.

From John Winthrop's seventeenth-century description of New England's "city on a hill" to Tocqueville's expositions on the uncanny nature of the nation's social order, American exceptionalism became and is still today national folklore. Antebellum Americans reaffirmed these presumptions. In his inaugural address Jefferson touted America as "the world's best hope," and Lincoln more than a half century later described the nation as "the last, best hope of earth." Language employed by the two figures who in some ways bracket the period under discussion communicates a shared awareness of the nation's historical uniqueness. The Americans born free of British colonial rule were imbued with a cultural understanding of what Joyce Appleby called "firstness." The first of an American species, the generation that reached adulthood by the early decades of the nineteenth century recognized their exceptional historical position in what was already regarded as an exceptional place.[106] Protectionists combined socially accepted notions regarding the uniqueness of America's historical, political, and economic conditions to construct an explicitly optimistic economic philosophy. In doing so, they aligned protectionism with a vital feature of antebellum culture.

Protectionists highlighted elements that contributed to America's distinct historical standing. First, the nation's democratic institutions promised unprecedented economic opportunity. Protectionists intimated antebellum assumptions regarding the benefits of democracy, and they incorporated an economics of democracy into their vision of hybrid capitalist industrial development. The protectionist brand of industrialization would be democratic. Protectionism grew increasingly popular in the 1830s and 1840s precisely during the so-called Age of Democracy.[107] Except for Rhode Island, Virginia, and Louisiana, by 1824 most property qualifications were dropped, granting nearly all adult white males the right to vote. Protectionists believed democratic government was genuinely responsible to the people's demands, political and economic. "Government is instituted to guard the interests of the nation confided to its care," Carey wrote.[108] In this way protectionism revealed the nation's political milieu and might be considered a form of economic democracy. Hamilton served as a starting point for most protectionists, but as social and political liberals they denied the conservative elitism and distrust of democracy typical of Federalist politics. Protectionists imagined the working masses in a more positive light. Higher wages meant there was no reason for labor to rebel, and thus no reason for capital to shriek in fear of the workingman. By strengthening labor, the rule of law and the sanctity of property were in fact confirmed.[109]

Most contemporaries subscribed to the general notion that the United States was the first nation with an enlightened, virtuous republican majority willing to sacrifice their individual economic interests for the common good. But the United States was also exceptional in that Americans expected its legislators to respond positively to voters' demands. The state represented a benevolent, patronizing institution that played a constructive role in harnessing domestic economic forces. British intellectual capitalism mistakenly assumed that political interference in the economy subverted the public welfare. Protectionists argued that the antistatist tone of laissez-faire was a reaction to experiences under the Old Regime, whereas Americans had no reason to oppose state meddling in the economy. An American protectionist state promised a fundamentally different economic experience from the colonial strictures of British mercantilism. The Constitution itself, Colton declared, was "enacted for the purpose of establishing a protective policy . . . to protect the persons and rights of the people."[110] In protectionist hybrid capitalism the strong arm of government was not feared. A positive state promoted prosperity, facilitated industrial expansion, and served as a paternal sponsor in the economy.[111]

The New Historians of Capitalism have emphasized this point in recent literature, urging scholars to recognize the significance of the activist state in national capitalist development, or what is sometimes referred to as a research agenda that "brings the state back" in narratives on the history of capitalism.[112] The implication here is that capitalist formation was an unnatural phenomenon, and thus state interference was essential to market creation. Southerners saw the alliance between state and industry manifested in tariff legislation as evidence of corruption, much in the same way that Marxist historians consider the state in capitalist societies an agent of bourgeois exploitation. To be sure, Francis Lowell lobbied Congress for minimum valuations tariffs in 1816, and Samuel Slater traveled to Washington to advocate restrictions in 1824.[113] Manufacturers crafted legislation to advance industry interests. But protectionist intellectuals offer little cause to believe that their arguments were swayed by the pecuniary ambitions of contemporary industrialists any more than Smith's *Wealth of Nations* was a propaganda piece for British merchants.

For Raymond and other protectionists, tariffs served first and foremost the interests of labor. Articulations of concern for workers were pervasive in protectionist literature, and imbued with an ostensibly sincere appreciation of the potential hazards occasioned by industrialization if left under a free-trade regime. In 1800, wage earners constituted approximately 12 percent of the labor force. Explosive growth in manufacturing, mainly in the Northeast, raised this figure to 40 percent by the Civil War, exceeding the number of self-employed, which historians estimate to have decreased from 57 percent to 37 percent. Roughly over this same period, real wages for domestic industrial labor, which were higher than European averages before 1840, began to mirror those paid to workers across the Atlantic by 1860.[114] Economic historians account for the shrinking wage gap by pointing to, among other factors, labor and capital immigration, intermittent financial and commercial crises, and specialization and the subsequent de-skilling of labor. Protectionists were not blind to these developments. Raymond called explicitly on the paternal hand of government to safeguard American labor. "So it is the duty of the legislator to find employment for all people." He charged Congress with unprecedented responsibility, "and if he cannot find them employment in agriculture and commerce, he must set them on manufacturing."[115]

The near-religious faith in American exceptionalism contributed to protectionist understanding of the historical uniqueness of domestic labor. But the exceptional circumstances were easily upset if American workers were exposed to competition from cheap foreign labor. Tariffs alone guaranteed labor's true place in antebellum society. The celebration of American labor matched long-standing cultural values that were most palpable in antebellum northern society.[116] The American worker, if protected by high tariffs, had no reason to fear the dismal conditions described by Malthus and Ricardo. This was not the capitalism of England. There workers were betrayed. But in an American tariff fortress, no sector of the population was promised greater prosperity than the laboring classes. By the 1850s the free-labor mantra emerged as one of the sacred principles of protectionist hybrid capitalism, serving as the capstone of national economic, social, and political life and thought, especially in Whig and Republican political economy.[117] Labor was imagined as an instrument for self-advancement, the source of all value, the fountain of improvement, and the cause of civilization's progress. Labor was not demoralized by endless competition, motivated by starvation, nor was labor Adam's curse. Neither was free labor in the North degraded as a source of shame, as it was treated in the slave South. Labor was a dignified calling eagerly responded to by all.

Free-labor ideology in antebellum protectionism was not a form of industrial-capitalist apologetics. Neither was it a dishonest effort to capitalize politically on the assumptions of naive workers. Instead, tariffs created a hybrid capitalist order intended to soften the social externalities of industrialization. Protectionism was as much a social creed as it was an industrial one.[118] For Raymond, protectionism was the remedy against unemployment. For others, tariffs assured what in modern parlance is called a living wage. Tony Freyer has shown how producers of all sorts interpreted constitutional and democratic politics as instruments to protect their local or regional "associational economy" against perceived threats from domestic and foreign capitalists.[119] Carey, Raymond, and other protectionists considered tariffs an honest effort to defend through democratic means the economic interests of constituents, namely white male producers. British laissez-faire had overestimated the importance of distribution and consumption, failing to acknowledge that the essence of men lay in the fruits of their labor. Labor's expression was its humanity. "In the eyes of modern political economy he [the laborer] is nothing, and can be nothing," one protectionist wrote, "because it takes no note of the qualities by which he is distinguished from the brute."[120] Eric Foner and Jeffrey Sklansky have demonstrated that the nation's transition to market society encouraged the creation of a wide range of nuanced moral and social identities that transcended earlier definitions based on traditional precapitalist property relations. The spread of wage-labor, according to Foner, meant that many Americans "experienced the expansion of capitalism not as an enhancement of the power to shape their world, but as a loss of control over their own lives."[121] For protectionists, ownership over one's labor formed the essence of selfhood. Malthus and Ricardo, protectionists argued, taught that labor was an instrument of capital, the human spirit behind labor's production an automated materialistic reaction that satisfied base desires. When protectionists emphasized that man was a producer first, then a consumer, they relegated ownership of material property to a subordinate social position and elevated control over one's labor as the quintessential value in determining social identity.

In their celebration of free labor, protectionists presented a radically different narrative of industrial capitalism from the somber accounts of southern reactionaries and of northern laborites like Byllesby and Skidmore. Protectionism reflected American economic culture in still other ways—it was the only school in the antebellum discourse that championed the rapid and comprehensive industrialization of the domestic economy. Protectionism was the period's clearest reflection of the American industrial *mentalité*. An evangelical optimism about industrial prospects permeates protectionist literature. If directed by effective tariff legislation, the industrial future held an economics of growth, not scarcity and stagnation. Carey argued that industry advanced society by cultivating the sciences, arts, and literature, and served as "the only sure foundation of national virtue, happiness, and greatness."[122] Manufacturers were, according to another protectionist, "the great agents and tokens of the increase of national opulence, and the progress of civilization."[123]

Neither did domestic labor have anything to fear about industrialization. Industrial workers were promised intrinsic and extrinsic rewards. According to Colton, labor was provided with "the best state of health in body and mind. . . . What industrial calling has not its quiet aspects by day, and its refreshing sleep at night?"[124] Industrial cities were not plagued by the "social problem." The nation's factory operative had more to hope for than to fear. If anything, manufactures in the United States improved the morality of labor, for no class in the young republic, according to one protectionist, was "more respectable and intelligent, or better educated."[125] The protectionist version of industrial hybrid capitalism offered workers generous conditions, starkly different from the satanic mills in Britain. "Europe is but a prison house for labor, forcing it to toil for bare subsistence," Colton discerned.[126] Coxe argued that domestic industry raised "a body of firm supporters of the constitutions and laws and the most respectable examples of the civic virtues."[127] That manufactures in the United States were unlike their European competitors was a popular notion shared by many. Charles Dickens, for instance, following his visit to Lowell in the 1830s described the contrast between American and European industry as one "between the Good and Evil, the living light and deepest shadow."[128]

More than review the stock arguments of free labor ideology, protectionist hybrid capitalism infused the labor theory of value with moral authority. The American worker, Colton argued, "occupies an elevated, influential, honorable position." To toil was the American fashion, its historical custom, that which provided one with distinction. "Labor, work, is the spirit, the genius of the American people. It was so from the beginning by of necessity; it became a fixed habit of the community; and has ever been a part of the morale of the country."[129] The contrast with southern notions of labor could not have been starker. The founding of the new republic had ushered in "a new era of labor . . . the true millennium of labor."[130] Only after the revolution from Britain was labor free to exercise its long-dormant republican virtue. "The breaking of the British sceptre was the installation of American labor in its rights; it was the foundation of an empire of working men; and from that hour, labor has been the great political power of the country. The event was a jubilee—the jubilee of labor."[131] Now extended the franchise, American labor wielded political along with social and economic powers. In Europe, labor was pitied, a victim to market spurts and stops, groveling at the foreman's boot for work at a meager rate. Classical doctrine betrayed labor's historic place in economic society. In the American republic of labor, workers were not simply the handmaiden of capital. Labor acted as an "independent agent."[132] Indeed, capital courted labor; it was dependent upon labor; labor was its master. In this environment labor "does not accept a price imposed, but commands its own price."[133]

Capital, however, had nothing to fear about labor's unprecedented power. Domestic conditions, if steered along a protectionist course, made Ricardian anxieties over class war a moot point, dispelled with countering claims of social-economic fluidity. The protectionist version of industrial capitalism was benign, packaged without fears of working-class revolt, Chartists, or *sans-culottes*. Indeed, capital and labor worked in harmonious unison, sharing practically identical interests; they were essentially one and the same. High tariffs engaged workers and capitalists in mutually beneficial relationships where increasing wages corresponded with augmented production and never infringed on profits. "The interests of the capitalist and the labourer are thus in perfect harmony with each other," one protectionist reported, "as each derives advantage from every measure that tends to facilitate the growth of capital, and to render labour productive, while every measure that tends to produce the opposite effect is injurious to both."[134] Writing in 1844, Colton declared: "Every American laborer can stand up proudly, and say, I AM THE AMERICAN CAPITALIST, which is not a metaphor but literal truth."[135] In protectionist hybrid capitalism, industrialization fostered cooperatist networks, minimized class distinctions, and assimilated capital and labor until the differences between the two were indiscernible.

American exceptionalism was further evidenced by the safety valve theory, which was widely accepted in northern intellectual culture and championed by land reformers.[136] American labor was unique precisely because it could access unclaimed lands, leveraging the workingman's power, and inhibiting European-style pauperism by offering workers an alternative to industrial employment. The safety valve concept buttressed protectionist claims that American industrialization would follow a course wholly distinct from the descriptions presented in British intellectual capitalism. Workers could, theoretically, abandon factories for western settlements, "go to the back-woods,"

Colton claimed, so that labor had "a security for its independence for ages to come."[137] America's continental expanse ensured balanced economic growth and the coexistence of an industrial and republican character. The widely presumed scarcity of domestic labor, combined with the absence of aristocratic institutions, fashioned a landscape free of rank and hereditary privilege, with social mobility encouraged by an equality of access to open fields where every citizen could fulfill republican dreams of proprietorship and economic independence.

Apprehension over the long-term fate of labor was symptomatic of a producer mentality prevalent in antebellum economic culture. Protectionist defense of labor was not presented as an attack on industrial capitalism. As Karl Polanyi has shown, tariffs shielded labor from the dehumanizing aspects of proletarianization and helped relay to the state society's expectations for softening labor's transition into what must have seemed like an unprecedented set of social and economic transformations. In the early nineteenth century, industrial capitalism was a historical novelty, having introduced impressive alterations to societies that had traditionally subordinated economic prerogatives to social systems. Perhaps most revolutionary was the creation of a labor market that commodified human productive energies.[138] What Polanyi referred to as "the liberal myth of collectivist conspiracy" interprets reforms like tariffs as manifestation of narrow class interests rather than a communal response to the weakening of traditional social values then under threat by market encroachment. "For the alleged commodity 'labor power' cannot be shoved about, used indiscriminately, or even left unused, without affecting also the human individual who happens to be the bearer of this peculiar commodity."[139] Protectionists understood that labor was inseparable from its human attendant, its spiritual and psychological agent. They resisted exposing labor to unfettered market mechanisms, few of which, protectionists charged, were even properly understood. Moreover, British intellectual capitalism, at least under the direction of Malthus and Ricardo, purported that market functions would inevitably conclude with labor's pauperization. Protectionists took these narratives seriously. It was impossible to ignore the threats described in British classicism, contemporary labor literature, and the political activism of workingmen in the North. Protectionists resisted market hegemony in an attempt to thwart, soften, or at least delay the supposed impending plight of labor.

In this way, protectionists aimed to save industrial capitalism from itself.

But this could only be accomplished through noncapitalist restrictions on an otherwise self-regulating domestic market. Protectionist hybrid capitalism was a reaction against the social calamities of British intellectual capitalism. Although Polanyi's discussion of nineteenth-century protectionism does not extend to antebellum America, what he referred to as the "double movement" helps explain the popularity of tariff policies in the domestic discourse. "While on the one hand markets spread all over the face of the globe and the amounts of goods involved grew to unbelievable proportions, on the other hand," Polanyi found, "a network of measures and policies was integrated into powerful institutions designed to check the action of the market relative to labor, land, and money."[140] In Britain, the "double movement" complemented national ambitions to extend liberal markets abroad while simultaneously pursuing domestic social reassurances to the participating but less fortunate laboring masses. When the United States withdrew from the shelter of the British system, domestic producers were subjected to foreign competitors. America's "double movement" is found in the antebellum protectionist matrix that juxtaposed industrial expansion at home and measures (tariffs) to protect domestic labor from exposure to international markets dominated by British interests. A liberal commercial order guaranteed intrusive competition from foreign industry and threatened labor with gluts, lower wages, industrial failures, unemployment, and displacement. Protectionist hybrid capitalism favored competitive commercial and industrial markets at home, but it demanded the extraction of America from international trade. Tariffs were posited as defensive instruments, protecting first, theoretically, the nation's "infant industry," and later in the antebellum period, labor. For protectionists, free trade with Britain was tantamount to labor's suicide, and with it the potentially devastating effects on the social and cultural fabric of the American experience. Industry was not the servant of commerce, as it was in British capitalism. And contrary to southern political economy, protectionist literature did not consider national prosperity dependent on access to overseas markets; rather its plans were directed toward domestic expansion, which could only be realized by insulating the economy.

By the 1850s, the tariff-for-labor argument increasingly supplanted protectionist claims that restrictions were required to guard infant industries. The gradual liberalization of commercial policy that followed the Compromise Tariff was interrupted by protectionist retrenchment in the tariff of 1842. But tariff legislation took a sharp liberal turn when James Polk won the 1844 election. In his first address to Congress, Polk established his administration's guiding principles on trade. "Discriminations should be within the revenue standard and be made with the view to raise money for the support of government."[141] Polk's message was influenced by his treasury secretary, Robert Walker, who offered a fuller exposition of free trade maxims in what is often touted as the antebellum liberal rebuttal to Hamilton's *Report*. Walker's 1845 "Report" and the tariff that followed in 1846 reduced rates to 26 percent, establishing a twelve-year period of relative free trade, or tariffs designed strictly for revenue purposes.[142] Emboldened by Democratic majorities in both houses, in 1857 free traders pushed subsequent legislation that further shrank tariff averages below 20 percent, the lowest rates of the nineteenth century. By then the nation was on the precipice of war—but not before the Panic of 1857 sent the national economy into a tailspin, cut federal revenues, and decreased industrial production by 7 percent.[143] It was no coincidence, protectionists charged, that the crisis began one month after the Tariff of 1857 became law.

The tariff debate of the 1850s was not the primary cause of the Civil War, but when Republicans presented pro-northern high-tariff platforms in the elections of 1856, 1858, and again in 1860, southerners keen on secession interpreted these measures as proof of the Republicans' sectionalist ambitions. These anxieties were confirmed when in the spring of 1860 Vermont representative Justin Morrill introduced to the Republican-controlled House revisions to the 1857 tariff. Morrill, a six-term representative and six-term senator, was one of the founders of the Republican Party. His bill was shelved by Democrats in the Senate but reintroduced in December, following Lincoln's election victory. When the South brought its mostly Democratic politicians home, Congress was left open to protective majorities. Morrill's tariff was signed into law by President Buchanan in early March 1861, two days before Lincoln's inauguration. By then, seven southern states had seceded, Jefferson Davis had been sworn in as provisional president of the Confederacy, and in April shots were fired at Fort Sumter. As if having a free hand in Congress was not enough, a war debt the size of which Americans had never seen contributed to calls for the Morrill tariff to be strengthened. It was, with little congressional debate, first in 1862, then in 1864, and again in 1865. At war's end, Republican-sponsored tariffs had raised average ad valorem rates on dutiable goods to 48 percent. After the war, Congress reneged on earlier promises to reduce restrictions once the exigencies of the conflict passed. For the remainder of the nineteenth century, average tariffs ranged between 40 and 45 percent, hovering around Civil War–era schedules, peaking in 1899 at 52 percent.[144]

Aside from the interludes of moderate tariff levels following the Compromise of 1833 and later the Walker tariff, antebellum America was, in the words of Paul Bairoch, "the mother country and bastion of modern protectionism."[145] An industrial Fortress Americana was erected. Despite the transformative developments to the antebellum economy between Hamilton's *Report* and the Civil War, protectionists offered a fairly consistent set of principles that transcended material forces. The tariff-for-labor position was salient throughout the period. Pragmatism, nationalism, and American exceptionalism and its myriad attachments were also central points across antebellum protectionist logic, as was the home market argument. The latter was made requisite by a series of historical factors. Throughout the antebellum period, protectionist ideology appealed directly to farmers. Jeffersonian homilies on the yeoman ideal had convinced many Americans that the nation's future wealth rested on its comparative advantage in agriculture and an international trade regime that opened overseas markets to domestic foodstuffs. America's natural advantages in agriculture seemed a sure bet, especially in light of contemporary conflicts in Europe. The seemingly endless succession of wars conscripted European farmers to the front and left fields across the Continent ruined. Europeans would fight again, and American farmers would be ready to feed them.

The admission of western states had by the middle decades of the antebellum era compelled protectionists to expand their appeals to agricultural interests, highlighting the benefits of tariffs to farmers. Protectionists were obliged to explain how industrial political economy spurred by tariffs was not antithetical to agriculture's sacred first place in American culture. Hamilton's *Report* initiated this line of argument by wedding manufacturers and farmers, with manufacturing serving as a kind of multiplier effect inciting agrarian production. His entreaties to farmers were given fuller exposition by the coauthor of the *Report*, Coxe, who recognized early the need to package tariffs in a theory that elicited sympathy from domestic agriculture.[146] Coxe was appointed assistant secretary to Hamilton in 1790. He also played a central role in Hamilton's plans for the Society for Establishing Useful Manufactures, a short-lived industrial project founded in New Jersey in 1791. Hamilton hoped the pilot program would serve as a model for a national manufacturing system, but the enterprise folded in 1796. Historians sometimes credit Coxe as one of the first sponsors of the domestic cotton textiles industry, since he was instrumental in schemes to essentially steal intellectual property in the form of industrial secrets from Britain, specifically the Arkwright model. And as one of the most prominent activists in the Pennsylvania Manufacturing Society, Coxe was a leading voice in the early protectionist movement. A savvy politician, he was a Whig at Annapolis, a Federalist under Washington, and a Democratic-Republican in Jefferson's administration. His relationship with Hamilton was contentious. During the writing of the *Report*, Hamilton drew on Coxe's knowledge of domestic manufacturers, but in 1795 the secretary described him as "too cunning to be wise. I have been so in the habit of seeing him mistaken that I hold his opinion cheap." These feelings were shared by John Quincy Adams, who styled Coxe a "wily, winding, subtle, and insidious character."[147]

Notwithstanding his personal attributes, Coxe was the first in a long line of antebellum protectionists to champion national self-sufficiency, otherwise known as the home market argument. Proprietors of land, Coxe argued, were provided "a very great benefit" from the expansion of manufacturing, since industry tends to "goad the whole landed interest to profitable exertion and production."[148] Factory workers in search of food, as well as industrialists in search of raw materials, Coxe reasoned, would bolster domestic demand for agrarian produce and subtract from what protectionists figured was an overstocked labor supply in agriculture. Coxe enthusiastically advertised machine technology and the factories that harnessed their powers. Always the promoter, Coxe couched his celebration of machine technology in a style of thought and language that comported with contemporary agrarian values by emphasizing how the exceptionality of American conditions allowed manufactures to exist seamlessly within America's bucolic paradise. In his *The Machine in the Garden*, Leo Marx highlighted the significance of Coxe in antebellum efforts to reconcile industrialization with the pastoral ideal, noting how "in arguing for the development of machine power, Coxe depicts it as 'naturally arising,' like agriculture, from the divine purpose invested in the New World landscape."[149] To bring, in the words of one protectionist, "the loom and the anvil to take their natural place by the side of the plough and the harrow."[150] The home market argument was the economic corollary to Marx's notion of the middle landscape, encouraging a cultural balance between the nation's economic sectors.

Writing in the 1820s, Mathew Carey expounded on Coxe's vision, arguing that without a complementary manufacturing sector agriculture faced an uncertain future.[151] Farmers and planters, according to Carey's line of reasoning, saw their products carried from port to port seeking buyers, expending great costs in transportation, only to be sold at dockside auctions. Overseas markets were glutted with American produce, triggering a fall in commodity prices. Moreover, agricultural specialization and over capitalization of lands inevitably exhausted soils. "The system of foreign trade, of itself, necessarily tends to impoverish the land already under cultivation . . . in order to maintain its rate of production."[152] The growth of manufacturing would even benefit southern slaveholders. Cotton "will then have a home market," another protectionist declared. "There is no interest that ought to hail the establishment of manufactures louder than this."[153] According to the home market logic, slavery and industry were not mortal enemies; the expansion of one was not predicated on the demise of the other.

The home market argument posited not only the preservation of agriculture's economic primacy; autarky also served internal, coastal, and foreign commercial interests. Protectionists crafted arguments to charm virtually every economic sector. On the whole, antebellum protectionists disparaged mercantile interests, but at various points they assured the public that merchants and industrialists were not rivals competing for income from a fixed fund. Rather the home market logic allowed for industrialization to enlarge the merchant's share of national wealth by opening new trading opportunities. Coastal and internal trade would increase, Coxe argued, if food staples and raw materials from the South and Midwest were provided with industrial markets in the North.[154] Likewise, domestic wares would need transport to the South and West.

The emphasis given to the self-sufficient home market drew protectionists into the logic of economic autarky. Protectionists were not imperialists interested in projecting American influence abroad. In essence, protectionism was the economic adjunct of Washington's Farewell Address. "Protection looks homeward. Free trade, under existing circumstances, looks abroad."[155] The isolationist tone of protectionist thought was colored with a patriotic zeal that reflected antebellum notions of nationalism, Anglophobia, and the desire to separate from the Old World.[156] "Home consumption, and a home market," Raymond put simply, "is, therefore, always to be preferred to a foreign one."[157] Economic isolationism was consistent with an overarching view that the world was a dangerous place. Throughout the antebellum period, protectionists adopted a Hobbesian view of foreign affairs anticipated by Hamilton, whereby international markets substituted as space for rivals to wage war. "The occasional occurrence of wars . . . must be calculated on as inevitable. . . . Every alternate year has been on an average a year of war," with deleterious consequences for the combatants' domestic economy.[158] Protectionists called for Americans to shun the outside. "All people must look at home first . . . and stop not short of securing the home market in its fullest extent to themselves. . . . The home market is like an inherited patrimony; we may claim it as belonging to us, as of right ours."[159]

Isolationism in the protectionist lexicon was a by-product of American exceptionalism. "No nation, ancient or modern," Mathew Carey argued, "ever possessed more solid advantages than are here enumerated."[160] Colton agreed when he declared, "Never, in the history of the world, did a nation occupy such a position, or have within its reach such means of wealth and power, as the United States."[161] The exceptional conditions afforded the potential for absolute economic independence, America being "a world in itself, and able by its ingenuity and skill to supply every luxury, as well as every necessity."[162] Protectionists grew increasingly isolationist both economically and intellectually as the antebellum period came to a close. The inward turn was featured in part to illustrate the ideological distinctions between protectionism and free-trade cosmopolitanism. "For the most part, ours is a different world from theirs," Colton declared. "Things here started different, have grown up different, and are different."[163]

This attitude reflected popular antebellum desires to break from the Old World, and it helps explain the continuity in principles expressed across protectionist literature. American liberal intellectual capitalism, in the North and South, was influenced by preexisting external ideological forces, mainly British classicism, which in the early nineteenth century underwent several stages of theoretical development as the science moved from Smith to Ricardo to Mill. Additionally, the British authors were compelled to treat contemporary social, political, and economic realities, and in the case of Malthus and Ricardo they participated in shaping British social and economic policy. British political economy interfered with laissez-faire ideology in America. By design American protectionist thought was insulated. Most of the stock tenets of antebellum protectionism were expressed by the early nineteenth century. Even

List, perhaps the single most influential foreign voice in the movement, did not unearth theoretical discoveries; rather he expounded on already established principles.

When Raymond finished his text in 1820, he believed it was the first economic treatise for the new nation. He aimed to divorce America, in his own words, "from the fetters of foreign authority—from foreign theories and systems of political economy."[164] The American School, as the protectionists called themselves, believed Old World economists were prejudiced by their social and political institutions and therefore incapable of writing economic theory applicable to the American experience. "It is morally impossible from the social position of European economists," Colton wrote, "that they should be able to adapt a system of political economy to American society."[165] Laissez-faire ideology was simply extraneous to the United States. Neither did laissez-faire convey an accurate understanding of economic phenomenon. European conditions simply did not allow for it. But in America, where the manifestations of the natural economic order followed an unfettered course, protectionists were afforded "much greater advantages for studying the science of political economy than Europeans."[166] American conditions, according to Raymond, engendered markets of the purest form, a material basis untouched by corrupt human institutions and artificial impediments.

The New World demanded a new political economy that reflected the distinct history and reality of the American economic experience. Raymond issued a call to action in his *Thoughts on Political Economy*. "Let those who are endowed with greater talents, exert them as faithfully in the same cause, and we shall not be under the necessity of importing foreign systems of political economy, whatever else we may continue to import."[167] For many Americans protectionism was that system. And for many Americans, Henry Carey, son of Mathew, crystallized the protectionist principles into a coherent hybrid capitalist ideology. In doing so, Carey offered the period's most formidable and popular theoretical challenge to laissez-faire intellectual capitalism, one that for many Americans represented the sharpest expression of the native economic mind.

6

HENRY CAREY, NATURE, AND THE DESTINY OF MAN

> Just as the savage must wrestle with Nature to satisfy his wants, to maintain and reproduce life, so must civilized man, and he must do so in all social formations and under all possible modes of production. With his development this realm of physical necessity expands as a result of his wants; but, at the same time, the forces of production which satisfy these wants also increase. Freedom in this field can only consist in socialized man, the associated producers, rationally regulating their interchange with Nature, bringing it under their common control, instead of being ruled by it as by the blind forces of Nature; and achieving this with the least expenditure of energy and under conditions most favorable to, and worthy of, their human nature.
>
> KARL MARX, *CAPITAL*

Henry Carey is to American protectionism what Adam Smith is to free trade. Carey united protectionist ideas into an interlocking ideology and, during his own time, was recognized as the most important thinker of the protectionist movement. More than any other antebellum economist, he drove protectionist thought to its furthest logical conclusion. Drawing on American exceptionalism, nationalism, free-labor ideology, and an optimistic vision of the natural economic order, Carey expounded on existing protectionist principles to turn British intellectual capitalism on its head. His political economy was based on a Whiggish interpretation of the American economic experience. It reflected important antebellum beliefs about the nation's economic destiny and help set the economy along a hybrid capitalist industrial trajectory. Not only did Carey's works lay bare the protectionist brand of American political economy, but in many ways his writings encapsulate the most authentic expression of the antebellum economic mind.

Born in Philadelphia in 1793, Henry Carey found his curiosity in economics sparked as a boy perusing the commercial tracts that passed through his father's publishing house. At twenty-eight he succeeded Mathew as a partner in the firm. In 1834 Henry retired from the printing business to launch a career as a public intellectual.

In protectionist circles Henry Carey was an icon, and his influence extended beyond America's borders. His works were translated into European languages and Japanese, and in Germany he was hailed as having revolutionized economic theory. His home in Philadelphia became a sort of Parisian salon, where Condy Raguet, Henry Vethake, Joseph Wharton, and E. Peschine Smith made regular visits. During the late 1850s Carey set out on a European tour, exporting protectionist ideas by participating in economic conferences where he met, among others, his German admirers and John Stuart Mill. And when Lincoln ascended to the White House, Carey became one of the president's chief economic advisors.[1]

Carey's intellectual development in some ways was analogous to the internal tensions of the antebellum discourse. Early in his career Carey was a professed adherent of Smithian laissez-faire. His 1840 three-volume *Principles of Political Economy* manifested a commitment to free-trade maxims. Indeed, Carey admired Smith, extolling him as "the great father of political economy."[2] But as Carey matured, he began to question the authority of the British thinkers, especially Malthus and Ricardo. "Need we then wonder," he wrote, "that by that school the field of economical science has recently been so reduced in its proportions that it is now limited to the consideration of the mere acts of buying cheaply and selling dearly, having thus become a sort of shopkeeping science."[3] If Smith were alive in the mid-nineteenth century, Carey speculated, the Scotsman would oppose the very science attributed to him.[4]

The decisive moment in Carey's cerebral evolution came as an epiphany one morning in the 1840s when, he told his nephew Henry Carey Baird, he "jumped out of bed, and dressing myself, was a protectionist from that hour."[5] Early indications of Carey's apostasy were revealed in his 1835 *Essay on the*

Rate of Wages. Like most Americans, he found no proof of Ricardo's dismal conclusions in prevailing domestic conditions. For Carey, American industrialization followed an alternative course. His refutation of the Ricardian theory of distribution hinged on a zealous faith in the exceptional circumstances enjoyed by American labor. American workers were eager to contribute to the nation's unparalleled productivity precisely because they were rewarded with a fair share of the national income. "No people," Carey found, "ever had stronger inducements, so none ever pursued their avocations with more earnestness." Contrary to Ricardo, higher wages were not subtracted from profits, neither were they taken from a fixed wages-fund. Instead, wages drew from an increasing pool of profits and capital. "Where wages are highest," Carey wrote simply, "there capital increases most rapidly."[6] Advances in manufacturing technologies promised increasing returns. Ricardo's so-called Iron Law of Wages and Law of Diminishing Returns were perhaps applicable to British circumstances, but they were not evident in the United States. Indeed, Carey found that the value of labor increased over time or, put another way, became more effective at exploiting capital. British classicists insisted labor was a passive agent, a tool of capital. But in the American industrial environment, labor exercised power over capital. Therefore, workers and capitalists engaged in enterprise in partnership, sharing higher yields and easier access to the comforts of life.

Like other protectionists, Carey countered most of the central principles of British classicism. His theory of wages was predicated on the belief that America lacked a permanent class structure. By the 1850s protectionists took an increasingly Whiggish tone in their interpretations of American industrial society. Carey celebrated free-labor ideology, arguing that labor, not capital, determined distribution outcomes, and touted social mobility as a hallmark of the young nation's economic experience. His wage doctrine widened the gap between protectionism and classical doctrine over theories of rent and profit. Ricardo maintained that as population and capital increased, humanity moved to cultivate less fertile lands, dwindling returns on capital and labor. Carey rejected this narrative. Part historical economics, part historical conjecture, Carey countered Ricardo's presumption that the earliest settlers cultivated the most fecund lands, requiring nominal investments in capital and labor. Instead, Carey posited that the most fertile lands were rarely the first to be tilled. Early settlements, selected for defensive purposes or plain expediency, required little clearing, seldom occupied a region's most alluvial soils, and generally afforded nominal returns on labor. These societies started at a productive disadvantage. Moreover, original settlements were typically founded during primitive stages of civilization, and lands were therefore planted using experimental tools and archaic agronomics. Only after a community felt secure did men venture out, from "the sides of the hills and mountains towards the rich lands at their feet: and everywhere, with the growth of numbers, penetrating the earth to reach the lower soils."[7] With each passing generation, humanity discovered more fertile lands and cultivated with more effective implements, generating larger returns for labor and capital.

More important, historical migratory patterns, according to Carey, pointed to human agency as the determinant factor in rents. Ricardian political economy was overturned by the historical thrust of the human spirit. Carey's theory of rent reflected contemporary Americans' enthusiasm over their capacity to control their economic fate through the more effective exploitation of nature's store. He rejected Ricardian assumptions that rent was dependent upon the "original and indestructible powers of the soil." Agricultural yields were in fact decided by man's imposition of labor power and capital on nature. "Labor and skill have been applied, and the difficulty is removed, a consequence of which is that [the lands] are becoming very valuable, although their fertility is no greater than before." The progressive force of human will, combined with agricultural technology, agronomics, and man's aptitude for specialized labor, meant that the greatest returns lay in the distant future. Like other protectionists, Carey denied the economics of stagnation claimed by classical authors and instead projected an economics of affluence. He infused his theory of rent with a buoyant optimism that struck squarely against Malthusian gloom. "We possess no means of measuring the extent of the powers of the earth," Carey wrote, then enthusiastically predicted, "It produces now vastly more than it did half a century since, and the close of the present century will see it rendered greatly more productive than at present."[8] Each successive generation builds upon the improvements of the previous one, assuring humanity of greater command over natural resources and increased opportunities for wealth.[9]

Carey's confidence mirrored antebellum attitudes. Nature afforded Americans an exceptional opportunity: to mold the continent to their liking and shape their nation's economic destiny. Returns were accelerated or slowed depending upon society's ability to, according to Carey, "combine their exertions for the increase of production and for mutual protection, thus rendering their labour more productive, and promoting the further increase of capital."[10] Heightened production rates were accelerated by the inclination in all men to gravitate toward one another and form associations, pooling human energies and recycling agricultural and industrial by-products. Rather than separate farms from factories, and subsequently reconnect them through the wasteful intermediaries of long-distance merchant trade, Carey advocated economic concentration. Human association was inherent to the march of civilization, stimulating greater social diversity of productive powers and a more refined, localized division of labor. The latter enlarged what Carey referred to as concentrated "motion" or "local action."[11]

With the help of his disciple E. Peschine Smith, Carey formulated his theory of association into an economic law of human society that fused organic chemistry, ecological studies, and protectionist political economy.[12] What Carey advanced was nothing short of an intellectual revolution in economic inquiry, and in the process he undermined the foundational tenets of classical doctrine with an alternative understanding of man's position in the natural economic order. In essence, Carey denaturalized economics. Economies were no longer predicated on nature's system. Extracting the nutritional values from land, digesting those nutrients, and reprocessing residual refuse back into the commercial and industrial ecosystems facilitated man's hegemony over the economy. Recycling nature's store was for Carey essential to civilization's progress. The theory of association served as the catalyst to man's newfound supremacy over the environment and, more important, man's control over the irrationality and unpredictability of market forces. Americans had mastered the natural order, and with it the market. Carey and Smith were hardly interested in conservationist methods for the sake of Mother Earth. Their objective was to optimize man's domination and exploitation of the environment. Put differently, man could employ nature against herself, and thereby liberate humanity from the Malthusian/Ricardian quagmire. The intensification of association, or the increase in exchanges generated by bringing together within a confined space the forces of production and consumption, advanced the accumulation of wealth. "The nearer the place of exchange, the less of labour and manure are wasted on the road, and the more uninterruptedly is labour applied. . . . The more distant the loom and the anvil, the more labour and manure are wasted."[13] When producers trade goods in distant markets, they have forfeited valuable residuals that would otherwise have been credited to a community's local resources. In short, distance precludes regeneration, or, in Carey's words, "the manure cannot be returned to the land."[14]

Carey chided merchant trade for inhibiting the process of association, slowing the accumulation of wealth, and subjecting man to nature's will. In this way, Carey distanced protectionism from traditional mercantilism. Foreign trade spoiled consolidation. His theory of association was also an explicit rejection of Ricardian notions of comparative advantage and the international division of labor. Carey complemented the isolationist spirit behind the home market argument. In fact, the Carey-Smith theory of association is a more mature theoretical reiteration of Coxe's autarkic program. Here Carey also displayed an intellectual debt to Adam Smith, who had expounded on the efficiencies of domestic markets in his *Wealth of Nations*.[15] Carey backed the abolition of long-distance trade since it widened the space between producers and consumers, limiting the extent of human association and exchange within a community.[16] Ever since the colonial era, the merchant had been a popular straw man in protectionist literature. Merchants were accused of various forms of economic thievery. Carey referred to merchants as "converters and exchangers" who nicked what farmers sowed, siphoned labor's wage, and imposed an "exhausted tax" on consumers.[17] In line with his theory of association, Carey found British intellectual capitalism antithetical to national economic development, since it led to the "centralization" of production and consumption. Inhibiting the diversity of national production caused a population to grow more specialized in certain industries, in turn encouraging dependence on foreign trade and preventing localized action from enhancing the community's regenerative powers. By widening the gap between producers and consumers, international commerce compelled local economic societies, especially workers, to become "more completely an instrument of trade."[18] Tariffs would mitigate the destructive tendencies of global trade by fostering regionalized divisions of labor, would secure workers and capitalists a higher return, and would stall domestic migration to western lands. Most important for Carey, tariffs would liberate America from the fetters and fluctuations of foreign markets.[19] His brand of hybrid capitalism, in short, was void of foreign trade.

Although Carey claimed his theory of association was an economic law, it was founded on an understanding of economic development that was specific to antebellum America—a universal law applicable only to a singular place. This would not have appeared as theoretically duplicitous to contemporaries. American exceptionalism was an ideological intransigent. The association theory echoed popular cultural perceptions that new technologies could be employed in novel and more productive ways against the natural environment. Moreover, Carey's version of hybrid capitalism, like earlier expressions of protectionism, relied on American economic exceptionalism in such a way as to minimize the threat that industrial machinery posed to labor, republican virtue, and the social order. As we saw with Coxe, industrial technology was celebrated as the harbinger of the modern age. The ultimate expressions of human reason, machines took on a progressive metaphysical idealism.[20] Machinery was the "great instrument of civilization," Carey declared, empowering Americans in their historical quest to bring nature's resources under their control.[21]

For Carey, earth was a passive agent; but extraction of nature's wealth depended upon man's ability to combine his powers of production and consumption. Proper coordination of these forces determined society's technological potency, which in turn established the capacity to mine from nature society's prosperity. "The earth is a great machine, given to man to be fashioned to his purpose. The more he fashions it, the better it feeds him, because each step is but preparatory to a new one more productive than the last; requiring less labour and yielding larger return. . . . He is obtaining a daily increased power over the various treasures of the earth."[22] Human agency pushed confidently into the future. Each stage of economic development introduced improvements; "man commences with the worst machinery and proceeds upward towards the best," Carey wrote. There was no way to tell how much the combined energies of labor, capital, and machinery would wrest from nature's reserve. In the distant future, Carey conjectured, Americans would employ technologies to subjugate the unknown powers of the earth, "powers so wonderfully great that it would be absurd, with our present limited knowledge, to attempt a definition of their extent."[23]

Carey's understanding of man's relationship with nature is his single most important philosophical contribution to antebellum political economy. Under Carey, protectionism emerged more explicitly as a political economy of optimism and growth precisely because humanity had reached the stage in its historical progress where it exercised dominance over nature. Carey's writings contrasted starkly with the central premises of Smithian laissez-faire. Free trade was based, in part, on the subtle yet fundamental point of skepticism about man's mental faculties. Eighteenth-century philosophical skepticism was the capstone bridging Smith's moral philosophy and his laissez-faire economics. The perceived inherent weakness of man's mind precluded attempts at controlling, manipulating, or even understanding the natural economic order. Smith relegated man to more humble cerebral pursuits. Free markets spun complicated webs of cause and effect into economic phenomena that ordinary individuals could not even begin to comprehend. Statesmen and ministers, no more adept in their understanding of economic experiences and trends, occupied halls of government separated by wide distances from local economies, making it virtually impossible to manage the natural economic order. Indeed, according to Smith, it was difficult even to appreciate our most immediate self-interest.

Carey refuted Smith's economics of philosophical skepticism. Instead he posited something akin to a common-sense school of economics in line with earlier protectionist values. The unknown for Smith was the natural economic order. Put differently, man was subject to nature's will because of the innate weakness of the mind. For Carey, the natural economic order was clearly discerned. The single unknown for Carey—the potential for material prosperity—extended rather than prescribed man's position vis-à-vis nature. Americans had at their disposal the intellectual and material powers to direct nature's course, or at the very least dominate nature's resources. In protectionist thought, nature was not something to fear. Rather nature's immeasurable treasures were open to man's exploitation.

The elder Carey and the generation of protectionists that wrote during the early national period had defined freedom through the establishment of national sovereignty and American independence from British economic and political neocolonialism. Henry Carey found this understanding of autonomy limited, bound by temporary political concerns that failed to comprehend the true meaning of human liberty. For the younger Carey, the scale and scope of freedom was extended to sovereignty over nature, the power of man to bend natural laws. This ontology of freedom maximized human agency through the exercise of human will over natural economic forces. Man is not free, Carey argued, if subject to nature's will. His discussion of rent and his theory of association point to humanity, not nature, as the impetus behind the economic order. "To the power of the earth . . . there are no limits. Her treasury overflows with the raw materials of food and clothing, and all she asks of man is that he will come and take them."[24] Malthus and Ricardo, Carey argued, did not realize man's ability to wring from nature what he desired. And Smith discounted entirely man's power to even discern nature's order.

British intellectual capitalism described man as a "mere brute animal." Carey countered by describing "the real man, the being made in the image of his Creator, fitted for becoming master of nature and an example worthy to be followed by those around him."[25] In an explicit reproof of Malthus, Carey figured "twice, or thrice, ten, or twenty, or fifty times the population could be supported, even with our present agricultural knowledge. . . . we cannot hesitate to admit that the productive power of land exists in measureless quantity."[26] The British economists had made the profound mistake of underestimating the powers of man. Higher concentrations of population did not threaten communities with the Malthusian trap. "If the powers of the earth to afford food be, as they probably are, absolutely incalculable, we may safely leave to future generations to settle the questions as to when population will press upon subsistence; as to the extent of the pressure; and the remedies that may then be required."[27] Malthus and Ricardo were blind to the "breath of the spirit" in man.[28] "Mr. Ricardo makes him," Carey wrote, "the victim of a sad necessity that precludes the existence of hope. He is destitute of power over the land, or over himself, and he can have no confidence in the future. The machine he uses must deteriorate."[29]

Carey's brand of protectionist hybrid capitalism stretched beyond economic analysis into an all-encompassing theory of human evolution. His expanded assessments of man's interchange with nature served as the springboard to launch attacks on British intellectual capitalism. British classicism, Carey found, "teaches, that all the evils of society are the result of one great force constantly impelling man in a wrong direction—increasing the number of mouths, as the machine by help of which, alone, they can be fed, diminishes in its powers."[30] Beginning with Smith, laissez-faire posited a universal order governed by laws that effected absolute command over the course of human affairs. For Smith, the natural order was benign. But Malthus and Ricardo slighted Smith's underlying optimism, forecasting instead posterity's catastrophe. The British authorities saw "the power of nature over man steadily increasing," Carey wrote, with man becoming "more and more her slave."[31] The British economists considered man neither affectionate nor intelligent, denying "the existence of the spirit itself." Man, in the classicist formula, "is nothing, and can be nothing, because it takes no note of the qualities by which he is distinguished from the brute."[32]

The economic relationship between man and nature was transformed in Carey's narrative. Economic society did not rely on Smith's benevolent Creator. Neither did Carey accept the Malthusian and Ricardian understanding that exchanges between nature and humanity were adversarial, so that the order established by Providence devolved toward self-destruction, leaving men weak and destitute. "The great Architect of the universe was no blunderer," Carey declared. "Can it be, then, that after having given to man all the faculties required for assuming the mastery of nature, it has been a part of His design, to subject him to absolute and irreversible laws, in virtue of which he must inevitably become nature's slave?"[33] For Carey, man reigned over nature. Her order was understood, her once troubling mystical and subliminal powers made "to serve the purpose of man—and with his coming we find the important difference that whereas all other animals were bound to continue forever the slaves of nature, he alone was gifted with the faculties required for enabling him to become her master, and to make her do his work." While Malthus and Ricardo looked to "the ultimate enslavement of man by nature," Carey inverted the sequence.[34] He told a sweeping narrative of the epic struggle between nature's material powers and the intellectual powers of humanity. "Matter and mind were to be brought face to face with each other, contending for mastery of the world; the former armed with powers so prodigious that words scarcely suffice for their enumeration and description; the latter at first so weak as to be deficient in many of the qualities by means of which even the lowest animals had been fitted for self-preservation." Earlier history demonstrated how nature's colossus bore down on man's frail and feeble intellect, bringing distress and privation to the ancient human circumstance. With time, civilization's march began and, "step by step, mind is seen gaining on its opponent, seizing his outworks and on the instant turning upon him the captured guns, each forward movement proving thus but simple preparation for a new and greater one."[35]

In Carey's dialogue with liberal intellectual capitalism the destiny of man held an inestimable improvement in the human condition. History was a story of man's progress, with each generation becoming more effective in subduing nature. The industrial revolution was the catalyst in Carey's narrative. "The life of man is a constant combat with nature, matter sometimes triumphing over mind, but the latter more frequently triumphing over the former, and always using the power thus acquired as a means of obtaining further triumphs."[36] This confidence represents a cultural bravado quintessentially American. Industrialization accelerated humanity's exploitation of nature, "constantly battering at her gates, and overthrowing her walls."[37] Carey's work solicited recognition of man's newly obtained dominance over nature.[38] "At every step there is an increased consciousness in man of the existence of power to improve his condition, producing increased desire of improvement. Desire produces determination, and determination creates power."[39] A more effective deployment of industrial technologies overpowered natural forces. "With each addition thereto, he finds less resistance to his further efforts; and hence it is, that each successive discovery proves to be but the precursor of newer and greater ones." "Each successive year," Carey continued, "thus augments the power of man, and with every new discovery utility is given to forces that now are being wasted. The more they are utilized—the more nature is made to labor in man's service—the less is the quantity of human effort required."[40] Market forces and the natural economic laws over which Smith, Malthus, and Ricardo found humanity powerless were cast in a new light by Carey. The market could be controlled, the natural order fashioned to benefit man, and nature's forces brought under man's dominion. The pessimism of the classical school seemed, if not entirely unwarranted, then certainly excessive. "The whole English politico-economical system," Carey maintained, was based on a theory "invented for the purpose of accounting for the poverty and wretchedness which are its necessary results."[41] Carey premised his political economy on the economics of growth.

The industrial optimism explicit in Carey's writings contributed to calls for a distinctly American political economy. A "really American policy," Carey wrote just after the Civil War.[42] The popularity of protectionist ideology and policy in the antebellum and post–Civil War periods indicates that American economic culture was primed for a paradigmatic shift, one severed from Old World traditions, and one that reflected the economics of the American conscience. For an American system of economic thought, protectionists believed the native mind needed to turn inward. Carey's protectionism reflected an understanding that the United States moved toward uncharted economic territories of unprecedented material prosperity.

Although Carey's brand of protectionist hybrid capitalism was in the main an expression of northern economic ambitions, it drew from an assortment of cultural and intellectual traditions that permeated much of American history. In no way did protectionists wish to overturn free markets in the domestic economy. Protectionism was, in essence, national hybrid capitalism—or, put differently, capitalism isolated from foreign markets. This is not the intellectual capitalism of Smithian economics. But the mixing of liberal and non-liberal values would not have struck contemporaries as ideologically inconsistent. Most southerners, after all, envisioned free markets without free labor. Northeastern free traders projected moral capitalism. And virtually every American liberal rejected Malthus and Ricardo. Each group professed a particular version of hybrid capitalism. Under Carey, protectionism combined various strains of the American economic mind into a single ideology. It made American exceptionalism the central piece of an overtly optimistic political economy and, in doing so, helped relieve domestic anxieties over the potential for the negative social consequences associated with industrialization. Protectionism promised to ease labor's transition into the industrial age. To be sure, in the antebellum discourse, protectionism was essentially the only ideology of American industrialization. By fusing these components into a unified school of economic thought, the protectionists cast a wide net, affording ideological consolation for practically every sector of society and, perhaps most important, meeting American aspirations for national independence and individual economic prosperity.

7

LIBERALISM, REPUBLICANISM, AND FINANCE

> Had a committee of clever men been selected to devise means by which the public might be tempted to engage in all manner of absurd projects, and be most easily duped and swindled, we do not know that they could have hit upon any thing half so likely to effect their object as the existing American banking system. It has no one redeeming quality about it, but is from beginning to end a compound of quackery and imposture.
>
> J. R. MCCULLOCH, *A DICTIONARY, PRACTICAL, THEORETICAL, AND HISTORICAL, OF COMMERCE AND COMMERCIAL NAVIGATION*

The antebellum debate over trade highlights the ideological forces wrestling for control over the nation's economic culture. Because American intellectual capitalism assumed hybrid forms, the tensions between competing schools of economic thought assumed unconventional categories of ideological distinction. Protectionists were at the head of an industrial hybrid capitalist surge, much like nineteenth-century British classicism, but they denied the liberal orthodox reliance on Smithian free trade. Northeastern liberals crafted a political economy geared toward free enterprise, but in stressing the ethical propriety of laissez-faire over its material benefits, they conjured a brand of intellectual capitalism that was largely outdated by the middle decades of the nineteenth century. The northeastern liberals clung to a religiously charged version of free trade just as transatlantic intellectual capitalism was turning secular. Southern free traders were committed to an international liberal commercial ideal, but their defense of slavery coupled with their opposition to industrialization indicates that their devotion to more modern forms of material and intellectual capitalism was compromised.

The disputes between protectionists and free traders were waged in ambiguous spaces across an ill-defined spectrum of contemporary capitalist thought and practice. Still, their positions grew more entrenched as the period neared its end. The rigid sectional forms of liberal and protectionist hybrid capitalism did not, however, extend into every category of the discourse. Chapter 4 demonstrates how southern reactionaries and northern laborites railed against manifestations of material and intellectual capitalism, engendering awkward intellectual associations between what today might be identified as staunchly conservative and progressive values. American economic thinkers mixed and matched principles that challenge conventional understandings of ideological coherence, drawing distinctions with their British predecessors and contemporaries, and combining values that posterity would find incompatible.

A comparable disordering of customary ideological categories emerged in the antebellum literature on finance, which too was marked by seemingly incongruent intellectual linkages. Economic historians recognize financial institutions as integral to the advancement of capitalist economies. In his study of modern business history, Joseph Schumpeter described financial instruments, particularly credit, as the *differentia specifica* of capitalism. "Most of the features . . . of capitalism would be absent from the economic and . . . cultural process of a society without credit creation."[1] Twenty-first-century historians have expanded on Schumpeter's emphasis by focusing on the centrality of financial institutions in the evolution of American capitalism. Robert Wright, for instance, wrote that finance was the "root cause" of economic growth in the antebellum period, the "heart of the mighty beast."[2] Today historians take for granted that finance was an essential factor in the spread of markets, and they extend their analyses beyond simple understandings of the institution itself to a more complete respect for "how deeply finance has penetrated into daily life" and "institutionalized the self-interested activity of investors as a compass for public systems."[3] These interpretations suggest a positive interface between capitalism and finance, or, put simply, material capitalism cannot exist without finance. Logically, it follows that the antebellum discourse, written precisely during the period in which financial institutions became fully embedded in America's economic experience, should exhibit a clear correspondence between intellectual capitalism and support for finance.

In the antebellum literature on finance and capitalism, however, Americans entertained perspectives that do not match this established, probative ideological relationship. The volume of economic writing directed at finance was immense, nearly equivalent to the amount of attention paid to trade and slavery. In it, Americans constructed dynamic dialogues that defy modern expectations, especially the type that simplify intellectual affinities into neat combinations of complementary systems of economic thought. These mixed philosophical arrangements further indicate the broad continuum on which the discourse was structured in its attempt to make sense of the economic and social attendants to market revolution.

Historians of American finance have paid considerable attention to the financial episodes of the 1830s. The parameters established during Jackson's so-called war on banks have been extended in both chronological directions to form broad generalizations about the entire antebellum period. One interpretation posits a neat division between two rival camps, with finance taking center stage in the discursive drama. These historians define the struggle as a kind of class conflict, adopting traditional Marxist paradigms of class bifurcation, with the enemies of finance pitted against an enterprising commercial elite bent on modernizing financial institutions and extending capitalism's reach. According to these writings, lower-class urban workers and farmers joined forces to wage war on financial capitalism; Jackson led them. The resistance crystallized in 1832 with Jackson's veto of the Bank of the United States. The veto was the showcase policy piece in a series of measures initiated by Jacksonian Democrats aimed at derailing the nation's financial course. Jackson's bombastic class rhetoric is evidence that the president and his supporters were targeting banks as part of a broader strategy to undercut capitalism. In his bank veto message to the Senate, Jackson lamented "that the rich and powerful too often bend the acts of government to their selfish purposes . . . to make the rich richer and the potent more powerful."[4] Suspicions of an aristocracy of banking marauders led King Mob, according to Charles Sellers, a proponent of this narrative, to whip up into a frenzy "a democratic challenge to bourgeois/middle class hegemony that is unparalleled in presidential annals" and to "politicize popular resistance to capitalist transformation by mobilizing patriarchal democracy against the money power."[5] In short, opposition to finance triggered a wider movement—a *Kulturkampf*—against the market revolution. This interpretation, first popularized by early twentieth-century Progressive historians, was made famous in Arthur Schlesinger's *The Age of Jackson*. Each confirmed stock Marxist interpretations on the ideological conflicts between finance, capitalism, and democracy, with an invigorated franchise enlisted in the avant-garde of a nineteenth-century anticapitalist crusade. In antebellum America, the intellectual opponents of finance were the enemies of capitalism.

A second strain in the historiography downplays the class-war/anticapitalist narrative of Jackson's campaign. Jackson wanted *more* banks, not fewer. Acting as a proxy of a profit-maximizing commercialized mass, Jackson exemplified an incipient breed of bourgeois individualism intent on democratizing capitalism, liberating markets, and facilitating access to more and cheaper credit. Capitalism came over on the first ships, so naturally all Americans privileged a robust financial sector; they did not organize against it. According to this narrative, intellectual capitalism championed material finance. An authority on this interpretation, Bray Hammond, wrote, "The millionaires created by the so-called Jacksonian revolution of 'agrarians' against 'capitalists'—of the democracy against the money-power—were richer than those they dispossessed, they were more numerous, they were quite as ruthless; and *laissez faire*, after destroying the monopolies and vested rights the Jacksonians decried, produced far greater ones."[6] Jackson's veto message, according to Richard Hofstadter's liberal consensus reading of antebellum history, "is not the philosophy of a radical leveling movement.... What is demanded is only the classic bourgeois ideal.... This is the philosophy of a rising middle class; its aim is not to throttle but to liberate business, to open every possible pathway for the creative enterprise of the people."[7] The antimonopolistic and antiaristocratic demonstrations employed by the foes of finance should not be mistaken for radical anticapitalism. In fact, the opposition movement deployed a rhetorical style that camouflaged its true intent, leaving historians to misread antebellum campaigns that ostensibly advocated restrictions on finance. Americans' commitment to an intellectual and material capitalism meant that manifestations of opposition—even calls for the wholesale abolition of finance—were veiled expressions of a wider consensus that aimed at unfettered market proliferation and confirmed social recognition of finance as an essential component of capitalist systems. In short, because Americans have always been capitalists, logically they worked to advance finance.

This chapter argues against both interpretations. First, as James Huston put it succinctly in his study of the Panic of 1857, "Americans of all political persuasions viewed banks as abnormal economic enterprises."[8] Contrary to the liberal consensus reading of antebellum economic literature, when contemporaries expressed hostility to finance, they meant it. Most contemporaries understood that material capitalism, in all its hybrid forms, extended a wide set of ancillary socioeconomic benefits, but most never quite understood what exactly the benefits of finance were. On the whole, many more Americans opposed than supported financial institutions. Second, this chapter features a middle, liberal, often neglected variant in histories of the antebellum opposition financial discourse. Contrary to modern perceptions that adjoin finance to capitalism, both material and intellectual, antebellum economists regularly conceptualized the two in separate and often conflicting spheres. Intellectual capitalism and finance were not kindred spirits. Antebellum liberal economists described financial institutions as obscure, shadowy, and not exactly legitimate. Even while they celebrated markets and capitalism in most other aspects, by and large American liberals opposed the financialization of antebellum society. The liberal opposition literature was heterogeneous, and it lacked a single authority. But most liberals possessed not an anticapitalist bone in their bodies. In fact, opposition to finance often served as testament to one's devotion to Smithian laissez-faire. Many envisioned capitalism without finance; others argued that finance was the enemy of free markets. Almost all liberal opponents conceptualized the free market as a mechanism to slow the expansion of finance. Put differently, intellectual capitalism was weaponized as a theoretical device against material finance.

Likewise, the strongest advocates of finance typically doubted that free-market mechanisms were reliable instruments to encourage financial development. The friends of finance wrote positively on the role of state intervention to administer a healthy and steady expansion of credit, debt, banks, corporations, stocks, and notes. State oversight ensured a more efficient and benign program of financial growth and fostered paternal supervision over what even the apologists for finance recognized as a potentially hazardous, albeit indispensable, sector of the antebellum economy. Few Americans who wrote seriously about finance, even its staunchest supporters, advocated unbridled proliferation. And almost every American gauged the speed at which antebellum financial institutions multiplied across the economic landscape to be dangerously unnatural. The proponents of finance enjoyed influence among policy makers, and as the record shows, they were remarkably successful in exercising this influence and overcoming the opposition. Still, some of the opponents and all of the advocates of financial institutions understood that some form of finance was compulsory, a necessary evil of sorts, and thus the literature is replete with policy reforms, bound by the complex, oftentimes indiscernible, ideological lines that fashioned the subsets of antebellum hybrid intellectual capitalism.

Within the opposition literature there also existed a strain of thought that drew inspiration from classical republican traditions with origins stretching to Augustan England. In working-class quarters in the Northeast, backwoods settlements along the Mississippi, and patriarchal plantations in the Old South, republican opponents of finance gave new life to a style of thought and language grounded in early eighteenth-century English political ideology. To this subcategory of opposition, antebellum republicans added a nuanced nineteenth-century commitment to liberal, Smithian-inspired economic values that comported with American intellectual hybrid capitalism. American critics signaled their evolution away from the most purist forms of republican thought by fitting elements of laissez-faire into a wider opposition movement directed explicitly against finance. Here, intellectual capitalism was combined with republican values to produce the period's most resilient form of antifinance thought.

Jackson's veto of the Bank of the United States, the seminal moment in antebellum finance history, was at least partially motivated by the president's understanding of the English republican tradition. "I do not dislike your Bank any more than all banks," Jackson wrote Bank president Nicholas Biddle in 1829, "but ever since I read the history of the South Sea Bubble I have been afraid of banks."[9] Jackson was referring to England's first major financial calamity and the first modern financial crisis of international significance.[10] The South Sea Bubble was also arguably the determinant event in the development of classical republican economic ideology. And in the Anglo-American historical imagination, the South Sea Bubble embodied everything that was wrong with financial capitalism.

To rival the Whig-dominated Bank of England, Tories chartered the South Sea Company in 1711 with rights to assume £9 million of government debt. The company's first ship, named after the Prince of Wales for his noteworthy investment, was launched in 1715. Despite enjoying, according to the company's charter, "the sole trade and traffic" to much of the Atlantic, from the beginning it was clear, at least to the company's directors, that the enterprise would function primarily as a financial undertaking. An ambitious £1.3 million bribery campaign persuaded Parliament to grant the company rights to issue an additional £32 million in bonds and annuities. When news of Parliament's decision reached Exchange Alley in London, it set off a firestorm of speculative bidding. In January 1720 company shares traded for £130. That summer shares peaked at over £1,000. The mania was fueled by credit. The company's initial offering sold 37,000 shares at a total price of approximately £13 million, yet only £2.75 million was collected. The second subscription sold 15,000 shares at £400 each, requiring a deposit of only 10 percent at the time of purchase.[11] London was engrossed in a stock-buying frenzy.

Credit and stocks were for most early eighteenth-century Englishmen a novelty. Credit was thought by some to be panacea, opening opportunities and removing traditional barriers to wealth and status. It also armed the state with new methods to finance England's costly wars by mortgaging future revenues through the sale of public debt. By 1720 England's debt reached £54 million, up from £3.1 million in 1691. Shares in the national debt were exchanged in secondary markets, and their values, along with shares in other joint-stock companies, were printed in the stock price listings in London's papers along with brokers' advertisements for their financial services. Quite a few Englishmen responded. Historians estimate that approximately 30,000 investors participated in the bubble market. By the early months of 1720, roughly £50 million was invested in these joint-stock companies, a tenfold increase from turn-of-the-century figures.[12] So-called bubble companies sprung up at a rapid pace. There was one "for insuring horses," another "for making salt water fresh," and one project "to carry on an undertaking of great advantage but nobody to know what it is."[13] Two months before the market crash, London's *Daily Post* reported: "The hurry of our stock-jobbing bubblers has been so great this week, that it has exceeded all that was ever known. . . . The general cry has been, 'For G . . . 's sake let us subscribe to something, we don't care what it is!'"[14] Coffeehouses swarmed with speculators buzzing about, buying and selling stocks with dreams of accumulating "vast sums of gold gained without toil or care."[15] The bull market offered no shortage of optimism or opportunism. Workers left their tools idle, and sailors abandoned ships, as all attention swung to stock jobbing.[16]

In August 1720 the bubble popped. Shares in the South Sea Company collapsed below £200. The following winter, candles and bonfires lit the London night sky as the public celebrated the sentencing of John Aislabie, chancellor of the exchequer in the government of King George I, to the Tower for his role in the South Sea fiasco. Much of London's financial elite was implicated. And as governor of the failed company who had personally profited by £86,000 from the first subscription, King George I, along with the entire administration of Robert Walpole, was suspected of nefarious dealings.[17] The financial crisis hastened what historians call "future shock," or a newfound awareness, anxiety, and distrust of the emerging financial economy.[18] Modern finance, it seemed, disrupted traditional social and political hierarchies, diminished the importance of customary forms of wealth creation like labor, agriculture, and manufacturing, imperiled personal independence through the accumulation of debt, fostered a culture of doubt and suspicion, and wrapped society in knotty networks of interdependent credit relations.

The South Sea Bubble also incited a republican brand of economic thought that had at its center opposition to finance.[19] Jackson's own anti-finance political economy was likely informed by the English protest writings of John Trenchard and Thomas Gordon. From 1720 until 1724 they penned essays for the *London Journal* later compiled in book form as *Cato's Letters*. Trenchard and Gordon were for most Americans the principal source of English opposition thought. "Quoted in every colonial newspaper from Boston to Savannah," according to one historian, and recommended by Benjamin Franklin for instruction in English grammar at the Philadelphia Academy, *Cato's Letters* circulated widely in early America.[20] Whether they realized it or not, a broad set of antebellum finance opposition writers repeated nearly the same arguments and used nearly the same rhetorical strategies as England's classical republicans. Although Americans interspersed classical republicanism with laissez-faire, the migration of early eighteenth-century English opposition thought to antebellum America indicates continuity in the formulation of a transatlantic anti-finance strain in republican political economy.[21]

In the antebellum republican conscience, financial institutions were the most dangerous outgrowth of commercialization. According to classical republican thought, commercialization, broadly defined, weakened the sociopolitical pursuit of civic virtue by way of the numerous distractions offered to citizens, mainly the self-interested quest for riches and the proliferation of choices in areas of luxury, vice, and general self-indulgence. Credit, as J. G. A. Pocock has shown, was viewed by republican critics as an institution founded entirely on irrational calculations, subjective imaginations, or speculative enthusiasms that swamped society with a "flood of fantasy" and contributed in powerful ways to the dissemination of a debased commercial ethic.[22] Political engagement and commercial social saturation were, according to classical republican theorists and their historians, inherently incompatible. Republican values and commercial enterprise fueled by credit were especially irreconcilable. Credit and debt, the twin scourges of modernity, made individuals and sovereigns slaves to financiers, corrupted legislators, forced the imposition of onerous taxes, and, most important, disabled the pursuit of civic virtue and endangered what contemporaries perceived to be the already precarious foundations of republican polity. The decline of the commonwealth, hastened by the commercialization and financialization of modern society, inevitably placed republican notions of political freedom at risk. Historically, the republican understanding of personal freedom consisted strictly of political values. Politics far outweighed economics in the traditional republican discourse. Freedom meant independence from arbitrary power, foreign or domestic, so that citizens could practice civic virtue. This republican version of freedom is contrary to the more modern and purely individualistic market-oriented conception of freedom that emphasizes the importance of, first and foremost, unhindered economic choice. Accordingly, John Locke, David Hume, and Adam Smith underwrote the early modern intellectual transition away from classical republican notions of political freedom toward a more liberal, economically focused understanding.[23]

Scholasticism, mercantilism, slavery, and classical republicanism were some of the early modern casualties of the emerging liberal economic order. Republicanism, like slavery, exhibited remarkable ideological and material flexibility in adapting to market imperatives.[24] American historians have shown that republicanism persisted in the nation's political and economic culture as an important intellectual force during the revolutionary and early national periods. Fewer historians have extended the "republican synthesis" beyond the Jacksonian era. Insurgent capitalism, which by 1840 had permeated virtually every aspect of antebellum society, is said to have purged the nation of its republican heritage. "A new generation of democratic Americans," described by Gordon Wood in his study of early American political culture, "was no longer interested in the revolutionaries' dream of building a classical republic of elitist virtue out of the inherited materials of the Old World. . . . People did not have to feel guilty anymore about pursuing their personal happiness here and now. Even the 'pursuit of gold' now had beneficial results."[25] Finance, the sine qua non of capitalism, delivered a decisive blow to republicanism as a social, cultural, and economic option. The strike was not fatal, however. Classical republican values persisted throughout the antebellum period as an ideological instrument directed at its original archenemy—finance—decades after America's capitalist turn. American republican anti-finance literature incorporated market-oriented values in traditional republican ideology to form something of a hybrid capitalist opposition. This helped unite a fresh, invigorated opposition to finance within the American liberal economic mind and pushed republicanism chronologically deeper into the period's history.

In early national America, republican opposition first surfaced in response to Alexander Hamilton's program for financial modernization. Hamilton's plan included the assumption of states' debts, discrimination in the repayment of revolutionary debt, increases in domestic excises and tariffs, funding of the national debt, and establishment of a national bank.[26] He declared credit the "invigorating principle."[27] When Hamilton's brainchild, a national bank, conceived in his *Report on Public Credit*, was brought to life by President Washington's pen in 1791, the nation was on the brink of a financial revolution. Hamilton touted the Bank of the United States as "an institution of primary importance to the prosperous administration of the finances" that facilitated "the augmentation of active or productive capital" and promised a boon to the national economy.[28] Investors responded enthusiastically. At the Bank's initial public offering, subscriptions totaling the entire $8 million available to the public were purchased within an hour.[29] Hamilton's scheme was based in part on the controversial point that "public debts are public blessings."[30] In his view, the modernization of domestic finance would improve America's credit rating, rally her standing in international capital markets, and attract foreign investment.[31] The latter saw a sharp increase the year Hamilton's Bank was established, and by 1803 almost 60 percent of the nation's sovereign debt was held in foreign hands, the highest proportion of the nineteenth century.[32] Trust in the nation's financial institutions was, according to Hamilton, "the palladium of public safety."[33] Hamilton's principal concern was political. He figured stability in capital markets would solicit support for the new government from domestic financiers. "To promote the increasing respectability of the American name," Hamilton wrote, "to cement more closely the union of the states . . . [and] to add to their security against foreign attack."[34] He argued that the proliferation of financial institutions would sustain economic growth, so long as proper oversight was provided by a coalition of ministers and bankers.

Hamilton's financial agenda raised a fury of inspired political opposition. From almost every corner surfaced vehement accusations and vile condemnations. He was, in the imagination of his assailants, Walpole reincarnated. Perhaps the most prominent of Hamilton's enemies sat across from him in Washington's cabinet—Thomas Jefferson. "Debt," according to the Jeffersonian scholar Herbert Sloan, "is the thread that runs through Thomas Jefferson's private life and public career . . . debt was a constant presence in Jefferson's personal affairs." Two years prior to drafting the Declaration of Independence, Jefferson had incurred liabilities stemming from the settlement of his father-in-law's estate. "I am overwhelmed," Jefferson later wrote, "at the prospect of the situation in which I may leave my family." Like many planters' in the Old Dominion, Jefferson's personal finances were in shambles. The never-ending architectural projects at Monticello, his taste for fine wines, his prodigious home library, and lackluster returns from his property holdings contributed to his troubles. But Jefferson's personal indebtedness was not the primary motivation behind his hostility toward finance. Like most republicans, he detested financial capitalism for the social, economic, political, and moral ramifications that accompanied it. The burdens of debt drowned a man's esteem, ruined his aspirations, and made him essentially a slave to his creditors. For Jefferson finance empowered moneygrubbing jobbers, encouraged dangerous speculation, curtailed honest labor, and accelerated the decline of republican economy. "Not only was debt an evil in itself," according to Sloan's account of Jefferson's opposition, "but, once again, it was leading to still other evils, and the worst of them, as Jefferson read the scene, was the undermining of the true principles of republican government."[35] Politically, debt posed the greatest danger. England served as the historical example for Jefferson. Even before the long wars with revolutionary France, in 1783 approximately 75 percent of Britain's budget serviced its debt.[36] What was once a virtuous constitutional monarchy had relinquished sovereignty to creditors and brokers, the nouveaux riches of a financier aristocracy that profited at the expense of liberty-loving English republicans, wrecking the commonwealth and tyrannizing the people with what Hamilton was now touting as a public blessing.

Jefferson came nearest to writing a treatise on economic philosophy with his *Notes on the State of Virginia* (1781). The celebrated tract serves as a seminal piece in the annals of American agrarianism, but few historians consider it a systematic work in political economy. Almost a decade after retiring to Monticello, Jefferson completed an English translation of Antoine Destutt de Tracy's *Traité de l'économie politique*, a book lined with economic commentary. He hoped Tracy's work would become standard reading for Americans.[37] It offers historians a glimpse into Jefferson's sometimes elusive and ever evolving mind. Tracy's opposition to finance, like Jefferson's, was couched in a liberal agrarian context that celebrated the benefits of free markets. International commerce, for Tracy, sped labor specialization and advanced human civilization. But the excessive issue of paper currency attendant on commercial economies was almost always followed by financial bust, threatening the free-market order, "for there is no longer any free exchanges." The Frenchman was a hard money advocate, believing the paper system "a theft of great magnitude" and of "absolutely no real value." Paper currency was constructed on fictitious promises, multiplied for corrupt purposes, and circulated to an excessive degree facilitating what Tracy considered the purposeful debasement of its value. "Paper money," Jefferson translated from the French, "is the most fatal of fraudulent bankruptcies." Banks provided the fund from which the fraud commenced. Institutions that tended toward concentration, the banking "privileged companies" did indeed serve an economic function, but at a cost few republics could bear. Like Jefferson, Tracy found that the sort of funding system then in vogue "has none of the advantages which are attributed to it; and rests on a false principle."[38]

Tracy, and by extension Jefferson, mirrored early nineteenth-century southern republicanism in its nearly indiscriminate abhorrence of finance. Indeed, early American clamoring against the expansion of finance was heard loudest in the South. Perhaps the sharpest critique in the opposition literature came from John Taylor of Caroline. Born in 1753 into the political elite of Virginia's gentry, Taylor was a confidant of Jefferson, a distant cousin of James Madison, and son-in-law to a signer of the Declaration of Independence. He served in the Virginia House of Delegates and in the United States Senate. During the Constitutional debates Taylor sided with the anti-Federalists, fearing the centralizing tendencies of the new government would establish an American aristocracy. Taylor was encouraged by Jefferson's promises of reform and retrenchment in the campaign of 1800. However, the conciliatory tone that Jefferson struck in his inaugural address raised doubts, and these suspicions were confirmed when Jefferson and later Madison exercised executive powers that were contrary to Taylor's strict interpretation of the Constitution. Midway through Jefferson's second term Taylor appeared to be more Jeffersonian than Jefferson himself. He led a movement of Old Republicans in their schism with the party. But the breach left Taylor alienated in Congress. Still, he authored a number of political, social, and economic tracts that exemplified southern republican opposition thought. He died in 1824 in Port Royal, Virginia, not far from where Fitzhugh took up residence five years later.[39]

The current of Taylor's intellectual stream was mostly negative, his mode critical. He helped launch a pattern of liberal republican opposition ideology that anticipated the anti-finance movement of the later antebellum period. Thus, like Jefferson, he embraced laissez-faire economics, celebrated the republican agrarian ideal, and at the same time repudiated finance. His primary point of opposition to finance rested on a critique of the relationship between financial institutions and legislatures. Protesting corrupt legislation, namely the corporate chartering system, was a hallmark of classical republicanism, but Taylor linked this principle to free-trade political economy. "By incorporations, great bodies politick, whole parties, and entire states, may be degraded into clientage, and bribed to obedience; and legislators themselves may participate in every bonus they bestow."[40] Like many republican critics of finance, Taylor pointed to English history for signs of what was to become of the United States. Following the Glorious Revolution, according to Taylor, Walpole and his parasitic cabal contrived the funding system founded on a debased logic that public credit engendered public faith and national credit was necessary for defense purposes. For Taylor this bore a striking resemblance to Hamilton's argument, and was resuscitated by entrepreneurial Republicans responsible for chartering the second national bank. Taylor explained, "no funding system ever defended a nation. It was invented in England to prop a revolution by corruption; extensively used to sacrifice the nation."[41] The ramifications of financial capitalism were evidenced in the recent history of the English economy—Taylor referenced the South Sea Bubble on several occasions—by financiers enslaving virtuous and hard-working farmers through oppressive taxation.[42] "The idle classes of the nobility, clergy, army, navy, bankers and national debt holders, with their servants and dependents, are the items of an aristocracy, which has reduced the agricultural class to a poor and powerless state, by the juggle of persuading it to buy high prices, by creating and maintaining these idle classes."[43] The original source of trouble was the creation of the English national debt. A "factitious wealth," Taylor called it, contrived "to compel land and labour or real wealth, to become its humble and obedient subject."[44] Once established, the national debt fostered "decay and impoverishment both in mind and fortune of the landed gentry, and an exchange of that honest, virtuous, patriotic and bold class of men, for an order of stock-jobbers in loans, banks, manufactories . . . and an infinite number of inferior tricks to get money, calculated to instil opposite principles."[45]

Mortgaging debts for posterity to pay with decades of taxes was a dramatic deviation from traditional notions of generational accountability. History exhibited a fundamental, natural order that bound generations together through the inheritance of land. Agriculture was the final socioeconomic bulwark against wholesale commercialization. Tangible property, stable in its value, land provided an honest, republican subsistence and maintained social allegiances by promises of subsequent yields cultivated through centuries of accumulated toil. Early antebellum republican opponents of finance like Taylor incorporated pastoral idealism into their critique of finance. In republican political economy, agriculture provided the source of all wealth. Therefore, the income of financiers was extracted from farmers. "Hence we see capital flying from the fields," Taylor wrote, "to the legal monopolies, banking and manufacturing. The laws have established a thousand modes by which capital will produce quicker and larger profits, than when employed in the slow improvements of agriculture." For the agrarian Taylor, farming offered society republican stability that transcended generations. Now in America, theretofore blessed with an agrarian republican economy, the paper contriver, "a sly thief, who empties your pockets under a pretense of paying your debt," fixed through legislative fiat schemes of aristocratic pillage.[46]

Taylor's commitment to republican agrarianism should not discount his attachment to free markets. He did not attack intellectual capitalism; he made war on financial corporations. A disciple of Adam Smith, according to Paul Conkin, Taylor "applauded economic ambition, consumptive goals, and profits as high as one can earn by honest labor and fair exchange."[47] The Virginian arrived at laissez-faire, much like the southern free traders, to maximize individual liberty and ensure the separation of political and economic institutions. For Taylor, it was not inconsistent to champion free markets while simultaneously attacking finance, in the same way southerners celebrated free trade but doubted industrialization. And to suggest, as Hammond has, that Taylor's opposition was based on an agrarian "ignorance of banking" is akin to historical patronizing.[48] These characterizations minimize the complexities of Taylor's republican distrust of finance. And they underestimate the extent and seriousness with which the liberal republican brand of opposition thought exercised influence in the antebellum literature.

Taylor penned his anti-finance tracts during an especially tumultuous time in early American finance. The second national bank that became the target of Jackson's wrath had its origins in congressional debates that started in 1814 and lasted until Madison signed its charter into law two years later. Calhoun pushed the act through Congress, aided by lobbying efforts from financiers and merchants responsible for funding the United States in the War of 1812.[49] Captain William Jones was named the Bank's first president. The onetime secretary of the navy, secretary of the treasury, and recent bankrupt steered the nation's most powerful financial institution along a course mapped for enriching the speculators that filled its board of directors. Jones was responsible for administrating the nation's credit, securing government deposits, regulating state banks and the notes they issued, and meeting the expectations of private investors who held stock in the national bank, which was after all a private corporation. Writing to Secretary of the Treasury William Crawford in 1817, Jones faulted the lending practices of the first national bank for being "circumscribed by a policy less enlarged, liberal, and useful than its powers and resources would have justified."[50] The newly established Bank was afforded an augmented treasure to pursue Jones's expansionist program. It was capitalized at $35 million, more than triple the amount of Hamilton's first Bank of the United States.

But the Bank experienced complications from the start. Stephen Girard, the single largest shareholder and one of five government-appointed directors, quickly grew disillusioned by the Bank's patronage, recalling how "intrigue and corruption had formed a ticket for twenty directors of the Bank of the United States who I am sorry to say appear to have been selected for the purpose of securing the presidency for Mr. Jones."[51] Girard headed a conservative faction on the board of directors committed to steering the financial colossus toward restraint and judicious lending practices. But expansionism was the order of the day. In an age when "bustle was the rule," the relentless entrepreneurialism Americans embodied and the speed with which most individuals expected to attain personal wealth outpaced the young banking system. Article I, Section 10 of the Constitution prohibited fiat currency, largely to prevent democratic state legislatures from issuing notes as a form of debtor's relief. Privately chartered state banks, numbering almost four hundred by 1818, assumed that responsibility with remarkable generosity, overissuing notes that the national bank and Treasury treated as equivalent to specie. Money was commodified, and its production and distribution turned into a profit-making enterprise.[52]

Pent-up entrepreneurial ambitions following years of Atlantic conflict sprung a commercial boom in the late 1810s, fueled by cheap credit, then bust, culminating in an economic crisis and the collapse of America's banking system. The free-for-all economy that distinguished the Era of Good Feelings ended with Jones's resignation from the national bank. Langdon Cheves, the Bank's new president, inherited a frightful situation. "The paper bubble is then burst," Jefferson wrote to John Adams in 1819. "This is what you and I, and every reasoning man, seduced by no obliquity of mind or interest, have long foreseen."[53] John Jacob Astor reported to Albert Gallatin just after the Panic of 1819 broke that "our merchants instead of shipping produce ship specie, so much so . . . that it is not without difficulty that specie payments are maintained. The different states are going on making more banks and I shall not be surprised if by and by there be a general blow up among them."[54]

Astor was right. Credit contracted, loans were called, prices collapsed, personal bankruptcies spiked, debtor prisons swelled, and properties liquidated in a whirlwind of financial catastrophe. One contemporary described the agony: "I have seen several men turned out of boarding houses, where their money would not be taken. They had no other recourse but to lodge in the woods, without any covering except their clothes. . . . A still greater misfortune than being paid with bad money is to be guarded against, namely, that of not being paid at all."[55] The federal bank, itself overextended, was woefully unprepared to manage the crisis. By the spring of 1819 it had more than $41 million in loans, $23 million in notes issued, with less than $3 million in specie reserve.[56] Cheves exacerbated troubles by enacting retrenchment policies, restricting credit, and ordering branches to collect specie at a time when hard money was scarce.

Cheves's deflationary measures saved the bank but incited a sharp social reaction. Many Americans blamed the economic crisis on financial institutions. Nonetheless, when the financial storms subsided, Americans pushed the democratization of finance to new heights during the 1820s. Agrarians and aristocrats aided in wanton overissue of credit and paper notes beyond anyone's imagination. This was particularly the case in the West, home of "wildcat banking," where specie scarcity hastened calls for cheap credit. In Kentucky, for instance, Hammond finds that the specie-to-note ratio was of "nothing to infinity."[57] Historians estimate that by the mid-1820s no less than 10 percent of banknotes in circulation were worthless. John Neal, a haberdasher, aptly characterized the commercial environment: "lie-cheat-swear-and pass counterfeit money-if occasionally required. . . . If you buy the devil, the sooner you sell him, the better."[58]

The modern financial economy, with its regional, national, and sometimes global credit networks, tied even the most disconnected market participants to the complexities of finance. Credit as a form of social mutuality, or trust, facilitated network-building in the commercial community, and credit offered numerous economic opportunities. As the historian Jeffrey Sklansky noted, "capitalism so conceived embodies a way of believing, a mode of creating confidence in a society of anonymous strangers, faceless institutions, and relentless instability."[59] Finance relied on trust—faith between creditor and borrower, buyer and seller, and capital and labor. But this trust occasioned opportunities for fraud: falsified accounting, counterfeiting, spreading unfounded rumors for personal gain . . . The lines between financial deceit and good-natured speculation were blurred. Finance confounded, alienated, and disillusioned. Credit also made individuals vulnerable to a sometimes arbitrary economic order where mutuality felt like dependency. Public attitudes toward finance, particularly debt and insolvency, began to change during the early 1800s. The traditional understanding that economic failure was punishment for personal indiscretions and moral culpability, for instance, was replaced by an awareness that insolvency could result from market pressures outside an individual's reach and that failure might even be inherent in the antebellum economic experience. Either way, credit and the debt that came with it challenged American ideals about personal autonomy, republican identity, and proprietorship.[60]

Taylor's laissez-faire but anti-finance position reflected contemporary structural changes taking place in the economy. And opponents like Taylor struggled to reconcile their affinity for free markets and their antagonism toward financial institutions. Their commitment to an idealized past marked by traditional interpersonal relations was shaken at its very foundations by financial capitalism. Liberal intellectual capitalism here was balanced against social conservatism. Americans agitated for market expansion, but they hesitated when confronted by capitalism's prodigal son, finance. To some historians, republican economic thinkers like Taylor were backward looking in all aspects of their thought. Gordon Wood, for instance, argues that republican ideology of the antebellum period was "essentially anti-capitalistic, a final attempt to come to terms with the emergent individualistic society that threatened to destroy once and for all the communion and benevolence that civilized men had always considered to be the ideal of human behavior."[61] Although Taylor's attachment to agrarianism and his hostility toward finance were imbued with conservative appeals, his commitment to free markets should not be overlooked. In the antebellum American mind, hybrid intellectual capitalism made room for improbable ideological concoctions. Taylor's agrarian social conservatism, republican politics, and laissez-faire economics were not mutually exclusive values; rather the fusion illustrates Americans' cerebral acrobatics in making sense of the financial Frankenstein born to insurgent capitalism.

Thomas Cooper helps exemplify the evolution of the antebellum liberal opposition discourse. As we saw in chapter 2, Cooper championed laissez-faire principles against protectionists. He attacked financial institutions for the same reason he criticized tariffs. Finance and tariffs were offspring of the same parents: corrupt legislators pandering to the interests of capitalists. Bank speculators and legislators, Cooper found, "have too much of a fellow feeling."[62] Cooper, however, broke from earlier republicans like Taylor in distinct ways. He integrated a more explicit defense of free-market institutions and avoided the agrarian eulogies that saturated Taylor's thought. Commercial society was not antithetical to republican values. Rather Cooper explained how the laissez-faire, negative state buttressed republican institutions by curbing the powers of government, both state and federal, altogether extracting legislatures from economic society, and thus limiting opportunities for financial-political malfeasance.[63]

Liberal republican opposition to finance was intimately connected to broader understandings of government. Cooper opposed the incorporation of banks on republican constitutional grounds. Corrupted legislators threatened the republican polity. "I am unshaken in my opinion," Cooper argued, "that every bank charter is unconstitutional: depriving the great majority of citizens of rights... and conferring exclusive privileges on another class, upon motives and pretences often fraudulent, seldom excuseable, never justifiable." Corporate limited liability especially, he charged, sanctioned "a mode of swindling" that sacrificed the earnings of decent laborers to the risk, misjudgment, and mismanagement of others. "I REST ON REPUBLICAN PRINCIPLES," Cooper declared; "a monopoly privilege, with the power of acquiring profit without limitation, conferred on persons whose liability to pay their debts does not extend beyond the share they possess in the joint stock of a privileged company, is a fraud on the honest and confiding part of the public." Corporate proprietors accumulated debts without incurring responsibility beyond their invested stake. What became conventional corporate practice by the middle decades of the nineteenth century was for Cooper a reproach against community trust. Absolving a man from repaying debt flew in the face of traditional standards of social and moral justice. "How then are they to know to what extent to trust this company, who may (as often has been done) divide their principal, as a dividend of annual profits, and then sell out to unsuspecting purchasers not in the secret?"[64]

Cooper's *Lectures on the Elements of Political Economy* was published in 1826, the same year as Jefferson's death, and the work signifies a kind of changing of the guard in the liberal republican opposition movement. By the 1830s critics of finance relied less on the agrarian romantics of earlier republicanism. As the nation matured economically and the slave question cemented political divisions, southern thought grew attached to an antistatist disposition, and with it an anticorporatist, strict-constructionist model. Classical republicanism supplemented laissez-faire. For Cooper, opposition to finance was wed a broader states' rights, pro-slavery ideology that sponsored curtailing all forms of political activism in the economy. Laissez-faire opposition to finance targeted rotten legislators granting bank charters for the same reasons it objected to lobbyist-inspired tariffs for manufactures.⁶⁵ "All this can be managed well enough without the interference of government or the legislature," Cooper declared, "who are seldom known to meddle but to do mischief. . . . we may surely venture in this new country to say, when our rulers attempt to regulate the private investment of capital, 'let us alone.'"⁶⁶

The elevation of finance to the center of the national discourse during Jackson's administration brought increased scrutiny of the acts of government that legislated banks into existence. Cooper directed special animus toward the corporatist model of bank charters. He favored free banking, or the end of chartered bank corporations with debt liabilities limited to their subscriptions. Americans sometimes preferred free banking because, according to one historian, "they had not developed any alternative." But for Cooper, free banking promised to pare the corrosive influence that banks exercised over legislatures, and thus served a liberal republican end. "I have no objection in great and expensive undertakings to joint stock companies," Cooper wrote, "but the common law of partnership is equity, viz: those who claim a dividend of unlimited profits, are liable to the loss."⁶⁷ Free banking, according to its proponents, encouraged conservative lending practices, as well as a return to traditional commercial responsibilities. In a manner akin to Malthus's support for cutting the dole, markets could rein in both commercial impropriety and excess, promising a slow, stable, more natural course.

Still, embedded in Cooper's free banking approach is a tacit if reluctant recognition of the economic necessity of financial institutions. In the five years that followed Jackson's war on banks, an additional two hundred banks were established, bringing the total above seven hundred. Over this period there was a 130 percent increase of notes in circulation, in the West a 100 percent increase, and even in the more conservative Northeast a 50 percent increase. All the while, specie reserves hovered around 4 percent. The free banking movement that started in New York and Michigan in the late 1830s eventually spread to other states. New York, which replaced Pennsylvania as the nation's financial center, enacted its free banking law in 1837. Within six months fifty applications were reviewed, of which fourteen requested charters lasting 400 years, two asked for a 1,000-year license, and one for a charter of 4,050 years.⁶⁸

Banks were the tip of the financial iceberg. The proliferation of banks corresponded with the spread of other financial and monetary institutions. In Europe corporations were long considered apparatuses of corruption that concentrated power in the hands of a privileged aristocracy. But in the United States, almost immediately following independence, state legislatures created corporations in record numbers. As Pauline Maier notes, America "rescued the corporation, an all-but-moribund institution in late eighteenth-century England, and utilized its capacity to empower individuals whose resources were unequal to their imaginations."[69] By 1830 there were approximately 10,000 business corporations in the United States, the first "corporate nation."[70] On the eve of the Civil War, that number had ballooned to 22,000. Stock exchanges in New York and Philadelphia traded corporate securities, debt, and commercial notes on margin and were informed by credit reporting agencies. Investment came from state and municipal governments, private banks, and foreign interests. The latter contributed approximately $374 million in capital by the mid-1850s, most of it invested in federal, state, and local debt, but also in railroads. In the late 1830s, the Camden and Amboy Railroad became the first American railroad company listed on the London Exchange. By then the Rothschilds and Barings had substantial holdings in American banks. A seemingly perpetual call for more credit could be heard throughout the antebellum period. The financial sector responded by facilitating information symmetry, monetizing, and integrating a national financial system that by 1860 had more than $6 billion invested in the domestic economy.[71]

The parallel emergence of an expanding financial sector with a burgeoning democracy necessitated that pro-banking factions and their elected officials explain publicly how exactly republican institutions were not in any way jeopardized by financial capitalism. The localized and shifting nature of antebellum politics occasionally distorted party lines, but historians typically grant that during the Jacksonian period the Whigs advocated the pro-finance position. Antebellum Whigs were, by and large, the intellectual descendants of Hamilton. According to Michael Holt, "consistently Whigs took the pro-corporation, pro-banking, and pro-paper-money side."[72] For most Whigs, and even soft-money Democrats, banks represented agents of progress. Banks provided a safe place for deposit, facilitated business by discounting commercial notes and collecting debts, issued credit to state governments for internal improvements, and furnished the economy with a circulating medium. Credit expanded prospects for wealth in every sector of the economy. For farmers, credit funded agronomic improvements; for merchants, credit encouraged trading partnerships between producers, distributors, and consumers; for manufacturers, credit underwrote new machinery. And through the democratization of finance, credit lubricated the levers of social mobility for the lower and middling orders aspiring to commercial success.[73] Despite what pro-bank factions claimed, however, outside of utilizing banknotes as a form of currency, few Americans had direct business intercourse with institutions of finance. In her study of antebellum New England banking, Naomi Lamoreaux finds banks acting more like investment clubs established by wealthy elites to fund the entrepreneurial endeavors of bank directors. Like most antebellum enterprises, banks were not large corporate conglomerates but family businesses that generally favored the private interests of the institution's principals and their close, typically familial associates.[74]

Along with defending banks, Whigs were charged with deflecting popular hostility toward corporations. Whigs touted corporations as providing a more structured and orderly mode of economic progress. They imagined corporations in an innocuous light, as mere associations of capital organized by honest entrepreneurs who voluntarily forged contractual relations with other interested parties. These contracts were made between equals, subject to the legislature's approval, and helped promote a sense of solidarity within the business community. According to Whig political economy, corporations not only advanced the interests of their shareholders but, by providing a service to the public, in theory fostered widespread economic improvement and thus served the long-term interests of the commonwealth.[75] Corporate charters were not confined to private businesses, either; they were granted for all types of ventures, from the establishment of local municipalities to turnpike, canal, and railroad companies, waterworks, insurance, benevolent societies, manufacturers, colleges, and of course banks. Across the antebellum period, charters were extended almost every day, no matter the legislature's political tilt. In 1808 a Massachusetts court ruled that the liability of stockholders for corporate debts was limited. Almost three decades later, the first general law of incorporation was passed in Connecticut.[76] General acts expedited corporate creation, allowing states to grant charters to business interests that did not promise to fulfill a particular public good and at least pretend to serve the community. The rapid pace at which corporations proliferated shows that many Americans, even during the Jacksonian age, harbored a Whiggish affinity for corporate entities.

The corporatization and financialization of the antebellum economy is not, however, evidence that American hostility toward finance was insignificant. Financial corporations developed in spite of the anti-finance consensus that marked the period's economic literature. Indeed, even Whig advocates of finance agreed that certain tendencies of financial institutions were so damaging to the social and economic fabric of America that they required close state oversight. The Whig model was driven by state initiatives, and set in a broader economic agenda hostile to market imperatives. This was finance without capitalism. Whigs backed the modernization of American financial institutions—comparable to their support for industry through tariffs—from a decidedly antimarket position. They had the appetite for financial capitalism, but only so long as finance was carefully managed by legislatures and conservative bank directors.

The New Englander Nathan Appleton exemplified ambiguities in the Whig position toward finance and markets. A "cotton Whig," financier, merchant, and principal of the Boston Associates, Appleton articulated the Whig case for government oversight of the financial sector. Born in New Hampshire in 1779, Appleton was one of the founders of the factory complexes at Waltham and Lowell and became a leader in American manufacturing. He also served in the Massachusetts House of Representatives, then was elected to Congress in the early 1830s as an anti-Jacksonian and later in the 1840s as a Whig. He died in Boston in 1861.[77]

Appleton's criticisms of banking echoed the anxieties of the nation's established commercial and industrial elite. Conservatives of his ilk took issue with the entrepreneurial upstarts—the American nouveaux riches of finance—that the financial revolution encouraged.[78] The spectacular and seemingly spontaneous fortunes that financiers amassed were said to spring from very "unnatural" economic circumstances. Appleton shared this concern with contemporary republican opponents, but he was no agrarian. In fact, agrarian hostility toward finance, he wrote, derived "from a superficial view of the subject."[79] Still, Appleton condemned reckless bank directors for abandoning moral responsibility in their business practices. "Banks are established as models of punctuality and honorable dealing; their notes have obtained circulation on the ground that the promise to furnish the coin on demand was of the most sacred character." New England Whigs like Appleton were reared in a culture instilled with a Puritan ethic, where political economy was taught as a branch of moral philosophy and stressed an early form of what business scholars today know as social responsibility.[80] As Sean Wilentz has demonstrated, Whigs mixed spiritual with material reforms, promoting state efforts to "help direct and even coerce individuals toward what they considered personal improvement."[81] Appleton's father, Isaac, was deacon at his local Congregational church for more than thirty years and raised Nathan along strict Calvinist lines. Business ethics influenced his understanding of finance, and he expected the same from others. Appleton called on bank directors, "selected from those of the highest standing in the mercantile community," to honor their "most solemn pledge" to pay in full the face value of their notes. Suspensions of payment in particular, once a rarity, now occurred with shameless regularity. Appleton described them as "an opiate, which if justifiable at all, can only be justifiable where the paroxysms are so violent as to endanger life." He condemned suspensions as "a broken promise," likening them to spiritual transgression. "It is difficult to perceive," Appleton continued, "how honorable men, holding the office of bank directors, can reconcile a continued suspension to a proper sense of moral obligation."[82]

Unlike the liberal republican critics, however, Appleton attached his patrician review of banking parvenus to lectures on the wider social and economic benefits provided by sound financial institutions. In typical Whig fashion, he described credit and paper currency as fundamental to the national economy. Contrary to hard-money activists, he saw paper currency as "an instrument of the first necessity to a nation. No trade or commerce can be carried on without it."[83] Neither were currency brokers parasites preying on unsuspecting workers. They afforded an essential and legitimate public service in processing notes disfavored by the community. To counter negligent directors of "wildcat" banks, Appleton recommended, in the words of one historian, "mechanisms for enforcing responsibility."[84] He favored restrictions on the ability of banks to issue currency, with a stringent specie-to-note ratio of 20 percent and a 3 percent tax on circulating notes. Appleton figured tighter ratios would reduce profitability for banks whose sole function was issuing notes for circulation, and thus discourage their spread. Moreover, banks should operate "under a surveillance" of business and legislators. "The whole security lies in A LARGE CAPITAL AND A SMALL CIRCULATION," Appleton emphasized. "It is exceedingly important that the legislature should preserve an entire control over the bank currency, by reserving the right to regulate, by any general law, the amount of bank issues in proportion to capital, and the description of bills which may be put in circulation."[85]

Whigs like Appleton craved a currency as permanently fixed as the yardstick and the pint. He aimed to abolish banks founded for speculative purposes. The supposed self-regulating virtues of the market should not prevent the more highly capitalized national and regional banks from policing the smaller country banks. Appleton's position reflected the conservative, entrenched economic interests that populated the elite ranks of the New England Whig party. These were not freebooting, footloose financial revolutionaries. Appleton exhibited little confidence in perfectly free-market mechanisms to properly administer financial expansion. But Whig opposition to the heedless proliferation of finance did not derive from republican concerns. Appleton shared with republican and laissez-faire opponents anxiety over the deleterious social residuals of unfettered finance. But Whigs preferred the nineteenth-century economy to Augustan England's. Appleton was, after all, one of the founders of American industrialization. Whigs envisioned guardianship over the modern American economy, with the state assuming paternal responsibility for sound growth. Banks, preferably large institutions headed by respectable, judicious, and incorruptible directors, secured by an "enlightened public opinion," and closely watched over by experienced and discerning legislators, would be managed effectively, Appleton asserted; "the public security requires it."[86]

Not all Whigs conformed to a statist program, however. Some even called for reforms based on free-market models. George Opdyke, onetime mayor of New York and a prominent figure in the Free Soil and Republican Parties, worked within free-market parameters to tighten the bonds between creditor and borrower. Born in 1805 in New Jersey, Opdyke grew familiar with banks as a young man through his business associations in New York's Chamber of Commerce.[87] He presented his views on finance in his 1851 *A Treatise on Political Economy*. A dry goods chain made Opdyke a millionaire; for a time his textile and merchandising businesses were the largest in New York City. And as a "conservative greenbacker," he later exercised influence over Lincoln's treasury secretary Salmon P. Chase.[88]

Opdyke was no extremist, but certain parts of his reforms were nothing short of radical. To be sure, he conformed to Whiggish standards by advocating restrictions on the financial system, including the elimination of all convertible notes, over the course of ten years, except bills issued by the national government, which would be irredeemable. This amounted to a national currency, similar to the Republican plan promulgated under the Legal Tender Act of 1862 that created the greenback. "The functions of money are so interwoven with the affairs of men," Opdyke found, "that its stability and uniformity of value are almost as essential to their prosperity as is the establishment and maintenance of the right of property itself." The national paper currency, according to Opdyke, "instead of being governed by natural laws, would be governed by positive law." Managing the currency was, after all, the charge of the government, delegated under the broad authority covered by the power of the purse.[89] Opdyke's work toward a national irredeemable currency epitomized the sometimes slippery ideological disposition of Whigs. The anti-tariff, big-city businessman was no anticapitalist; nor does he come across as an entrepreneur thirsting for cheap credit. Rather Opdyke was genuinely interested in neutralizing the social evils engendered by finance. Like other republican opponents, Opdyke believed that the paper currency system, which he compared to "the chance-like uncertainties of the gambling table," promoted "idleness, dissipation, improvidence and other vicious habits." Most disturbingly, he argued, finance bred a business culture of moral malfeasance. Opdyke likened credit markets to a game of hide and seek. "As the matter now stands . . . it is accounted meritorious to evade the payment of an honest debt." Opdyke continued, "Creditors look more to the law than to the honesty or honor of their debtors for the enforcement of payments; and while such is the case we must expect that evasions of payment will be regarded as skillful achievements over the law and the sagacity of creditors, rather than as acts of dishonor."[90]

Under these circumstances, the abolition of laws for the collection of debt seemed the only viable option. This would ensure that creditors investigate fully their borrower's requests and capacity for repayment. Extensions of credit, and its collection, would rest on the decency and moral constitution of men rather than on legal recourse. "Increase the demand for integrity of character, frugality and diligence, by basing credits exclusively upon them, and you will soon stimulate and develope these desirable qualities of character to such a degree that any one who should prove so far deficient therein as to refuse the payment of a debt . . . would be utterly discountenanced in all respectable society." Curtailing state involvement in creditor-debtor disputes and forcing lenders to exercise discretion in credit extensions promised a moderate, more prudent set of banking standards, and with it a more subdued expansion of financial institutions. The desire to reinstate traditional methods of credit networks based on intimate, symbiotic relations evoked earlier republican ideals of civic and social moralism. Opdyke aimed at curbing the buccaneering banking practices that from his perspective were damaging to market mechanisms within the financial sector. "Increase the demand for virtue and you will increase the supply; enlarge its rewards, and you will not fail to improve its quality, and thereby elevate the national standard of morality."[91] But by removing legal institutions from the process of debt collection, later antebellum opponents like Opdyke placed greater emphasis on market imperatives than earlier republicans like Taylor. Opdyke employed republican opposition as a medium to advance laissez-faire within the financial sector and thus curb the economically and socially destructive features of finance. His ultimate goal, unlike earlier republican critics of finance, was not reversion to an agrarian ideal or absolute abolition of banks. Rather, liberal republicanism for Opdyke was a means to sanitize financial markets of their immoral tendencies and cultivate a sound, ethical commercial class.

Whigs were not immune to this particular brand of liberal republican finance. Richard Hildreth exemplifies this point. Born in 1807, Hildreth was a prolific writer, most notably of a six-volume *History of the United States*, published between 1849 and 1852. Harvard educated, abolitionist, poet, essayist, moral philosopher, and founder and editor of the Boston-based Whig paper *Atlas*, Hildreth presented his views of American finance in his 1840 work *Banks, Banking, and Paper Currencies*.[92] In it he offered what stands as the most acute Whig endorsement of free banking. His enthusiasm for Smithian laissez-faire while opposing financial corporatism conflicted with conventional Whig thinking on banks. Hildreth advocated free markets as a means to spur growth in the financial sector. Whiggish support of financial institutions did not necessitate abandonment of laissez-faire principles. Hildreth's free-market critique of finance indicates that some Whigs shared traditional liberal republican concerns over the supposed corrosive nature of state-finance relations. His writings conform to the traditional binary association between finance and intellectual capitalism. Put differently, with Hildreth, intellectual capitalism compelled financial capitalism.

Hildreth criticized state and national legislatures for disrupting the otherwise natural and sound operations of financial institutions. Most state intervention in the financial sector originated in some form of political chicanery. Jackson's bank war, for instance, was "for the purpose of creating a new bank, the stock of which might be shared among their friends and partisans." The state banks, or "pet banks," that fought against Biddle's behemoth were rewarded with the redistribution of federal deposits—the "spoils of victory" according to Hildreth.[93] New York banks were shown preference. By 1835 three Wall Street banks held more than $5 million in federal funds.[94] Hildreth anticipated corruption. Legislative favoritism crossed party lines too, he charged: "It was most amply justified by the practice of all our legislative bodies, which have ever been in the constant habit of confining the grant of bank charters to influential persons of the prevailing political party."[95] Hildreth's assessment harkened back to republican anxieties over the potential abuse occasioned by conspiring politicians and financiers. But Hildreth was no Jeffersonian. He found that traditional agrarian hostility toward banks stemmed from Jefferson's reading of the Physiocrats, who, Hildreth determined, "never had much knowledge of commerce, and who always regarded it with suspicion if not with contempt."[96]

Hildreth's repudiation of political finance was rare for antebellum Whigs. His anticorporatist, laissez-faire criticisms of the banking system showcased the complexities in the Whig financial discourse. They also indicated a lack of consensus within the pro-finance movement. Hildreth believed banks ought not "to lie at the mercy of ignorant and reckless politicians, or at the mercy, no less to be deprecated, of a few purse-proud, domineering, dictatorial bank directors," but rather be "controlled and guided by . . . the Laws of Trade—laws which do not act by jerks and starts . . . but by a constant, steady, gentle, yet inevitable pressure."[97] These recommendations amounted to free banking. However, laissez-faire banking reforms would not necessarily hasten the proliferation of financial institutions. Multiply the number of banks, Hildreth calculated, and the ensuing competition would limit fraud and mismanagement, foster intra-sector equilibrium, and mitigate the speculative proclivities of financiers. He disparaged the federal bank, referring to it as a "sort of absolute monarch," anointed with a national charter that prejudiced ordinary Americans and investors into accepting at face value its reports of business acumen and solvency. Only by abolishing the monopoly control of the national bank, along with promulgating general laws for bank incorporations, could market forces check profligate circulation of notes through regular calls for redemption.[98] His admiration for banks as agents of economic progress combined with his desire to see the financial sector freed from the fetters of the state comports with what historians understand as the conventional alliance between intellectual capitalism and financial institutions, but in the antebellum discourse, Hildreth's markets-finance nexus makes him an intellectual anomaly.

Hildreth's and Appleton's essays on banking were published during cataclysmic financial flashpoints in American history. By the middle decades of the antebellum period most Americans had acclimated themselves to the commercial cycles of boom and bust, but few could imagine the ferocity of the coming collapse. The bubble burst first in New Orleans in March 1837. By summer the contagion had metastasized north to New York. Banks across the country suspended payments, and then shut their doors. Commodity prices dropped 40 percent, New York cotton prices fell by 50 percent, real estate values plummeted, and states were unable to pay the interest on debts accumulated over the boom period through lavish spending on internal improvements.[99] Bullion was hoarded, the unemployed scrambled for charitable relief, and according to one contemporary report, "Some died of starvation. Some were frozen to death. Many, through exposure and privation, contracted fatal diseases."[100] Material hard times took a toll on hearts and minds as well—asylums listed financial trauma as one of the leading causes of insanity. The economy rebounded for a brief period in 1838 only to crash again in 1839. A full recovery would take more than a decade. In 1841, to ease the pain of impoverished Americans and yet gain politically from the economic crisis, Whigs pushed through Congress the National Bankruptcy Act. One in every hundred adult white males took advantage of the new measure, filing 41,000 bankruptcies in the eighteen months before the law was repealed.[101]

Peter Temin, an economic historian, has largely discounted what contemporaries attributed as the causes of the 1837 calamity. Jackson's "war on banks," though misguided, did not precipitate the crisis. Rather an inauspicious confluence of events tied to, among other things, the spike and subsequent collapse in global cotton prices, disruptions in the international silver trade traced to Chinese demand for opium, and the apparent mismanagement of specie reserves by the Bank of England initiated a string of events that brought financial affliction across the Atlantic economy, of which the United States was a casualty. "The economy was not the victim of Jacksonian politics;" Temin concludes, "Jackson's policies were the victims of economic fluctuations."[102] Whigs thought otherwise, placing blame squarely on the shoulders of Jackson. Jessica Lepler's cultural history of the panic demonstrates how Whigs deflected culpability away from individual financiers and sought remedy for the crisis by reversing Jackson's program of decentralization. The panic, according to Whigs, was caused by ill-advised government policies—the abandonment of Hamiltonian political economy—and could only be fixed through effective state-sponsored management. Conservative, institutionalist bankers and merchants in the Northeast advocated paternal-state rescue, imploring Biddle to serve as a lender of last resort. But Biddle's temple of finance on Philadelphia's Chestnut Street was eviscerated by Jackson's removal of government deposits. Renamed under its new charter as the United States Bank of Pennsylvania, it stopped specie payments in 1839 and again the following year, declared bankruptcy in 1841, and was handed over to trustees.[103]

Jacksonian Democrats, themselves eager to shape the narrative, argued that the administration's policies had purposely delegated financial responsibility to individuals. In the highly politicized atmosphere of the 1830s financial discourse, the Jacksonian brand of intellectual capitalism held American citizens, especially financiers, responsible for the vicissitudes of commercial fluctuations. Laissez-faire Whig anomalies like Hildreth confirmed this logic, Hildreth writing in 1840 that commercial downturns were inevitable: "They are one of those evils which flesh is heir to; they may be alleviated, but cannot be radically cured.... In countries where trade and manufactures are at a low ebb, the great mass of the people always remain in that state of destitution and idleness which is witnessed with us only at the moment of some great commercial crisis—a crisis which soon passes by and gives place to the state of prosperity by which it was preceded."[104]

Calls for the laissez-faire reforms suggested by Hildreth were amplified in the liberal-republican opposition movement of the later antebellum period (1830–1860), though they were pursuing fundamentally different ends. Free-market reforms were intended to moderate, or in some cases reverse entirely, the influence of finance. They drew on traditional republican opposition thought traced to Taylor, illustrating the chronological range of classical republicanism. "The great Banking bubble of America was the same in principle as the South Sea Bubble," declared William Gouge, a respected Jacksonian free marketer, "but of longer continuance, and involved in it the fortunes of the whole community."[105] But the liberal opposition movement of the later antebellum period widened its attacks on finance to include a nuanced set of denunciations that challenged, in different ways, the bedrock principles on which the financial system rested. Still others understood that finance was an inescapable feature of the free-market system that they cherished, and employed an exaggerated version of Smithian laissez-faire as a vehicle to check financial proliferation.

The later antebellum liberal opponents identified many of the same points of criticism as earlier republicans, with equal emphasis paid to the moral depravity of banks. Financial institutions encouraged a frantic social psychosis that surrendered all rational thought. Financiers employed "every art of cajolery and allurement ... excited a thirst for speculation ... until it increased to a delirious fever, and men, in the epidemic frenzy of the hour, wildly rushed upon all sorts of desperate adventures."[106] Profligate extensions of credit and specious expansions of paper money induced, one wrote, "a reckless fanatical spirit of speculation, unparalleled, perhaps, in the history of the world."[107] Finance also normalized debased conventions in commercial affairs that undermined social morality and justice. The financial system was "wrong in principle, and must be ruinous in its effects on the integrity, the morals and the ultimate prosperity of a people."[108]

And later antebellum liberal critics kept to the traditions of republican political economy by focusing contempt on credit. Credit created a socioeconomic order founded on fantasy and delusion. "A very uncertain and fluctuating thing," credit contorted reality by warping personal and social estimations of wealth.[109] Mental and emotional lunacy were offshoots of a frenetic credit-filled atmosphere "that madden the brains of whole communities," casualties of a banking system, "the insane root that takes the reason prisoner."[110] Credit also transformed the social divisions of labor, pushing Americans to shun traditional forms of respectable employment. The plow stood idle, the merchant square vacant, and the workshop silent, "while to those employed in the paper money laboratories, the temptations to fraud and peculation are so strong, and the opportunities so inviting, that many men of ordinary honesty are thereby turned into rogues."[111] In short, credit disturbed the otherwise natural, positive social enhancements of market-driven economic development. Credit was also damned for its association with debt. Indebtedness was akin to slavery, the person and property of debtors subjugated to the whims of creditors. A source of humiliation and shame, debt signified the worst kind of oppression, for a debtor was always "reduced to the condition of his [creditor's] bondsman or serf.... Debt is the prolific mother of crime; it taints the course of life in all its streams."[112]

But the later antebellum liberal opponents broke from earlier republican rhetorical customs by intensifying claims that finance undermined free-market institutions. Finance was, in essence, capitalism's profligate son. Here, intellectual capitalism was retooled against finance. As Americans grew more familiar with the internal operations of banks they began to better understand, as they saw it, the machinations that financiers routinely employed to upset the natural order of free markets. The later antebellum republican-liberal opposition literature also focused on the supposed evils of paper currency. Paper notes represented fictitious values, at times redeemable for fractions of their alleged worth, at other times not redeemable at all, but at all times a "fraudulent system of money making out of rags." A banknote was "paper trash" of "no intrinsic value, and which a breath of public suspicion may at any time destroy."[113] Critics charged that specie convertibility was a farce. It was tacitly understood that paper notes were not backed by specie reserves but rather arbitrary values that left society in a state of flux, fixed to a sliding scale that measured human fantasies rather than commercial reality. "All men of ordinary sagacity know that the representative character of convertible paper money is, in part at least, an ingenious fiction."[114] Indeed, as one cynic wrote, "the whole amount of the precious metals scattered throughout the world, would scarcely be sufficient to redeem the paper credits of the United States."[115]

The tirades against finance, and paper notes in particular, should not be mistaken for anticapitalist invective. Indeed, the liberal opposition insisted that by restricting financial institutions, a more durable free market would emerge, promoting the interests of business and labor and encouraging economic growth. The period's most influential reformer, William Gouge, illustrates the dynamics between Jacksonian-era laissez-faire and finance. A journalist and publisher by trade, Gouge also worked intermittently in the Treasury Department for thirty years. His 1833 *The Curse of Paper-Money and Banking; or, A Short History of Banking in the United States of America*, according to Dorfman, was "the bible" of the Jacksonian hard-money movement and earned Gouge an international reputation on banking.[116] Gouge also edited the Jacksonian *Journal of Banking*. There he repeated the standard Jacksonian maxim "We are friendly to free banking." But Gouge was referring only to banks of deposit, lending, and discount, not to the free issue of notes. "Free competition in paper money banking would be little more than a competition of cunning," fostering a commercial environment that was "essentially evil."[117] Gouge's writings captured the blurred lines of ideological distinction found in the opposition to finance. His denunciations of corporate banks, and his opposition to financial institutions in general, were couched in the parlance of Smithian laissez-faire. He imagined himself a "disinterested political economist" helping Americans understand that the prevailing economic difficulties were the effects of "a Banking System resting on principles fundamentally erroneous."[118]

The opening pages of his *Short History* cited Smith as an authority on banking. Gouge wrote how Smith had delineated the advantages of Scotland's financial system, "carried on by *unincorporated* companies, each of the members of which is responsible, in his whole personal and real estate, for the whole amount of the debts due by the company."[119] Smith advocated a mixed currency, which included limitations on the circulation of notes under £5, as well as what Jacksonians like Gouge interpreted as a free-bank system. The banking industry seemed suited for joint-stock corporations, Smith argued, since company charters were typically inclusive of strict governing constitutions, rendering them "more tenacious of established rules than any private copartnery." These shall be granted, however, without "any exclusive privilege," or exemption "from some of the general laws which take place with regard to all their neighbours." Smith offered this recommendation after discussing the South Sea Company and other examples of British firms granted exclusive trading rights that, he noted, were almost always marked by "negligence and profusion." Competition between banks, Smith found, "obliges all of them to be more circumspect in their conduct." Besides, "if any branch of trade," including banking, "be advantageous to the public, the freer and more general the competition, it will always be the more so." Still, Smith, cognizant of the "frequent bankruptcies to which ... beggarly banks must be liable," and knowing full well the potential for "very great calamity" attending an excessive circulation of notes, did advocate legislative checks on finance. "But those exertions of the natural liberty of a few individuals, which might endanger the security of the whole society, are, and ought to be, restrained by the laws of all governments; of the most free, as well as of the most despotical."[120] Banking, after all, was no different from any other economic sector, "as simple in its nature as the trade in flour or the trade in tobacco, and ought to be conducted on the same principles." Like Smith, Gouge argued that the natural economic order was governed by mechanisms "in general so uncertain as frequently to baffle all calculations," tying society, with or without its consent, to "the seesaw of fortune. Now we go up, and now we go down."[121] Banking, industry, and commerce conformed to natural cycles. A government that attempted to control nature's design did so at its peril. "Half the evils of society," Gouge announced, "arise from the attempts of government to do that which ought to be done by individuals."[122] To restore the natural order, let competition serve as the final regulator, and the laws of supply and demand be the determinant of value.

Historians have erred in suggesting that Gouge's hard-money program advanced labor/agrarian extremism.[123] Rather Gouge's writings demonstrate that the hard-money movement articulated criticisms compatible with laissez-faire values. Gouge sought reforms aimed at preserving and strengthening market institutions, shorn of what he perceived were the contaminating influences of corporate finance. For Jacksonians like Gouge, finance was the enemy of capitalism. Gouge's ideas were not conceived in a philosopher's closet, either. His recommendations had practical, real-world policy significance. "Make gold and silver coin the exclusive money of the country," Gouge declared, and "the evils of the system would be greatly diminished."[124] In 1835 Jackson's treasury secretary Levi Woodbury proposed legislation prohibiting the circulation of banknotes under $10. A bill was introduced in Congress, sponsored by James Polk, but defeated along party lines. Combined with the 1836 Specie Circular that required federal land sale transactions to be made only in gold and silver, Gouge helped shape the monetary system and contributed to the growing legitimacy of the hard-money movement by outlining the feasibility of abolishing paper money.[125]

The Massachusetts lawyer Lysander Spooner further illustrates the range of antebellum liberal opposition culture. Spooner's criticisms were reminiscent of republican conventions; however, they were marked by an unequivocal allegiance to laissez-faire values. Born in 1808, he spent years as a young man under the legal tutelage of future Suffolk County chief justice Charles Allen.

Later he served for a short period as a clerk at Gallatin's National Bank of New York, but his education in finance was shaped by the Panic of 1837. At the time, Spooner was speculating in Ohio land. The crisis sent him back to his father's farm in rural Massachusetts to mull over possible reforms. He published his ideas in *Poverty, Its Illegal Causes and Legal Cure* (1846) and *The New System of Paper Currency* (1861). Today Spooner is remembered as one of America's most prolific philosophical anarchists. His political economy expressed an anarcho-capitalist bent, determined to maximize individual liberties through an absolutist form of free-market economics.[126]

To fix finance, Spooner focused on alterations to the procedures behind debt settlement. Spooner's measures were reminiscent of earlier republican demands to reestablish credit networks on a more intimate basis. But his program was broader in scope and, if implemented, would have reconstructed the entire financial system on a strict laissez-faire model. At the maturation of a debt, Spooner argued, the borrower ought to be liable only for what he could muster at that moment. Since debt was the equivalent of a value purchased by creditors, subject to rise or fall throughout the term of the loan, its value, like all property, was exposed to market risks and thus carried the potential for variation. A lender assumed as much risk and responsibility for a debt as the borrower. Debt, Spooner figured, "has no legal obligation, and generally no moral one, beyond the means of the debtor to pay at the time the debt becomes due." Since none could predict what might become of an enterprise, all contracts and obligations made without provisioning for "all the contingencies and accidents that may occur to defeat his purposes" were "void from the beginning." Moreover, if capital is lent for purposes that appear to be "a manifest impossibility," it is an "immoral and absurd contract," and thus invalid at inception.[127] Spooner called for the abolition of laws regulating the collection of debt. Doing so would tighten credit and incline lenders to inspect the substance of a borrower's plans, and return banking to a romanticized age marked by symbiotic and ethical commercial relations. "When a capitalist loans money to a laborer . . . he does not look, for himself, into the merits of the enterprise as he would if he knew that his ultimate security for his capital depended solely upon the success of the enterprise, instead of depending also upon the subsequent earnings of the laborer."[128] Spooner articulated absolute confidence in the market to provide creditors with perfect information about the industry and integrity of individual borrowers. And in doing so, Spooner stands out as the essential representation of an exaggerated free-banking ideologue.

Theophilus Fisk, editor of freethinking journals, public lecturer, and Bostonian labor leader, also contributed to contemporary bonds between anti-finance and laissez-faire. During the Jacksonian era Fisk passed his time voicing a fiery dislike for all things related to finance. "I therefore feel it my bounden duty," he wrote, "to oppose all banks except such as the Almighty made—fishing banks and sand banks—and all shares, but the plough share."[129] Fisk's hostility toward finance, however, was not premised on an anticapitalist bias as historians have suggested.[130] "I am not an agrarian in the perverted sense of the term," he declared to an audience at Charleston in 1837. He assured readers of his laissez-faire credentials by commending Ricardo as "seldom in the wrong." What drove Fisk to pen impassioned anti-finance tracts was what he perceived were the monopolistic tendencies of bank charters. "It is the artificial inequality alone that I oppose, created by partial legislation, by monopolies and exclusive privileges—it is the granting of exclusive favors by the legislature to a privileged nobility." Corporate charters emboldened "speculating gamesters" across the nation, "like swarms of locusts," performing a "cold calculation, which is carried into all the relations of society."[131] Fisk captured the conventional Jacksonian Democratic position by advocating economic equality of opportunity, not an equality of economic conditions. Legislatures thwarted these efforts. They were besieged by corruptive influences in the form of bank directors, creating gross disparities of wealth through the legalized fraud of paper money. "Among all the labor saving machines invented by human ingenuity to enable men to grow rich without earning any thing," Fisk railed on, "that of manufacturing money out of paper rags holds the highest place in the estimation of many." A committed libertarian, he carried the badge of the common man when he announced, "I go for equal laws, equal rights, equal means of acquiring property *by honest labor (not by legislation,)* equal burdens and equal benefits. I would neither rob the few for the benefit of the many, nor plunder the many for the benefit of the few."[132]

Fisk gave expression to the equal rights campaign that climaxed in the 1830s. These efforts were centralized under the banner of the short-lived Locofoco movement, founded in 1835 and named after a new type of match that the radical group ignited to relight Tammany Hall after conservative Democrats shut the gas. The strength of the party came from the poorer wards of

New York, mainly artisans, mechanics, and labor activists disillusioned with what they considered were Jackson's half-measures at reform. Their mission, according to Fitzwilliam Byrdsall, the organization's recording secretary, was to counter the corporatist, soft-money Democrats that controlled Tammany. The "Methodists of Democracy," the Locofocos declared that the current "system of finance in general use . . . ought to be abolished with the least practical delay."[133] Formally, its Declaration of Principles aimed at restoring the original intentions of the Constitution, that is, equal rights, simple government, and a metallic currency, all of which were, by the 1830s, undermined by "a leagued band of paper-promise coiners" operating a "cheating game of hazard" and a "mean mode of robbery" through corporate trickery.[134]

The surest method to destroy the paper system was to "let credit alone."[135] Providence implanted in all men the competitive principle, which should be granted full exercise in every sector of the economy, but especially in banking. Corporatist-inspired banking legislation effectively "pronounced the great Architect to be a bungler," and like "beasts of prey lying in wait for the honest laborers of society," bank marauders left no choice for the republican, liberty-loving citizen but to sacrifice the Christian God at the altar of Mammon. Clinton Roosevelt, an attorney, economist, newspaper editor, and early leader of the movement, transmitted the seriousness of Locofoco intentions, declaring in his *Principia of Social Science*, "we require not a partial change, but a thorough destruction of the present peculating banking system."[136] These were New York's laborites determined to stop financial encroachment, commercial expansionism, and industrial development, through the strict observance of an antimonopolist, Smithian inspired laissez-faire.[137]

The campaign for equal rights found its most powerful voice, although he was never officially a member of the Locofocos, in William Leggett. Leggett lived an eventful yet abbreviated life. Born in 1801 in Savannah, Georgia, as a young man he attended Georgetown College. The failure of his father's business shortened his enrollment there, and Leggett soon joined the navy. When Leggett abandoned his post to fight a duel, the midshipman was court-martialed, imprisoned, and at twenty-four dismissed from the service. In 1828 he moved to New York, where he found work as a theatrical and literary critic for local papers. William Cullen Bryant recognized talent in Leggett, hiring him as a writer for the *Evening Post*. Leggett was, however, hindered by yellow fever contracted while he was in the navy, and the disease ended his life just before his fortieth birthday.[138] Leggett's critique of finance was published in two widely read periodicals that he established in the late 1830s, the *Plaindealer* and the *Examiner*.

As Jeffrey Sklansky has shown, Leggett helped antebellum Americans better conceptualize financial phenomena by distinguishing between economic realities, namely markets, and economic abstractions: credit, paper bills, and corporate bank charters. Finance flooded minds with delusion, erasing the boundaries between fact and fiction. "Men, now-a-days," Leggett observed, "go to bed deeming themselves rich, and wake in the morning to find themselves stripped of even the little they had."[139] His mission was to pull back the curtain, lay bare the financial fraud, and bring to center stage the Jacksonian era's great moral economic drama. Leggett's own *Plaindealer* was patterned after the London *Examiner*, an early nineteenth-century weekly that commented on economics, politics, society, and theater. His earlier work as a theater critic versed him in a literary style that set up the melodrama between capitalism's dual antagonists—the idealized marketplace and wicked finance.[140] Banking encouraged a "fever of speculation ... the moral epidemic of the land," spread by the moneyed aristocracy that now abandoned "the deluded men whom their deceitful lures seduced so far upon the treacherous sea of credit."[141]

Leggett wrote many of his economic tracts in the spring of 1837, just as the nation was teetering toward crisis. Sklansky notes that Leggett contributed to the antebellum belief that "financial panic and economic depression represented the corruption, and not the completion, of the sovereignty of the market."[142] For Leggett, banks were the problem; markets were the solution. He further solidified the intellectual union between laissez-faire and anti-finance in the antebellum literature. His writings are additional indication that the later antebellum opposition was fully committed to the market regime. Competitive markets were encouraged by resisting the spread of financial institutions. These values were hardly outside of contemporary conventional wisdom. In fact, by the late 1830s they were fundamental to American economic thought. For Leggett, the "sister doctrines" of republicanism and laissez-faire were reciprocating ideologies. The campaign against banks was for Leggett the most important front in the struggle for human freedom. The American banking system was "an essentially aristocratic institution," inimical to democracy and contrary to the canons of equal rights. It was the latter that

Leggett was most concerned with, for the subversion of equal rights posed the greatest challenge to republican society. In an article defending Jackson's war on banks, Leggett articulated his stock maxims: "The universal political equality of mankind, the intelligence and integrity of the great mass of the people, and the absolute right of the majority to govern."[143] Financial interests threatened to usurp political power and enslave the public, Leggett warned, with "their tendency to build up a privileged order, and to concentrate all wealth and power in the hands of a few."[144] "Let the Banks perish! Let the monopolists be swept from the board! Let the whole brood of privileged money-changers give place to the hardy offsprings of commercial freedom, who ask for no protection but equal laws, and no exemption from the shocks of boundless competition."[145]

An unbending commitment to laissez-faire was the driving force behind Leggett's pleas for republican equal rights. "Is there any thing in the nature of banking," Leggett asked, "which makes it an exception to the universal rule, that enterprise and competition are the best regulators of trade?"[146] His criticisms of finance were comparable to Smith's censures of mercantilism. "Protect their persons and property," Leggett declared, legislate uniform and general laws, "and all the rest they can do themselves."[147] He cited Say and Stewart, and pointed to Smith's "immortal work" to validate his belief that laissez-faire and republican government advanced "the largest liberty; . . . both are equally opposed to all special privileges and immunities; and both would leave men to manage their own affairs, in their own way, so that they did not invade each others natural rights."[148] Leggett called for banking to be "left open to the free competition of all who choose to enter into that pursuit."[149] Mixing government and business inevitably led to partial legislation that spoiled market purity. Purge society of the "unholy alliance between politics and banking," Leggett demanded, and "let commerce, and let the currency . . . regulate themselves."[150]

In an 1837 *Plaindealer* article Leggett explained the omnipotent character of the natural economic order and the shortcomings of legislation in its attempts to manage economic phenomena. "While trade is in prosperous operation, it seems governed by laws as fixed and harmonious and to most minds as inscrutable, as those of the universe. Each link in the mighty chain, each part of the prodigious whole, performs its allotted office, and contributes to the grand result—the improvement of the physical and intellectual condition of mankind." Employing language analogous to Smithian philosophical skepticism, Leggett continued: "But when derangement takes place, when any thing occurs to interrupt the harmonious movement, such are the mutual relations and dependence of the various parts, that the inquirer is bewildered in his attempts to investigate the cause of the confusion."[151] Directives promulgated by "ignorant legislators" attempted "to control what is in its nature uncontrollable, and should be as free as air."[152] In short, markets worked best when left alone. "Leave trade to its laws, as we leave water to the laws of nature, and both will eventually be equally certain to find their proper level."[153] Free markets inspired stability, while state interference precipitated financial seduction, fictional wealth, commercial fantasy, and disequilibrium, since it "forces credit out of its natural channel."[154] Leggett discovered that by liberating financial markets from state management "the simple order of nature" would be left to bend organically to universal commands. "That is most excellent," Leggett declared, "which comes nearest to the simplicity of nature."[155]

Leggett's admiration for laissez-faire coupled with his underlying reticence toward financial institutions demonstrates that the bonds between intellectual capitalism and finance in the popular historical imagination were mostly absent in antebellum writings. For opponents like Leggett, finance was not an essential element of market economies. And the dichotomies maintained in the historiography between republicanism and capitalism, and finance and statism, mask the complexities of the anti-finance movement. Such was the nature of hybrid intellectual capitalism. Furthermore, to imply that the free banking proposals of Gouge, Spooner, and Leggett are illustrative of a disingenuous strategy to advance the pecuniary interests of state-bank directors is simply inaccurate. Neither was the opposition literature stocked with working-class agitators calling for across-the-board revolution. By categorizing the opposition literature into two distinct, class-based interest groups, historians have discounted important theoretical developments in the discourse. Criticisms of finance provided a vehicle for opponents to articulate broader, more nuanced economic philosophies.

Antebellum Americans constituted this nation's earliest generations to experience modern financial capitalism. These interactions were unprecedented, sometimes confusing occurrences that conjured up novel responses and inspired a broad assortment of ideological categories. And the anti-finance movement was inclusive of a wide range of personalities. Even high-brow free-trade academics articulated sharp misgivings about finance. Henry Vethake, for instance, complained that banking speculation excited "a corrupt spirit of gambling."[156] And Jacob Cardozo disparaged paper money for afflicting the world "with a moral evil" more "pestilent and dreadful" than anything that had passed before it.[157] On the opposite end of the ideological spectrum, George Frederick Holmes denounced "the financial dragons" as "absolutely fatal to public morals" and said they were "utterly antagonistic to political order or the permanent prosperity of States, and must prove the ruin of all governments. . . . They are consuming the vitals of society, and rendering the continuance of social order an impossibility."[158]

In his Farewell Address, Jackson offered parting counsel on how best to deal with the financial menace. "The paper-money system and its natural associations—monopoly and exclusive privileges—have already struck their roots too deep in the soil, and it will require all your efforts to check its further growth and to eradicate the evil." Jackson cautioned the public against designing men in finance who "will seek by every artifice to mislead and deceive the public servants."[159] Then as in more recent times, serious hostility was directed at financial institutions. Anti-finance sentiment has always been a staple of the American economic mind. Resistance toward finance was so ubiquitous in the antebellum discourse that the opposition literature constituted American convention.

In this way, finance is a bit of an economic-cultural anomaly. Since colonial times Americans have tacitly accepted even the most socially destructive and politically corrupt externalities of material capitalism. Episodic remonstrations against working conditions, inflation, monopolies, unemployment, and the like are given voice according to the ebbs and flows of economic cycles. But opposition to finance was the consistent theme in American economic intellectual culture. This is not to say the movement to modernize American financial institutions was without support. America emerged as a leader in global finance because of its pro-bank interests. Finance developed in spite of the opposition. If anything, the antebellum literature on finance indicates the detachment in American economic culture between ideology and practice. And like the debate over industry and trade, the financial literature was remarkably diverse, hampering development of a consensus. This is partly owed to the multiplicity of personal financial experiences that shaped the lives of Americans caught in the middle of significant economic transformation. Republicanism, liberalism, and Whiggish statism were just a few of the ideological platforms vying to help Americans better understand the period's transition into modern financial capitalism. The commonalities manifested in the Anglo-American republican literature, like the similarities found between antebellum and later-day financial reformers, show the historical persistency and centrality of finance in the modern sociocultural economic experience. Taken together, they reflect the rational and sometimes irrational responses to financial institutions that were, and still are, transformative, engrossing, and dauntingly complex.

8

CONCLUSION

THE OLD AND THE NEW IN AMERICAN ECONOMICS

In the inaugural 1892 issue of the *Journal of Political Economy*, J. Laurence Laughlin, an economics professor at the University of Chicago, attributed what he called a "new-born interest in economics" to the public controversy over currency and banking.[1] After the Civil War, the rapid expansion of financial institutions continued, hastened by Republicans and northeastern businessmen eager to impose uniformity on the national monetary system, reduce sovereign liabilities, and encourage industrial growth.[2] Americans understood that the stability of financial institutions was imperative for economic prosperity, yet combinations of hostility and ambivalence toward finance remained a persistent theme, just as it had been during the antebellum period. The debate continued over, among other things, the advantages of a redeemable national currency, the dangers of bank monopolies, and the government's role in regulating financial markets. And these issues were again tied to wider concerns about virtue and corruption, agrarians and aristocrats, and soft and hard money. Intermittent economic crises, the Great Depression of 1873 and the Panic of 1893, both tied to volatility in financial markets, intensified the debate and, according to Irwin Unger, a historian of Reconstruction-era finance, "generated frustrations and aggression just short of the social flash point."[3]

Since the nation's founding, and more recently during the Great Recession, financial institutions have provoked complex and energized agitations. Nearly one hundred years of American ascendancy in *haute finance* has not quelled anxieties. In the twenty-first century those who embrace and even cherish the multilayered value system undergirding free markets have expressed difficulty swallowing the financial pill. As it was in the beginning, is now, and likely shall ever be, Americans have awkward relations with debt and credit, bills and stocks, banks and bourses. And much of the dialectic, language, and framework set to help understand their position in the financial order can be traced to the antebellum literature.

In that same article, Laughlin noted how the nation's recent industrial unrest, "the strikes and the activity of labor organizations," rendered a "leavening of economic apathy throughout the whole country."[4] America's primacy in international finance largely coincided with its industrial preponderance. The latter was tied, again, inexorably, to trade policy. The postbellum debate over commercial policy further institutionalized the protectionist agenda, so that, in the words of Frank Taussig, "all feeling of opposition to high import duties almost entirely disappeared. The habit of putting on as high rates as any one asked had become so strong that it could hardly be shaken off; and even after the war, almost any increase of duties demanded by domestic producers was readily made."[5] Across the nineteenth-century battle of economic ideas, the protectionists triumphed. The moderate tariff of 1846 was an American laissez-faire moment in a century otherwise dominated by protectionism. The United States did not effectively participate in the global trading community until the early twentieth century.[6] And even into the post–World War II era, as the political scientist Arthur Stein has shown, America never assumed Britain's mantle of leadership in universal free trade. Rather, through a series of multilateral commercial treaties with its Cold War allies, the United States advanced an international political economy, Stein writes, "founded on asymmetric bargains that permitted discrimination. . . . The agreements that lowered tariff barriers led not to free trade, but freer trade. In the process, they legitimated a great deal of mercantilism and protectionism."[7]

And, as Giovanni Arrighi has suggested, the protectionists were right. Economic hegemony could be attained, over the long term, by insulating the nation's industrial energies and concentrating them toward the development of a home market.[8] In a country supplied with what in the late nineteenth century must have still seemed like immeasurable stores of natural resources, an expanding consumer base, and endless supplies of labor, protectionists could promise that restricting foreign competition in domestic markets would yield vast accumulations of industrial capital. Henry Carey's erudite writings on the inherent limitations of the Smithian natural order of liberty, his repudiation of Ricardian and Malthusian scarcity, and his celebration and defense of the laboring masses were largely ignored by postbellum Republican political coalitions that tied disparate groups for disparate reasons to tariff legislation.[9] But the tariff-for-labor argument that was championed by antebellum protectionists and intended to soften the social transition into an industrial economy was raised again, directed at successive generations of uprooted, mostly agricultural, immigrant workers largely unaccustomed to, but made subject of, the increasingly disciplined, standardized, and scientifically managed factory regime.[10]

The vertically and horizontally integrated firms that controlled the nation's commanding heights during the Gilded Age internalized markets of production and distribution, as Alfred Chandler demonstrated, through bureaucratic management and the mechanistic operations of corporate visible hands.[11] These too deserved protection, according to tariff proponents, for the same defensive reasons that antebellum infant industries did. A dynamic economy, after all, always had infant industries. Their appeals for higher tariffs were rewarded mightily, in 1883, 1890, 1922, and most infamously in 1930 with the Smoot-Hawley tariff.[12] Throughout the long nineteenth century and into the early decades of the twentieth, tariffs sheltered American manufacturers from British attempts at free trade globalization, countered "ruinous competition" from overseas, and bought American firms time to leverage their competitive positions at home, in preparation for discriminative entry into foreign markets after World War II.[13]

In the later nineteenth century, protectionist ideology was cemented in the nation's political and economic culture. It was also afforded a somewhat more auspicious intellectual setting, at least in American academia, which by the start of the twentieth century was splitting from classical conventions.[14] In 1885 John Bates Clark, then a Christian socialist and later a neoclassical professor at Columbia University, published his *The Philosophy of Wealth*, credited with initiating the American marginalist revolution in theoretical economics. Clark found value to be a measurement of utility determined by a series of subjective calculations, both personal and social. In the process, Clark, and the British economist William Stanley Jevons, helped overthrow the classical theory of value. Clark's critique of the classical canon extended beyond the theory of value, however. The emergence of industrial and financial conglomerates gave Clark reason to doubt classical assumptions of perfect competition, and he insisted that humanity was driven by motives other than pure economics. His quest for an economics "middle ground" perpetuated the already established antebellum tradition of exposing British classicism to critical revision.[15]

The post–Civil War breach with classicism was given further impetus by a full-fledged methodological rift, again emulating standards set by antebellum economists. Clark, like many American students at the time, studied in Germany and brought back to the United States an appreciation of historical economics. German universities were then excited by the historicism of Leopold von Ranke, and students of Wilhelm Roscher and Gustav von Schmoller in particular were instructed to challenge the a priori inductions of ahistorical classicism.[16] American students of the historical school imported the German *Methodenstreit* to the domestic discourse. Like the antebellum protectionists, the New School economists clamored for a more historically minded political economy. Friedrich List is the obvious conduit, but Henry Carey was by the second half of the nineteenth century celebrated in Germany for having activated that nation's historical-nationalism methodological turn in economics.[17] The controversy over method came to a head in 1885 when the so-called New School—young economists influenced by German historicism—established the American Economic Association, of which Clark was a principal founder. An early prospectus listed as its first principle "that the doctrine of *laissez-faire* is unsafe in politics and unsound in morals."[18] Its founding constitution declared, among other things, "We regard the state as an agency whose positive assistance is one of the indispensable conditions of human progress." And on the progression of the economics discipline generally, the New School conceded: "While we appreciate the work of former economists, we look not so much to speculation as to the historical and statistical study of actual conditions of economic life."[19]

Henry Carter Adams, the first PhD graduate of Johns Hopkins, an economics professor at various universities, and later president of the American Economic Association, declared shortly after his two-year sojourn in Germany the need for "an American Political Economy."[20] In this way, Adams echoed calls of earlier protectionists. There are clear ties between the principles of the New School and antebellum protectionist ideology. Both envisioned the state as a facilitator of economic development, and both believed democratic institutions should be employed to promote the people's economic interests.

Both emphasized the inductive method, arguing that economic theory was dependent upon prevailing social, political, and economic conditions, and both favored practical solutions over universal laws.[21]

Postbellum American economic thought and policy demonstrate that the intellectual trajectory of protectionism extended well beyond the antebellum discourse. Moreover, late nineteenth-century economic and political realities suggest that the principal policy objective of antebellum protectionists—American economic and political sovereignty—was accomplished. Still, the mission of protectionists was not a complete success. Antebellum protectionists were motivated in part by a desire to steer American industrialization along a course fundamentally different from the British example, especially with regard to the condition of labor. What was most feared, the degradation of the working class, was realized under the nineteenth-century protectionist regime. The fact that tariffs failed to preserve labor's sacred place in American culture, and instead bolstered an industrial order dominated by corporate gigantism, however, speaks more to their lack of perfect foresight and their near religious faith in American exceptionalism than to an underhanded effort to advance the Robber Baron agenda.

Only in the decades following the Civil War did American thinkers begin to accept that the progress of American industrialization would model Britain's. The United States, it seemed, was not that exceptional. By then, a rising intellectual tide spanning the Atlantic recognized the proletariat of Marx, and before long the industrial revolution was mythologized as social catastrophe.[22] The social difficulties wrought on labor by industrialization were criticized most poignantly in the post–Civil War discourse not by the protectionist disciples of Carey but in an emerging body of labor/socialist literature, much of which was anticipated by Langton Byllesby and Thomas Skidmore. The original identification of problems with industrialization by Byllesby and Skidmore, as well as by southern reactionaries like Fitzhugh and Holmes, seemed at least partially vindicated when late nineteenth-century labor leaders identified the same problems. Ironically, some of the voices historians conventionally counted as least progressive in the antebellum literature were, after the Civil War, seen by some as prophetic.

But the reforms suggested by antebellum anticapitalist thinkers like Byllesby and Skidmore and Fitzhugh and Holmes were first and foremost expressions of a conservative disposition. This was especially true of the southern reactionaries. Both sets aimed at preserving a world upset by capitalist revolution, so that when posterity catalogues the labor ideology of Byllesby and Skidmore as revolutionary, these classifications obscure the material and intellectual context in which their works were written. The same ideological dialectic applies to the antebellum protectionists. Mathew Carey, Raymond, Colton, Henry Carey, and the entire cadre of protectionists aimed at preservation through restriction. To be sure, protectionists championed a hybrid form of intellectual and material industrial capitalism, but their energies were also focused on shielding labor from unfettered markets. To preserve and protect, the advocates of tariffs, and Byllesby and Skidmore, as well as the republican opponents of finance, channeled a producerist, craftsman mentality, a proprietary capitalism that retained the respect and dignity of labor, emphasized a traditionalist appreciation for the common good, and defended the promises of individual and national independence embedded in the principles of 1776.

Smithian-inspired intellectual capitalism was the revolutionary force in the antebellum discourse. The American economists who wrote against the Scotsman and his classical progeny, namely Malthus and Ricardo and the economic order they ostensibly sanctified, imbued their ideologies with conservative properties. Their end was the salvation of economic traditions then being torn asunder by market revolution. Even Henry Carey, whose protectionist brand of hybrid intellectual capitalism featured industrial transformation, discovered true liberty in freedom from the tyranny of Smith's "natural system of liberty"—man versus nature—by corralling and subjugating insurgent market forces unleashed by the modern economy. Emergent material capitalism was arguably the most significant life-altering development for antebellum Americans. Not every reformer, however, was a socialist. Rather, as Richard White has argued, "they simply imagined other capitalisms."[23]

This was true even for the period's closest adherents to British classicism. Antebellum liberals were a mixed lot. But as this book has shown, the American liberal discourse was not dominated by Smithian laissez-faire, and was routinely inviting of alternative, hybrid intellectual capitalist forms. But even liberal expressions of antebellum political economy were marked by a conservative temperament. Southern laissez-faire, though wedded to a liberal, negative-state political platform, aimed ultimately at the preservation of archaic slavery. And the northeastern evangelical brand of laissez-faire was tied to the traditional moral instructions of the Church. Neither institution—slavery or the Church—is typically interpreted as a trailblazer in liberal modernity.

The persistency of conservative attachments is a central component of early American economic thought. Shortly after the Civil War, laissez-faire ideology experienced something akin to an intellectual coup d'état when conservatives became liberal capitalists, in what Clinton Rossiter described as "the great train robbery of American intellectual history."[24] The laissez-faire political economy of the British sociologist Herbert Spencer commanded influence in the American public sphere. The Enlightenment economic laws of nature that the British classicists made famous were refashioned as evolutionary laws of natural selection. Smithian liberalism, intended to expand freedoms by subverting traditional feudal and mercantilist institutions, was packaged as a defense of an industrial capitalist regime, and Smith's moral imperatives promising universal fraternity and fellow feeling were replaced with the survival of the fittest. Dugald Stewart's earlier attempt to domesticate Smith, to dispel the radical interpretations that Tories assigned to the *Wealth of Nations*, was realized, but inverted, by postbellum laissez-faire conservatives. The revolutionary ideals of individualism and the negative state, precisely the ones that Stewart sought to discount and disconnect from events in Jacobin France, and in the process assuage Smith's more conservative readers, were precisely the ideals celebrated in postbellum American laissez-faire literature. By the end of the nineteenth century, Smithian intellectual capitalism had evolved into an ideological vehicle to preserve the political economic status quo, a much different status quo from the one that existed in 1776.

Liberal political economy became conservative, or at least partly conservative, as Rossiter argued. It was certainly not the conservatism of Fitzhugh. "Where they [postbellum laissez-faire economists] clearly strayed from Conservatism was in their glorification of rugged individualism and consequent disregard for the community, their choice of struggle over harmony and contract over status as the bases of sound human relations, their fatuous optimism and confidence in progress . . . and their unabashed, all-pervading materialism." Revolutionary intellectual capitalism, by the 1870s infused with social Darwinian naturalism, had superseded the political economy of traditional early American conservatism. "Individual striving, not collective effort; acquisition, not enjoyment; conflict, not harmony; self-interest, not fraternal sympathy; competition, not co-operation—these were the preferences of God and nature."[25] The epic struggle between man and nature that preoccupied the minds of classicists and protectionists was exchanged in the postbellum laissez-faire conservative discourse for the man-versus-the-state dialectic. And Spencer and his American laissez-faire disciples surrendered man to natural forces, much in the same way that Smithian-inspired intellectual capitalism had a century earlier.

The appointment of Charles Dunbar to the chair of political economy at Harvard in 1871 marked the first position of its kind in American academia. Five years later, in the widely read summary essay on American economic thought referenced at the start of this book, Dunbar concluded that antebellum economists had contributed "nothing towards developing the theory of political economy."[26] While the professionalization of economic analysis at American institutions of higher learning may have begun in earnest with Dunbar's appointment, this book demonstrates that during the antebellum period the discipline was pursued, inside and outside of academia, with great intensity, and was inclusive of an extensive, rich, and dynamic range of ideological and theoretical positions. Antebellum economists exhibited originality and inquisitiveness and were relevant participants in the domestic and Atlantic public spheres. They worked, in a manifestly nonlinear manner, toward the formulation of an economic science suited to the American experience. In no way was the American economic mind insulated from Old World influences. In fact, the antebellum economists were in constant dialogue with European, particularly British thinkers. And although British laissez-faire wielded influence over antebellum economic thought, classical orthodoxy never dominated the domestic discourse.

An awareness of the ideological differences between antebellum economists provides a clearer measure of American intellectual culture and can improve our understanding of how the economic dialogue helped set the narrative for the political discord that culminated with the Civil War. And by appreciating the complexities and contrasts within the economic literature, we find historical insight into how Americans perceived material and intellectual capitalism in all its varied, hybrid forms. Capitalism, however defined, was and still is the defining feature of the American experience. Antebellum endeavors at making sense of capitalist phenomena, like the earlier attempt made by Smith, were sensible of the past, captured the power struggles of the present, and embodied hopes for the future. Smith offered a paradigm, which the Americans refashioned and in most cases abandoned, opting instead to construct native economic ideologies that matched American realities. These were sometimes disjointed, occasionally contradictory, and almost always unrehearsed. Joyce Appleby explained how "capitalism caused a crisis of meaning" for contemporaries and historians, its origins and functions both liberating and constraining, divine and satanic, and calculating and irrational.[27] To recover historical meaning we must first recognize capitalism as an intellectual cultural system, shaped by the existing material forces that antebellum economists sought to explain. Fortunately, as this book illustrates, the antebellum economic literature is prodigious, perhaps owing to the shortage of professionalization in the field, which essentially encouraged everyone to be their own economist, but also likely owing to what Tocqueville described as the American "independence of the mind," that instinct "to mistrust the judgment of others, and to seek the light of truth nowhere but in their own understanding."[28] In this regard, at least, the lack of economy practiced by antebellum political economists is still paying historical dividends.

NOTES

Chapter 1. Introduction: Capitalism and Antebellum Thought

1. Robert Gallman, "Economic Growth and Structural Change in the Long Nineteenth Century," in *The Long Nineteenth Century*, vol. 2 of *The Cambridge Economic History of the United States*, ed. Stanley L. Engerman and Robert E. Gallman (Cambridge: Cambridge University Press, 1996), 5–8.

2. George Rogers Taylor, *The Transportation Revolution, 1815–1860* (New York: Rinehart, 1951), 247; Robert Margo, "The Labor Force in the Nineteenth Century," in Engerman and Gallman, *The Long Nineteenth Century*, 208, 213–214; Stanley Engerman and Kenneth Sokoloff, "Technology and Industrialization, 1790–1914," in Engerman and Gallman, *The Long Nineteenth Century*, 369; Douglas A. Irwin, *Clashing over Commerce: A History of US Trade Policy* (Chicago: University of Chicago Press, 2017), 197; Douglass C. North, *The Economic Growth of the United States, 1790–1860* (1961; New York: W. W. Norton, 1966), 165.

3. Christopher Clark, "The Agrarian Context of American Capitalist Development," in *Capitalism Takes Command: The Social Transformation of Nineteenth-Century America*, ed. Michael Zakim and Gary J. Kornblith (Chicago: University of Chicago Press, 2012), 14; Alan L. Olmstead and Paul W. Rhode, "Cotton, Slavery, and the 'New History of Capitalism,'" *Explorations in Economic History* 67 (2018): 13; Allan Kulikoff, *The Agrarian Origins of American Capitalism* (Charlottesville: University Press of Virginia, 1992).

4. Susan Previant Lee and Peter Passell, *A New Economic View of American History* (New York: W. W. Norton, 1979), 71–79, 282, summarizes the data and literature on the economic impact of turnpikes, canals, steamboats, and railroads. See Taylor, *Transportation Revolution*, 85; Albert Fishlow, "Internal Transportation in the Nineteenth and Early Twentieth Centuries," in Engerman and Gallman, *The Long Nineteenth Century*, 560–561, 564, 580; Walter Johnson, *River of Dark Dreams: Slavery and Empire in the Cotton Kingdom* (Cambridge, MA: Belknap Press of Harvard University Press, 2013), 73; John Lauritz Larson, *Internal Improvement: National Public Works and the Promise of Popular Government in the Early United States* (Chapel Hill: University of North Carolina Press, 2001); Robert E. Lipsey, "U.S. Foreign Trade and the Balance of Payments, 1800–1913," in Engerman and Gallman, *The Long Nineteenth Century*, 687–688.

5. Giovanni Arrighi, *The Long Twentieth Century: Money, Power, and the Origins of Our Times*, 2nd ed. (London: Verso, 2010), xi; Niall Ferguson, *The Ascent of Money: A Financial*

History of the World (London: Allen Lane, 2008), 3; Thomas Piketty, *Capital in the Twenty-First Century*, trans. Arthur Goldhammer (Cambridge, MA: Belknap Press of Harvard University Press, 2014).

6. Bray Hammond, *Banks and Politics in America, from the Revolution to the Civil War* (Princeton, NJ: Princeton University Press, 1957), 698; Howard Bodenhorn, *A History of Banking in Antebellum America: Financial Markets and Economic Development in an Era of Nation-Building* (Cambridge: Cambridge University Press, 2000), 182; Hugh Rockoff, "Banking and Finance, 1789–1914," in Engerman and Gallman, *The Long Nineteenth Century*; Seth Rockman, "What Makes the History of Capitalism Newsworthy?," *Journal of the Early Republic* 34, no. 3 (2014): 450.

7. William H. Sewell Jr., "A Strange Career: The Historical Study of Economic Life," *History and Theory* 49, no. 4 (2010): 149; Kenneth Lipartito, "Reassembling the Economic: New Departures in Historical Materialism," *American Historical Review* 121, no. 1 (2016): 101–107; Joyce Oldham Appleby, "The Vexed Story of Capitalism Told by American Historians," *Journal of the Early Republic* 21, no. 1 (2001); Naomi R. Lamoreaux, "Rethinking the Transition to Capitalism in the Early American Northeast," *Journal of American History* 90, no. 2 (2003); Paul A. Gilje, "The Rise of Capitalism in the Early Republic," *Journal of the Early Republic* 16, no. 2 (1996): 159–162. Albert Fishlow and Robert Fogel were pioneers in cliometric studies. See, for instance, Albert Fishlow, *American Railroads and the Transformation of the Ante-Bellum Economy* (Cambridge, MA: Harvard University Press, 1965); Robert William Fogel and Stanley L. Engerman, *Time on the Cross: The Economics of American Negro Slavery* (Boston: Little, Brown, 1974); Simon Kuznets, *Modern Economic Growth: Rate, Structure, and Spread* (New Haven, CT: Yale University Press, 1966).

8. Sewell, "A Strange Career," 154–155. American social historians were inspired by the works of Eric Hobsbawm, E. P. Thompson, and Christopher Hill. Besides Charles Sellers, *The Market Revolution: Jacksonian America, 1815–1846* (New York: Oxford University Press, 1991), and Sean Wilentz, *Chants Democratic: New York City and the Rise of the American Working Class, 1788–1850* (New York: Oxford University Press, 1984), other important social histories of the antebellum economy include Ruth Schwartz Cowan, *A Social History of American Technology* (Oxford: Oxford University Press, 1997); Seth Rockman, *Scraping By: Wage Labor, Slavery, and Survival in Early Baltimore* (Baltimore: Johns Hopkins University Press, 2009); Walter Licht, *Industrializing America: The Nineteenth Century* (Baltimore: Johns Hopkins University Press, 1995).

9. Lipartito, "Reassembling the Economic," 101.

10. Rockman, "What Makes the History of Capitalism Newsworthy?," 447. Zakim and Kornblith, *Capitalism Takes Command*, captures many of the trends in the New History of Capitalism, as does Sven Beckert and Christine Desan, eds., *American Capitalism: New Histories* (New York: Columbia University Press, 2018). See also Eric Hilt, "Economic History, Historical Analysis, and the 'New History of Capitalism,'" *Journal of Economic History* 77, no. 2 (2017): 511–536.

11. Rockman, "What Makes the History of Capitalism Newsworthy?," 442.

12. Pierre-Samuel Du Pont's *De l'origine et des progrès d'une science nouvelle* (1768) is arguably the first history of modern political economy, or what by the late nineteenth century became known as economics. Du Pont covered thirteen years of economic thought, originating with the Physiocrats, of which he considered himself a member. J. R. McCulloch's *A*

Discourse on the Rise, Progress, Peculiar Objects, and Importance, of Political Economy (1825) traces the science from antiquity to nineteenth-century Britain. McCulloch's work was the first of its kind in the English language. See Oreste Popescu's "On the Historiography of Economic Thought: A Bibliographical Survey" in *The Historiography of Economics*, ed. Mark Blaug (Aldershot, Hants.: Edward Elgar, 1991).

13. Antebellum Americans used the terms "capitalists" and "capital," but "capitalism" was not elevated to an ism in popular Atlantic parlance until the late nineteenth century, and then usually as a pejorative by socialists. William Thackeray's 1854 novel *The Newcomers* is commonly identified as the first to use the term.

14. Donald Winch, "Adam Smith's 'Enduring Particular Result': A Political and Cosmopolitan Perspective," in *Wealth and Virtue: The Shaping of Political Economy in the Scottish Enlightenment*, ed. István Hont and Michael Ignatieff (Cambridge: Cambridge University Press, 1983).

15. Jacob Viner suggests this in his survey of laissez-faire thought, "The Rise of Cost in a System of Economic Liberalism," in *The Long View and the Short*, ed. Viner (Glencoe, IL: Free Press, 1958), 121–122.

16. Beckert and Desan, *American Capitalism*, 4.

17. Louis Hartz, *The Liberal Tradition in America: An Interpretation of American Political Thought since the Revolution* (New York: Harcourt, Brace, 1955), 18; Zakim and Kornblith, *Capitalism Takes Command*, 1.

18. Ernest Campbell Mossner and Ian Simpson Ross, eds., *The Correspondence of Adam Smith* (Oxford: Clarendon Press, 1977), 102, 186, 251. Smith corresponded with members of Parliament, and the *Wealth of Nations* inspired legislation. For Smith's impact on parliamentary debates in the 1780s, see C. R. Fay, *Great Britain from Adam Smith to the Present Day* (London: Longmans, Green, 1950), 15–17.

19. Smith's association with Hume seems to have negatively impacted the immediate reception of the *Wealth of Nations*. One month after its publication, Hume died. While the public was attentive to news about the American Revolution, Smith's correspondence indicates his own attention was directed toward the controversies surrounding the posthumous publication of Hume's writings, especially *Dialogues concerning Natural Religion*.

20. Emma Rothschild, *Economic Sentiments: Adam Smith, Condorcet, and the Enlightenment* (Cambridge, MA: Harvard University Press, 2001), 52–55. For the intellectual culture of the Scottish Enlightenment, see Richard B. Sher, *Church and University in the Scottish Enlightenment: The Moderate Literati of Edinburgh* (Princeton, NJ: Princeton University Press, 1985).

21. Dugald Stewart, *Account of the Life and Writings of Adam Smith* (1793), in Adam Smith, *Essays on Philosophical Subjects*, ed. W. P. D. Wightman and J. C. Bryce (Oxford: Clarendon Press, 1980), 311.

22. E. G. West, *Adam Smith* (New Rochelle, NY: Arlington House, 1969), 166. A sample of the historiography on Smith might include Joseph Cropsey, *Polity and Economy: With Further Thoughts on the Principles of Adam Smith* (South Bend, IN: St. Augustine's, 2001); Andrew Stewart Skinner, *A System of Social Science: Papers Relating to Adam Smith*, 2nd ed. (Oxford: Clarendon Press, 1996); Vivienne Brown, *Adam Smith's Discourse: Canonicity, Commerce, and Conscience* (New York: Routledge, 1994); Charles L. Griswold Jr., *Adam Smith and the Virtues of Enlightenment* (Cambridge: Cambridge University Press, 1999); Glenn R. Morrow, *The Ethical and Economic Theories of Adam Smith* (New York: Longmans, Green, 1923); Donald

Winch, *Adam Smith's Politics: An Essay in Historiographic Revision* (Cambridge: Cambridge University Press 1978); J. Ralph Lindgren, *The Social Philosophy of Adam Smith* (The Hague: Nijhoff, 1973).

23. Stewart, *Life and Writings of Adam Smith*, 322.

24. Richard F. Teichgraeber III, "Adam Smith and Tradition: The *Wealth of Nations* before Malthus," in *Economy, Polity, and Society: British Intellectual History, 1750–1950*, ed. Stefan Collini, Richard Whatmore, and Brian Young (Cambridge: Cambridge University Press, 2000), 103.

25. Charles Gide and Charles Rist, *History of Economic Doctrines from the Time of the Physiocrats to the Present Day*, trans. Robert Richards (Boston: D. C. Heath, 1915), which argues that Smith is the "true founder" of political economy (50); Fay, *Great Britain from Adam Smith*, 5–6; Douglas A. Irwin, *Against the Tide: An Intellectual History of Free Trade* (Princeton, NJ: Princeton University Press, 1996), 89–116; Jacob Viner, "Adam Smith and Laissez-faire," in *The Long View and the Short*.

26. See John Rae, *Life of Adam Smith* (1895; New York: A. M. Kelley, 1965); Ian Ross, "The Physiocrats and Adam Smith," in *François Quesnay (1694–1774)*, ed. Mark Blaug (Aldershot, Hants.: Edward Elgar, 1991), 2: 213–215; Ronald L. Meek, "Physiocracy and Classicism in Britain," in *The Economics of Physiocracy*, ed. Meek (Cambridge, MA: Harvard University Press, 1963), 345–363, for discussions of the relationship between Smith and the French economists. "Laissez-faire" is associated with the Physiocrats, but the term is attributed to Vincent de Gournay, an eighteenth-century French economist who was not a Physiocrat. See also Elizabeth Fox-Genovese, *The Origins of Physiocracy* (Ithaca, NY: Cornell University Press, 1976); Gianni Vaggi, *The Economics of Francois Quesnay* (Durham, NC: Duke University Press, 1987).

27. Sidney Fine, *Laissez Faire and the General-Welfare State: A Study of Conflict in American Thought, 1865–1901* (Ann Arbor: University of Michigan Press, 1956), 47, notes that in American academia, political economy was tied to laissez-faire ideology by 1865.

28. John Maynard Keynes, *The General Theory of Employment, Interest, and Money* (New York: Harcourt, Brace, 1936), 3, emphasis in original.

29. Charles Dunbar, "Economic Science in America, 1776–1876," *North American Review* 122, no. 250 (1876): 140, 146; Joseph A. Schumpeter, *History of Economic Analysis* (Oxford: Oxford University Press, 1954), 514, 519; John Kenneth Galbraith, *The Affluent Society* (Boston: Houghton Mifflin, 1958), 48. A. W. Coats, *On the History of Economic Thought* (London: Routledge, 1992), 342, gives a recent expression of this argument: "Indeed, in a sense they were too inventive, too ready to scrap or modify existing ideas in response to some new intellectual impulse or the pressure of current concerns, and unwilling to undertake sustained analysis. Hence, their thoughts on economic subjects were rarely expressed in mature, consistent and systematic form."

30. Joseph Dorfman, *The Economic Mind in American Civilization*, vols. 1–2, *1606–1865* (New York: Viking, 1946). Book 2, "From Independence to Jackson," and book 3, "From Jackson to the Civil War," cover the periods dealt with here.

31. Dorfman, *Economic Mind*, 1: ix, x–xi.

32. Richard Hofstadter, *The American Political Tradition and the Men Who Made It* (1948; New York: Vintage, 1974), xxviii; this Hofstadter work and Hartz, *The Liberal Tradition in America*, are classic iterations of the liberal consensus view. See John Lauritz Larson's *The*

Market Revolution in America: Liberty, Ambition, and the Eclipse of the Common Good (Cambridge: Cambridge University Press, 2010) for a recent expression of this view.

33. Paul K. Conkin, *Prophets of Prosperity: America's First Political Economists* (Bloomington: Indiana University Press, 1980). Besides Dorfman and Conkin, see Michael J. L. O'Connor, *Origins of Academic Economics in the United States* (New York: Columbia University Press, 1944); J. F. Normano, *The Spirit of American Economics: A Study in the History of Economic Ideas in the United States Prior to the Great Depression* (New York: John Day, 1943); Ernest Teilhac, *Pioneers of American Economic Thought in the Nineteenth Century*, trans. E. A. J. Johnson (New York: Macmillan, 1936); Frank A. Fetter, "The Early History of Political Economy in the United States," *Proceedings of the American Philosophical Society* 87, no. 1 (1943); William J. Barber, ed., *Economics and Higher Learning in the Nineteenth Century* (New Brunswick, NJ: Transaction, 1993); Malcolm Rutherford, ed., *The Economic Mind in America: Essays in the History of American Economics* (London: Routledge, 1998); Michael Hudson, *Economics and Technology in 19th-Century American Thought* (New York: Garland, 1975); Judith Goldstein, *Ideas, Interests, and American Trade Policy* (Ithaca, NY: Cornell University Press, 1993); James L. Huston, *Securing the Fruits of Labor: The American Concept of Wealth Distribution* (Baton Rouge: Louisiana State University Press, 1998); Allen Kaufman, *Capitalism, Slavery, and Republican Values: Antebellum Political Economists, 1819–1848* (Austin: University of Texas Press, 1982); Samuel Barbour, James Cicarelli, and J. E. King, *A History of American Economic Thought: Mainstream and Crosscurrents* (London: Routledge, 2017).

34. Conkin, *Prophets of Prosperity*, viii, 312.

35. Richard C. Edwards, "Economic Sophistication in Nineteenth Century Congressional Tariff Debates," *Journal of Economic History* 30, no. 4 (1970): 805.

36. Conkin, *Prophets of Prosperity*, 17.

37. Ibid.

38. Jessica M. Lepler, *The Many Panics of 1837: People, Politics, and the Creation of a Transatlantic Crisis* (Cambridge: Cambridge University Press: 2013), 253.

39. Jacob Viner, "Fashion in Economic Thought," in Viner, *Essays on the Intellectual History of Economics*, ed. Douglas A. Irwin (Princeton, NJ: Princeton University Press, 1991), 193.

40. Rockman, *Scraping By*, 11.

41. Adam Smith, *An Inquiry into the Nature and Causes of the Wealth of Nations* (1776; repr., New Rochelle, NY: Arlington House, 1966), 2: 290–297, 301–302, 325–326.

42. Sven Beckert and Seth Rockman, introduction to *Slavery's Capitalism: A New History of American Economic Development*, ed. Beckert and Rockman (Philadelphia: University of Pennsylvania Press, 2016), 10.

43. Daniel Walker Howe, "Charles Sellers, the Market Revolution, and the Shaping of Identity in Whig-Jacksonian America," in *God and Mammon: Protestants, Money, and the Market, 1790–1860*, ed. Mark A. Noll (Oxford: Oxford University Press, 2002), 54–70; O'Connor, *Origins of Academic Economics*, 3–6, 64–106.

44. Dorothy Ross, *The Origins of American Social Science* (Cambridge: Cambridge University Press, 1991); Arthur Alphonse Ekirch Jr., *The Idea of Progress in America, 1815–1860* (New York: Columbia University Press, 1944); Carl Russell Fish, *The Rise of the Common Man, 1830–1850* (New York: Macmillan, 1927).

45. Beckert and Rockman, *Slavery's Capitalism*, 9.

46. Taken from Joyce Appleby's *The Relentless Revolution: A History of Capitalism* (New York: W. W. Norton, 2010).

47. Karl Marx, *Manifesto of the Communist Party* (1848), in *The Marx-Engels Reader*, ed. Robert C. Tucker (New York: W. W. Norton, 1978), 475.

48. Jeffrey Sklansky, "William Leggett and the Melodrama of the Market," in Zakim and Kornblith, *Capitalism Takes Command*, 204.

49. For instance, Sellers, *The Market Revolution*; Arthur M. Schlesinger Jr., *The Age of Jackson* (Boston: Little, Brown, 1945); Harry Watson, *Liberty and Power: The Politics of Jacksonian America*, rev. ed. (New York: Hill and Wang, 2006); John Ashworth, *Slavery, Capitalism, and Politics in the Antebellum Republic*, vol. 1, *Commerce and Compromise, 1820-1850* (Cambridge: Cambridge University Press, 1995); Sean Wilentz, *The Rise of American Democracy: Jefferson to Lincoln* (New York: W. W. Norton, 2005); Hammond, *Banks and Politics*.

50. J. G. A. Pocock, *The Machiavellian Moment: Florentine Political Thought and the Atlantic Republican Tradition* (Princeton, NJ: Princeton University Press, 1975), ix; Caroline Robbins, *The Eighteenth-Century Commonwealthman: Studies in the Transmission, Development, and Circumstance of English Liberal Thought from the Restoration of Charles II until the War with the Thirteen Colonies* (Cambridge, MA: Harvard University Press, 1959); Isaac Kramnick, *Bolingbroke and His Circle: The Politics of Nostalgia in the Age of Walpole* (Cambridge, MA: Harvard University Press, 1968).

51. The exceptions are Stuart Banner, *Anglo-American Securities Regulation: Cultural and Political Roots, 1690-1860* (Cambridge: Cambridge University Press, 1998); Wilentz, *Chants Democratic*; Major L. Wilson, "The 'Country' versus the 'Court': A Republican Consensus and Party Debate in the Bank War," *Journal of the Early Republic* 15, no. 4 (1995).

52. Besides Pocock, see Bernard Bailyn, *The Ideological Origins of the American Revolution* (Cambridge, MA: Belknap Press of Harvard University Press, 1967); Gordon S. Wood, *The Creation of the American Republic* (Chapel Hill: University of North Carolina Press for the Institute of Early American History and Culture, Williamsburg, VA, 1969); Drew R. McCoy, *The Elusive Republic: Political Economy in Jeffersonian America* (Chapel Hill: University of North Carolina Press, 1980).

Chapter 2. Laissez-Faire in the American Tradition

1. "Political Economy," *Southern Review* 8, no. 16 (1832): 493.

2. Samuel Fleischacker, "Adam Smith's Reception among the American Founders, 1776-1790," *William and Mary Quarterly* 59, no. 4 (2002): 7; William J. Barber, ed., *Economists and Higher Learning in the Nineteenth Century* (New Brunswick, NJ: Transaction, 1993), 15; Paul K. Conkin, *Prophets of Prosperity: America's First Political Economists* (Bloomington: Indiana University Press, 1980), 17; Joseph Dorfman, *The Economic Mind in American Civilization*, vols. 1-2, *1606-1865* (New York: Viking, 1946), 2: 512; Herbert E. Sloan, *Principle and Interest: Thomas Jefferson and the Problem of Debt* (1995; Charlottesville: University of Virginia Press, 2001), 245; Michael J. L. O'Connor, *Origins of Academic Economics in the United States* (New York: Columbia University Press, 1944), 20-22, 111. Richard F. Teichgraeber III's "Adam Smith and Tradition: The *Wealth of Nations* Before Malthus," in *Economy, Polity, and Society: British Intellectual History, 1750-1950*, ed. Stefan Collini, Richard Whatmore, and Brian Young (Cambridge: Cambridge University Press, 2000), offers insight on the early reception of Smith.

3. John Lauritz Larson, *The Market Revolution in America: Liberty, Ambition, and the Eclipse of the Common Good* (Cambridge: Cambridge University Press, 2010), 144; Roy C. Smith, *Adam Smith and the Origins of American Enterprise: How America's Industrial Success Was Forged by the Timely Ideas of a Brilliant Scots Economist* (New York: St. Martin's Press, 2002), 201; John Steele Gordon, *An Empire of Wealth: The Epic History of American Economic Power* (New York: HarperCollins, 2004), 67.

4. Larson, *Market Revolution in America*, and C. Donald Johnson, *The Wealth of a Nation: A History of Trade Politics in America* (Oxford: Oxford University Press, 2018), are recent expressions.

5. Alfred F. Chalk, "Relativist and Absolutist Approaches to the History of Economic Theory," in *The Historiography of Economics*, ed. Mark Blaug (Aldershot, Hants.: Edward Elgar, 1991), 60.

6. Thomas Jefferson to Thomas Mann Randolph, May 30, 1790, in *The Writings of Thomas Jefferson*, ed. Andrew Lipscomb (Washington, DC: Thomas Jefferson Memorial Association of the United States, 1903), 8: 31.

7. Dorfman, *Economic Mind*, 1: 112; Merle Curti, *The Growth of American Thought*, 2nd ed. (New York: Harper, 1951), 224; Michael Hudson, *Economics and Technology in 19th-Century American Thought* (New York: Garland, 1975), 22–33; Barber, *Economists and Higher Learning*, 4–5; Dorfman, *Economic Mind*, 2: 512; Stewart Davenport, *Friends of the Unrighteous Mammon: Northern Christians and Market Capitalism, 1815–1860* (Chicago: University of Chicago Press, 2008), 19–73; O'Connor, *Origins of Academic Economics*, 78–94. On the influence of Christianity in American liberal culture, see James T. Kloppenberg, "The Virtues of Liberalism: Christianity, Republicanism, and Ethics in Early American Political Discourse," *Journal of American History* 74, no. 1 (1987).

8. O'Connor, *Origins of Academic Economics*, 78–94.

9. Dorothy Ross, *The Origins of American Social Science* (Cambridge: Cambridge University Press, 1991), 36.

10. O'Connor, *Origins of Academic Economics*, 106.

11. Max Weber, "The Protestant Sects and the Spirit of Capitalism" (1905), in *From Max Weber: Essays in Sociology*, ed. and trans. H. H. Gerth and C. Wright Mills (New York: Oxford University Press, 1946), 321.

12. Daniel Walker Howe, afterword to *God and Mammon: Protestants, Money, and the Market, 1790–1860*, ed. Mark A. Noll (Oxford: Oxford University Press, 2002), 295–298.

13. Robin Klay and John Lunn, "Protestants and the American Economy in the Postcolonial Period: An Overview," in Noll, *God and Mammon*, 39–40.

14. Jacob Viner, "Fashion in Economic Thought," in Viner, *Essays on the Intellectual History of Economics*, ed. Douglas A. Irwin (Princeton, NJ: Princeton University Press, 1991), 190; A. W. Coats, *On the History of Economic Thought* (London: Routledge, 1992), 343; William Letwin, *The Origins of Scientific Economics: English Economic Thought, 1660–1776* (London: Methuen, 1963), 81, 147–148; Margaret Schabas, *The Natural Origins of Economics* (Chicago: University of Chicago Press, 2005), 2, 12; Joyce Oldham Appleby, *Economic Thought and Ideology in Seventeenth-Century England* (Princeton, NJ: Princeton University Press, 1978), 54.

15. Daniel Walker Howe, "Charles Sellers, the Market Revolution, and the Shaping of Identity in Whig-Jacksonian America," in Noll, *God and Mammon*, 63.

16. Boyd Hilton, *The Age of Atonement: The Influence of Evangelicalism on Social and Eco-

nomic Thought, 1785–1865 (Oxford: Clarendon, 1988); Maxine Berg, "Progress and Providence in Early Nineteenth-Century Political Economy," *Social History* 15, no. 3 (October 1990); Donald Winch, *Riches and Poverty: An Intellectual History of Political Economy in Britain, 1750–1834* (Cambridge: Cambridge University Press, 1996); Charles Dunbar, "Economic Science in America, 1776–1876," *North American Review* 122, no. 250 (1876): 140, 146.

17. John Brett Langstaff, *The Enterprising Life: John McVickar, 1787–1868* (New York: St. Martin's Press, 1961), 74.

18. McCulloch's essay "Political Economy" appeared in the *Encyclopaedia Britannica*, 6th ed. (1824), and helped establish Ricardian principles as orthodoxy.

19. John McVickar, *Outlines of Political Economy: Being a Republication of the Article upon That Subject Contained in the Edinburgh Supplement to the "Encyclopedia Britannica"* (1825; repr., New York: A. M. Kelley, 1966), 160.

20. J[ohn] McVickar, *Introductory Lecture to a Course of Political Economy: Recently Delivered at Columbia College* (London: John Miller, 1830), i, 9. For examples of the cosmopolitan and benign nature of trade in Adam Smith, see *An Inquiry into the Nature and Causes of the Wealth of Nations* (1776; repr., New Rochelle, NY: Arlington House, 1966), 2: 66–67, 71–75, 124, and *Lectures on Jurisprudence*, ed. R. L. Meek, D. D. Raphael, and P. G. Stein (Oxford: Clarendon, 1978), 391, 538.

21. Eliga Gould, "War by Other Means: Mercantilism and Free Trade in the Age of the American Revolution," in *American Capitalism: New Histories*, ed. Sven Beckert and Christine Desan (New York: Columbia University Press, 2018), 285–290; C. R. Fay, *Great Britain from Adam Smith to the Present Day* (London: Longmans, Green, 1950), 31–34.

22. Joseph Dorfman and R. G. Tugwell, "John McVickar: Christian Teacher and Economist," in *Early American Policy: Six Columbia Contributors*, ed. Dorfman and Tugwell (New York: Columbia University Press, 1960), 116, 131–132.

23. Adam Smith, *The Theory of Moral Sentiments* (1759; repr., New York: A. M. Kelley, 1966), 3–6, 10–16, 56, 70–86, 161–172, 497; Smith, *Lectures on Jurisprudence*, 352, 538–539; Charles L. Griswold Jr., *Adam Smith and the Virtues of Enlightenment* (Cambridge: Cambridge University Press, 1999), 288, 297–298; T. D. Campbell, *Adam Smith's Science of Morals* (London: Allen and Unwin, 1971), 89–104, 136–146, 197–198.

24. Smith, *Theory of Moral Sentiments*, 86.

25. McVickar, *Introductory Lecture*, 5–7.

26. Hilton, *Age of Atonement*; Berg, "Progress and Providence," 366–369; Winch, *Riches and Poverty*, 223–241.

27. Anthony Howe, "Restoring Free Trade: The British experience, 1776–1873," in *The Political Economy of British Historical Experience, 1688–1914*, ed. Donald Winch and Patrick K. O'Brien (Oxford: Oxford University Press, 2002), 212; Frank Thistlethwaite, *The Anglo-American Connection in the Early Nineteenth Century* (Philadelphia: University of Pennsylvania Press, 1959), 33; Robert Kelley, *The Transatlantic Persuasion: The Liberal-Democratic Mind in the Age of Gladstone* (New York: Knopf, 1969).

28. Marc-William Palen writes, "By the 1840s, so too were Cobdenism and abolitionism enmeshed within the American North," and "These northern subscribers to Cobdenism were the vanguard of the Victorian American free-trade movement," in *The "Conspiracy" of Free Trade: The Anglo-American Struggle over Empire and Economic Globalisation, 1846–1896* (Cambridge: Cambridge University Press, 2016), 21. The free-trade abolitionists—Joshua

Leavitt, Harriet Martineau, Henry Ward Beecher, Ralph Waldo Emerson, William Lloyd Garrison—that Palen argues were at the fore of the American free trade movement are not included in this work.

29. Deborah Bingham Van Broekhoven, "Suffering with Slaveholders: The Limits of Francis Wayland's Antislavery Witness," in *Religion and the Antebellum Debate over Slavery*, ed. John R. McKivigan and Mitchell Snay (Athens: University of Georgia Press, 1998), 211.

30. Eric Williams, *Capitalism and Slavery* (Chapel Hill: University of North Carolina Press, 1944). Sven Beckert, *Empire of Cotton: A Global History* (New York: Knopf, 2014) is the most complete expression. See Trevor Burnard for an insightful criticism, "Slavery and British Industrialisation: The 'New History of Capitalism' and Eric Williams' *Capitalism and Slavery*," www.history.ucsb.edu/wp-content/uploads/Slavery-and-British-Industrialisation.docx.

31. Palen writes, "Cobdenism's mid-century American arrival introduced a new free-trade tradition," in *"Conspiracy" of Free Trade*, 12.

32. Roger Hamilton Brown, *The Republic in Peril: 1812* (New York: Columbia University Press, 1964), 177–191.

33. McVickar, *Introductory Lecture*, 9.

34. Joseph Blau, introduction to *The Elements of Moral Science*, by Francis Wayland, ed. Blau (Cambridge, MA: Belknap Press of Harvard University Press, 1963), xii–xv; O'Connor, *Origins of Academic Economics*, 77; Dorfman, *Economic Mind*, 2: 758–767; William J. Barber, "Political Economy from the Top Down: Brown University," in Barber, *Economists and Higher Learning*, 74.

35. Francis Wayland, *The Elements of Political Economy* (New York: Leavitt, Lord, 1837), vi, 138–139.

36. Wayland, *Elements of Moral Science*, 345–348.

37. Wayland, *Elements of Political Economy*, 124–125, 329.

38. Ibid., 170–171, 90.

39. Ibid., 90, 173.

40. Wayland, *Elements of Political Economy*, 30.

41. Ibid., 161, 173, 117.

42. Blau, introduction to *Elements of Moral Science*, xlii.

43. Wayland, *Elements of Moral Science*, 60.

44. McVickar, *Outlines of Political Economy*, 90–91.

45. R. H. Tawney, *Religion and the Rise of Capitalism* (New York: Harcourt, Brace, 1926), 89–131; Eric MacGilvray, *The Invention of Market Freedom* (Cambridge: Cambridge University Press, 2011), 83–89; Kloppenberg, "Virtues of Liberalism," 9, 10, 18, 28; Naomi R. Lamoreaux, "Rethinking the Transition to Capitalism in the Early American Northeast," *Journal of American History* 90, no. 2 (2003): 443–448, 454; Stephen Innes, *Creating the Commonwealth: The Economic Culture of Puritan New England* (New York: W. W. Norton, 1995); Henry William Spiegel, ed., *The Rise of American Economic Thought* (Philadelphia: Chilton, 1960), 6; E. A. J. Johnson, *American Economic Thought in the Seventeenth Century* (London: P. S. King, 1932); J. E. Crowley, *This Sheba, Self: The Conceptualization of Economic Life in Eighteenth-Century America* (Baltimore: Johns Hopkins University Press, 1974).

46. T. W. Hutchison, *On Revolutions and Progress in Economic Knowledge* (Cambridge: Cambridge University Press, 1978), 54–57; Winch, *Riches and Poverty*, 19–22, 354–356.

47. Schabas, *Natural Origins of Economics*, 2.

48. Karl Polanyi, *The Great Transformation: The Political and Economic Origins of Our Time* (1944; Boston: Beacon, 2001); Appleby, *Economic Thought and Ideology*; Letwin, *Origins of Scientific Economics*, 10–13, 131–143, 161–180; MacGilvray, *Invention of Market Freedom*, 77–80; Cathy Matson and Peter Onuf, "Toward a Republican Empire: Interest and Ideology in Revolutionary America," *American Quarterly* 37, no. 4 (1985): 498–509.

49. Joseph Dorfman and R. G. Tugwell, "Francis Lieber: German Scholar in America," in Dorfman and Tugwell, *Early American Policy*, 249–257; Dorfman, *Economic Mind*, 2: 865–870.

50. Francis Lieber, *Essays on Property and Labour as Connected with Natural Law and the Constitution of Society* (1841; repr., New York, 1854), 41, 71, 76, 152, 183.

51. Francis Lieber, "Leading Truths in Political Economy," *De Bow's Review* 15, no. 2 (1853): 190.

52. Francis Lieber, "Notes on the Fallacies of American Protectionism" (1869), in *The Miscellaneous Writings of Francis Lieber*, vol. 2, *Contributions to Political Science*, ed. Daniel C. Gilman, (Philadelphia: J. B. Lippincott, 1881), 455.

53. Lieber, "Leading Truths," 190.

54. Lieber, "Notes on the Fallacies," 454.

55. Dorfman, *Economic Mind*, 2: 877; Lieber to de Tocqueville, November 20, 1839, in *The Life and Letters of Francis Lieber*, ed. Thomas Sergeant Perry (Boston: J. R. Osgood, 1882), 141. Lieber later had the official title of his post changed from "history and political economy" to "history and political science." His rules of war helped shape international treaties, including the Geneva Convention.

56. Lieber, "Notes on the Fallacies," 394, 401, 426, 453, 420.

57. "Sketch of the Life and Character of Condy Raguet," *Merchant's Magazine*, December 1842, 543–544; Malcolm Rogers Eiselen, *The Rise of Pennsylvania Protectionism* (1932; New York: Garland, 1974), 92–98.

58. Condy Raguet, *The Principles of Free Trade, Illustrated in a Series of Short and Familiar Essays Originally Published in the* Banner of the Constitution (1840; repr., New York: A. M. Kelley, 1969), 3, 4, 27, 28, 54, 56.

59. Ibid., 2, 77, 354–355, 220, 226, 326.

60. William S. Belko, *The Triumph of the Antebellum Free Trade Movement* (Gainesville: University Press of Florida, 2012); Eiselen, *Rise of Pennsylvania Protectionism*; Douglas A. Irwin, *Against the Tide: An Intellectual History of Free Trade* (Princeton, NJ: Princeton University Press, 1996).

61. Albert Gallatin, "Memorial of the Committee Appointed by the Free Trade Convention, 1832," in *Selected Writings of Albert Gallatin*, ed. E. James Ferguson (Indianapolis: Bobbs-Merrill, 1967) 413, 430, 438.

62. Belko, *Triumph*, 160.

63. Conkin, *Prophets of Prosperity*, 28. Jacob Cardozo's and Thomas Cooper's free-trade texts were published in 1826.

64. Belko, *Triumph*, 160, 161.

65. Ibid., 11.

66. Leonard C. Helderman, "A Social Scientist of the Old South," *Journal of Southern History* 2, no. 2(1936): 151; James Fieser, ed., *The Life and Philosophy of George Tucker*, 4 vols. (Bristol: Thoemmes Continuum, 2004), 2: vii–xiv; Tipton R. Snavely, *George Tucker as Political Economist* (Charlottesville: University Press of Virginia, 1964), 1–3.

67. Besides *The Theory of Moral Sentiments*, for examples of Smith's skepticism and epistemology see his *The History of Astronomy* and *of the External Senses*, in Adam Smith, *Essays on Philosophical Subjects*, ed. W. P. D. Wightman and J. C. Bryce (Oxford: Clarendon Press, 1980).

68. Smith, *History of Astronomy*, 43, 34.

69. Smith, *Theory of Moral Sentiments*, 459; Andrew Stewart Skinner, *A System of Social Science: Papers Relating to Adam Smith*, 2nd ed. (Oxford: Clarendon Press, 1996), 37–41.

70. Smith, *Theory of Moral Sentiments*, 239, 341.

71. Smith, *Wealth of Nations*, 2: 290.

72. Smith, *Theory of Moral Sentiments*, 265.

73. E. J. Hundert, "Sociability and Self-Love in the Theatre of Moral Sentiments: Mandeville to Adam Smith," in Collini, Whatmore, and Young, *Economy, Polity, and Society*, 34–35; Emma Rothschild, *Economic Sentiments: Adam Smith, Condorcet, and the Enlightenment* (Cambridge, MA: Harvard University Press, 2001), 10–26; Joyce Appleby, *Inheriting the Revolution: The First Generation of Americans* (Cambridge, MA: Belknap Press of Harvard University Press, 2000), 56; Gordon S. Wood, *The Creation of the American Republic, 1776–1787* (Chapel Hill: University of North Carolina Press for the Institute of Early American History and Culture, Williamsburg, VA, 1969), 604–608; Gordon S. Wood, *The Radicalism of the American Revolution* (New York: Knopf, 1992), 294–296; Drew R. McCoy, *The Last of the Fathers: James Madison and the Republican Legacy* (Cambridge: Cambridge University Press, 1989), 36–66; David F. Prindle, *The Paradox of Democratic Capitalism: Politics and Economics in American Thought* (Baltimore: Johns Hopkins University Press, 2006), 26; Joyce Appleby, *Capitalism and a New Social Order: The Republican Vision of the 1790s* (New York: New York University Press, 1984), 32; Jeffrey Sklansky, *The Soul's Economy: Market Society and Selfhood in American Thought, 1820–1920* (Chapel Hill: University of North Carolina Press, 2002), 5–6, 20; Milton Friedman, *Capitalism and Freedom* (1962; Chicago: University of Chicago Press, 2002); David Hume, "Of Civil Liberty" (1742), in *Essays Moral, Political, and Literary*, ed. Eugene F. Miller, rev. ed. (Indianapolis: Liberty Fund, 1987).

74. George Tucker, "On the Illusions of Fancy" (1804), in Fieser, *Life and Philosophy*, 2: 100–102; see also Tucker, "Contemporary Fame" (1830), in Fieser, *Life and Philosophy*, 2: 130.

75. George Tucker, *Political Economy for the People* (1860; repr., New York: A. M. Kelley, 1970), 42; Gary Hull, "The Prospect of Man in Early American Economic Thought, 1800–1850" (PhD diss., University of Maryland, 1969), 133–136.

76. George Tucker, *Progress of the United States in Population and Wealth in Fifty Years with an Appendix Containing an Abstract of the Census of 1850* (1855; repr., New York: A. M. Kelley, 1964), 14.

77. Tucker, *Political Economy*, 107, 115, 119, 120.

78. George Tucker, *The Laws of Wages, Profits and Rents Investigated* (1837; repr., New York: A. M. Kelley, 1964), 48–49; Snavely, *George Tucker as Political Economist*, 153.

79. Michael O'Brien, *Conjectures of Order: Intellectual Life and the American South, 1810–1860* (Chapel Hill: University of North Carolina Press, 2004), 2: 877; Clement Eaton, *The Freedom-of-Thought Struggle in the Old South*, rev. ed. (New York: Harper and Row, 1964); Eugene D. Genovese, *The Slaveholders' Dilemma: Freedom and Progress in Southern Conservative Thought, 1820–1860* (Columbia: University of South Carolina Press, 1992).

80. Smith, *Wealth of Nations*, 1: 89, also 411–416; Smith, *Lectures on Jurisprudence*, 185, 523–526.

81. J. D. B. De Bow, "Free Trade and Direct Taxation," *De Bow's Southern and Western Review* 27, no. 4 (1857): 386.

82. James Oakes, *The Ruling Race: A History of American Slaveholders* (New York: Knopf, 1982), 225.

83. Important twentieth-century works in the history of the political economy of antebellum slavery include Kenneth M. Stampp, *The Peculiar Institution: Slavery in the Ante-bellum South* (New York: Knopf, 1956); Eugene D. Genovese, *The World the Slaveholders Made: Two Essays in Interpretation* (New York: Pantheon, 1969); Eugene D. Genovese, *Roll, Jordan, Roll: The World the Slaves Made* (New York: Pantheon, 1974); Eugene D. Genovese, *The Political Economy of Slavery: Studies in the Economy and Society of the Slave South* (New York: Pantheon, 1965); Gavin Wright, *The Political Economy of the Cotton South: Households, Markets, and Wealth in the Nineteenth Century* (New York: W. W. Norton, 1978), 2, 12, 142; Laurence Shore, *Southern Capitalists: The Ideological Leadership of an Elite, 1832–1885* (Chapel Hill: University of North Carolina Press, 1986); Wilfred Carsel, "The Slaveholders' Indictment of Northern Wage Slavery," *Journal of Southern History* 6, no. 4 (1940); William E. Dodd, "The Social Philosophy of the Old South," *American Journal of Sociology* 23, no. 6 (1918).

84. Corn, small grains, and hay were antebellum America's most valuable agricultural commodities. See Alan L. Olmstead and Paul W. Rhode, "Cotton, Slavery, and the 'New History of Capitalism,'" *Explorations in Economic History* 67 (2018): 13.

85. Stampp, *Peculiar Institution*, 45, 82, 43, 56, 78.

86. Edward E. Baptist, *The Half Has Never Been Told: Slavery and the Making of American Capitalism* (New York: Basic Books, 2014), xxii. Many of the explicit and implicit claims regarding the relationship between capitalism and slavery made popular by the New Historians of Capitalism have been challenged. See, for instance, Olmstead and Rhode, "Cotton, Slavery," 1–17.

87. Adam Rothman, *Slave Country: American Expansion and the Origins of the Deep South* (Cambridge, MA: Harvard University Press, 2005), 223; Edward E. Baptist, "Toward a Political Economy of Slave Labor: Hands, Whipping-Machines, and Modern Power," in *Slavery's Capitalism: A New History of American Economic Development*, ed. Sven Beckert and Seth Rockman (Philadelphia: University of Pennsylvania Press, 2016), 35, 52; Caitlin Rosenthal, "Slavery's Scientific Management: Masters and Managers," in Beckert and Rockman, *Slavery's Capitalism*, 62–80; Bonnie Martin, "Neighbor-to-Neighbor Capitalism: Local Credit Networks and the Mortgaging of Slaves," in Beckert and Rockman, *Slavery's Capitalism*, 108; Edward E. Baptist, "Toxic Debt, Liar Loans, Collaterized and Securitized Human Beings, and the Panic of 1837," in *Capitalism Takes Command: The Social Transformation of Nineteenth-Century America*, ed. Michael Zakim and Gary J. Kornblith (Chicago: University of Chicago Press, 2012), 81–85.

88. Walter Johnson, *River of Dark Dreams: Slavery and Empire in the Cotton Kingdom* (Cambridge, MA: Belknap Press of Harvard University Press, 2013), 5; Robert William Fogel, *Without Consent or Contract: The Rise and Fall of American Slavery* (New York: W. W. Norton, 1989), 32–33, 87. Alfred D. Chandler Jr. argues plantations served as an early example of the managerial enterprise. He describes the plantation overseer as the "first salaried manager in the country" in *The Visible Hand: The Managerial Revolution in American Business* (Cambridge, MA: Belknap Press of Harvard University Press, 1977), 65.

89. Fogel, *Without Consent or Contract*, 30; Wright, *Cotton South*, 91, 96.

90. Douglass C. North, *The Economic Growth of the United States, 1790–1860* (1961; New York: W. W. Norton, 1966), 233; Olmstead and Rhode, "Cotton, Slavery" 13. The figure representing the value of Southern slaves is contested. Matthew Karp, for instance, writes, "In 1860 the value of southern slaves amounted to $3 billion, far more than all the 'railways and cotton manufactures' in America combined," in *This Vast Southern Empire: Slaveholders at the Helm of American Foreign Policy* (Cambridge, MA: Harvard University Press, 2016), 151.

91. Thomas Piketty, *Capital in the Twenty-First Century*, trans. Arthur Goldhammer (Cambridge, MA: Belknap Press of Harvard University Press, 2014), 159–160.

92. North, *Economic Growth*, 68–69.

93. David Christy, "Cotton Is King: Slavery in the Light of Political Economy," in *Cotton Is King, and Proslavery Arguments*, ed. E. N. Elliott (1860; repr., New York: Johnson, 1968), 215; Wright, *Cotton South*, 91.

94. O'Connor, *Origins of Academic Economics*, 48; O'Brien, *Conjectures of Order*, 2: 896; John Roscoe Turner, *The Ricardian Rent Theory in Early American Economics* (New York: New York University Press, 1921), 54–57; Abram C. Flora Jr., "Economic Thought in South Carolina, 1820–1860" (PhD diss., University of North Carolina, 1957), 2–3, 34, 35; B. F. Kiker, "The Economic Ideas of Thomas Cooper," in *South Carolina Economists: Essays on the Evolution of Antebellum Economic Thought*, ed. B. F. Kiker and Robert J. Carlsson (Columbia: University of South Carolina Press, 1969), 44–46.

95. Jefferson quoted in Daniel Walker Howe, *What Hath God Wrought: The Transformation of America, 1815–1848* (New York: Oxford University Press, 2007), 459. Cooper's other important works include "The Scripture Doctrine of Materialism" (1823) and "A View of the Metaphysical and Physiological Arguments in Favor of Materialism" (1781).

96. Thomas Cooper, *Lectures on the Elements of Political Economy*, 2nd ed. (1830; repr., New York: A. M. Kelley, 1971), 332–333.

97. Thomas Cooper, *Two Tracts: On the Proposed Alteration of the Tariff; and On Weights and Measures* (Charleston, 1823), 5.

98. Cooper, *Lectures*, 253.

99. J. B. Say, *Treatise on Political Economy* (1803; repr., Philadelphia: Grigg and Elliot, 1824), xix–xx. Say's work was standard reading for American free traders; see O'Connor, *Origins of Academic Economics*, 23, 121, 124.

100. Karp, *This Vast Southern Empire*, 5, 2, 100, 198.

101. John Majewski, *Modernizing a Slave Economy: The Economic Vision of the Confederate Nation* (Chapel Hill: University of North Carolina Press, 2009), 3, 160, 10, 80, 129, 21.

102. Richard Franklin Bensel, *Yankee Leviathan: The Origins of Central State Authority in America, 1859–1877* (Cambridge: Cambridge University Press, 1990), 95, 13.

103. Douglas A. Irwin, *Clashing over Commerce: A History of US Trade Policy* (Chicago: University of Chicago Press, 2017), 169–184.

104. Lawrence A. Peskin, *Manufacturing Revolution: The Intellectual Origins of Early American Industry* (Baltimore: Johns Hopkins University Press, 2003), 40–47, 79.

105. Majewski writes: "Secession, then, was something more than a conservative 'counter-revolution' against liberal, egalitarian forces emanating from the North and Europe"; secessionists were driven by a "modernizing impulse" (*Modernizing a Slave Economy*, 10, 160). Majewski qualifies his arguments at several points, notably saying that secessionists "synthesized both free trade and protectionist arguments" (128) in calling for lower duties on European

goods and high tariffs on northern goods, though it remains unclear how this is liberal economic policy. Majewski also notes how secessionists inserted an injunction against protective tariffs (131). The various legislative efforts that were driven by statist secessionists prior to the conflict never garnered majority support.

106. Cooper, *Two Tracts*, 7, 5.

107. Thomas Cooper, "Political Arithmetic, No. II" (1798), in *Philosophical Writings*, by Thomas Cooper, ed. Udo Thiel, vol. 2, *Political Essays* (Bristol: Thoemmes Continuum, 2001), 50.

108. Cooper, *Two Tracts*, 21.

109. Nicholas Onuf and Peter Onuf argue that the debate over commercial policy split the nation and "gave rise to conflicting conceptions of union and nation," in *Nations, Markets, and War: Modern History and the American Civil War* (Charlottesville: University of Virginia Press, 2006), 117, 260. John Ashworth argues that the tensions were spawned by regions' different labor systems, in *Slavery, Capitalism, and Politics in the Antebellum Republic*, vol. 1, *Commerce and Compromise, 1820–1860* (Cambridge: Cambridge University Press, 1995), 13. James M. McPherson emphasizes the differences in economics and society between the North and South in his introduction to *The Battle Cry of Freedom: The Civil War Era* (New York: Oxford University Press, 1988). And Richard Bensel argues, "Even without attempting to abolish slavery outright, the advent of a Republican administration promised potentially lethal changes in the political economy in which the institution [slavery] operated," in *Yankee Leviathan*, 24. The New Historians of Capitalism challenge the conventional understanding of the divide between North and South by pointing to the capitalist and, in some cases, industrial nature of the southern economy; see Karp, *This Vast Southern Empire*, 151, 202, and John Majewski, "Why Did Northerners Oppose the Expansion of Slavery? Economic Development and Education in the Limestone South," in Beckert and Rockman, *Slavery's Capitalism*.

110. Onuf and Onuf, *Nations, Markets, and War*, 10, 174–182, 260–262.

111. Richard Hofstadter's chapter "John C. Calhoun: Marx of the Master Class," in *The American Political Tradition and the Men Who Made It* (1948; New York: Vintage, 1974), 86–117, is a significant piece in the historiography. On the nullification crisis see Sean Wilentz, *The Rise of American Democracy: Jefferson to Lincoln* (New York: W. W. Norton, 2005), 374–379; Arthur M. Schlesinger Jr., *The Age of Jackson* (Boston: Little, Brown, 1945), 33–34, 95–96; Ashworth, *Slavery, Capitalism, and Politics*, 1: 135–136, 202–203, 333–335; Harry Watson, *Liberty and Power: The Politics of Jacksonian America*, rev. ed. (New York: Hill and Wang, 2006), 117–119, 129–131; Merrill D. Peterson, *Olive Branch and Sword: The Compromise of 1833* (Baton Rouge: Louisiana State University Press, 1982).

112. North, *Economic Growth*, 123, 191, 195; Wright, *Cotton South*, 15–24.

113. Peter H. Lindert and Jeffrey G. Williamson, "American Incomes before and after the Revolution," *Journal of Economic History* 73, no. 3 (2013): 725–765; Baptist, "Political Economy of Slave Labor," 54.

114. Calhoun to Samuel Ingham, July 23, 1828, in *The Papers of John C. Calhoun*, vol. 10, ed. Clyde N. Wilson and W. Edwin Hemphill (Columbia: University of South Carolina Press, 1977), 402.

115. Calhoun to John McLean, July 10, 1828, in *Papers*, 10: 397.

116. John C. Calhoun, "Exposition and Protest," in *Papers*, 10: 456.

117. Joseph J. Persky, *The Burden of Dependency: Colonial Themes in Southern Economic*

Thought (Baltimore: Johns Hopkins University Press, 1992), 52; Bruno Gujer, "Free Trade and Slavery: Calhoun's Defense of Southern Interests against British Interference, 1811–1848" (PhD diss., University of Zurich, 1971), 23–43.

118. Brian Schoen, *The Fragile Fabric of Union: Cotton, Federal Politics, and the Global Origins of the Civil War* (Baltimore: Johns Hopkins University Press, 2009), 72–92; Brian Schoen, "Calculating the Price of Union: Republican Economic Nationalism and the Origins of Southern Sectionalism, 1790–1828," *Journal of the Early Republic* 23, no. 2 (2003): 190–206; Gujer, "Free Trade and Slavery," 23–30.

119. Schoen, "Price of Union," 200–203; Persky, *Burden of Dependency*, 52–53.

120. Calhoun to Micah Sterling, September 1, 1828, in *Papers*, 10: 415.

121. Irwin, *Clashing over Commerce*, 165–167.

122. Seth Rockman, "Negro Cloth: Mastering the Market for Slave Clothing in Antebellum America," in Beckert and Desan, *American Capitalism*, 171–180.

123. "Speech of Mr. McDuffie against the Prohibitory System," *Southern Review* 8, no. 15 (1831): 216.

124. Persky provides insightful analysis of McDuffie's ideas in *Burden of Dependence*, 57–68.

125. Calhoun to Samuel Ingham, October 30, 1830, in *The Papers of John C. Calhoun*, vol. 11, ed. Clyde N. Wilson (Columbia: University of South Carolina Press, 1978), 252.

126. Imports and exports were related, but most economic historians find that antebellum tariffs had a marginal impact on the price of cotton, over which the South enjoyed a virtual monopoly. As Douglas Irwin has shown, the tariff did contribute to increased returns on northern capital and lowered land values throughout the country. But, he notes, "the South lost a small amount, in the aggregate, from import duties, but those losses were probably concentrated on a few politically influential landowners," *Clashing over Commerce*, 196.

127. John C. Calhoun, "Speech on the Force Bill," in *The Papers of John C. Calhoun*, vol. 12, ed. Clyde N. Wilson (Columbia: University of South Carolina Press, 1978), 65.

128. Calhoun, "Exposition and Protest," 492, 506, 526.

129. John C. Calhoun, "Rough Draft of an Address to the People of South Carolina," in *Papers*, 11: 272.

130. On Calhoun's republicanism see Lacy K. Ford, "Republican Ideology in a Slave Society: The Political Economy of John C. Calhoun," *Journal of Southern History* 54, no. 3 (1988): 421–422.

131. John C. Calhoun, "The Tariff," *Southern Quarterly Review* 1, no. 2 (1842): 514–515.

132. Appleby, *Capitalism and a New Social Order*, 39–47; Allan Kulikoff, *The Agrarian Origins of American Capitalism* (Charlottesville: University Press of Virginia, 1992).

133. Smith, *Wealth of Nations*, 1: 403. Also, "The capital employed in agriculture, therefore, not only puts into motion a greater quantity of productive labour than any equal capital employed in manufactures, but in proportion, too, to the quantity of productive labour which it employs, it adds a much greater value to the annual produce of the land and labour of the country, to the real wealth and revenue of its inhabitants. Of all the ways in which a capital can be employed, it is by far the most advantageous to the society" (1: 388). David McNally, *Political Economy and the Rise of Capitalism: A Reinterpretation* (Berkeley: University of California Press, 1988), xii–13; Vivienne Brown, *Adam Smith's Discourse: Canonicity, Commerce, and Conscience* (New York: Routledge, 1994), 173–179; Schabas, *Natural Origins of Economics*, 99–100.

134. The development of a manufacturing-centered export economy was not the root cause of the anti–Corn Law movement; rather it was a result of it. The most systematic treatment of the Corn Laws debate, as well as Ricardo's influence over it, remains Boyd Hilton's *Corn, Cash, Commerce: The Economic Policies of Tory Governments, 1815-1830* (Oxford: Oxford University Press, 1977). Also, A. Howe, "Restoring Free Trade"; Richard F. Teichgraeber III, *"Free Trade" and Moral Philosophy: Rethinking the Sources of Adam Smith's "Wealth of Nations"* (Durham, NC: Duke University Press, 1986); William Grampp, *The Manchester School of Economics* (Stanford, CA: Stanford University Press, 1960); Norman McCord, *The Anti-Corn Law League, 1838-1846* (London: Allen and Unwin, 1953); Paul A. Pickering and Alex Tyrrell, *The People's Bread: A History of the Anti–Corn Law League* (London: Leicester University Press, 2000). For an alternative view, see Bernard Semmel, *The Rise of Free Trade Imperialism: Classical Political Economy, the Empire of Free Trade and Imperialism, 1750-1850* (Cambridge: Cambridge University Press, 1970).

135. Hilton, *Corn, Cash, Commerce*, 182-183, 306-312; Berg, "Progress and Providence," 366-369.

136. Hume quoted in Semmel, *Rise of Free Trade Imperialism*, 148.

137. Anna Gambles, *Protection and Politics: Conservative Economic Discourse, 1815-1852* (London: Royal Historical Society, 1999), 42, 51, 69, 77, 183-185, 207, 217-218.

138. Raguet, *Principles of Free Trade*, 151.

139. Calhoun, "Exposition and Protest," 480.

140. Ford, "Republican Ideology in a Slave Society," 421.

141. Hofstadter, *American Political Tradition*, 86.

142. Hartz, *Liberal Tradition in America*, 197.

143. Fogel, *Without Consent or Contract*, 218, estimates that total losses to the British economy from the suppression of the Atlantic slave trade were equal to domestic expenditures for poor relief between 1837 and 1844.

144. Karp, *This Vast Southern Empire*, 133. Karp implies that British abolitionism worked together with British mercantilism. This is odd, considering that British free traders (anti-mercantilists) were abolitionists.

145. Olmstead and Rhode, "Cotton, Slavery" 3-8.

146. Schoen, *Fragile Fabric of Union*, 191.

147. Olmstead and Rhode, "Cotton, Slavery" 11.

Chapter 3. Progress and Poverty: Malthus and Ricardo in America

1. See Anthony Brewer's discussion of Richard Cantillon's ideas on population, *Richard Cantillon: Pioneer of Economic Theory* (London: Routledge, 1992), 36-44. Also, Physiocratic population theory was grounded in materialism theory; see François Quesnay, *Corn* (1757), *Hommes* (1757), and *Miscellaneous Extracts* (1758), in *The Economics of Physiocracy: Essays and Translations*, ed. Ronald L. Meek (Cambridge, MA: Harvard University Press, 1963), 66-67, 84, 88.

2. Adam Smith, *The Theory of Moral Sentiments* (1759; repr., New York: A. M. Kelley, 1966), 264-265.

3. Peter Linebaugh, *The London Hanged: Crime and Civil Society in the Eighteenth Century* (Cambridge: Cambridge University Press, 1992), 8.

4. E. A. Wrigley, "The Growth of Population in Eighteenth-Century England: A Conundrum Resolved," *Past & Present* 98, no. 1 (1983): 124, 127.

5. For a synopsis of Malthus's career and writings see Donald Winch, *Riches and Poverty: An Intellectual History of Political Economy in Britain, 1750–1834* (Cambridge: Cambridge University Press, 1996), chapters 8–12.

6. Thomas Malthus, *An Essay on the Principle of Population*, ed. Geoffrey Gilbert (Oxford: Oxford University Press, 2008), 12–13.

7. Thomas Robert Malthus, *An Essay on the Principle of Population: The 1803 Edition*, ed. Shannon C. Stimson (New Haven, CT: Yale University Press, 2018), 418. This paragraph was omitted from the 1806 and later editions.

8. Malthus, *Principle of Population* (Oxford 2008 edition), 58.

9. George Johnson Cady, "The Early American Reaction to the Theory of Malthus," *Journal of Political Economy* 39, no. 5 (1931): 632. For a list of references in contemporary journals, see Dennis Hodgson, "Malthus' *Essay on Population* and the American Debate over Slavery," *Comparative Studies in Society and History* 51, no. 4 (2009): 747.

10. On the relationship between Malthusianism and Smithian laissez-faire, see Winch, *Riches and Poverty*, 224, 269. Francis Wayland and John McVickar accepted Malthus and Ricardo at face value, but their optimism pointed their thinking in another direction; see John Roscoe Turner, *The Ricardian Rent Theory in Early American Economics* (New York: New York University Press, 1921), 74.

11. Joseph J. Spengler's assessment in "Population Doctrines in the United States, I: Anti-Malthusianism," *Journal of Political Economy* 41, no. 4 (1933): 435, that the Americans misunderstood Malthusianism is inaccurate.

12. James Russell Gibson Jr., *Americans versus Malthus: The Population Debate in the Early Republic, 1790–1840* (New York: Garland, 1989), 27.

13. Benjamin Franklin, "Observations Concerning the Increase of Mankind and the Peopling of Countries" (1755), in *Essays on General Politics, Commerce, and Political Economy*, ed. Jared Sparks (1836; repr., New York: A. M. Kelley, 1971), 313.

14. Franklin, "Observations Concerning the Increase," 313.

15. On the belief in exceptionalism in American intellectual history, see Dorothy Ross, *The Origins of American Social Science* (Cambridge: Cambridge University Press, 1991); Seymour Martin Lipset, *American Exceptionalism: A Double-Edged Sword* (New York: W. W. Norton, 1996); Jonathan A. Glickstein, *American Exceptionalism, American Anxiety: Wages, Competition, and Degraded Labor in the Antebellum United States* (Charlottesville: University of Virginia Press, 2002).

16. Franklin, "Observations Concerning the Increase," 311.

17. Sidney Sherwood, "Tendencies in American Economic Thought," *Johns Hopkins Studies* 15, no. 12 (1897): 10.

18. Michael J. L. O'Connor, *Origins of Academic Economics in the United States* (New York: Columbia University Press, 1974), 160. Joseph J. Spengler, "Population Theory in the Ante-Bellum South," *Journal of Southern History* 2, no. 3 (1936): 36.

19. Francis Wayland, *The Elements of Political Economy* (New York: Leavitt, Lord, 1837), 340.

20. Gibson, *Americans versus Malthus*, argues that the Americans met Malthus with the machine. Americans perceived industrialization as the harbinger of unprecedented growth,

and thus, capable of sustaining large populations. See also Edmond Cocks, "The Malthusian Theory in Pre–Civil War America: An Original Relation to the Universe," *Population Studies* 20, no. 3 (1967): 351–352; Spengler, "Anti-Malthusianism," 437–439.

21. Francis Bowen, *The Principles of Political Economy Applied to the Condition, the Resources, and the Institutions of the American People* (1856; repr., New York: Garland, 1974), 141.

22. Turner, *Ricardian Rent Theory*, 34, 112.

23. For instance, Alexander H. Everett, *New Ideas on Population, with Remarks on the Theories of Malthus and Godwin* (1826; repr., New York: A. M. Kelley, 1970), 40; E. Peschine Smith, *A Manual of Political Economy* (1853; repr., New York: Garland, 1974), 50–75; Daniel Raymond, *The Elements of Political Economy*, 2nd ed. (1823; repr., New York: A. M. Kelley, 1964), 2: 71–80; Daniel Raymond, *Thoughts on Political Economy* (Baltimore: F. Lucas, 1820), 88, 129, 367–368, 379. Protectionists' optimism, and especially their refutation of diminishing returns, is highlighted in chapters 6 and 7 below.

24. Margo J. Anderson, *The American Census: A Social History* (New Haven, CT: Yale University Press, 1990), 8–10.

25. Gibson, *Americans versus Malthus*, 96–103.

26. L[oammi] Baldwin, *Thoughts on the Study of Political Economy, as Connected with the Population, Industry, and Paper Currency of the United States* (1809; repr., New York: A. M. Kelley, 1968), 67.

27. Samuel P. Newman, *The Elements of Political Economy* (1835; repr., Clifton, NJ: A. M. Kelley, 1973), 203, 66.

28. Ibid., 254–255.

29. Eric H. Walther, *The Fire-Eaters* (Baton Rouge: Louisiana State University Press, 1992), 204–205; Spengler, "Population Theory," 373.

30. James Oakes, *The Ruling Race: A History of American Slaveholders* (New York: Knopf, 1982), 57–104.

31. Walter Johnson, *River of Dark Dreams: Slavery and Empire in the Cotton Kingdom* (Cambridge, MA: Belknap Press of Harvard University Press, 2013), 84–87.

32. Oakes, *Ruling Race*, 57–77, 154–170.

33. Amy Dru Stanley, "Slave Breeding and Free Love: An Antebellum Argument over Slavery, Capitalism, and Personhood," in *Capitalism Takes Command: The Social Transformation of Nineteenth-Century America*, eds. Michael Zakim and Gary J. Kornblith (Chicago: University of Chicago Press, 2012), 139.

34. Robert William Fogel, *Without Consent or Contract: The Rise and Fall of American Slavery* (New York: W. W. Norton, 1989), 124.

35. J. D. B. De Bow, "Notes on Political Economy," *De Bow's Southern and Western Review* 36, no. 4 (1855): 422–423.

36. J. D. B. De Bow, *The Industrial Resources, Statistics, &c. of the United States and More Particularly of the Southern and Western States*, 3rd. ed. (1854; repr., New York: A. M. Kelley 1966), 1: 12.

37. Ibid., 1: 69.

38. J. D. B. De Bow, "The Non-Slaveholders of the South: Their Interest in the Present Sectional Controversy Identical with That of the Slaveholders" (1861), in *Slavery Defended: The Views of the Old South*, ed. Eric L. McKitrick (Englewood Cliffs, NJ: Prentice-Hall, 1963), 72; Ross, *American Social Science*, 32.

39. De Bow, "Non-Slaveholders of the South," 72.

40. Spengler, "Anti-Malthusianism," 435.

41. George Tucker, *Progress of the United States in Population and Wealth in Fifty Years With an Appendix Containing an Abstract of the Census of 1850* (1855; repr.: New York: A. M. Kelley, 1964), iii, 27.

42. George Tucker, "On Density of Population," in *Essays on Various Subjects of Taste, Morals, and National Policy* (Georgetown, DC: Joseph Milligan, 1822), 82.

43. Ibid., 76.

44. Leonard C. Helderman, "A Social Scientist of the Old South," *Journal of Southern History* 2, no. 2 (1936): 167.

45. "The Malthusian Theory Discussed in a Correspondence between Alexander Everett and Prof. George Tucker May 14, 1844" (1845), in Everett, *New Ideas on Population*, 298. Tucker later restated his Malthusian position: "As population advances, and the means of subsistence become comparatively more difficult of attainment, a portion of the community must pass from a dearer to a cheaper mode of subsistence, or the population must become stationary," in *Political Economy for the People* (1859; repr., New York: A. M. Kelley, 1970), 80.

46. "The Malthusian Theory Discussed," 299.

47. See also George Tucker, *The Laws of Wages, Profits and Rents Investigated* (1837; repr., New York: A. M. Kelley, 1964), 32, 117–120, 155.

48. Hodgson, "Malthus' *Essay on Population*," 748.

49. Laurence Shore, *Southern Capitalists: The Ideological Leadership of an Elite, 1832–1885* (Chapel Hill: University of North Carolina Press, 1986), 26–28; Hodgson, "Malthus' *Essay on Population*," 744, 747.

50. Thomas Cooper, *Lectures on the Elements of Political Economy* (1831; repr., New York: A. M. Kelley, 1971), 273, 276.

51. Joseph J. Spengler, "Population Doctrines in the United States. II. Malthusianism," *Journal of Political Economy* 41, no. 5 (1933): 646; Hodgson, "Malthus' *Essay on Population*," 747–751.

52. Lowell Harrison, "Thomas Roderick Dew: Philosopher of the Old South," *Virginia Magazine of History and Biography* 57, no. 4 (1949): 390.

53. Joseph Dorfman, *The Economic Mind in American Civilization*, vols. 1–2, *1606–1865* (New York: Viking, 1946), 1: 895–896.

54. Michael O'Brien, *Conjectures of Order: Intellectual Life and the American South, 1810–1860* (Chapel Hill: University of North Carolina Press, 2004), 2: 888.

55. Thomas R. Dew, *Lectures on the Restrictive System* (1829; repr,, New York: A. M. Kelley, 1969), 39, 46, 30, 195.

56. William S. Belko, *The Triumph of the Antebellum Free Trade Movement* (Gainesville: University Press of Florida, 2012), 75. Belko offers insightful analysis of Dew's economic thought, 76–92.

57. Shore, *Southern Capitalists*, 26–27.

58. Thomas R. Dew, *Review of the Debate in the Virginia Legislature of 1831 and 1832* (Westport, CT: Negro Universities Press, 1979), 53.

59. Ibid., 56, 53.

60. Dew, *Lectures on the Restrictive System*, 26, 153, 144.

61. Ibid., 146, 153.

62. Malthus to E. D. Clark, 1807, quoted in Seymour Drescher, *The Mighty Experiment: Free Labor versus Slavery in British Emancipation* (Oxford: Oxford University Press, 2002), 43.

63. For analysis of the American reception of Ricardo, see Turner, *Ricardian Rent Theory*.

64. Joseph Dorfman, "Henry Vethake: Jacksonian Ricardian," in *Early American Policy: Six Columbia Contributors*, ed. Joseph Dorfman and R. G. Tugwell (New York: Columbia University Press, 1960), 155.

65. Ricardo in 1822, quoted in *The Works and Correspondence of David Ricardo*, ed. Piero Sraffa with M. H. Dobb, 11 vols. (Cambridge: Cambridge University Press, 1951–1955), 10: 36. For discussion of Ricardo's *Principles*, see the editors' introduction to *Works and Correspondence* in vol. 1; also John Cunningham Wood, ed., *David Ricardo: Critical Assessments* (1985; London: Routledge, 1991); T. W. Hutchison, *On Revolutions and Progress in Economic Knowledge* (Cambridge: Cambridge University Press, 1978), 54–56; Charles Gide and Charles Rist, *History of Economic Doctrines from the Time of the Physiocrats to the Present Day*, trans. Robert Richards (Boston: D. C. Heath, 1915), 139–160.

66. T. R. Malthus, *Principles of Political Economy*, ed. John Pullen (Cambridge: Cambridge University Press, 1989), 1: 23.

67. Ricardo, *The Principles of Political Economy and Taxation*, in *Works and Correspondence*, 1: 67, 102.

68. Ibid., 1: 126, 122, 335.

69. Margaret Schabas, *The Natural Origins of Economics* (Chicago: University of Chicago Press, 2005), 113–119, 124, 129–134.

70. Ricardo, *Principles of Political Economy and Taxation*, 1: 126.

71. Turner, *Ricardian Rent Theory*, 67; Dorfman, "Henry Vethake: Jacksonian Ricardian," 155.

72. Dorfman, "Henry Vethake: Jacksonian Ricardian"; Paul Conkin, *Prophets of Prosperity: America's First Political Economists* (Bloomington: Indiana University Press, 1980), 133–134.

73. Turner, *Ricardian Rent Theory*, 71.

74. Henry Vethake, *The Principles of Political Economy*, 2nd ed. (1844; repr., New York: A. M. Kelley, 1971), 283.

75. Ibid., 407, 404, 230, 303.

76. Ibid., 283, 258, 225, 404.

77. A sect of British neo-Ricardians/Ricardian Socialists, discussed briefly in the next chapter, emerged during the 1820s and 1830s. They interpreted the labor theory of value to attack industrialization. See Noel W. Thompson, *The People's Science: The Political Economy of Exploitation and Crisis, 1816–1834* (Cambridge: Cambridge University Press, 1984); Esther Lowenthal, *The Ricardian Socialists* (New York: Columbia University Press, 1911); George J. Stigler, "Ricardo and the 93% Labor Theory of Value," *American Economic Review* 48, no. 3 (1958).

78. Vethake, *Principles of Political Economy*, 327–331.

79. Turner, *Ricardian Rent Theory*, 72.

80. Vethake, *Principles of Political Economy*, 73.

81. Edward Pessen, *Jacksonian America: Society, Personality, and Politics*, rev. ed. (Homewood, IL: Dorsey, 1978), 86.

82. Edward Pessen, *Riches, Class, and Power before the Civil War* (Lexington, MA: D. C. Heath, 1973), 34, 35–128.

83. Conkin, *Prophets of Prosperity*, 126; Dorfman, *Economic Mind*, 2: 37.
84. Vethake, *Principles of Political Economy*, 90–93.
85. Joseph Dorfman, introduction to Vethake, *Principles of Political Economy*, 11.
86. Vethake, *Principles of Political Economy*, 94, 93, 230–303.
87. Ibid., 70, 71, 74; Conkin, *Prophets of Prosperity*, 126; Dorfman, *Economic Mind*, 2: 37.
88. Lacy K. Ford Jr., *The Origins of Southern Radicalism: The South Carolina Upcountry, 1800–1860* (New York: Oxford University Press, 1988); Wilfred Carsel, "The Slaveholders' Indictment of Northern Wage Slavery," *Journal of Southern History* 6, no. 4 (1940); Jonathan A. Glickstein, *Concepts of Free Labor in Antebellum America* (New Haven, CT: Yale University Press, 1991); Eric Foner, *Free Soil, Free Labor, Free Men: The Ideology of the Republican Party before the Civil War* (Oxford: Oxford University Press, 1970); William Sumner Jenkins, *Pro-Slavery Thought in the Old South* (Chapel Hill: University of North Carolina Press, 1935). See chapter 5 below for further discussion.
89. Barnett A. Elzas, *The Jews of South Carolina: From the Earliest Times to the Present Day* (Philadelphia: Lippincott, 1905), 177.
90. Melvin M. Leiman, *Jacob N. Cardozo: Economic Thought in the Antebellum South* (New York: Columbia University Press, 1966), 73–87, 27–28.
91. The equivalent today would be about fifty dollars.
92. Jacob Cardozo, "The Tariff—Its True Character and Effects Practically Illustrated" (1830), in *Notes on Political Economy* (1826; repr., New York: A. M. Kelley, 1972), 212, 191; O'Brien, *Conjectures of Order*, 2: 919.
93. Cardozo, "The Tariff," 212.
94. Leiman, *Jacob N. Cardozo*, 39; Dorfman, *Economic Mind*, 2: 558; Abram C. Flora Jr., "Economic Thought in South Carolina, 1820–1860" (PhD diss., University of North Carolina, 1957), 12.
95. Cardozo, *Notes on Political Economy*, iii.
96. Ibid., 8–9, 66–72, 136; Allen Kaufman, *Capitalism, Slavery, and Republican Values: Antebellum Political Economists, 1819–1848* (Austin: University of Texas Press, 1982), 127–129.
97. Cardozo, *Notes on Political Economy*, 36, 52, 8.
98. Ibid., 38, 137.
99. Ibid., 124, iii.
100. Conkin, *Prophets of Prosperity*, 111.
101. Hutchison, *Revolutions and Progress*, 54–58, 77–79, 90.

Chapter 4. The Crisis of Free Society: The Southern and Northern Reactionaries

1. Jonathan A. Glickstein, *American Exceptionalism, American Anxiety: Wages, Competition, and Degraded Labor in the Antebellum United States* (Charlottesville: University of Virginia Press, 2002), 20–26, 38–44; Jonathan A. Glickstein, *Concepts of Free Labor in Antebellum America* (New Haven, CT: Yale University Press, 1991), 142–159; Eric Foner, *Free Soil, Free Labor, Free Men: The Ideology of the Republican Party before the Civil War* (Oxford: Oxford University Press, 1970), xi–xxv; William Sumner Jenkins, *Pro-Slavery Thought in the Old South* (Chapel Hill: University of North Carolina Press, 1935), 298; Laurence Shore, *Southern Capitalists: The Ideological Leadership of an Elite, 1832–1885* (Chapel Hill: University of North

Carolina Press, 1986), 17; James L. Huston, *The Panic of 1857 and the Coming of the Civil War* (Baton Rouge: Louisiana State University Press, 1987), 99–100; Eugene D. Genovese, *The Slaveholders' Dilemma: Freedom and Progress in Southern Conservative Thought, 1820–1860* (Columbia: University of South Carolina Press, 1992), 6, 35–37, 56–57; Lacy J. Ford Jr., *The Origins of Southern Radicalism: The South Carolina Upcountry, 1800–1860* (New York: Oxford University Press, 1988), 353–362; Wilfred Carsel, "The Slaveholders' Indictment of Northern Wage Slavery," *Journal of Southern History* 6, no. 4 (1940).

2. Fitzhugh to Holmes, March 27, 1855, Holmes Letterbook, Duke University Library, quoted in Eugene D. Genovese, *The World the Slaveholders Made: Two Essays in Interpretation* (New York: Pantheon, 1969), 130.

3. Fitzhugh to President Buchanan, June 1858, quoted in Joseph Dorfman, *The Economic Mind in American Civilization*, vols. 1–2, *1606–1865* (New York: Viking, 1946), 2: 933.

4. James Oakes, *The Ruling Race: A History of American Slaveholders* (New York: Knopf, 1982), 197–198. Radical pro-slavery thought is discussed in Eric H. Walther, *The Fire-Eaters* (Baton Rouge: Louisiana State University Press, 1992); John Ashworth, *Slavery, Capitalism, and Politics in the Antebellum Republic*, vol. 1, *Commerce and Compromise, 1820–1850* (Cambridge: Cambridge University Press, 1995), 216–228; Paul Finkelman, *Defending Slavery: Proslavery Thought in the Old South: A Brief History with Documents* (Boston: Bedford, 2003).

5. Genovese, *World the Slaveholders Made*, 129.

6. George Fitzhugh, *Cannibals All!; or, Slaves without Masters* (1857; Cambridge, MA: Belknap Press of Harvard University Press, 1988), 132–133, 69.

7. George Fitzhugh, *Sociology for the South; or, The Failure of Free Society* (1854; repr., New York: B. Franklin, 1965), 178.

8. Fitzhugh, *Cannibals All!*, 253–254.

9. Fitzhugh, *Sociology for the South*, 10, 178, 265.

10. Ibid., 23.

11. Ibid., 20.

12. Genovese, *World the Slaveholders Made*, 168, 184–190; Ashworth, *Slavery, Capitalism, and Politics*, 1: 230, 232.

13. Fitzhugh, *Cannibals All!*, 202–203, 18, 16.

14. Ibid., 76.

15. Fitzhugh, *Sociology for the South*, 70–71.

16. Ibid., 38.

17. Ibid., 226.

18. Fitzhugh, *Cannibals All!*, 23.

19. Ashworth, *Slavery, Capitalism, and Politics*, 1: 230.

20. Harvey Wish, *George Fitzhugh, Propagandist of the Old South* (Baton Rouge: Louisiana State University Press, 1943), 20.

21. Ashworth, *Slavery, Capitalism, and Politics*, 1: 231.

22. Fitzhugh, *Cannibals All!*, 201; Fitzhugh, *Sociology for the South*, 43.

23. Fitzhugh, *Cannibals All!*, 94.

24. Fitzhugh, *Sociology for the South*, 46.

25. Genovese is associated with this interpretation.

26. Oakes, *The Ruling Race*, 195, 218–220, 173.

27. Harry L. Watson, "Slavery and Development in a Dual Economy: The South and the

Market Revolution," in *The Market Revolution in America: Social, Political, and Religious Expressions, 1800–1880*, ed. Melvyn Stokes and Stephen Conway (Charlottesville: University Press of Virginia, 1996), 49.

28. The description of Fitzhugh's home is found in C. Vann Woodward, introduction to Fitzhugh, *Cannibals All!*, xii.

29. Louis M. Hacker, *The Triumph of American Capitalism: The Development of Forces in American History to the End of the Nineteenth Century* (New York: Simon and Schuster, 1940), 290–291; Ford, *Origins of Southern Radicalism*, 72–84.

30. Oakes, *The Ruling Race*, 84–87.

31. William Howard Russell, *My Diary, North and South* (Boston: T. O. H. P. Burnham, 1863), 179.

32. Watson, "Slavery and Development," 64.

33. Southern dissident culture during the Civil War era seems to have exaggerated class distinctions in the rebel armies. James M. McPherson's *Battle Cry of Freedom: The Civil War Era* (New York: Oxford University Press, 1988) finds "the greater tendency of men from its poorest upcountry regions to skedaddle, desert, or otherwise avoid Confederate service" (615).

34. George Fitzhugh, "The Impending Fate of the Country," *De Bow's Southern and Western Review* 2, no. 6 (1866): 567–569.

35. Fitzhugh, *Sociology for the South*, 10.

36. Louis Hartz, *The Liberal Tradition in America: An Interpretation of American Political Thought Since the Revolution* (New York: Harcourt, Brace, 1955), 184; Clinton Rossiter, *Conservatism in America: The Thankless Persuasion*, 2nd ed. (New York: Knopf, 1962), 124. See also Wish, *George Fitzhugh*.

37. Neal C. Gillespie, *The Collapse of Orthodoxy: The Intellectual Ordeal of George Frederick Holmes* (Charlottesville: University Press of Virginia, 1972).

38. George Frederick Holmes, "Capital and Labor," *De Bow's Southern and Western Review* 22, no. 2 (1857): 256.

39. W. J. Cash, *The Mind of the South* (New York: Knopf, 1941); Clement Eaton, *The Freedom of Thought Struggle in the Old South* (New York: Harper, 1964); William Dodd, "The Social Philosophy of the Old South," *The American Journal of Sociology* 23, no. 6 (1918); William Robert Taylor, *Cavalier and Yankee: The Old South and American National Character* (New York: Braziller, 1961); Richard Hofstadter, *Anti-Intellectualism in American Life* (New York: Knopf, 1963).

40. George Frederick Holmes, "Carlyle's Latter-Day Pamphlets," *Southern Quarterly Review* 18, no. 2 (1850): 329, 354.

41. Ibid., 354; George Frederick Holmes, "The Nineteenth Century," *Southern Literary Messenger* 17, no. 8 (1851): 460.

42. Holmes, "The Nineteenth Century," 461.

43. George Frederick Holmes, "Failure of Free Societies," *Southern Literary Messenger* 21, no. 3 (1855): 133.

44. Holmes, "The Nineteenth Century," 460, 465.

45. George Frederick Holmes, "Greeley on Reforms," *Southern Literary Messenger* 17, no. 5 (1851): 263.

46. George Frederick Holmes, "Slavery and Freedom," *Southern Quarterly Review*, n.s., 1, no. 1 (1856): 81, 84.

47. Alan L. Olmstead and Paul W. Rhode, "Cotton, Slavery, and the 'New History of Capitalism,'" *Explorations in Economic History* 67 (2018): 7–8; Stanley Lebergott, "Wage Trends: 1800–1900," in *Trends in the American Economy in the Nineteenth Century*, comp. National Bureau of Economic Research (Princeton, NJ: Princeton University Press, 1960), 457.

48. Holmes, "Carlyle's Latter-Day Pamphlets," 345. Edmund Ruffin expands on this point in *The Political Economy of Slavery; or, The Institution Considered in Regard to Its Influence on Public Wealth and the General Welfare* (1853), in Finkelman, *Defending Slavery*, 67–73.

49. George Frederick Holmes, "Speculation and Trade," *Southern Quarterly Review*, n.s., 1, no. 1 (1856): 23.

50. Holmes, "The Nineteenth Century," 461.

51. George Frederick Holmes, "Review of Uncle Tom's Cabin," in *Slavery Defended: The Views of the Old South*, ed. Eric L. McKitrick (Englewood Cliffs, NJ: Prentice-Hall, 1963), 106; Holmes, "Slavery and Freedom," 71, 73, 86–88, 93; Holmes, "Greeley on Reforms," 260.

52. Oakes, *The Ruling Race*, 229, 207–208.

53. Holmes, "The Nineteenth Century," 466.

54. Holmes, "Carlyle's Latter-Day Pamphlets," 328, 351.

55. Ibid., 331.

56. Holmes, "Greeley on Reforms," 260.

57. Henry Hughes, *Treatise on Sociology, Theoretical and Practical* (1854; repr., New York: Negro Universities Press, 1968), 186, 123; Michael O'Brien, *Conjectures of Order: Intellectual Life and the American South, 1810–1860* (Chapel Hill: University of North Carolina Press, 2004), 2: 966–969.

58. James Hammond, "Mud-sill Speech," in Finkelman, *Defending Slavery*, 67, 86–88.

59. Ruffin, *Political Economy of Slavery*, 68, 67.

60. Walther, *The Fire-Eaters*, 267–268.

61. William H. Herndon to Jesse W. Weik, October 28, 1885, *Herndon on Lincoln: Letters*, ed. Douglas L. Wilson and Rodney O. Davis (Urbana, IL: Knox College Lincoln Studies Center, 2016), 159.

62. Gillespie, *Collapse of Orthodoxy*, 202–203, 210, 204.

63. *American Historical Review* 3, no. 2 (1898): 392.

64. Hartz, *Liberal Tradition in America*, 197.

65. Ibid., 176.

66. Sven Beckert and Seth Rockman, introduction to *Slavery's Capitalism: A New History of American Economic Development*, ed. Becker and Rockman (Philadelphia: University of Pennsylvania Press, 2016), 14; Edward E. Baptist, "Toward a Political Economy of Slave Labor: Hands, Whipping-Machines, and Modern Power," in Beckert and Rockman, *Slavery's Capitalism*, 40, 44–45.

67. Olmstead and Rhode, "Cotton, Slavery, and the 'New History of Capitalism,'" 17.

68. Mark A. Lause, *Young America: Land, Labor, and the Republican Community* (Urbana; University of Illinois Press, 2005), 2; Walter Hugins, *Jacksonian Democracy and the Working Class: A Study of the New York Workingmen's Movement, 1829–1837* (Stanford, CA: Stanford University Press, 1967), 112–128, for occupational affiliations in the Working Men's Party.

69. Sean Wilentz, *Chants Democratic: New York City and the Rise of the American Working Class, 1788–1850* (New York: Oxford University Press, 1984), 17.

70. Ibid., 30–60, 107–132.

71. Timothy Messer-Kruse, *The Yankee International: Marxism and the American Reform Tradition, 1848–1876* (Chapel Hill: University of North Carolina Press, 1998). Historians debate the existence of an anticapitalist class consciousness among antebellum industrial labor. Sean Wilentz finds a "class-conscious, inter-ethnic New York labor movement of the mid-1830s" in *Chants Democratic*, 9. Wilentz's assessment is supported by Carl N. Degler, "The Locofocos: Urban 'Agrarians,'" *Journal of Economic History* 16, no. 3 (1956); James Roger Sharp, *The Jacksonians versus the Banks: Politics in the States after the Panic of 1837* (New York: Columbia University Press, 1970); John M. McFaul, *The Politics of Jacksonian Finance* (Ithaca, NY: Cornell University Press, 1972); John Ashworth, *'Agrarians' and 'Aristocrats': Party Political Ideology in the United States, 1837–1846* (1982; repr., Cambridge: Cambridge University Press, 1987); Arthur M. Schlesinger Jr., *The Age of Jackson* (Boston: Little, Brown, 1945); Charles Sellers, *The Market Revolution: Jacksonian America, 1815–1848* (New York: Oxford University Press, 1991); Jamie L. Bronstein, *Land Reform and Working-Class Experience in Britain and the United States, 1800–1862* (Stanford, CA: Stanford University Press, 1999). Edward Pessen describes the labor leaders as "uncommon" in *Most Uncommon Jacksonians: The Radical Leaders of the Early Labor Movement* (Albany: State University of New York Press, 1967). Joseph Dorfman and Walter Hugins argue that the heterogeneity of the working class precluded formation of a single ideological pattern and that in general the leaders of the movement were laissez-faire entrepreneurs; see Dorfman, "The Jacksonian Wage-Earner Thesis," *American Historical Review* 54, no. 2 (1949); Hugins, *Jacksonian Democracy and the Working Class*.

72. Bronstein, *Land Reform*, 113; Wilentz, *Chants Democratic*, 340–343.

73. Joseph Dorfman, introduction to *Observations on the Sources and Effects of Unequal Wealth, with Propositions Towards Remedying the Disparity of Profit in Pursuing the Arts of Life and Establishing Security in Individual Prospects and Resources*, by L[angton] Byllesby (1826; repr., New York: Russell and Russell, 1961). Discussion of Byllesby is found in Paul K. Conkin, *Prophets of Prosperity: America's First Political Economists* (Bloomington: Indiana University Press, 1980), 234–246; Martin J. Burke, *The Conundrum of Class: Public Discourse on the Social Order in America* (Chicago: University of Chicago Press, 1995), 84–86; John Lauritz Larson, *The Market Revolution in America: Liberty, Ambition, and the Eclipse of the Common Good* (Cambridge: Cambridge University Press, 2010), 146–147; Wilentz, *Chants Democratic*, 164–167; Dorfman, *Economic Mind*, 2: 638–641.

74. Conkin, *Prophets of Prosperity*, 234.

75. Conkin, *Prophets of Prosperity*, 234–236, covers Byllesby under the chapter title "Agrarians." Dorfman's introduction to Byllesby's *Observations* describes the work as "the first systematic American treatise" on Owenism (9).

76. Byllesby, *Observations*, 23, 52, 30.

77. Ibid., 53.

78. Bruce Laurie, *Artisans into Workers: Labor in Nineteenth-Century America* (New York: Hill and Wang, 1989), 65.

79. Byllesby, *Observations*, 76–94.

80. Ibid., 110, 117.

81. Dorfman, "The Jacksonian Wage-Earner Thesis," 306.

82. Rossiter, *Conservatism in America*, 6–7.

83. Noel W. Thompson, *The People's Science: The Political Economy of Exploitation and*

Crisis, 1816-1834 (Cambridge: Cambridge University Press, 1984); Esther Lowenthal, *The Ricardian Socialists* (New York: Columbia University Press, 1911); George J. Stigler, "Ricardo and the 93% Labor Theory of Value," *The American Economic Review* 48, no. 3 (1958).

84. Byllesby, *Observations*, 121.

85. Wilentz, *Chants Democratic*, 167.

86. For a sympathetic biography of Skidmore, see Amos Gilbert, *A Sketch of the Life of Thomas Skidmore* (1834; Chicago: C. H. Kerr, 1984). Other analyses of Skidmore include Conkin, *Prophets of Prosperity*, 237–239; Wilentz, *Chants Democratic*, 182–187; Dorfman, *Economic Mind*, 2: 641–645.

87. Thomas Skidmore, *The Rights of Man to Property!* (1829; repr., New York: B. Franklin, 1966), 8.

88. Ibid., 37, 136, 56, 4.

89. Ibid., 255, 283, 246–247, 228, 346.

90. Ibid., 121, 130. Some of Skidmore's proposals are repeated in his shorter work, *Moral Physiology Exposed and Refuted* (New York: Skidmore and Jacobs, 1831).

91. Wilentz, *Chants Democratic*, 187.

92. Dorfman, "The Jacksonian Wage-Earner Thesis," 300.

93. Skidmore, *Rights of Man to Property!*, 273–275.

94. Wilentz, *Chants Democratic*, 195–198, 202–208; Pessen, *Most Uncommon Jacksonians*, 60–61.

95. Stephen Simpson, *The Working Man's Manual: A New Theory of Political Economy, on the Principle of Production the Source of Wealth* (Philadelphia: T. L. Bonsal, 1831), 44–45, 70, 83.

96. John Pickering, *The Working Man's Political Economy: Founded upon the Principle of Immutable Justice and the Inalienable Rights of Man; Designed for the Promotor of National Reform* (1847; repr., New York: Arno, 1971), 9, 55, 66, 38, 45.

97. Holmes, "The Nineteenth Century," 466.

98. Ibid., 466.

99. François Furstenberg, "Beyond Freedom and Slavery: Autonomy, Virtue, and Resistance in Early American Political Discourse," *Journal of American History* 89, no. 4 (2003). For a sweeping review of modern understandings of economic freedoms, see Eric MacGilvray, *The Invention of Market Freedom* (Cambridge: Cambridge University Press, 2011).

100. Karl Marx, *Value, Price and Profit: Addressed to Working Men* (1865), in *The Portable Karl Marx*, ed. Eugene Kamenka (New York: Viking, 1983), 423–424; Ruffin, *Political Economy of Slavery*, 74; Fitzhugh, *Sociology for the South*, 48.

Chapter 5. An American Political Economy

1. Richard W. Thompson, *The History of Protective Tariff Laws* (Chicago: R. S. Peale, 1888), 38, which describes the petitioners as tradesmen, mechanics, and others from Baltimore.

2. William H. Michael and Pitman Pulsifer, comps., *Tariff Acts Passed by the Congress of the United States from 1789 to 1895, Including All Acts, Resolutions, and Proclamations Modifying or Changing Those Acts* (Washington, DC: United States Government Printing Office, 1896), 9; Douglas A. Irwin, *Clashing over Commerce: A History of U.S. Trade Policy* (Chicago: University of Chicago Press, 2017), 72–77.

3. George Washington, "First Annual Address," in *A Compilation of the Messages and Papers of the Presidents, 1789-1897*, comp. James D. Richardson, 10 vols. (Washington, DC: United States Government Printing Office, 1896-1899), 1: 65.

4. The exceptions are F. W. Taussig, *The Tariff History of the United States*, 8th ed. (1931; New York: Capricorn, 1964); Lawrence A. Peskin, *Manufacturing Revolution: The Intellectual Origins of Early American Industry* (Baltimore: Johns Hopkins University Press, 2003); Percy Ashley, *Modern Tariff History: Germany-United States-France*, 3rd ed. (1920; New York: H. Fertig, 1970); Judith Goldstein, *Ideas, Interests, and American Trade Policy* (Ithaca, NY: Cornell University Press, 1993); Richard C. Edwards, "Economic Sophistication in Nineteenth Century Congressional Tariff Debates," *Journal of Economic History* 30, no. 4 (1970); Malcolm Rogers Eiselen, *The Rise of Pennsylvania Protectionism* (1932; New York: Garland, 1974); Michael Hudson, *Economics and Technology in 19th-Century American Thought* (New York: Garland, 1975); Edward Stanwood, *American Tariff Controversies in the Nineteenth Century*, 2 vols. (1903; New York: Garland, 1974); Joseph Dorfman, *The Economic Mind in American Civilization*, vols. 1-2, *1606-1865* (New York: Viking, 1946); James L. Huston, *Securing the Fruits of Labor: The American Concept of Wealth Distribution* (Baton Rouge: Louisiana State University Press, 1998). More recently, tariffs have been studied as political coalition building and evaluation of international trade theory. For instance, Benjamin J. Cohen and Charles Lipson, eds., *Issues and Agents in International Political Economy: an* International Organization *Reader* (Cambridge, MA: MIT Press, 1999); Robert Gilpin, *Global Political Economy: Understanding the International Economic Order* (Princeton, NJ: Princeton University Press, 2001).

5. Douglas A. Irwin, *Against the Tide: An Intellectual History of Free Trade* (Princeton, NJ: Princeton University Press, 1996), 3.

6. Matthew Josephson, *The Politicos, 1865-1896* (New York: Harcourt, Brace, 1938), 112.

7. There is an implicit judgment that the free-trade position occupied a higher moral plank. Jonathan J. Pincus, *Pressure Groups and Politics in Antebellum Tariffs* (New York: Columbia University Press, 1977), begins his work on tariffs and political coalition building with the following: "The term 'Free trade,' like 'Virginity,' refers to one condition only, whereas 'Protection' covers a multitude, as does 'Sin.' This book is an investigation into the morphology of the sin of Protection, not into the conditions of a fall from Grace" (1). Also Robert W. McGee, *A Trade Policy for Free Societies: The Case Against Protectionism* (Westport, CT: Quorum, 1994), "The only two kinds of trade are free trade and restricted trade.... If trade is restricted because of some tariff, quota, or antidumping policy, it is the result of special interests (producers) going to the legislature to seek the hand of government to protect them from foreign competitors.... protectionist policies are an abuse of governmental power" (vii-viii).

8. Michael J. L. O'Connor, *Origins of Academic Economics in the United States* (New York: Columbia University Press, 1944), 21.

9. Karl Marx, "Contribution to the Critique of Hegel's *Philosophy of Right*: Introduction" (1844), in *The Marx-Engels Reader*, ed. Robert C. Tucker (New York: W. W. Norton, 1978), 57.

10. Andrew Shankman, "Capitalism, Slavery, and the New Epoch: Mathew Carey's 1819," in *Slavery's Capitalism: A New History of American Economic Development*, ed. Sven Beckert and Seth Rockman (Philadelphia: University of Pennsylvania Press, 2016), 260.

11. Frank William Taussig, *Some Aspects of the Tariff Question* (Cambridge, MA: Harvard University Press, 1915), 365.

12. Peskin, *Manufacturing Revolution*; E. A. J. Johnson, *American Economic Thought in the Seventeenth Century* (London: P. S. King, 1932), 11–18, 253–255, 268–269; Eliga Gould, "War by Other Means: Mercantilism and Free Trade in the Age of the American Revolution," in *American Capitalism: New Histories*, ed. Sven Beckert and Christine Desan (New York: Columbia University Press, 2018), 285–298; Steve Pincus, "Rethinking Mercantilism: Political Economy, the British Empire, and the Atlantic World in the Seventeenth and Eighteenth Centuries," *William and Mary Quarterly* 69, no. 1 (2012): 4–7; William Appleman Williams, "The Age of Mercantilism: An Interpretation of the American Political Economy, 1763 to 1828," *William and Mary Quarterly* 15, no. 4 (1958): 421–422.

13. Cathy D. Matson and Peter S. Onuf, *A Union of Interests: Political and Economic Thought in Revolutionary America* (Lawrence: University Press of Kansas, 1990), 7. A sample of the literature on Hamilton includes Gerald Stourzh, *Alexander Hamilton and the Idea of Republican Government* (Stanford, CA: Stanford University of Press, 1970); Stanley Elkins and Eric McKitrick, *The Age of Federalism: The Early American Republic, 1788–1800* (Oxford: Oxford University Press, 1993); Peter McNamara, *Political Economy and Statesmanship: Smith, Hamilton, and the Foundation of the Commercial Republic* (DeKalb: Northern Illinois University Press, 1998); E. James Ferguson, *The Power of the Purse: A History of American Public Finance, 1776–1790* (Chapel Hill: University of North Carolina Press for the Institute of Early American History and Culture at Williamsburg, VA, 1961).

14. Alexander Hamilton, *Report on Manufactures* (1791), in *The Works of Alexander Hamilton*, ed. Henry Cabot Lodge (New York: G. P. Putnam's Sons, 1903), 4: 71, 78, 98. The home-market argument is discussed in full toward the end of this chapter.

15. Ibid., 4: 85, 97, 95, 139, 84, 130–131.

16. Ibid., 4: 101.

17. See ibid., 4: 100–101; Liah Greenfeld, *The Spirit of Capitalism: Nationalism and Economic Growth* (Cambridge, MA: Harvard University Press, 2001), 386, 388–391, 396–397.

18. Stanley Engerman and Kenneth Sokoloff, "Technology and Industrialization, 1790–1914," in *The Long Nineteenth Century*, vol. 2 of *The Cambridge Economic History of the United States*, ed. Stanley L. Engerman and Robert E. Gallman (Cambridge: Cambridge University Press, 2000), 398–399; Irwin, *Clashing over Commerce*, 78–84.

19. Ashley, *Modern Tariff History*, 140; Maurice G. Baxter, *Henry Clay and the American System* (Lexington: University Press of Kentucky, 1995), 19; George B. Curtiss, *Protection and Prosperity: An Account of Tariff Legislation and Its Effect in Europe and America* (1896; repr., New York: Garland, 1974), 2: 572.

20. For a list of articles included in the tariffs of 1816, see Taussig, *Tariff History*, 30, 41, 43, 50–51.

21. Jefferson to Benjamin Austin, January 9, 1816, in *The Writings of Thomas Jefferson*, ed. Andrew A. Lipscomb, 20 vols. (Washington, D. C.: Thomas Jefferson Memorial Association of the United States, 1904–1905), 14: 392.

22. Nicholas Onuf and Peter Onuf, *Nations, Markets, and War: Modern History and the American Civil War* (Charlottesville: University of Virginia Press, 2006), 17, 157–163; Steven Watts, *The Republic Reborn: War and the Making of Liberal America, 1790–1820* (Baltimore: Johns Hopkins University Press, 1987), xvii, 230–232, 310, 316; George Dangerfield, *The Awakening of American Nationalism, 1815–1828* (New York: Harper and Row, 1965); Roger Hamilton Brown, *The Republic in Peril: 1812* (New York: Columbia University Press, 1964).

23. [Nathaniel A. Ware], *Notes on Political Economy as Applicable to the United States, by a Southern Planter* (1844; repr., New York: A. M. Kelley, 1967), 217.

24. Friedrich List, *National System of Political Economy* (1841), trans. G. A. Matile (1856; repr., New York: Garland, 1974), 403.

25. "Memorial to the Senate" (1831), in *Journal of the Proceedings of the Friends of Domestic Industry*, ed. Alexander Everett (1831; repr., New York: Garland, 1974), 176.

26. Friedrich List, *The Natural System of Political Economy* (1837), ed. and trans. W. O. Henderson (London: F. Cass, 1983), 47.

27. List, *National System of Political Economy*, 378; Tench Coxe, *A Brief Examination of Lord Sheffield's Observations on the Commerce of the United States: In Seven Numbers, with Two Supplementary Notes on American Manufactures* (Philadelphia: Carey, Stewart, 1792), 33–40, 57–58.

28. Friedrich List, *Outlines of American Political Economy, in a Series of Letters* (1827), in *Life of Friedrich List, and Selections from His Writings*, by Margaret Hirst (1909; repr., New York: A. M. Kelley, 1965), 178; Calvin Colton, *The Junius Tracts* (1844; repr., New York: Garland, 1974), 37; List, *National System of Political Economy*, 62.

29. Andrew Stewart, *The American System: Speeches on the Tariff Question, and on Internal Improvements* (1872; repr., New York: Garland, 1974), 167.

30. Kenneth Wyer Rowe, *Mathew Carey: A Study in American Economic Development* (Baltimore: Johns Hopkins Press, 1933), 429–435; Cathy Matson, "Mathew Carey's Learning Experience: Commerce, Manufacturing, and the Panic of 1819," *Early American Studies* 11, no. 3 (2013): 455–485; Stephen Meardon, "'A Reciprocity of Advantages': Carey, Hamilton, and the American Protective Doctrine," *Early American Studies* 11, no. 3 (2013): 431–454.

31. Mathew Carey, *Addresses of the Philadelphia Society for the Promotion of National Industry* (1820; repr., New York: Garland, 1974), 185, 189, 152.

32. For biographical information on Colton, see Dorfman, *Economic Mind*, 2: 777–779; Michael Hudson, introduction to *Public Economy for the United States*, by Calvin Colton (1848; repr., New York: A. M. Kelley, 1969), v–xvi.

33. Colton, *Public Economy*, 63.

34. Brougham in House of Commons, April 9, 1816, quoted in *Niles' Weekly Register* (Baltimore), December 28, 1816, 284.

35. Alexander Everett, *British Opinions on the Protecting System, Being a Reply to Strictures on That System, Which Have Appeared in Several Recent British Publications* (Boston: Nathan Hale, 1830), 3.

36. Colton, *Public Economy*, 95–97.

37. Calvin Colton, *The Rights of Labor* (1846; repr., New York: Garland, 1974), 89.

38. Colton, *Public Economy*, 94.

39. Mathew Carey, *Autobiographical Sketches in a Series of Letters Addressed to a Friend* (1829; repr., New York: Arno, 1970), ix.

40. Willard Phillips, *Propositions Concerning Protection and Free Trade* (1850; repr., New York: A. M. Kelley, 1968), 163.

41. Ware, *Notes on Political Economy*, 97–98.

42. Everett, *British Opinions on the Protecting System*, 13.

43. Colton, *Public Economy*, 93, 94.

44. Colton, *Rights of Labor*, 74, 89; List, *Natural System of Political Economy*, 140.

45. Bernard Semmel, *The Rise of Free Trade Imperialism: Classical Political Economy, the Empire of Free Trade and Imperialism, 1750–1850* (Cambridge: Cambridge University Press, 1970), 157. For an alternative view, see Boyd Hilton's *Corn, Cash, Commerce: The Economic Policies of Tory Governments, 1815–1830* (Oxford: Oxford University Press, 1977).

46. List, *Outlines of American Political Economy*, 148

47. M. Carey, *Addresses*, 182, 17.

48. E. Peschine Smith, *A Manual of Political Economy* (1853; repr., New York: Garland, 1974), iii.

49. Ware, *Notes on Political Economy*, 1.

50. M. Carey, *Addresses*, 17.

51. Colton, *Public Economy*, 17, 20, 95.

52. Phillips, *Propositions Concerning Protection and Free Trade*, 8, 33, 108.

53. M. Carey, *Addresses*, 183.

54. Thomas Reid, *An Inquiry into the Human Mind on the Principles of Common Sense* (1764), ed. Derek R. Brooks (University Park: Penn State University Press, 2000), 216, 32; Henry F. May, *The Enlightenment in America* (Oxford: Oxford University Press, 1976), 121, 132, 342–346; Daniel J. Boorstin, *The Lost World of Thomas Jefferson* (New York: Henry Holt, 1948); Ralph Henry Gabriel, *The Course of American Democratic Thought: An Intellectual History since 1815* (New York: Ronald, 1940), 9–10, 26.

55. J. F. Normano, *The Spirit of American Economics: A Study in the History of Economic Ideas in the United States Prior to the Great Depression* (New York: John Day, 1943), 196.

56. Colonial political economy valued practical measures over theory. See Johnson, *American Economic Thought*, 9–11, 16, 27–29; Stephen Innes, *Creating the Commonwealth: The Economic Culture of Puritan New England* (New York: W. W. Norton, 1995); Arthur Schlesinger Jr., "Ideas and the Economic Process," in *American Economic History*, ed. Seymour E. Harris (New York: McGraw-Hill, 1961), 7–8.

57. Robert V. Remini, *Andrew Jackson* (New York: Twayne, 1966), 17–19; Richard Hofstadter, *Anti-Intellectualism in American Life* (New York: Knopf, 1963), 155.

58. Edward Pessen, *Jacksonian America: Society, Personality, and Politics*, rev. ed. (Homewood, IL: Dorsey, 1978), 28.

59. Hofstadter, *Anti-Intellectualism in American Life*, 147–155.

60. Pessen, *Jacksonian America*, 25.

61. George Tucker's estimate, "On American Literature," in *Essays on Various Subjects of Taste, Morals, and National Policy* (Georgetown, DC: Joseph Milligan, 1822), 41–45.

62. Fanny Trollope, *Domestic Manners of the Americans* (1832), ed. Pamela Neville-Sington (London: Penguin, 1997), 255.

63. Martin Öhman, "The Statistical Turn in Early American Political Economy: Mathew Carey and the Authority of Numbers," *Early American Studies* 11, no. 3 (2013). Edwin R. A. Seligman, *Essays in Economics* (New York: Macmillan, 1925), 135, notes that American interest in statistics was first taken in 1806 with Samuel Blodget's *Economica: A Statistical Manual for the United States of America*. The American Statistical Association was founded in 1839. By the Civil War most states had bureaus for statistical accumulation; see Carl Abbott, *Boosters and Businessmen: Popular Economic Thought and Urban Growth in the Antebellum Middle West* (Westport, CT: Greenwood, 1981), 109, 111, 203.

64. Colton, *Public Economy*, 398–399.

65. Quoted in Michael Hudson, introduction to E. P. Smith, *Manual of Political Economy*, 11.

66. T. W. Hutchison, *On Revolutions and Progress in Economic Knowledge* (Cambridge: Cambridge University Press, 1978), 54, 55.

67. Erik Grimmer-Solem, *The Rise of Historical Economics and Social Reform in Germany, 1864–1894* (Oxford: Clarendon Press, 2003), 6; Joseph A. Schumpeter, *History of Economic Analysis* (Oxford: Oxford University Press, 1954), 808, 812; Joseph Dorfman, "The Role of the German Historical School in American Economic Thought," *American Economic Review* 45, no. 2 (1955); Richard T. Ely, "A Decade of Economic Theory," *Annals of the American Academy of Political and Social Science* 15, no. 2 (1900): 96–101; Sidney Fine, *Laissez Faire and the General-Welfare State: A Study of Conflict in American Thought, 1865–1901* (Ann Arbor: University of Michigan Press, 1956), 198–221.

68. William Notz, "Friedrich List in America," *American Economic Review* 16, no. 2 (1926): 264.

69. W. O. Henderson, *Friedrich List, Economist and Visionary, 1789–1846* (London: F. Cass, 1983), 59.

70. Greenfeld, *Spirit of Capitalism*, 200. An English translation of *Das Nationale System der Politischen Oekonomie* was first published in the United States in 1856; see note 24.

71. Henderson, *List, Economist and Visionary*, 88.

72. Louis L. Snyder, *Roots of German Nationalism* (Bloomington: Indiana University Press, 1978), 17, 2; Henderson, *List, Economist and Visionary*, 145.

73. Notz, "Friedrich List in America," 264; Ugo Rabbeno, *American Commercial Policy* (London: Macmillan, 1895), 346–347; Schumpeter, *History of Economic Analysis*, 807–812; Henry William Spiegel, *The Growth of Economic Thought* (Englewood Cliffs, NJ: Prentice-Hall, 1971), 421–424; Charles Gide and Charles Rist, *History of Economic Doctrines from the Time of the Physiocrats to the Present Day*, trans. Robert Richards (Boston: D. C. Heath, 1915), 379–395; J. Laurence Laughlin, "The Study of Political Economy in the United States," *Journal of Political Economy* 1, no. 1 (1892): 6–8.

74. James Hamilton, April 19, 1827, *Congressional Register of Debates*, 20th Congress, 1st Session, 2432.

75. Friedrich List, "Introduction to the National System of Political Economy," in Hirst, *Life of Friedrich List*, 290–292.

76. List, *National System of Political Economy*, 188, 70.

77. Ibid., 73; List, *Outlines of American Political Economy*, 148.

78. List, *Outlines of American Political Economy*, 214–215.

79. List, *National System of Political Economy*, 272, 424.

80. Ibid., 263, 157.

81. List, *Outlines of American Political Economy*, 155; List, *National System of Political Economy*, 62.

82. List, *Outlines of American Political Economy*, 155.

83. Giovanni Arrighi, *The Long Twentieth Century: Money, Power, and the Origins of Our Times*, 2nd ed. (London: Verso, 2010) 71; Gustav von Schmoller, *The Mercantile System and Its Historical Significance*, trans. W. J. Ashley (New York: Macmillan, 1896), 50; Onuf and Onuf, *Nations, Markets, and War*, 6, 17, 157–158, 176, 182, 246–247.

84. List, *Outlines of American Political Economy*, 203.

85. Onuf and Onuf, *Nations, Markets, and War*, 157–170, 247, 260–262; Greenfeld, *Spirit of Capitalism*, 200–203.

86. List, *National System of Political Economy*, 200, 262.

87. List, *Outlines of American Political Economy*, 212.

88. List, *Natural System of Political Economy*, 40; List, *Outlines of American Political Economy*, 161.

89. Adams quoted in Daniel Raymond, *The Elements of Political Economy*, 2nd ed. (1823; repr., New York: A. M. Kelley, 1964), 1: v; Gary Hull, "The Prospect of Man in Early American Economic Thought, 1800–1850," (PhD diss., University of Maryland, 1969), 50.

90. Charles Patrick Neill, *Daniel Raymond: An Early Chapter in the History of Economic Theory in the United States* (Baltimore: Johns Hopkins Press, 1897), 47, 56, 57, 63.

91. Dorfman, *Economic Mind*, 2: 566 (quote); Kenneth Lundberg, introduction to Raymond, *Elements of Political Economy*; Donald Frey, "The Puritan Roots of Daniel Raymond's Economics," *History of Political Economy* 32, no. 3 (2000); Neill, *Daniel Raymond*, 47–49.

92. Daniel Raymond, *Thoughts on Political Economy* (Baltimore: F. Lucas, 1820), 9, 58.

93. Raymond, *Thoughts on Political Economy*, 128, 49.

94. Raymond, *Elements of Political Economy*, 1: 47–50, 33.

95. Ibid., 2: 228.

96. Ibid., 2: 201, 222.

97. Allen Kaufman, *Capitalism, Slavery, and Republican Values: Antebellum Political Economists, 1819–1848* (Austin: University of Texas Press, 1982), 65.

98. A. P. Lerner, "The Symmetry Between Import and Export Taxes," *Economica*, n.s., 3 no. 11 (1936).

99. Murray N. Rothbard, *The Panic of 1819: Reactions and Policies* (1962; Auburn, AL: Ludwig von Mises Institute, 2007), 26–29, argues the crisis does not illustrate modern business cycles.

100. Raymond ignored the influx of foreign currency and thus the contributions to domestic currency reserves because of cotton exports. Eric Hilt, "Economic History, Historical Analysis, and the 'New History of Capitalism,'" *Journal of Economic History* 77, no. 2 (2017): 518.

101. Seth Rockman, "Negro Cloth: Mastering the Market for Slave Clothing in Antebellum America," in Beckert and Desan, *American Capitalism*, 173.

102. M. Carey, quoted in Taussig, *Tariff History*, 107.

103. Taussig, *Tariff History*, 80.

104. Baxter, *Henry Clay and the American System*, 21, 26–27, 65, 194–199. For histories of the 1828 and 1832 tariffs, and the compromise of 1833, see Stanwood, *American Tariff Controversies*, 1: 243–410, 2: 1–37; Taussig, *Tariff History*, 110–114. For the 1842 tariff, see Irwin, *Clashing Over Commerce*, 183–185.

105. List, *Outlines of American Political Economy*, 166–167.

106. Joyce Appleby, *Inheriting the Revolution: The First Generation of Americans* (Cambridge, MA: Belknap Press of Harvard University Press, 2000), 23. On American exceptionalism see Seymour Martin Lipset, *American Exceptionalism: A Double-Edged Sword* (New York: W. W. Norton, 1996); Jonathan A. Glickstein, *American Exceptionalism, American Anxiety: Wages, Competition, and Degraded Labor in the Antebellum United States* (Charlottesville: University of Virginia Press, 2002).

107. Richard P. McCormick, *The Second American Party System: Party Formation in the Jacksonian Era* (Chapel Hill: University of North Carolina Press, 1966); Sean Wilentz, *The Rise of American Democracy, Jefferson to Lincoln* (New York: W. W. Norton, 2005), 309. On the expansion of the suffrage during the Jacksonian era, see Lee Benson, *The Concept of Jacksonian Democracy: New York as a Test Case* (Princeton, NJ: Princeton University Press, 1961); Dixon Ryan Fox, *The Decline of Aristocracy in the Politics of New York, 1801–1840* (1919; repr., New York: Harper Torchbooks, 1965).

108. M. Carey, *Addresses*, 86; also Mathew Carey, *The New Olive Branch; or, An Attempt to Establish an Identity of Interest between Agriculture, Manufactures, and Commerce* (1821), in *Essays on Political Economy; or, The Most Certain Means of Promoting the Wealth, Power, Resources, and Happiness of States, Applied Particularly to the United States* (1822; repr., New York: A. M. Kelley, 1968), 376.

109. Alexander Everett, "Address of the Friends of Domestic Industry Assembled in Convention at New York, Oct. 26, 1831, to the People of the United States," in Everett, *Friends of Domestic Industry*, 21.

110. Colton, *Rights of Labor*, 15–16.

111. Edwards, "Economic Sophistication," 815, 820.

112. Beckert and Desan, *American Capitalism*, 8–11; Jeffrey Sklansky, "The Elusive Sovereign: New Intellectual and Social Histories of Capitalism," *Modern Intellectual History* 9, no. 1 (2012): 243–244.

113. Pincus, *Pressure Groups and Politics*, 51.

114. Robert Margo, "The Labor Force in the Nineteenth Century," in Engerman and Gallman, *The Long Nineteenth Century*, 224; John Ashworth, *Slavery, Capitalism, and Politics in the Antebellum Republic*, vol. 1, *Commerce and Compromise, 1820–1850* (Cambridge: Cambridge University Press, 1995), 85.

115. Raymond, *Elements of Political Economy*, 2: 242.

116. James L. Huston, *The Panic of 1857 and the Coming of the Civil War* (Baton Rouge: Louisiana State University Press, 1987), 101; George B. Mangold, *The Labor Argument in the American Protective Tariff Discussion* (1908: repr., New York: Arno, 1971); Huston, *Securing the Fruits of Labor*, 175–176, 248–250; Daniel Walker Howe, *The Political Culture of the American Whigs* (Chicago: University of Chicago Press, 1979), 190.

117. Eric Foner, *Free Soil, Free Labor, Free Men: The Ideology of the Republican Party before the Civil War* (Oxford: Oxford University Press, 1970), 12–17; Huston, *Securing the Fruits of Labor*, 175–178, 187, 248–251.

118. James L. Huston, "A Political Response to Industrialism: The Republican Embrace of Protectionist Labor Doctrines," *Journal of American History* 70, no. 1 (1983); Karl Polanyi, *The Great Transformation: The Political and Economic Origins of Our Time* (1944; Boston: Beacon, 2001), 160–162; Jeffrey Sklansky, *The Soul's Economy: Market Society and Selfhood in American Thought, 1820–1920* (Chapel Hill: University of North Carolina Press, 2002).

119. Tony A. Freyer, *Producers versus Capitalists: Constitutional Conflict in Antebellum America* (Charlottesville: University Press of Virginia, 1994), 4–11, 36–39, 69, 91.

120. Henry Charles Carey, *Principles of Social Science* (1858–1859; repr., New York: A. M. Kelley, 1963), 1: 31.

121. Foner, *Free Soil*, xvii; Sklansky, *The Soul's Economy*, 5–8, 20–25.

122. M. Carey, *Addresses*, 22.

123. Francis Bowen, *The Principles of Political Economy Applied to the Condition, the Resources, and the Institutions of the American People* (1856; repr., New York: Garland, 1974), 91.

124. Colton, *Junius Tracts*, 106.

125. P. T. Jackson, "Report on the Manufactures of Cotton," in Everett, *Friends of Domestic Industry*, 110.

126. Colton, *Rights of Labor*, 64.

127. Tench Coxe, *A Statement of the Arts and Manufactures of the United States of America, for the Year 1810* (1814; repr., Elmsford, NY: Maxwell, 1971), liii.

128. Charles Dickens, *American Notes for General Circulation* (1842; repr., London: Penguin, 2000), 80.

129. Colton, *Public Economy*, 281, 282.

130. Colton, *Junius Tracts*, 106.

131. Colton, *Public Economy*, 282–283.

132. Colton, *Rights of Labor*, 7.

133. Colton, *Junius Tracts*, 105.

134. Henry Charles Carey, *Principles of Political Economy* (1837–1840; repr., New York: A. M. Kelley, 1965), 1: 339; Louis Hartz, *The Liberal Tradition in America: An Interpretation of American Political Thought since the Revolution* (New York: Harcourt, Brace, 1955), 108–112; Ashworth, *'Agrarians' and 'Aristocrats': Party Political Ideology in the United States, 1837–1846* (1982; repr., Cambridge: Cambridge University Press, 1987), 65–69; Richard Hofstadter, *The American Political Tradition and the Men Who Made It* (1948; New York: Vintage, 1974), 132–135.

135. Colton, *Junius Tracts*, 107, emphasis in original.

136. Henry Nash Smith, *Virgin Land: The American West as Symbol and Myth* (Cambridge, MA: Harvard University Press, 1950), 240. Eric Foner finds that "it was eastern farmers, not wage earners in crowded cities, who were able to take advantage of the offer of free land" (*Free Soil*, 32).

137. Colton, *Rights of Labor*, 7.

138. Polanyi, *The Great Transformation*, 43–49, 67, 72–77.

139. Ibid., 158, 160–162, 76.

140. Ibid., 79.

141. James Polk, inaugural address to Congress, March 4, 1845, quoted in Stanwood, *American Tariff Controversies*, 2: 42.

142. Robert J. Walker, "Report from the Secretary of the Treasury on the State of Finances, etc." (1845), in *State Papers and Speeches on the Tariff*, ed. F. W. Taussig (Cambridge, MA: Harvard University, 1892); Stanwood, *American Tariff Controversies*, 2: 59; Taussig, *Tariff History*, 114–115; Thompson, *History of Protective Tariff Laws*, 393–404.

143. Irwin, *Clashing over Commerce*, 204–206.

144. Stanwood, *American Tariff Controversies*, 2: 132; Taussig, *Tariff History*, 527–528.

145. Paul Bairoch, *Economics and World History: Myths and Paradoxes* (Chicago: University of Chicago Press, 1993), 32.

146. Jacob E. Cooke, "Tench Coxe, Alexander Hamilton, and the Encouragement of American Manufactures," *William and Mary Quarterly* 32, no. 3 (1975): 379; Meardon, "'A Reciprocity of Advantages,'" 431–454; Peskin, *Manufacturing Revolution*, 94–96; Virgle Glenn Wilhite, *Founders of American Economic Thought and Policy* (New York: Bookman, 1958), 214.

147. Alexander Hamilton to Oliver Wolcott, August 8, 1795, *Works of Alexander Hamilton*, 8: 355; John Quincy Adams, *Memoirs of John Quincy Adams, Comprising Portions of His Diary from 1795 to 1848*, ed. Charles Francis Adams, 12 vols. (Philadelphia: J. B. Lippincott, 1874–1877), 4: 370.

148. Coxe, *Statement of the Arts and Manufactures*, xiv.

149. Leo Marx, *The Machine in the Garden: Technology and the Pastoral Ideal in America* (1964; Oxford: Oxford University Press, 2000), 160.

150. Henry C. Carey, *The Harmony of Interests, Agricultural, Manufacturing, and Commercial* (1851; repr., New York: A. M. Kelley, 1967), 190.

151. M. Carey, *The New Olive Branch*, 343.

152. E. P. Smith, *Manual of Political Economy*, 203.

153. Ware, *Notes on Political Economy*, 124–125.

154. Coxe, *Statement of the Arts and Manufactures*, xx–xxi; M. Carey, *Addresses*, 61–64.

155. H. Carey, *Harmony of Interests*, 196.

156. For anti-British sentiment in antebellum thought, see J. G. Cook, *Anglophobia: An Analysis of Anti-British Prejudice in the United States* (Boston: Four Seas, 1919).

157. Raymond, *Thoughts on Political Economy*, 128.

158. Everett, *British Opinions on the Protecting System*, 41.

159. Ware, *Notes on Political Economy*, 88.

160. Mathew Carey, "Address to the Farmers of the United States on the Ruinous Consequences to Their Vital Interests of the Existing Policy of This Country" (1821), in *Essays on Political Economy*, 414; M. Carey, *Addresses*, 145; Mathew Carey, "Report of a Philadelphia Committee: American Manufactures" (1816), in *Essays on Political Economy*, 226–227.

161. Colton, *Public Economy*, 536.

162. Colton, *Rights of Labor*, 75.

163. Colton, *Public Economy*, 156.

164. Raymond, *Thoughts on Political Economy*, v.

165. Colton, *Rights of Labor*, 4.

166. Raymond, *Elements of Political Economy*, 2: 395–396.

167. Raymond, *Thoughts on Political Economy*, vi.

Chapter 6. Henry Carey, Nature, and the Destiny of Man

1. Discussions on Carey include Andrew Dawson, "Reassessing Henry Carey (1793–1879): The Problems of Writing Political Economy in Nineteenth-Century America," *Journal of American Studies* 34, no. 3 (2000); Rodney J. Morrison, "Henry C. Carey and American Economic Development," *Transactions of the American Philosophical Society* 76, no. 3 (1986); A. D. H. Kaplan, *Henry Charles Carey: A Study in American Economic Thought* (Baltimore: Johns Hopkins Press, 1931); George Winston Smith, *Henry C. Carey and American Sectional Conflict* (Albuquerque: University of New Mexico Press, 1951).

2. Henry Charles Carey, *The Unity of Law; as Exhibited in the Relations of Physical, Social, Mental and Moral Science* (1872; repr., New York: A. M. Kelley, 1967), 282.

3. Henry Carey, "Our Resources" (1865), in *Miscellaneous Works of Henry C. Carey*, 2 vols. (1883; repr., New York: B. Franklin, 1967), 2: 22–23.

4. Carey, *Unity of Law*, 30.

5. Henry Carey Baird, "Carey and Two of His Recent Critics, Eugen v. Böhm-Bawerk and Alfred Marshall," *Proceedings of the American Philosophical Society Held at Philadelphia for Promoting Useful Knowledge* 29 (1891): 171.

6. Henry Charles Carey, *Essay on the Rate of Wages* (1835; repr., New York: A. M. Kelley, 1965), 145, 23, 32, 83, 88, 90, 23.

7. Henry Charles Carey, *The Past, the Present, and the Future* (1847; repr., New York: A. M. Kelley, 1967), 48.

8. Henry Charles Carey, *Principles of Political Economy*, 4 pts. in 3 vols. (1837–1840; repr., New York: A. M. Kelley, 1965), 1: 46, 130.

9. Ariel Ron, "Henry Carey's Rural Roots: 'Scientific Agriculture' and Economic Development in the Antebellum North." *Journal of the History of Economic Thought* 37, no. 2 (2015): 263–275.

10. Henry Carey, *Principles of Political Economy*, 3: 252.

11. Henry Charles Carey, *Principles of Social Science*, 3 vols. (1858–1859; repr., New York: A. M. Kelley, 1963), 1: 292.

12. E. Peschine Smith studied at Columbia and Harvard, was professor of mathematics at Rochester, worked in the federal government as commissioner of immigration, and between 1871 and 1876 was special advisor in Japan. Ten percent of Smith's work *A Manual of Political Economy* was quoted verbatim in Carey's *Principles of Social Science*.

13. Henry C. Carey, *The Harmony of Interests, Agricultural, Manufacturing, and Commercial* (1851; repr., New York: A. M. Kelley, 1967), 49.

14. Carey, *Principles of Social Science*, 1: 367.

15. Ibid., 1: 294. For a discussion of protectionist use of Smith's *Wealth of Nations* to advance the home-market argument, see Nicholas Onuf and Peter Onuf, *Nations, Markets, and War: Modern History and the American Civil War* (Charlottesville: University of Virginia Press, 2006), 264–266.

16. Carey, *Harmony of Interests*, 101, 136, 147, 198; Carey, *Principles of Social Science*, 1: 186, 211, 263, 377, 369–370.

17. Carey, *Principles of Social Science*, 1: 213. Carey thought New England ignored his works, writing, "I have just now found my system adopted . . . in the College de France—It has made its way steadily in Europe, and yet you might . . . search all the journals of New England, for twenty years without finding the slightest evidence that their writers had known of its existence" (Carey to Abner P. Peabody, March 23, 1858, quoted in G. W. Smith, *Carey and American Sectional Conflict*, 55).

18. Carey, *Harmony of Interests*, 83; Carey, *Principles of Social Science*, 2: 40.

19. Henry Carey, "Reconstruction: Industrial, Financial, and Political" (1867), in *Miscellaneous Works*, 2: 9.

20. David E. Nye, *American Technological Sublime* (Cambridge, MA: MIT Press, 1994), 56–60; Leo Marx, *The Machine in the Garden: Technology and the Pastoral Ideal in America* (Oxford: Oxford University Press, 2000), 192–214; John F. Kasson, *Civilizing the Machine: Technology and Republican Values in America, 1776–1900* (New York: Grossman, 1976), 41–47, 111–114.

21. Carey, *Principles of Social Science*, 1: 137; Carey, *Harmony of Interests*, 78.

22. Carey, *The Past, the Present, and the Future*, 95.

23. Carey, *Principles of Social Science*, 1: 137, 91.

24. Ibid., 2: 38.
25. Carey, *Unity of Law*, 61, vii.
26. Carey, *Principles of Political Economy*, 1: 130.
27. Ibid., 3: 62.
28. Carey, *Unity of Law*, 62.
29. Carey, *The Past, the Present, and the Future*, 248.
30. Carey, *Principles of Social Science*, 3: 279.
31. Ibid., 3: 134, 147.
32. Carey, *Principles of Social Science*, 1: 31.
33. Ibid., 1: 232; 3: 232, 265.
34. Ibid., 1: 71, 418.
35. Carey, *Unity of Law*, 158–159.
36. Ibid., 154.
37. Carey, *Principles of Social Science*, 3: 332.
38. William Cronon, *Nature's Metropolis: Chicago and the Great West* (New York: W. W. Norton, 1991); L. Marx, *The Machine in the Garden*.
39. Carey, *The Past, the Present, and the Future*, 54.
40. Henry Carey, "Money: A Lecture Delivered before the New York Geographical and Statistical Society" (1857), in *Miscellaneous Works*, 1: 11.
41. Carey, *Harmony of Interests*, 64.
42. Henry Carey, "Our Future," in *Miscellaneous Works*, 1: 6–7.

Chapter 7. Liberalism, Republicanism, and Finance

1. Joseph A. Schumpeter, *Business Cycles: A Theoretical, Historical, and Statistical Analysis of the Capitalist Process* (New York: McGraw-Hill, 1939), 223–234.
2. Robert E. Wright, *The Wealth of Nations Rediscovered: Integration and Expansion in American Financial Markets, 1780–1850* (New York: Cambridge University Press, 2002), 7, 193. More recently Wright argued: "Financial capital is the trail left behind as capitalism wended its way through the forests of economic history. The causes of capitalism are too complex, too contested, and too little understood to resolve here"; see his "Capitalism and the Rise of the Corporation Nation," in *Capitalism Takes Command: The Social Transformation of Nineteenth-Century America*, ed. Michael Zakim and Gary J. Kornblith (Chicago: University of Chicago Press, 2012), 146.
3. Sven Beckert and Christine Desan, eds., *American Capitalism: New Histories* (New York: Columbia University Press, 2018), 10–11.
4. Andrew Jackson, "Bank Veto," in *The Statesmanship of Andrew Jackson as Told in His Writings and Speeches*, ed. Francis Newton Thorpe (New York: Tandy-Thomas, 1909), 174–175.
5. Charles Sellers, *The Market Revolution: Jacksonian America, 1815–1846* (New York: Oxford University Press, 1991), 313; Arthur M. Schlesinger Jr., *The Age of Jackson* (Boston: Little, Brown, 1945); John Ashworth, *'Agrarians' and 'Aristocrats': Party Political Ideology in the United States, 1837–1846* (1982; repr., Cambridge: Cambridge University Press, 1987); John Ashworth, *Slavery, Capitalism, and Politics in the Antebellum Republic*, vol. 1, *Commerce and Compromise, 1820–1850* (Cambridge: Cambridge University Press, 1995), 289–315.
6. Bray Hammond, *Banks and Politics in America, from the Revolution to the Civil War*

(Princeton, NJ: Princeton University Press, 1967), 345–346; Joseph Dorfman, *The Economic Mind in American Civilization*, vols. 1–2, *1606–1865* (New York: Viking, 1946), 2: chap. 24; Daniel Walker Howe, *What Hath God Wrought: The Transformation of America, 1815–1848* (New York: Oxford University Press, 2007), 380–393.

7. Richard Hofstadter, *The American Political Tradition and the Men Who Made It* (1948; New York: Vintage, 1974), 78.

8. James L. Huston, *The Panic of 1857 and the Coming of the Civil War* (Baton Rouge: Louisiana State University Press, 1987), 46.

9. Jackson to Nicholas Biddle, November 1829, in *The Correspondence of Nicholas Biddle Dealing with National Affairs, 1807–1844*, ed. Reginald Charles McGrane (Boston: Houghton Mifflin, 1919), 93.

10. On the importance of the South Sea Bubble in Anglo-American economic history, see Charles P. Kindleberger, *Manias, Panics, and Crashes: A History of Financial Crises* (New York: John Wiley, 2000), 122; John Carswell, *The South Sea Bubble* (London: Cresset, 1960), 271–272; Peter M. Garber, *Famous First Bubbles: The Fundamentals of Early Manias* (Cambridge, MA: MIT Press, 2000), 11–12, 115; Richard Dale, *The First Crash: Lessons From the South Sea Bubble* (Princeton, NJ: Princeton University Press, 2004), 102; Bruce G. Carruthers, *City of Capital: Politics and Markets in the English Financial Revolution* (Princeton, NJ: Princeton University Press, 1996), 83–85; Malcolm Balen, *A Very English Deceit: The Secret History of the South Sea Bubble and the First Great Financial Scandal* (London: Fourth Estate, 2003); Larry Neal, *The Rise of Financial Capitalism: International Capital Markets in the Age of Reason* (Cambridge: Cambridge University Press, 1990); Margaret Patterson and David Reiffen, "The Effects of the Bubble Act on the Market for Joint Stock Shares," *Journal of Economic History* 50, no. 1 (1990).

11. Carswell, *The South Sea Bubble*, 46; Garber, *Famous First Bubbles*, 11–12, 115; Dale, *The First Crash*, 102; Carruthers, *City of Capital*, 83–85.

12. Neal, *Rise of Financial Capitalism*, 20–23.

13. Charles Mackay, *Extraordinary Popular Delusions and the Madness of Crowds* (1841; New York: Farrar, Straus and Giroux, 1972), 63, which lists eighty-six "bubble companies."

14. Quoted in Virginia Cowles, *The Great Swindle: The Story of the South Sea Bubble* (New York: Harper, 1960), 139.

15. Gent. J. B., *A Poem Occasioned by the Rise and Fall of the South Sea Company: Humbly Dedicated to the Merchant-Adventurers Trading in the South-Sea* (London, 1720).

16. *Scandal No Argument: An Oxford Annuitant's Letter to Sir Richard Steele, in Answer to the Crisis of Honesty* (London: Chapman, 1720).

17. Cowles, *The Great Swindle*, 40.

18. J. G. A. Pocock, ed., *The Political Works of James Harrington* (Cambridge: Cambridge University Press, 1977), 138.

19. J. G. A. Pocock, *The Machiavellian Moment: Florentine Political Thought and the Atlantic Republican Tradition* (Princeton, NJ: Princeton University Press, 1975), chaps. 11–15.

20. Elizabeth Christine Cook, *Literary Influences in Colonial Newspapers, 1704–1750* (1912; repr., Port Washington, NY: Kennikat, 1966), 3; Bernard Bailyn, *The Ideological Origins of the American Revolution* (Cambridge, MA: Belknap Press of Harvard University Press, 1967), 44; Henry F. May, *The Enlightenment in America* (Oxford: Oxford University Press, 1976), 39–41; Caroline Robbins, *The Eighteenth-Century Commonwealthman: Studies in the Transmission, Development, and Circumstance of English Liberal Thought from the Restoration of Charles*

II until the War with the Thirteen Colonies (Cambridge, MA: Cambridge University Press, 1961), 385; Bernard Cottret, ed., *Bolingbroke's Political Writings: The Conservative Enlightenment* (New York: St. Martin's, 1997), 1, 10.

21. Bailyn, *Ideological Origins*; Gordon S. Wood, *The Creation of the American Republic, 1776–1787* (Chapel Hill: University of North Carolina Press for the Institute of Early American History and Culture, Williamsburg, VA, 1969); Lance Banning, *The Jeffersonian Persuasion: Evolution of a Party Ideology* (Ithaca, NY: Cornell University Press, 1978); Drew R. McCoy, *The Elusive Republic: Political Economy in Jeffersonian America* (Chapel Hill: University of North Carolina Press for the Institute of Early American History and Culture, Williamsburg, VA, 1980); Sean Wilentz, *Chants Democratic: New York City and the Rise of the American Working Class, 1788–1850* (New York: Oxford University Press, 1984); Pocock, *The Machiavellian Moment*, 423; Stuart Banner, *Anglo-American Securities Regulation: Cultural and Political Roots, 1690–1860* (Cambridge: Cambridge University Press, 1998); Major L. Wilson, "The 'Country' versus the 'Court': A Republican Consensus and Party Debate in the Bank War," *Journal of the Early Republic* 15, no. 4 (1995).

22. Pocock, *The Machiavellian Moment*, 457.

23. This paragraph draws heavily from Eric MacGilvray's *The Invention of Market Freedom* (Cambridge: Cambridge University Press, 2011).

24. Sean Wilentz's *Chants Democratic* shows how workers in New York City incorporated republican values to mitigate the pressures of industrial markets. Richard B. Latner, "Preserving 'the Natural Equality of Rank and Influence': Liberalism, Republicanism, and Equality of Condition in Jacksonian Politics," in *The Culture of the Market: Historical Essays*, ed. Thomas L. Haskell and Richard F. Teichgraeber III (Cambridge: Cambridge University Press, 1993); Cathy Matson and Peter Onuf, "Toward a Republican Empire: Interest and Ideology in Revolutionary America," *American Quarterly* 37, no. 4 (1985): 498–522; and Wilson, "The 'Country' versus the 'Court'" emphasize republicanism as a powerful influence in the Jacksonian era.

25. Gordon S. Wood, *The Radicalism of the American Revolution* (New York: Knopf, 1992), 569, 359.

26. The synopsis of Hamiltonian finance draws on Peter McNamara, *Political Economy and Statesmanship: Smith, Hamilton, and the Foundation of the Commercial Republic* (DeKalb: Northern Illinois University Press, 1998), 113–127; Stanley Elkins and Eric McKitrick, *The Age of Federalism: The Early American Republic, 1788–1800* (Oxford: Oxford University Press, 1993), 110–144; Louis M. Hacker, *Alexander Hamilton in the American Tradition* (New York: McGraw-Hill, 1957), 128–186; E. James Ferguson, *The Power of the Purse: A History of American Public Finance, 1776–1790* (Chapel Hill: University of North Carolina Press for the Institute of Early American History and Culture at Williamsburg, VA, 1961), 337–343; Gerald Stourzh, *Alexander Hamilton and the Idea of Republican Government* (Stanford, CA: Stanford University, 1970).

27. Alexander Hamilton, *Public Credit* (1795), in *The Works of Alexander Hamilton*, ed. Henry Cabot Lodge (New York: G. P. Putnam's Sons, 1903), 3: 294. See also Alexander Hamilton, *First Report on Public Credit* (1790), in *Works*, 2: 232–233, 295–298.

28. Alexander Hamilton, *National Bank* (1790), in *Works*, 3: 388–390.

29. Hammond, *Banks and Politics*, 123.

30. The "public debts are public blessings" passage reads in its entirety: "A national debt, if it is not excessive, will be to us a national blessing. It will be a powerful cement of our union.

It will also create a necessity for keeping up taxation, to a degree which, without being oppressive, will be a spur to industry, remote as we are from Europe, and shall be from danger" (Hamilton to Robert Morris, *Works of Alexander Hamilton*, 3: 387).

31. On Hamilton's plan to tie the interest of financiers to the public credit, see Hamilton to Morris, *Works*, 3: 338, 360. For Hamilton's defense of the assumption of the states' debt, see his *First Report on Public Credit*, 2: 227, 228, 244, 246–248.

32. Lance Davis and Robert Cull, "International Capital Movements, Domestic Capital Markets, and America Economic Growth, 1820–1914," in *The Long Nineteenth Century*, vol. 2 of *The Cambridge Economic History of the United States*, ed. Stanley L. Engerman and Robert E. Gallman (Cambridge: Cambridge University Press, 2000), 737, 741.

33. Hamilton to George Washington, in *Works of Alexander Hamilton*, 2: 426.

34. Hamilton, *Public Credit*, 3: 232.

35. Herbert E. Sloan, *Principle and Interest: Thomas Jefferson and the Problem of Debt* (1995; Charlottesville: University of Virginia Press, 2001), 3, 11, 180.

36. Giovanni Arrighi, *The Long Twentieth Century: Money, Power, and the Origins of Our Times*, 2nd ed. (London: Verso, 2010), 164.

37. Jefferson previously worked with Tracy on the latter's English translation and publication in the United States of *Commentaire sur "l'Esprit des lois" de Montesquieu*; see Sloan, *Principle and Interest*, 204–205.

38. Antoine Louis Claude Destutt de Tracy, *A Treatise on Political Economy: To Which is Prefixed a Supplement to a Preceding Work on the Understanding; or, Elements of Ideology: With an Analytical Table, and an Introduction on the Faculty of the Will* (1817), in *Psychology of Political Science: With Special Consideration for the Political Acumen of Destutt de Tracy*, ed. John M. Dorsey (Detroit: Center for Health Education, 1973), 92, xxi, 94, xxi, xxvii.

39. Garrett Ward Sheldon and C. William Hill Jr., *The Liberal Republicanism of John Taylor of Caroline* (Madison, NJ: Associated University Presses, 2008); Eugene TenBroeck Mudge, *The Social Philosophy of John Taylor of Caroline: A Study in Jeffersonian Democracy* (New York: Columbia University Press, 1939); Robert E. Shalhope, *John Taylor of Caroline: Pastoral Republican* (Columbia: University of South Carolina Press, 1980).

40. John Taylor, *Construction Construed and Constitutions Vindicated* (1820; repr., New York: Da Capo, 1970), 89.

41. John Taylor, *An Inquiry into the Principles and Policy of the Government of the United States* (London: Routledge and Kegan Paul, 1814), 222–223.

42. Taylor references the South Sea Bubble in *Construction Construed*, 192, and *Arator: Being a Series of Agricultural Essays, Practical and Political* (Baltimore: J. Robinson, 1817), 252.

43. Taylor, *Arator*, 12.

44. Taylor, *Inquiry into the Principles*, 238.

45. Taylor, *Arator*, 24.

46. Ibid., 29, 43.

47. Paul K. Conkin, *Prophets of Prosperity: America's First Political Economists* (Bloomington: Indiana University Press, 1980), 61.

48. Hammond, *Banks and Politics*, 35, 741.

49. Ibid., 227–232.

50. Sean Wilentz, *The Rise of American Democracy: Jefferson to Lincoln* (New York: W. W. Norton, 2005), 206.

51. Girard to a stockholder meeting, October 28, 1816, quoted in John Bach McMaster, *The Life and Times of Stephen Girard, Mariner and Merchant* (Philadelphia: J. P. Lippincott, 1918), 2: 314–315.

52. Woody Holton, "The Capitalist Constitution," in Beckert and Desan, *American Capitalism*, 36–46; Murray N. Rothbard, *The Panic of 1819: Reactions and Policies* (1962; Auburn, AL: Ludwig von Mises Institute, 2007), 11.

53. Jefferson to Adams, November 7, 1819, in *The Writings of Thomas Jefferson*, ed. Andrew A. Lipscomb, 20 vols. (Washington, D. C.: Thomas Jefferson Memorial Association of the United States, 1904–1905), 15: 224.

54. Astor to Gallatin, March 14, 1818, in *Major Problems in the Early Republic, 1787–1848: Documents and Essays*, ed. Sean Wilentz (Lexington, MA: D. C. Heath, 1992), 337.

55. *James Flint on Hard Times* (1820), in Wilentz, *Major Problems*, 338.

56. Hammond, *Banks and Politics*, 258.

57. Ibid., 282. Hammond describes wildcat banks well: free banks "monetized the state debts by purchasing bonds with their own circulating notes and then disappeared in order to avoid having to redeem the notes. They had to be hunted for in the woods, among the retreats of wild cats. Their cash reserves were sometimes kegs of nails and broken glass with a layer of coin on top. Specie exhibited to the examiners at one bank was whisked through the trees to be exhibited at another the next day" (601).

58. Joyce Appleby, *Inheriting the Revolution: The First Generation of Americans* (Cambridge, MA: Belknap Press of Harvard University Press, 2000), 86.

59. Jeffrey Sklansky, "The Elusive Sovereign: New Intellectual and Social Histories of Capitalism," *Modern Intellectual History* 9, no. 1 (2012): 244.

60. Edward J. Balleisen, *Navigating Failure: Bankruptcy and Commercial Society in Antebellum America* (Chapel Hill: University of North Carolina Press, 2001); Bruce H. Mann, *Republic of Debtors: Bankruptcy in the Age of American Independence* (Cambridge, MA: Harvard University Press, 2002); Scott A. Sandage, *Born Losers: A History of Failure in America* (Cambridge, MA: Harvard University Press, 2005); Cathy Matson, "The Ambiguities of Risk in the Early Republic," *Business History Review* 78, no. 4 (2004): 597, 601, 604; Jessica M. Lepler, *The Many Panics of 1837: People, Politics, and the Creation of a Transatlantic Financial Crisis* (Cambridge: Cambridge University Press, 2013), 82–85, 124, 144, 154, 216.

61. Wood, *Creation of the American Republic*, 418.

62. Thomas Cooper, *Lectures on the Elements of Political Economy*, 2nd ed. (1830; repr., New York: A. M. Kelley, 1971), 178.

63. Cooper, *Lectures*, 194–195, 78. By the 1820s Cooper had largely abandoned the agrarianism of his earlier publications; see "Foreign Commerce" (1813), in *Philosophical Writings, by Thomas Cooper*, ed. Udo Thiel (Bristol: Thoemmes Continuum, 2001), 1: 161–165.

64. Cooper, *Lectures*, 178, 247, 251, 251. Cooper actually supported Biddle in his quarrel with Jackson. For Cooper, executive overreach was the greater threat.

65. Abram C. Flora Jr., "Economic Thought in South Carolina, 1820–60," (PhD diss., University of North Carolina, 1957), 68–120.

66. Cooper, *Lectures*, 252–253.

67. Lepler, *Many Panics of 1837*, 179; Cooper, *Lectures*, 252.

68. Hammond, *Banks and Politics*, 563. Between 1830 and 1837, 347 banks were chartered; see Reginald Charles McGrane, *The Panic of 1837: Some Financial Problems of the Jacksonian*

Era (Chicago: University of Chicago Press, 1924), 13; Wright, *Wealth of Nations Rediscovered*, 159; Jane Knodell, "Rethinking the Jacksonian Economy: The Impact of the 1832 Bank Veto on Commercial Banking," *Journal of Economic History* 66, no. 3 (2006): 544–554. By comparison, in England there were approximately 440 banks in 1845, and in Scotland 24; see Robert Harry Inglis Palgrave, ed., *Dictionary of Political Economy* (London: Macmillan, 1894–1895), 2: 91–95.

69. Pauline Maier, "The Revolutionary Origins of the American Corporation," *William and Mary Quarterly* 50, no. 1 (1993): 83.

70. Wright, "Corporate Nation," 149.

71. Wright, *Wealth of Nations Rediscovered*, 7, 15, 82, 90, 128, 130–132; John Steele Gordon, *An Empire of Wealth: The Epic History of American Economic Power* (New York: HarperCollins, 2004), 200; Richard Sylla, "Monetary Innovation in America," *Journal of Economic History* 42, no. 1 (1982): 26; Banner, *Anglo-American Securities Regulation*, 163, 192, 196; Howard Bodenhorn, *A History of Banking in Antebellum America: Financial Markets and Economic Development in an Era of Nation-Building* (Cambridge: Cambridge University Press, 2000), 85, 162, 167; William Gerald Shade, *Banks or No Banks: The Money Issue in Western Politics, 1832–1865* (Detroit: Wayne State University Press, 1972), 37.

72. Michael F. Holt, *The Rise and Fall of the American Whig Party: Jacksonian Politics and the Onset of the Civil War* (Oxford: Oxford University Press, 1999), 68. It seems Whigs and Democrats equally lacked political principles when it came to their position on finance. There were exceptions to Whig support for banks. James Roger Sharp, *The Jacksonians versus the Banks: Politics in the States after the Panic of 1837* (New York: Columbia University Press, 1970), provides state-by-state analyses of how Whigs viewed banks, indicating banks often did not provide for a party litmus test. In Louisiana, for instance, Whigs offered moderate support for banks and sometimes expressed reservations. Arthur Charles Cole, *The Whig Party in the South* (Washington, DC: American Historical Association, 1913), shows that many southern Whigs before the Panic of 1837 were anti-bank. Edward Pessen, *Jacksonian America: Society, Personality, and Politics*, rev. ed. (Homewood, IL: Dorsey, 1978), 214–217, shows that both Whigs and Democrats lacked ideological consistency. Lee Benson, *The Concept of Jacksonian Democracy: New York as a Test Case* (Princeton, NJ: Princeton University Press, 1961), 93–94, notes that Van Buren's Albany Regency originally attacked the antimonopoly position. During the Van Buren, Harrison, and Tyler administrations, 90 percent of Whigs in Congress supported national bank bills; see Ashworth, *Slavery, Capitalism, and Politics*, 1: 401. Conservative Democrats opposed Van Buren's Independent Treasury, and the Locofocos did not endorse a candidate in the election of 1836; see Walter Edward Hugins, *Jacksonian Democracy and the Working Class: A Study of the New York Workingmen's Movement, 1829–1837* (Stanford, CA: Stanford University Press, 1960), 43.

73. Naomi R. Lamoreaux and Christopher Glaisek, "Vehicles of Privilege or Mobility? Banks in Providence, Rhode Island, during the Age of Jackson," *Business History Review* 65, no. 3 (1991), 521.

74. Naomi R. Lamoreaux, *Insider Lending: Banks, Personal Connections, and Economic Development in Industrial New England* (Cambridge: Cambridge University Press, 1994), 1–7, 28, 32,159; Naomi R. Lamoreaux, "Banks, Kinship, and Economic Development: The New England Case," *Journal of Economic History* 46, no. 3 (1986).

75. Daniel Walker Howe, *The Political Culture of the American Whigs* (Chicago: University of Chicago Press, 1979), 182.

76. Sellers, *The Market Revolution*, 54.

77. For a discussion of Appleton's investments and political involvement in antebellum banking, see Robert F. Dalzell Jr., *Enterprising Elite: The Boston Associates and the World They Made* (Cambridge, MA: Harvard University Press, 1987), 93–97.

78. Lamoreaux, *Insider Lending*, 18–19, 37.

79. Nathan Appleton, *An Examination of the Banking System of Massachusetts, in Reference to the Renewal of the Bank Charters* (Boston: Stimpson and Clapp, 1831), 43.

80. Archie Carroll, Kenneth Lipartito, James Post, and Patricia Werhane, eds., *Corporate Responsibility: The American Experience* (Cambridge: Cambridge University Press, 2012).

81. Wilentz, *Rise of American Democracy*, 489.

82. Nathan Appleton, *Remarks on Currency and Banking: Having Reference to the Present Derangement of the Circulating Medium in the United States*, 3rd ed. (Boston: J. H. Eastburn, 1857), 16–17.

83. Ibid., 14.

84. Dalzell, *Enterprising Elite*, 97.

85. Appleton, *Banking System of Massachusetts*, 39, 21, 47, emphasis in original.

86. Ibid., 45.

87. Dorfman, *Economic Mind*, 2: 755–757; "George Opdyke Dead: Death of a Prominent Citizen and Former Mayor of New-York," *New York Times*, June 13, 1880.

88. Joseph Dorfman, "George Opdyke and the Tradition of Managed Money," in George Opdyke, *Treatise on Political Economy* (1851; repr., Clifton, NJ: A. M. Kelley, 1973), 19.

89. Opdyke, *Treatise on Political Economy*, 300, 303.

90. Ibid., 295, 315, 318.

91. Ibid., 318.

92. Arthur M. Schlesinger Jr., "The Problem of Richard Hildreth," *New England Quarterly* 13, no. 2 (1940).

93. Richard Hildreth, *Banks, Banking, and Paper Currencies* (1840; repr., New York: Greenwood, 1968), 87.

94. There were ninety-one "pet banks" by 1837. See Hammond, *Banks and Politics*, 419–420; Peter Temin, *The Jacksonian Economy* (New York: W. W. Norton, 1969), 60–63.

95. Hildreth, *Banks, Banking, and Paper Currencies*, 84; Lamoreaux, *Insider Lending*, 44.

96. Hildreth, *Banks, Banking, and Paper Currencies*, 109.

97. Ibid., 153.

98. Ibid., 172, 146–148.

99. Douglass C. North, *The Economic Growth of the United States, 1790–1860* (1961: New York: W. W. Norton, 1966), 232.

100. McGrane, *Panic of 1837*, 132.

101. Balleisen, *Navigating Failure*, 79, 124.

102. Temin, *Jacksonian Economy*, 17, 174–177; Lepler, *Many Panics of 1837*, 54–55.

103. Lepler, *Many Panics of 1837*, 107–108, 150–153, 162, 187–188, 211; Hammond, *Banks and Politics*, 501.

104. Hildreth, *Banks, Banking, and Paper Currencies*, 164.

105. William M. Gouge, *The Curse of Paper-Money and Banking; or, A Short History of Banking in the United States of America* (1833; repr., New York: Greenwood, 1968), 87.

106. William Leggett, "Thoughts on the Causes of the Present Discontents," in *Democrat-*

ick Editorials: Essays in Jacksonian Political Economy, by William Leggett, ed. Lawrence H. White (Indianapolis: Liberty, 1984), 97.

107. Theophilus Fisk, *Labor the Only True Source of Wealth; or, The Rottenness of the Paper Money Banking System Exposed, Its Sandy Foundations Shaken, Its Crumbling Pillars Overthrown* (1837; repr., New York: n.p., 1970), 8.

108. Fitzwilliam Byrdsall, *History of the Loco-Foco or Equal Rights Party* (1842; repr., New York: B. Franklin, 1967), 139.

109. William M. Gouge, *The Journal of Banking, July 1841–July 1842* (1842; repr., London: Routledge, 1996), 228.

110. William Leggett, "Fancy Cities," in *A Collection of the Political Writings of William Leggett*, ed. Theodore Sedgwick (1840; repr., New York: Arno, 1971), 2: 86, 103 (borrowing from Banquo in *Macbeth* I.iii).

111. Opdyke, *Treatise on Political Economy*, 293.

112. Fisk, *Labor the Only True Source of Wealth*, 15, quoting "A Father's Confession," *Fraser's Magazine* 11 (May 1835), 576, and Benjamin Disraeli, *Henrietta Temple: A Love Story* (London: H. Colburn, 1837).

113. Theophilus Fisk, *The Banking Bubble Burst; or, The Mammoth Corruptions of the Paper Money System Relieved by Bleeding* (Charleston: Wentworth Street, 1837), 24; Fisk, *Labor*, 18.

114. Opdyke, *Treatise*, 288.

115. Stephen Simpson, *The Working Man's Manual: A New Theory of Political Economy, on the Principle of Production the Source of Wealth* (Philadelphia: T. L. Bonsal, 1831), 143.

116. Joseph Dorfman, "William H. Gouge and the Formation of Orthodox American Monetary Policy," in William Gouge, *A Short History of Paper Money and Banking* (1833; repr., New York: A. M. Kelley, 1968), 5; Benjamin G. Rader, "William M. Gouge: Jacksonian Economic Theorist," *Pennsylvania History* 30, no. 4 (1963): 443–453.

117. Gouge, *The Journal of Banking*, 387.

118. Dorfman, "William H. Gouge," 25; Gouge, *The Journal of Banking*, 3.

119. Gouge, *Short History of Paper Money*, vi, emphasis in original.

120. Adam Smith, *An Inquiry into the Nature and Causes of the Wealth of Nations* (1776; repr., New Rochelle, NY: Arlington House, 1966), 1: 346–347, 353; 2: 361–362, 346.

121. Gouge, *Short History of Paper Money*, 117, 32.

122. Gouge, *The Journal of Banking*, 195.

123. Hammond, *Banks and Politics*, 608–612, suggests this by positioning his analysis of Gouge alongside agrarian opposition characterized as disingenuous. Schlesinger, *Age of Jackson*, 117–121, offers this inference by situating Gouge in the context of radical labor.

124. Gouge, *Curse of Paper-Money and Banking*, 113, 179.

125. Gouge's book was described by Schlesinger as "an instant success" (*Age of Jackson*, 118). It went through several editions within his lifetime. Woodbury initiated the prohibition of notes under $20; see John M. McFaul, *The Politics of Jacksonian Finance* (Ithaca, NY: Cornell University Press, 1972), 172–174.

126. Dorfman, *Economic Mind*, 2: 674.

127. Lysander Spooner, *Poverty, Its Illegal Causes and Legal Cure* (1846; repr., New York: Da Capo, 1971), 65, 66.

128. Ibid., 31; also Lysander Spooner, *The New System of Paper Currency* (Boston: A. Williams, 1861), 43.

129. Fisk, *Labor the Only True Source of Wealth*, 30.
130. Schlesinger, *Age of Jackson*, 169.
131. Fisk, *Labor the Only True Source of Wealth*, 8, 7.
132. Ibid., 17, 4.
133. Schlesinger, *Age of Jackson*, 190–200; Byrdsall, *History of the Loco-Foco*, vi, 101.
134. Byrdsall, *History of the Loco-Foco*, 111, 141, 147.
135. Ibid., 149.
136. Clinton Roosevelt, *Principia of Social Science* (New York: n.p., 1889), 47.
137. Carl N. Degler, "The Locofocos: Urban 'Agrarians,'" *Journal of Economic History* 16, no. 3 (1956), 333.
138. For a discussion of Leggett, see Marvin Meyers, *The Jacksonian Persuasion: Politics and Belief* (Stanford, CA: Stanford University Press, 1957), chap. 9; Hugins, *Jacksonian Democracy and the Working Class*, 88; Dorfman, *Economic Mind*, 2: 653–654; Jeffrey Sklansky, "William Leggett and the Melodrama of the Market," in Zakim and Kornblith, *Capitalism Takes Command*.
139. Leggett, "Present Discontents," 98.
140. Sklansky, "Leggett and the Melodrama," 200.
141. Leggett, "Present Discontents," 98.
142. Sklansky, "Leggett and the Melodrama," 221.
143. William Leggett, "Extremes Unite," in *Political Writings*, 1: 272.
144. William Leggett, "Monopolies," in *Political Writings*, 1: 140.
145. William Leggett, "The Crisis," in *Democratick Editorials*, 130.
146. William Leggett, "Theory and Practice," in *Democratick Editorials*, 168.
147. William Leggett, "The Reserved Rights of the People," in *Democratick Editorials*, 8.
148. William Leggett, "The Sister Doctrines," in *Democratick Editorials*, 287, 36–37.
149. William Leggett, "Small Notes and the State Banking System," in *Political Writings*, 1: 57.
150. William Leggett, "Connection of State with Banking," in *Political Writings*, 2: 306.
151. William Leggett, "The Pressure—The Cause of It—And the Remedy," in *Democratick Editorials*, 116.
152. Leggett, "Fancy Cities," 105.
153. William Leggett, "Why Is Flour So Dear?," in *Democratick Editorials*, 94.
154. William Leggett, "Morals of Legislation," in *Democratick Editorials*, 53.
155. William Leggett, "The Natural System," in *Political Writings*, 2: 334.
156. Henry Vethake, *The Principles of Political Economy*, 2nd ed. (1844; repr., New York: A. M. Kelley, 1971), 184.
157. Jacob Cardozo, *Notes on Political Economy* (1826; repr., New York: A. M. Kelley, 1972), 91.
158. George Frederick Holmes, "Speculation and Trade," *Southern Quarterly Review*, n.s., 1, no. 1 (1856): 12, 27–28.
159. "Jackson's Farewell Address," in Thorpe, *Statesmanship of Andrew Jackson*, 512–513.

Chapter 8. Conclusion: The Old and the New in American Economics

1. J. Laurence Laughlin, "The Study of Political Economy in the United States," *Journal of Political Economy* 1, no. 1 (1892): 4.
2. Irwin Unger, *The Greenback Era: A Social and Political History of American Finance*,

1865–1879 (Princeton, NJ: Princeton University Press, 1964); Richard Franklin Bensel, *Yankee Leviathan: The Origins of Central State Authority in America, 1859–1877* (Cambridge: Cambridge University Press, 1990), chaps. 4–5; Richard Franklin Bensel, *The Political Economy of American Industrialization, 1877–1900* (Cambridge: Cambridge University Press, 2000), chap. 6.

3. Unger, *Greenback Era*, 404.

4. Laughlin, "Study of Political Economy," 5.

5. F. W. Taussig, *The Tariff History of the United States*, 8th ed. (1931; New York: Capricorn, 1964), 166.

6. Judith Goldstein, *Ideas, Interests, and American Trade Policy* (Ithaca, NY: Cornell University Press, 1993), 81–131; Bensel, *Political Economy of American Industrialization*, 457–460; Taussig, *Tariff History*, 170–276; Paul Bairoch, *Economics and World History: Myths and Paradoxes* (Chicago: University of Chicago Press, 1993), 32, 53; Percy Ashley, *Modern Tariff History: Germany–United States–France*, 3rd ed. (1920; New York: H. Fertig, 1970), 181–204.

7. Arthur A. Stein, "The Hegemon's Dilemma: Great Britain, the United States, and the International Economic Order," in *Theory and Structure in International Political Economy*, ed. Charles Lipson and Benjamin J. Cohen (Cambridge, MA: MIT Press, 1999), 287.

8. Giovanni Arrighi, *The Long Twentieth Century: Money, Power, and the Origins of Our Times*, 2nd ed. (London: Verso, 2010), 62.

9. Bensel, *Political Economy of American Industrialization*, 457–460; Joanne Reitano, *The Tariff Question in the Gilded Age: The Great Debate of 1888* (University Park: Pennsylvania State University Press, 1994), 26–39, 52–59.

10. Herbert G. Gutman, "Work, Culture, and Society in Industrializing America, 1815–1919," *American Historical Review* 78, no. 3 (1973): 542–546; David Montgomery, *The Fall of the House of Labor: The Workplace, the State, and American Labor Activism, 1865–1925* (Cambridge: Cambridge University Press, 1987), 192–250.

11. Alfred D. Chandler Jr., *The Visible Hand: The Managerial Revolution in American Business* (Cambridge, MA: Belknap Press of Harvard University Press, 1977).

12. Taussig, *Tariff History*, 230, 251; Goldstein, *Ideas, Interests, and American Trade Policy*, 118–133.

13. Arrighi, *Long Twentieth Century*, 299–304.

14. Postbellum protectionists complained about the abundance of free trade literature in America and the liberal disposition of its professors. In 1876 a list of the ten "most saleable works on political economy" registered John Stuart Mill's *Principles of Political Economy* and Smith's *Wealth of Nations* at the top; see Joseph Dorfman, *The Economic Mind in American Civilization*, vol. 3, *1865–1918* (New York: Viking, 1949), 81. Joseph Wharton established the nation's first business school at the University of Pennsylvania, in part so students would learn "the doctrine that the nation is bound to take care of its own," i.e., protectionism. Quoted in Reitano, *Tariff Question*, 52.

15. Sidney Fine, *Laissez Faire and the General-Welfare State: A Study of Conflict in American Thought, 1865–1901* (Ann Arbor: University of Michigan Press, 1956), 200, 198–221; Richard T. Ely, "A Decade of Economic Theory," *Annals of the American Academy of Political and Social Science* 15, no. 2 (1900): 96–101; T. W. Hutchison, *On Revolutions and Progress in Economic Knowledge* (Cambridge: Cambridge University Press, 1978), chaps. 3–4; Samuel Barbour, James Cicarelli, and J. E. King, *A History of American Economic Thought: Mainstream and Crosscurrents* (London: Routledge, 2017), 154–156.

16. Henry William Spiegel, *The Growth of Economic Thought* (Englewood Cliffs, NJ: Prentice-Hall, 1971), 421–424; Joseph A. Schumpeter, *History of Economic Analysis* (Oxford: Oxford University Press, 1954), 807–812; Erik Grimmer-Solem, *The Rise of Historical Economics and Social Reform in Germany, 1864–1894* (Oxford: Clarendon Press, 2002), 122–126; Michael Hudson, introduction to *National System of Political Economy*, by Friedrich List (1841; repr., New York: Garland, 1974), 13.

17. A. D. H. Kaplan, *Henry Charles Carey: A Study in American Economic Thought* (Baltimore: Johns Hopkins Press, 1931), 1.

18. Richard T. Ely, "The American Economic Association, 1885–1909," *American Economic Association Quarterly* 11, no. 1 (1910): 57.

19. Ibid., 49.

20. Henry Carter Adams, "The Position of Socialism in the Historical Development of Political Economy," *Penn Monthly* 10 (April 1879): 294.

21. Fine, *Laissez Faire and the General-Welfare State*, 198–221.

22. D. C. Coleman, *Myth, History and the Industrial Revolution* (London: Bloomsbury, 1992), 3–36.

23. Richard White, "Utopian Capitalism," in *American Capitalism: New Histories*, ed. Sven Beckert and Christine Desan (New York: Columbia University Press, 2018), 120.

24. Clinton Rossiter, *Conservatism in America: The Thankless Persuasion*, 2nd ed. (New York: Knopf, 1962), 128; Richard Hofstadter, *Social Darwinism in American Thought* (Boston: Beacon, 1955); Fine, *Laissez Faire and the General-Welfare State*, 30–65; Eric MacGilvray, *The Invention of Market Freedom* (Cambridge: Cambridge University Press, 2011), 165–193.

25. Rossiter, *Conservatism in America*, 154, 152.

26. Charles Dunbar, "Economic Science in America, 1776–1876," *North American Review* 122, no. 250 (1876): 140.

27. Joyce Oldham Appleby, *Economic Thought and Ideology in Seventeenth-Century England* (Princeton, NJ: Princeton University Press, 1978), 6, 20–21, 279.

28. Alexis de Tocqueville, *Democracy in America*, trans. Henry Reeve (1835; New York: Bantam, 2000), 516.

INDEX

Abolitionism: American Protestantism and, 34; in Britain, 35-36, 71-72; northeastern laissez-faire and, 34-36; southern laissez-faire and, 72
Adams, Henry Carter, 237
Adams, John, 56, 158, 207
Adams, John Quincy, 152, 154, 163, 176
Agriculture: expansion in antebellum America, 2
Albany Regency, 124
American Economic Association, 237
American exceptionalism, 19-20, 79, 165
American political economy: break from British classicism, 13, 18-19, 75-76, 91; conformity to Smithian laissez-faire, 10-12, 28-29; conservatism of, 239-40; contribution to economic discourse, 12-13; German historicism and, 237; historians on, 10-12; protectionism and, 140, 179; sectionalism in American laissez-faire and, 18, 36, 44, 53, 72-73, 76; transformation of postbellum economic liberalism and, 240-41
Anti-Corn Law League, 36, 72; free trade and, 68; support for British manufactures and, 68
Anti-intellectualism, 151-52
Appleton, Nathan, 214, 220; on banking, 214; as conservative, 214-15; on paper currency, 215-16; on suspension of payments, 215
Astor, John Jacob, 207

Baird, Henry Carey, 181
Baldwin, Henry, 161
Baldwin, Laommi, 80; American exceptionalism in, 81; on the census of 1810, 80; on population, 81
Banking: expansion in antebellum America, 207, 211; free banking, 211, 224
Bank of England, 197, 220

Bank of the United States, 194, 197, 201, 206; Panic of 1819 and, 208; Panic of 1837 and, 221
Bentham, Jeremy, 40
Biddle, Nicholas, 42, 197, 219, 221
Bolingbroke, Henry St. John, 24
British classicism, 10; industrialism and, 67-68
British Evangelicalism, 32, 39
Brougham, Henry, 147
Bryant, William Cullen, 228
Buchanan, James, 105, 174
Burke, Edmund, 8
Byllesby, Langton, 21, 104, 125-26, 133, 134, 238; as conservative, 128-29; on distribution, 127; on finance, 127; Gray and, 129; on labor theory of value, 126-27; on manufacturing technology, 127; political economy of, 126-28
Byrdsall, Fitzwilliam: equal rights and, 228

Calhoun, John, 44, 56, 62, 161, 163, 206; on industrialization, 69-70; laissez-faire and, 64, 67; on the negative state, 66; nullification and, 63, 66, 164; protectionism of, 63-64, 144; republicanism of, 66, 70; states' rights and laissez-faire and, 66; on tariffs, 64, 66
Capitalism: and agrarianism, 67; in American history, 7, 195, 241; democracy and, 50; emergence in antebellum America, 1-3; historians of, 4-5; intellectual capitalism, 6, 9-10, 16; laissez-faire and, 9; as revolutionary, 22, 136, 242; slavery and, 17
Cardozo, Jacob, 98, 158; American political economy and, 101; on distribution, 100; on finance, 232; on labor theory of value, 99; laissez-faire and, 99; on rent, 100; on Ricardo, 99-100; on tariffs, 98-99

Carey, Henry, 60, 181, 235; American exceptionalism and, 182, 186; as founder of American political economy, 21, 180–81, 190; as founder of American protectionism, 21, 140, 180; on British political economy, 188–90; on distribution, 182; freedom and, 187; historicism and, 237; hybrid capitalism and, 181, 186, 188, 191; on increasing returns, 188; on international trade, 185; on population, 183; man vs. nature and, 184, 186–90; optimism of, 183; on rent, 182–83; on Smith, 181, 185, 187; on theory of association, 184

Carey, Mathew, 146, 158; Anglophobia of, 146–47; on British political economy, 150–51; democracy and, 166; home market and, 177; industrialization and, 169; on international trade, 177; Smith, 150; on Smith's influence in antebellum America, 148; on Tariff of 1828, 164

Chalmers, Thomas, 32, 39

Chase, Salmon, 216

Cheves, Langdon, 207, 208

Clark, James Bates, 236, 237; marginalism and, 236

Clay, Henry, 65, 164; American System and, 162

Cobden, Richard, 68; Cobden Club, American chapter, 36

Colonial economic thought, 40, 141

Colton, Calvin, 147, 167, 179; American exceptionalism and, 170, 178; Anglophobia of, 147; on British trade policy, 149; free labor ideology and, 170–72; harmony of interests and, 171; nationalism in, 147; on Smith, 148; on Smith's influence in antebellum America, 148; statistics and, 152

Confederacy: trade policy of, 59–60, 72

Conkin, Paul: on Byllesby, 126; consensus history and, 12–13; on Taylor, 206

Consensus historians: on American history and capitalism, 7, 123; on finance, 195; on tariffs, 138

Cooper, Thomas, 44, 56, 154, 155, 161; agrarianism of, 61; deconstruction of state and, 57–58; definition of national wealth, 61; on finance, 209–11; on free banking, 211; on industrialization, 61–62; on limited liability, 210; on population, 87; skepticism of, 57; states' rights and laissez-faire and, 57–58, 61

Corn Laws, 67–68, 71, 72, 149; Ricardo and, 92

Corporations: expansion in antebellum America, 212, 213; Whig support for, 213

Cotton: in antebellum economy, 55–56; diplomacy and, 60, 71; political economy of, 55–56, 60, 71; Staple Growth theory and, 55

Coxe, Tench, 146, 176, 186; home market and, 175–77; on industrialization, 170, 176

Crawford, William, 206

Credit: as fantasy, 222, 229; republican opposition to, 200; as social mutuality, 208, 212

Darwinism, 240

Davis, Jefferson, 174

De Bow, J. D. B., 82; on industrialization, 85; on population, 84–85; on slavery and republicanism, 84; as southern promotionalist, 82, 85

Debt: in England, 198–99; liberal opposition to, 223, 226; perceptions of bankruptcy and, 208; republican opposition to, 200

Dew, Thomas Roderick, 88, 158; debate in the Virginia Legislature and, 1831, 89; at the Free Trade Convention, 1831, 88; on industrialization, 90; on laissez-faire, 88; on population, 88–90

Dickens, Charles, 170

Distribution of wealth: in antebellum America, 95–96

Dorfman, Joseph: on American political economy, 11–12; on Byllesby, 128; consensus history and, 11; on Gouge, 223; on Ricardo's influence in America, 91; on Skidmore, 132

Douglass, Frederick, 84

Dunbar, Charles: on American political economy, 10, 241

Du Pont, Pierre-Samuel, 244n12

Embargo of 1807, 36, 64, 143

Evans, George Henry, 125, 133

Everett, Alexander: on British trade policy, 149; debate with George Tucker, 87; on influence of British political economy in antebellum America, 148

Finance: capitalism and, 23, 191–95, 218, 231; expansion in antebellum America, 3; historians on, 23–25, 193–95, 209, 231; liberal opposition to, 219, 224–25, 227–31; liberal republican opposition to, 25, 196, 209–10, 221–22, 223; in postbellum America, 234; republican opposition to, in America, 23, 197, 199–201; republican opposition to, in England, 24, 199; Whig opposition to, 196; Whig support of, 212–16

INDEX

Fisk, Theophilus: and equal rights, 227; on finance, 227
Fitzhugh, George, 21, 121, 134, 238; anti-intellectualism of, 114; on bourgeois liberalism, 106-7, 110; as conservative, 114; on industrialization, 108-9; influence in antebellum America, 105; racism of, 109; slavery as positive good and, 107, 111; slavery as socialism and, 135; on Smith, 107-8; on socialism, 110
Franklin, Benjamin: *Cato's Letters* and, 199; on population, 78-79
Free Trade Convention, 45-47, 60, 94; Dew's influence in, 88-89
Friedman, Milton, 50
Fulton, Robert, 2

Galbraith, John Kenneth: on American political economy, 10-11
Gallatin, Albert, 89, 207; at Free Trade Convention, 46; Free Trade *Memorial* and, 46-47, 89
Garrison, William Lloyd, 35, 84
Girard, Stephen, 206, 207
Glorious Revolution, 204
Gordon, Thomas, 24, 199
Gouge, William, 221, 223, 231; on free banking, 224-25; hard money and, 225; on Smith, 224
Gray, John: labor theory of value and, 129
Great Depression of 1873, 234
Great Recession, 234

Hamilton, Alexander, 23, 154, 174, 176, 212; Bank of the United States and, 201; debt and, 201; as founder of protectionism, 141, 143; home market and, 142, 175; on manufactures, 142; national credit and, 201; nationalism of, 142; on Physiocracy, 141; tariffs and, 143
Hamilton, James, 154
Hammond, James, 120; mud-sill speech and, 120
Harrington, James, 24
Harrisburg Convention, 154, 163
Hartz, Louis, 7, 122; on Fitzhugh, 114
Hildreth, Richard, 218; on commercial cycles, 221; on finance, 219; free banking and, 218, 219-20; on Jackson, 219
Historical School of Economics, 153
Hofstadter, Richard: consensus history and, 12; on Jackson's bank war, 195
Holmes, George Frederick, 21, 114, 238; on bourgeois liberalism, 115-16, 119, 134; during the Civil War, 121-22; on finance, 232; on free labor, 116-17; on industrialization, 117-18; on laissez-faire, 115-16; on political economy, 115; socialism and, 116, 134
Homestead Act, 1862, 125
Hughes, Henry, 105; on slavery, 120; statism of, 120
Hume, David, 8, 18, 50, 51, 200; on *Wealth of Nations*, 8
Hume, Joseph, 68
Hybrid capitalism, 14-21, 29, 52, 73-74, 75, 101-2, 192-93, 209; Henry Carey and, 186-88, 191; finance and, 193, 197, 209, 231; northeastern laissez-faire and, 17-18; protectionism and, 20-21, 136, 140, 164, 166-68, 170-73, 188, 191, 239; southern laissez-faire and, 17-18, 71, 83; Tucker and, 52; Vethake and, 98

Industrialization: expansion in antebellum America, 2, 124, 167
Ingersoll, Charles, 154
Intellectual capitalism: Adam Smith as founder of, 6, 9-10; definition of, 10

Jackson, Andrew, 132, 163, 206, 220, 225; anti-intellectualism and, 151-52; Bank Veto and, 194; Farewell Address of, 232; Force Bill and, 164; removal of government deposits and, 221; on the South Sea Bubble, 197
Jay's Treaty, 143
Jefferson, Thomas, 27, 36, 48, 55, 67, 143, 154, 165; on Cooper, 56; debt and, 202-3; on finance, 202-3; on manufactures, 144-45; on the Panic of 1819, 207; trade restrictions and, 143; on the *Wealth of Nations*, 28
Jevons, William Stanley, 236
Jones, William, 206, 207

Keynes, John Maynard: on British classicism, 10

Labor movement, antebellum, 124, 267n71
Lafayette, Marquis de, 146, 153, 154
Land reform: in antebellum America, 125; in Britain, 125
Legal Tender Act of 1862, 217
Leggett, William, 228; equal rights and, 230; on finance, 229-30; free banking and, 230; laissez-faire and, 230-31
Lerner, Abraham: Lerner Symmetry Theorem, 161

Lieber, Francis, 41, 42; liberal cosmopolitanism and, 42–44; liberal universalism and, 43; natural law and, 42; Lieber Code and, 43; on private property, 42
Lincoln, Abraham, 121, 165, 181
List, Friedrich, 153–54; American exceptionalism and, 165; Anglophobia of, 155; historicism and, 155, 237; home market and, 156; nationalism of, 155–57; on political economy, 155–58; on Smith, 155; statism of, 156; Zollverein and, 154
Locke, John, 7, 41, 200
Locofocos, 227; equal rights and, 228; on finance, 228
Lowell, Francis, 167

Madison, James, 50, 137, 143, 154, 203, 206; the Non-Intercourse Act and, 143
Malthus, Thomas, 6, 39, 46, 75–76, 81, 82, 86–87, 89, 188; abolitionism and, 90; on American population growth, 78; British Evangelism and, 31; influence of *Essay on the Principle of Population*, 77; on population, 77–78; relationship with Ricardo, 92; on *Wealth of Nations*, 9
Manchester School of Economics, 68
Mandeville, Bernard, 50
Marshall, John, 154, 158
Marx, Karl, 5, 6, 22, 123, 178, 238; on protectionism, 138–39; on slavery, 135
McCulloch, J. R., 32, 192; on *Wealth of Nations*, 9
McDuffie, George, 65, 73; Forty Bales doctrine, 65; states' rights and laissez-faire and, 66
McVickar, John, 32, 44; on abolitionism, 34; liberal cosmopolitanism and, 32–34, 36–37; moral philosophy and, 34, 40; natural law and, 41; religion and, 41
Mill, John Stuart, 31, 40, 153, 181
Monroe, James, 154
Morrill, Justin, 174

National Bankruptcy Act, 1841, 220
National Reform Association, 133
New Economic Historians, 4
New Historians of Capitalism, 5, 7, 13, 123; definition of capitalism and, 5; on protectionism, 167; on slavery, 17, 54–55; on Williams's *Slavery and Capitalism*, 35
Newman, Samuel: on population, 81–82
New School Economists, 237; the American Economic Association and, 237

Northeastern laissez-faire: break from British political economy, 40, 75, 91; as conservative, 29–30; decline in postbellum America, 73; in higher education, 18, 29–31; moral philosophy and, 18, 29–31, 41; religion and, 18, 29, 31
Northern laborites, 22, 104; as conservative, 23, 104, 133, 135–36, 239; land reform and, 125; relation to southern reactionaries, 22–23, 133–36; socialism and, 21–22
Nullification, 164. *See also* Calhoun, John

Opdyke, George, 216; on currency reforms, 217; on debt collection, 217–218; on finance, 218
Owens, Robert Dale, 125, 133

Panic of 1819, 162, 207
Panic of 1837, 164, 220; historians on, 220–21
Panic of 1857, 174, 196
Panic of 1893, 234
Physiocracy, 6, 100, 141, 219; laissez-faire and, 9; *Wealth of Nations* and, 67
Pickering, John: political economy of, 133
Pocock, J. G. A., 24, 200
Polanyi, Karl: double movement and, 173; on tariffs, 172
Polk, James, 174, 225
Population: in antebellum America, 1, 76; in nineteenth-century England, 76
Progressive historians: on Jackson's bank war, 195; on tariffs, 138
Protectionism, 136; American exceptionalism and, 165–66, 171–72, 178; in American history, 139–40, 164; as American political economy, 20, 140, 165, 178–79; Anglophobia of, 145–46; anti-intellectualism of, 151; break from British political economy and, 20; as conservative, 239; democracy and, 166–67; harmony of interests and, 171; historians on, 138–39, 269n7; historicism and, 153; home market and, 175–77; industrialization and, 21, 169–70; on influence of British political economy in America, 146, 149, 288n14; isolationism and, 177; labor and, 168–70, 172–73, 238; on population, 80; in postbellum America, 174–75, 235–36, 238; in post-WWII America, 235; pragmatism of, 151; in revolutionary period, 140–41; safety valve theory and, 171; statistics and, 152–53

Quesnay, François, 67

Raguet, Condy, 45, 181; agrarianism of, 69; on protectionism, 45
Ranke, Leopold von, 237
Raymond, Daniel, 158, 161; American political economy and, 179; home market and, 177; nationalism of, 160; on political economy, 159; on protectionism, 160; on slavery, 158; on Smith, 159–60; statism of, 160, 168; tariff and specie imports and, 162–63
Reid, Thomas, 151
Republicanism: historians on, 24–25, 197, 200; opposition to finance, 24–25; in English thought, 24, 199–201
Ricardian Socialists, 129
Ricardo, David, 5, 6, 31, 32, 40, 75, 91, 99, 153, 182, 188; in British political economy, 92; on distribution, 93; influence in antebellum America, 91; relationship with Malthus, 92; on rent, 92, 97; on *Wealth of Nations*, 9
Roosevelt, Clinton: on finance, 228
Roscher, Wilhelm, 237
Rossiter, Clinton, 128, 240; on Fitzhugh, 114
Ruffin, Edmund, 120; the Civil War and, 121; on industrialization, 121; slavery as socialism and, 135

Say, Jean-Baptiste, 42, 52, 230; divorce of economics and politics and, 58; influence in antebellum America, 46, 148
Schmoller, Gustav von, 156, 237
Schumpeter, Joseph: on American political economy, 10; on credit, 193
Scottish School of Common Sense, 151
Sedition Act, 56
Seven Years' War, 141
Simpson, Stephen, 132; political economy of, 132
Skidmore, Thomas, 21, 104, 129–30, 134, 238; abolition of classes and, 131; abolition of inheritance and, 131; agrarianism of, 130; labor theory of value and, 130; property rights and, 130
Slater, Samuel, 167
Slavery: as capitalism, 54–55, 82, 112; cost of slave vs. free labor, 117; in the Old South, 63, 112; as paternalism, 111–13; slave as capital and labor, 83–84; slave breeding and, 84
Smith, Adam, 6, 16, 29, 46, 51, 75, 135, 142, 153, 200, 239; agrarianism of, 67, 257n133; on banking, 224–25; as founder of intellectual capitalism, 6, 9–10; historical influence of, 9; influence in American history, 11–13, 27–28; laissez-faire and, 49–50; moral philosophy and, 30, 33; on population, 76; principles of, 6; reception in Britain, 8; relationship to Physiocrats, 67; skepticism of, 48–50, 187; on slavery and free labor, 53; on sympathy, 49
Smith, E. Peschine, 181, 278n12; theory of association, 184
Socialism. *See* Northern laborites
Southern laissez-faire: Anglophobia of, 72; break from British political economy and, 72, 91; as conservative, 70; decline in postbellum America and, 73; role of cotton trade and, 53–56; sectionalism of, 53–54, 62; secularism of, 44; slavery and, 44, 53, 83–84; states' rights and, 58, 62–61, 66; as statist, 59
Southern reactionary thought, 21–22, 104–5; as conservative, 23, 104–6, 118, 122–23, 133–36, 239; decline in postbellum America, 122; influence in antebellum America, 105, 112; slavery and, 22; relation to northern laborites, 22–23, 133–34
South Sea Bubble, 24, 197–99, 205, 221, 224
Specie Circular, 225
Spencer, Herbert, 73, 240, 241
Spooner, Lysander, 225, 231; on debt collection, 226; on finance, 226–27
Stewart, Dugald, 9, 230, 240; *Wealth of Nations* and, 8, 30
Sumner, William Graham, 73

Tammany Hall, 124, 227, 228
Tariff: of 1789, 137; of 1816, 144; of 1820 (Baldwin), 161; of 1824, 162–63; of 1827 (Woolens Bill), 65, 163; of 1828 (Abominations), 45, 56, 63, 65, 163–64; of 1833 (Compromise), 47, 60, 164, 173, 175; of 1842 (Black), 164, 173; of 1846 (Walker), 47, 60, 148, 174, 175, 235; of 1857, 174; of 1861 (Morrill), 174; of 1930 (Smoot-Hawley), 236; Civil War and, 174, 256n109; Congressional sectionalism over, 161–63; historians on, 138–39; impact on cotton prices, 257n26; minimum valuations and, 164; in postbellum America, 175; as source of federal revenue, 143, 162; in the twentieth century, 235
Taylor, John, 203; agrarianism and, 205; debt in English history and, 204–5; on finance, 204–5, 209; laissez-faire and, 206

Tocqueville, Alexis de, 95, 165, 242
Tod, John, 162
Tracy, Antoine Destutt de: Jefferson and, 203; on finance, 203
Trade: expansion in antebellum America, 3
Transportation: expansion in antebellum America, 2
Treaty of Ghent, 144, 145
Trenchard, John, 24, 199
Trollope, Fanny, 152
Tucker, George, 47–48, 57, 73; debate with Alexander Everett and, 87; on population, 85–87; on protectionism, 52; skepticism of, 51; on slavery, 52; statistics and, 52; theory of value, 51
Tyler, John, 164

United States Bank of Pennsylvania, 221

Van Buren, Martin, 163
Vethake, Henry, 93, 101, 181; American exceptionalism and, 95–97; conservatism of, 97; on finance, 232; hybrid capitalism and, 98; laissez-faire and, 94; moral philosophy and, 94; on rent, 97
Viner, Jacob, 14

Walker, Robert, 174
Walpole, Robert, 199
War of 1812, 33, 55, 144, 147
Washington, George, 137, 177, 201
Wayland, Francis, 37, 46, 73; on abolitionism, 34–35; on laissez-faire, 39; liberal cosmopolitanism and, 38; natural law and, 41; moral philosophy and, 37; optimism of, 39; on population, 79; on protectionism, 39; religion and, 37–39, 41
Weber, Max, 31
Webster, Daniel, 154
Wharton, Joseph, 181, 288n14
Wigfall, Louis T., 113
Williams, Eric, 35
Winthrop, John, 40, 165
Woodbury, Levi, 225
Working Men's Party, 123–25, 130, 132

CHRISTOPHER W. CALVO teaches American history at Florida International University and Gulliver Preparatory in Miami, Florida.